THE ORIGINS OF THE CRIMEAN WAR

ORIGINS OF MODERN WARS

General editor: *Harry Hearder*

THE ORIGINS OF
THE CRIMEAN WAR

David M. Goldfrank

LONGMAN
London and New York

LONGMAN GROUP UK LIMITED,
Longman House, Burnt Mill,
Harlow, Essex CM20 2JE, England
and Associated Companies throughout the world.

Published in the United States of America
by Longman Publishing, New York

© Longman Group UK Limited 1994

First published 1994

ISBN 0 582 490545 CSD
ISBN 0 582 490553 PPR

British Library Cataloguing-in-Publication Data
A catalogue record for this book is
available from the British Library

Library of Congress Cataloging-in-Publication Data
Goldfrank, David M.
    The origins of the Crimean War / David M. Goldfrank.
        p. cm. – (Origins of modern wars)
    Includes bibliographical references and index.
    ISBN 0-582-49054-5 (cased). – ISBN 0-582-49055-3 (paper)
    1. Crimean War, 1853-1856–Causes.   2. Crimean War, 1853-1856
    –Diplomatic history.   3. Europe–Politics and
    government–1848-1871.   I. Title.   II. Series.
    DK215.G57   1993
947'.073–dc20

Set 5B in Bembo Roman
Produced by Longman Singapore Publishers (Pte) Ltd
Printed in Singapore

Contents

Contents

Contents

List of tables

List of Maps

Editor's Foreword

Professor Goldfrank's study of the origins of the Crimean War is both immensely scholarly and intellectually exciting, in that it grapples successfully with a subject of considerable complexity. The war was the first between the Great Powers since Waterloo, and there was to be no other between more than two of the Great Powers until 1914, if Italy in 1866 can be dismissed as being not yet a 'Great Power'. Goldfrank considers the war to have been 'somewhat bizarre' for several reasons, one of which was the reluctance of the Tsar to come to terms, when it would surely have been to his advantage to do so. As the eleventh volume in the series, then, the origins of the Crimean War provide an intriguing study.

One striking value of Goldfrank's work is his willingness to consider what, with reference to the First World War, was once called the 'war guilt' question. The 'war guilt' approach between the two world wars became unfashionable because of the animosity it aroused, with the unfortunate result that historians became shy of passing value judgements on the origins of the First World War. After 1945 everyone was ready to concede that Hitler had been responsible for the Second World War, with only A.J.P. Taylor raising some original, if infuriating, questions.

That individual political leaders can be charged with responsibility for the Crimean War Goldfrank does not doubt. Nor is he mealy-mouthed about it: Nicholas I was 'more responsible than any other person for the Crimean War' (p. 284). It is a conclusion reached after an exhaustive study of Russian, French, British, Austrian, German and even Swedish and Belgian archives, and a consideration of the roles of the other principal actors, and of their servants among the diplomats. Earlier, Goldfrank points out that Nicholas was 'more interested in the military side of things' (p. 229). But the Tsar was more than simply an unimaginative military leader. Goldfrank refers to Nesselrode's 'mystification and cult of the Emperor in a despatch that the latter approved': 'The true thinking of the Emperor . . . is of a higher order than one can comprehend in Constantinople, and perhaps, elsewhere . . . His Majesty . . . obeys his conscience' (p. 150). An autocrat in command of vast armies, who 'obeys his conscience' only, is a terrifying phenomenon in history.

But Goldfrank shows clearly the failings of the British and French also. The British public, in particular, was in one of its phases of jingoism, though the term had not yet been invented. Goldfrank makes the interesting point that Napoleon III's government tried to pretend to its public that its policy was more pacific than it really was, while the British government endeared itself to its public by pretending that it was more aggressive than it really was. Clarendon, the Foreign Secretary, Goldfrank points out, 'lied through his teeth', in saying: 'We want nothing for our trade, and we fear nothing for our Indian possessions.' (p. 264). But Goldfrank is less severe on Clarendon, Stratford Canning and British policy generally than was Paul Schroeder's *Austria, Great Britain and the Crimean War*, which was published in 1972.

I must not give the impression, however, that Professor Goldfrank is concerned exclusively with apportioning blame. On the contrary, he shows convincingly how economic factors and the breakdown of the Concert of Europe after 1848 provided a setting for the war, and concludes: 'both nationalism and the counter-revolution were pervasive forces during 1848–53, but they did not have to result in a Russo-Turkish or Crimean War' (p. 282). Earlier he had commented that the weakening of the Concert of Europe had made 'unilateral strident moves by the Great Powers' possible, but none of them had 'rational grounds for provoking a war'. 'Only an irrational impulse, one sufficiently powerful to override simple considerations of other states' interests and the balance of power would set off war under these circumstances' (p. 77).

Harry Hearder

Acknowledgements

The author would like to express his gratitude to (1) the International Research and Exchanges Board (IREX), the Association of Professional Schools of International Affairs (APSIA), and the Provost's Office, Graduate School, School of Foreign Service, History Department, and Russian Area Studies Program of Georgetown University for travel and research support; (2) two graduate research assistants for the background chapters, Karen Taylor-Brovkin and Theresa Safon; (3) the staffs at the European archives and libraries he utilized, and especially those in Russia, who have been labouring in recent years under very difficult conditions – among them, L.A. Murashova, formerly of the Russian Foreign Ministry Archive (AVPR), and I.M. Florianova of the Naval Archive (TsGAVMF); (4) his encouraging and helpful Georgetown colleagues – including two historians who read earlier versions of this manuscript, Professors Aviel Roshwald and Richard Stites;★ (5) his engaging graduate students – in particular, Douglas Brown, Paul Heinemann, David Rich and (now) Professors Hubertus Jahn and Michael Smith; (6) specialists in Russian and European diplomatic history, many of whose invaluable works appear here in the notes and bibliography and two of whose do not – A.V. Ignatiev and V.N. Ponomarev; (7) his patient wife Jane; and (8) his first erudite teachers – his parents, Sylvia and the late Max Goldfrank.

★Gratitude for specific help is also due to Professors Adhip Chaudhuri (India), James Collins (methods), Peter Dunkley (England), Thomas Helde (Diplomatic), Sandra Horvath-Peterson (France), Ronald Johnson (US), Andrzej Kaminski (Polish Emigration), Alan Karras (US), Jo Ann Moran (mentalities), Kathryn Olesko (German), Marcus Rediker (methods), John Ruedy (Middle East), James Shedel (Austria), and Howard Spendelow (Russo-Chinese Relations).

Introduction

THE PROBLEM: I – A SICK MAN IN A SICK WORLD

On the evening of 9 January 1853, Nicholas I, Emperor and Autocrat of all the Russias, took aside Hamilton Seymour, Minister Plenipotentiary of the Queen of England to the court of St Petersburg, and said to him:[1]

> The affairs of Turkey are in a very disorganized condition. The country itself seems to be falling to pieces. The fall will be a great misfortune, and it is very important that England and Russia should come to a perfectly good understanding upon these affairs, and that neither should take any decisive step of which the other is not apprised.
>
> Note, that we have a sick man in our arms, a very sick man. It will be, I tell you frankly, a great misfortune, if one of these days he disappears, especially before all of the necessary dispositions are taken. But now is not the time to speak of this.

'Sickness' in politics or societies is a subjective quality. In 1853 the multinational Ottoman Empire of about 23 million Muslims and Christians was 'sick' for the same basic reason that the multinational Soviet Union was 'sick' in the 1980s. The economy was neither modern nor remotely competitive with the advanced countries in the manufacturing sector. The better-educated among the Turks (the chief nationality) were dissatisfied with the backwardness of the realm. Significant elements among the other peoples desired their own states and were attracted to destabilizing movements of nationalism and populism.

The development of modern secular institutions in Turkey had been slow compared to Europe. The Sultan was still theoretically all powerful under Allah, limited only by religious law. Legality

1

in the modern Western sense still hardly existed. Real and mobile property were not yet secure from arbitrary confiscation. Provincial governors or pashas usually held power of life and death over the local inhabitants, unless checked by special overseers or foreign consuls. Taxation and administration were hopelessly corrupt and inefficient. There were bankers, but no chartered banks.

The poorly educated Sultan Abdülmecid shared his power with a Council of Ministers, who represented the governing élite. A few of them were fairly well-educated. For major legislation and declarations of war, the Sultan had to consult an expanded Grand Council which also included some provincial governors, retired officials and religious leaders. This provided for a consensus within a very narrow Muslim élite, mainly Turks, though the Bosnians, Albanians, Arabs and Kurds also adhered to the Islamic faith.[2]

Medieval patterns of thought survived in the Ottoman Empire well into the nineteenth century, and the Islamic establishment was almost frozen in time. Over 16,750 young people pursued traditional Islamic law and theology in Constantinople alone in 1853, while only about 3,350 Muslim boys between ten and fifteen were studying in the sixty or so secondary Western-style schools established after 1839.[3] A Western-influenced press, however, had started in 1834, and the Translation Bureau of the Foreign Ministry served as a *de facto* institute of higher learning, out of which Western-oriented reformers emerged. Still the general sense among informed Turks that the West was superior in every respect was matched by a traditionalist defiance that blocked meaningful reform.

The military was the only domain that had allowed Western learning to penetrate the Naval and Military Engineering Schools dating from the late eighteenth century, before the nineteenth century. Added to these were the Military Medical Academy (1827), the Military Academy (1834) and the Staff College (1849). This was all too little and too late. Although the Turks had Europe's fourth largest army and fleet (220,000 regular troops and six battleships, on paper at least), they were economically and culturally incapable of matching potential enemies, and Turkey was no longer a 'Great Power'. All the same, the Turkish élite as a whole wished to retain the empire and, if possible, regain especially the Muslim territories lost to Russia.

If the empire was a traditional patrimonial despotism, it was also exceptionally porous, with economic, religious and cultural ties in all directions.[4] This made Ottoman rule over Christians especially problematic. Few Muslims wished to grant civil equality to native

Christians – Greeks, Bulgarians, Serbs, Romanians and Armenians – who were outside the central power structure and could not serve in the army or navy. The typical Turk felt that a *gâvur* (unbeliever) was a *gâvur*, and to the devil with modern European notions. On the other hand, Christians enjoyed the religious and administrative autonomy of the millet system, Serbs and Romanians even being governed by native princes. Most Ottoman Christians, the Armenians excepted, were (Greek) Orthodox, the official cult of Russia. Other Armenians lived across Turkey's north-eastern border with Russia as well. About half of all of these Christians were within striking distance of Russia's powerful army and Black Sea fleet. Some would have welcomed civil equality with Muslims, but those living in compact zones really desired full autonomy or independence. The combination of foreign wars and domestic unrest that modernization was bound to produce could easily explode the Ottoman Empire. This is why the Russian Tsar more than once said that if he withheld the hand that sustained the Sultan, the Ottoman Empire – at least the Christian sectors – would collapse.[5]

That mid-century Turkey was a 'sick man' is beyond doubt, but were the other societies of the world healthy? Both terms are immensely subjective. The health of British India and the English addiction to tea required a war to force the sale of opium to China against the wishes of the Chinese government.[6] The health of the British textile industry relied on the cotton produced by Afro-American slaves in the United States. The health of the English peerage and British agriculture allowed the starvation of millions of Irish in the great potato famine. The health of French democracy led to its abolition by the man whom the French overwhelmingly elected president by universal male suffrage. The health of the Russian state required serfdom, twenty-five-year terms for army conscripts, and discrimination against the religions of up to one third of the population and against the cultural aspirations of such large nationalities as the Ukrainians. The health of the balance of power in Europe required the continued suppression of Poland as a state, the forced inclusion of some north Germans within Denmark, and half a dozen nationalities within Austria. According to the liberal standards of the day, these conditions were all sick. According to the conservatives of the day, the liberals were sick, and radicals simply evil.

The truth in what Nicholas said to Seymour is that Britain and Russia together could determine the immediate fate of the Ottoman Empire. If London and St Petersburg saw eye to eye, then Ottoman sickness would not lead to war. But these two did not agree, and within less than fifteen months of this conversation, England and Russia were at war over the Ottoman Empire. So were France and Russia. So, of course, were the Turks and Russia. The goal of this book is to explain how this came about and elucidate some of the causes.

THE PROBLEM: II – REASONS WHY?[7]

On the simplest level, the Crimean War in its origin was just like the recent Gulf War. *A* occupied the territory of *B* on the heels of a dispute over *X*. Then *C* told *A* to leave, sooner rather than later. *A* tried to find a third-party negotiated expedient that allowed for a retreat with some concrete gain. *C* refused *A*'s conditions, set a military timetable, and attacked the home territory of *A*.

Of course the Crimean War was far more complicated: it was really two wars and also a diplomatic struggle. First there was a Russo-Turkish war, beginning, some might argue, with Russia's unopposed invasion of Moldavia and Wallachia, leading in four months to ambitious Turkish counterattacks with limited Anglo-French and Austrian armed diplomatic support. The conflict then developed into a coalition war, in which the French and especially the British not only fought on behalf of Turkey, but also pursued their own expansionist aims. In addition, Austria initiated an intricate diplomatic strategy to limit the extent of both wars. Students of this war thus have had no trouble finding defensive grounds for Russia's initial military moves against Turkish forces and aggressive bases for Anglo-French and Austrian support of Turkey and even for Turkey's responses to Russian moves.

Indeed the Crimean War originated within the context of the nineteenth-century developments of industrial capitalism, nationalism, and imperialism, shifts in the European balance of power, the 'Great Game' – the rivalry between England and Russia stretching halfway across the globe, the Eastern Question with its legacy of Russo-Turkish hostility, the tensions and dislocations created by the revolutions of 1848–49 – including the revival of French Bonapartism, and the growing divergence between Western Europe and Russia after 1815. Consequently the war was the product of a series of extra-European issues and forces as well as of the same root problems that led to the wars of Italian and German unification between 1848 and 1871.

The *A–B–C* model and the big picture, however, do not explain how the war itself arose. For this we must turn to three strange phenomena: the Holy Places dispute, the Menshikov mission to Constantinople, and the Vienna peace process. The first was a squabble between two of the world's greatest powers, France and Russia, over the respective rights of two great branches of Christianity in the Holy Land. The second pitted the diplomacy of Russia against the interests of Turkey, Britain, and Austria, as well as France. The third was a futile Great Power attempt to find a peaceful solution to what had become a Russo-Turkish quarrel, while the Turks, the weakest of all the concerned states, prepared to fight.

Behind these events lie some of the eternal questions about the origins of wars. Do they result primarily from the dynamics of domestic politics and the ambitions of individual leaders or ambassadors? Can the struggles between rival embassies abroad lead the home countries into war? Similarly can lesser states force their Great Power protectors into armed conflict? What, then, is the role of public opinion? Is it merely the tool of politicians who are determined to go to war?

The Crimean War has appeared to many observers from the very moment of its outset to have been unnecessary, stupid and the product of malice and misunderstandings. Having studied history most of my life, I am not certain that I know what *necessary* means, when states are in conflict, but I can say that I have always found the Crimean War to be somewhat bizarre. My fresh investigation of original documents from fourteen countries, including, especially, Russia, has rendered the origin of this war understandable, but, from the standpoint of what we normally consider to be modern, still bizarre. I would be surprised if, after going through the following nineteen chapters, the reader will not agree that this war would have been avoided if the leadership of every major power in 1853 had acted rationally in its own imperialistic interests. Such rationality, after all, is the least that we citizens of Great Power states should demand of our leaders for our own selfish interests, if for nothing else.

But what to do when another Great Power starts to act irrationally against its own interest . . .? Read this and weep, for there was, besides reason, *unreason why*.

NOTES

1. Seym. to Rus., 11 Jan. 1853 (*CORR* I.98).
2. For Turkey at this time, Bernard Lewis, *The Emergence of Modern Turkey* (London 1961/1965), pp. 55–113; Davison *ROE*:1–70.

3. David B. Ralston, *Importing the European Army. The Introduction of European Military Techniques and Institutions into the Extra-European World, 1600–1914* (Chicago 1990), pp. 62–4.

4. Cf. Alfred Rieber, 'The Persistent Conditions of Russian Foreign Policy: an Interpretative Essay', *The Traditions of Imperial Russian Foreign Policy* (ed. Hugh Ragsdale, forthcoming), employs the notion of porous frontiers as a permanent factor in Russian foreign policy, but it applies similarly to Austria, Turkey, and other states as well.

5. Nes. to Brw., 8/20★ Dec. 1849 (TsGADA III/115).

6. Gerald S. Graham, *The China Station, War and Diplomacy. 1830–1860* (Oxford 1978), pp. 103–4.

7. Cf. Alfred Lord Tennyson's 'The Charge of the Light Brigade', and two book titles: Cecil Woodham-Smith, *The Reason Why* (New York 1954); Norman Rich, *Why the Crimean War? A Cautionary Tale* (Hanover/London 1985).

★Readers should note that the use of soliduses throughout the text denotes old Russian/new western dates.

PART ONE
The Setting

CHAPTER ONE
Western Questions – The Home Fronts

EUROPE'S HEGEMONY

In the middle of the nineteenth century the world was much less inhabited and developed than today, but the differences among regions and culture zones were just as striking. Only about 1.2 billion people were alive. One-third lived in China, one-third in the rest of Asia, a twelfth in Africa, and a fortieth in Latin America – altogether about 950 million. On the other hand, 265 million Europeans and North Americans resided in the regions where international power was concentrated.

The population of Europe and North America was unevenly divided among the major states: about 60 million in the Russian Empire, 35 million in France, 33 million in the German states excluding Austria, 30 million in the conglomerate domains of the Austrian Emperor, 26 million in Great Britain, 19 million in the Italian states excluding Austrian Venetia and Lombardy, 15 million in Spain, and maybe 10 million in European Turkey. The United States had only about 23 million.[1]

Europe as a whole and each of its major states were divided into regions of greater and lesser development in culture and in the organization of technology, economic life, administration, and politics. Great Britain had the highest level of industrialization and urbanization in the world and about 70 per cent male literacy, more than twice that of Japan, the most advanced non-Western society. The corresponding rates for France, Germany and the more advanced part of Austria were about 55 per cent, and for white males in the United States, 90 per cent. The backward parts of Austria were more like Russia, where less than 20 per cent of the men could read.

On the other hand, even within the most advanced parts of the non-Western world, traditionally educated upper classes, literate state officials, and religious leaders tried to limit intercultural contacts and innovations to what was militarily useful. In most of Latin America, native élites, sharing in a conservative European culture, by and large maintained the Iberian colonial administration. Specialization and production for the world market did not enable any of these societies to operate within the more advanced world as equal partners.

Indeed the European world bristled with zones of cultural and economic dynamism. The development of steam power and its application to mining, manufacture and transportation gave an over-whelming advantage to the developed sectors of the European world. Eventually, the non-Europeans were going to be compelled, as one East Asian put it, to adopt the Europeans' 'putrid' calendar and wear their 'filthy' clothing.

The history of international competition from 1492, when Columbus sailed to Santo Domingo, until 1853, when the American Admiral Perry steamed to Japan, illustrates the political aspect of the Western Question for the non-Western world. In 1492 the imperialism of several Asian, African and American states flourished along with those of Europe. By 1853 five European and one North American state marched, rode or sailed off with the great prizes at the political expense of the others. When Europeans lost, it was to each other. Together, under Britain's *de facto* leadership, the advanced countries presented the rest of the world with a political, legal, commercial, scientific and military culture, that, as the Japanese soon discovered, could be beaten only by being joined.

WAYS AND MEANS OF PRODUCTION

A materialist would argue that the key Western Question for the West and non-West alike lay in the technical and social organization of production. More effective circulation of money, instruments of credit, distribution of goods and capital formation went hand in hand with the more efficient tools. As is the case today, the qualitative contrasts among these forms of production and the quantitative differences among societies possessing these forms determined the economic and political ranking of states. In contrast to a century earlier, the most backward of the major European powers around 1850 was well advanced over any non-Western society, except Japan.[2]

Industrialization was the chief measure of advancement and the bearer of what made the West so different from its own past, not to say the rest of the world. The results could be seen in all sorts of machinery, railroads, steamships with first paddle wheels and then screw propellers, larger and stronger wrought-iron bridges, iron-frame buildings, increased newspaper circulation, the telegraph, mass production of rifles, breech-loading ordnance (artillery), and war steamers. The Great Exhibition of 1851, housed in a huge hall built of iron and glass (rebuilt as the Crystal Palace), was testimony to a new British-led industrial civilization.

To grasp the 'modern' world of *c.* 1850 and its mechanisms more accurately, however, one should also bear in mind the degree to which animal, human and wind power still prevailed and improved. For example, in 1852, Britain's 25,000 sail carried 143 tons per craft, while the 1,270 steamers could ferry only 14 per cent more per ship. In France, the 1830s and the 1840s were the most intense decades ever for the construction of canals. Mountainous Austria witnessed a massive expansion of her primary road system for horse-drawn vehicles from the latter eighteenth century onward.[3]

A variety of pre-modern modes of production still flourished in the great states of Europe and North America of 1850. Small-scale agriculture, forestry, animal husbandry, fishing, crafts and the putting-out system were everywhere. Serf labour powered much of Russia's agriculture, industry, and mining; agrarian slavery prevailed in the US South; tenant-farming was widespread in British ruled Ireland; and large scale agriculture with free labour was practised on many English and Prussian estates, as well as in Austria, where former serfs were hit with additional payments for their recently acquired freedom.[4]

The immensely contrasting incidence of advancement was a crucial factor in the power potential of various states. Britain's 14,150 power-looms and 240,000 handlooms of 1820 had changed to 250,000 and 40,000 respectively in 1850, by which time there were 4.5 million industrial workers, nine times more than in Russia.[5] In 1850 Britain probably had more than half of the world's steam power and produced more than half the world's pig iron, even though the railroad system of the United States was almost one-third longer. This speaks for Britain's all-round development. Russia, by contrast, even when the St Petersburg–Moscow line was completed in 1851, had only 25 per cent the gross and 3 per cent the per capita amount of railways found in the agrarian American South, and no more mechanized industry than tiny Belgium. Russia thus possessed a very weak technical basis for its reputedly greatest army in the world.

Standards of living, even in advanced countries, were low in contrast to today. Although in England and the United States they were roughly twice what an average person needed to feed and house himself adequately according to 1850 standards, many working people lived well below the 'poverty line', especially on the European continent.[6] The seasonal or semi-employed reserve proletariat, very poor rural and urban labourers, were ubiquitous figures, but indispensable to the functioning of the economies. Widespread low standards of living for the majority explain why predatory, expansionist ventures normally generated more support than opposition. Life was still quite cheap. On the other hand, the civilization of industrialization was one of periodic food shortages and hardship, utopian nostalgia and rising expectations for working people, so even the advanced states were sitting on potential social powder kegs.[7]

COMMERCE AND ITS AMBITIONS

Industrial and financial power translated into commercial power, Great Britain being by far the greatest trading nation, especially for suppliers of raw materials, foodstuffs and specialized craft products. In turn, the Russian, Ottoman and Chinese Empires, India, Latin America and the United States, respectively accounted for 3.5, 5.5, 5, 11.75, 15.5 and 20 per cent of British external commerce. This extra-European 'lion's share' of trade created for Britain a world-wide 'empire in all but name'.[8] As foreign trade constituted about 35 per cent of GNP, the British were very touchy about anything, including other states' armies, fleets or fiscal and industrial policies that might disrupt or threaten this commerce.

Britain was also by far the leading foreign investor, overseas credit holdings having mushroomed from £24.6 million (12 per cent of GNP) in 1816 to £218 million (41.5 per cent of GNP) in 1851. The French, in contrast, held only about £25 million (5 per cent of GNP), most of it in neighbouring Spain, Belgium and Italy. The United States, in greater contrast, owed a net £44 million (10.5 per cent of GNP).[9]

Almost all of Britain's foreign wars had been connected with commerce. As rivals raised tariffs to develop their industries, though, Britain turned to an 'imperialism of free trade', which accommodated competitors, forged ahead with better production techniques, and forced open the markets of backward states, sometimes with gunboats and landing parties.[10] The predominance and utility of the British fleet for all trading powers, the commercial and financial dependence of the United States upon Britain, and the unwillingness of the French after Napoleon to risk any more maritime disasters all contributed to the remarkable fact that 1815 was the last year that any rivalries among the three great North Atlantic powers led to war. The residue of self-righteous hostility among them had ceded to enlightened self-interest, and a spiteful co-imperialism prevailed, whereby the maritime powers supported each other's commercially inspired gunboat diplomacy.

France, Prussia and Austria avoided Britain's commercial clutch and had their own special trading zones, French and Prussian industry also benefiting from Britain's relative free trade policies. Prussia's chief commercial concern was developing the German Zollverein or Customs Union, which also dominated Holland's commerce (32 per cent), and, together with France, Belgium's (26 per cent each). Austria, which included Lombardy and Venetia at this time, was, along with France, Turkey's second largest commercial partner. Austria also predominated in the border regions in the Balkans, and traded heavily with the other northern and central Italian states.[11]

France and Germany, as well as the United States, could think in terms of becoming first-rate economic powers. American 'Manifest Destiny' envisioned expansion across the Pacific to capture and develop Asian markets.[12] War with Mexico had just settled the major issues in the future south-west and California, while prudent negotiations with Britain produced the same results in the Oregon Territory. The French were cashing in on their new acquisition in Algeria, and some of them looked hungrily toward Belgium. Simultaneously, their Prussian counterparts hoped to unite Germany and turn the Zollverein into a political unit, and were not averse to taking over Belgium's railroads.[13] The leading Austrian economic thinking sought an impossible Vienna-dominated union with Germany, as well as more realistic expansion to the south, in the Balkans or Italy. North Italian capitalists and politicians in both Lombardy and independent Piedmont-Sardinia had similar ambitions towards central and southern Italy.[14] Almost all of Europe's war scares and wars involving Belgium, Germany, and Italy during 1848–71 can be traced in part to these designs of political economy, but to single out the economic factor is to tread on slippery turf.[15]

Russia was in a unique position, needing exports to pay off debts and import machinery, but with foreign trade only about 5 per cent of GNP, as compared to 17–20 per cent for Germany, France, the United States and the Ottoman Empire.[16] Protecting her weak industries with high tariffs, Russia was hence the most autarchic great power, but lacked economic leverage. On the other hand, relative autarchy created the freedom to operate outside the British-led, capitalist-imperialistic system of the mid-nineteenth century, as well as the pipe-dream of establishing a vast commercial empire along the borders from Turkey to northern China.[17] Russia's only genuinely natural allies were states that depended upon her for support of prevailing domestic structures.

The sole place where Russian economic interests and diplomatic problems seriously intersected was at the Sulina Channel at the mouth of the Danube. Russia could hinder steamboat traffic there by obstructing the dredging process to the benefit of grain exports from Odessa. This hurt Austria, the Ottoman Empire, the latter's Romanian Principalities and, eventually, England, and created a community of interest against a specific Russian policy by 1850.[18] However, this issue was not likely to lead England or any other state to provoke an expensive war with another major power. Given the prevailing monetary policies, negotiations and temporary losses were much more reasonable.

FINANCE AND ITS LIMITS

The monetary systems of the major powers were based on the old metallic principles that had served the Dutch and British so well for almost two centuries and now made the major powers cautious. Only the under-taxed, under-governed, and resource-rich United States courted fiscal anarchy by lacking a national bank, leading to great booms and busts and the generation of all sorts of venture capital, but not expensive foreign policies. In contrast the states of Europe were exceedingly cautious in the fiscal realm, except during emergencies. Money was the real and not so hidden king, and the Russian Tsar himself would not tinker with the good credit that his government had in the Amsterdam and London money markets. Consequently, even Britain suffered from a relative money shortage, while Austria and Russia were truly capital starved. France launched her innovative capital-generating Crédit foncier and Crédit mobilier only in 1852.[19]

Not least among the advantages of stable currencies, however, was a willingness to store money in savings banks, which enjoyed a remarkable development in most of Europe in the first half of the nineteenth century. Overall, sound private banking was most developed in Britain and growing. Total British deposits in 1844 were 150 per cent of the state budget; in 1855, they reached 240 per cent of the peacetime budget. This meant that money could be generated and loans subscribed whenever the London Cabinet deemed it necessary. British military allocations increased five to seven times in 1854, the initial year of the Crimean War, while France's and Russia's barely doubled.[20] Most other states needed a huge reserve of precious metals to raise sound money quickly. Even so rich a country as France or so vast a one as Russia, not to say so financially strapped a realm as Austria, had to be cautious about launching costly foreign adventures.

GOVERNANCE: THE WESTERN PART OF THE WEST

In general, conscious activism and the application of recent learning to the solution of specific domestic and foreign policy tasks distinguished Western states from non-Western ones, since all states were organized to protect property and the prevailing social structure. However, within this rubric there were vast differences among the great powers, as in the economic realm.

The limited British monarchy had the most stable representative institution, Parliament, but was no democracy. Only about 8–9 per cent of adult men had the vote, while 35–50 per cent of the parliamentary elections were uncontested.[21] The hereditary crown under Queen Victoria carried some weight, and, prodded by her German relatives, the queen was attempting to revive royal prerogatives.[22] Her Majesty's ministers, however, only paid lip-service to her office and tended to do as they chose as individuals or as a Cabinet.

An élite of landed aristocrats, upper bourgeois, and middle-class commoners of genuine talent succeeded in providing political continuity and stability. A small number of select schools and universities contributed to this, as their graduates dominated the political leadership of all the major groupings by forming a network of power-brokers and political operators, whose rivalries and disputes were balanced by their social ties.[23] Traditions of liberty kept the Home Office less powerful than the typical Ministry of the Interior on the

Continent, but it was sufficiently powerful to ensure social peace and the breaking of labour strikes.

The British press was the most developed in Europe, the rather moderate (London) *Times*, with its daily circulation of 40,000 in 1852, having seized the leadership in world journalism. The public often learned of important foreign news as soon as or even before the Foreign Office did. The various sectors of British opinion had their daily or periodical organs, and the major ones were 'all read in the clubs'. [24] The informal organizations of 'the City' (the London financial district) lent a strong voice to business interests. Moreover, the dichotomy between economic development and political disenfranchisement, the disparity between the rich and the working poor, dependence upon overseas trade and empire, and the workings of the free press made nationalism a key integrating force.

Politics at the centre were somewhat fluid due to shifting alliances, the two-party system of Conservatives (Tories) and Whigs (Liberals) having broken down over the issue of tariffs. The ex-Tory Peelites, by abolishing the restrictive Corn Laws in 1846, had helped to defuse the popular Chartist movement that demanded both democracy and cheap food; but the programme for radical political reform was still on the table. [25] In Parliament, Conservatives, Peelites ('Liberal–Conservatives'), and Liberals comprising Whigs, Radicals and Irish deputies manoeuvred under a handful of headstrong leaders to form and retain coalitions, which threatened to break down over special religious or fiscal interests. [26]

After Peel's death in 1850, the most powerful English politician was the ex-Tory Whig, Viscount Henry Palmerston, Foreign Secretary for most of 1831–51, who knew how to play upon nationalist sentiment and snipe at those who challenged him. It was risky for any government to face the charge of not defending English interests abroad. Regardless of who was in office, England would not sleep for very long if the home islands, commerce or the Empire even appeared to be threatened. [27]

Across the Channel, the French republic was a new democracy, born in the revolutionary events of 1848; but it was only a democracy on paper, because it was counter-revolutionary and required absolutist and dictatorial legacies for survival. Subversive ideas found eager listeners in the countryside as well as the cities, but troops were on hand for use against revolutionaries. The Ministry of the Interior, inherited from the Imperial dictatorship of Napoleon I, remained almost a law unto itself, dedicated to order, very powerful in the prefectures, and given to cooperating with the local notables and influencing elections. Troublemakers, against whom there were 'moral judgements', were jailed, exiled or shipped off to prisons in Algeria or Guyana. Labour organizations or corporations operated 'on the margins of the law', due to the enforcement of anti-union statutes, such as the Le Chapelier law of 1791.[28]

The central administration in Paris had been attempting to rule and regulate the entire country since the first Napoleon, and the concentration of money in Paris and élite education in a few *grandes écoles* were focal points of continuity at the top.[29] The conservative National Assembly, elected in 1849 on universal manhood suffrage, was a powerful legislature through 1851, and the press was almost completely free – at least temporarily. Radical political clubs, however, were suppressed. Furthermore, in 1850 the Assembly gave the local Catholic clergy a watchdog role over state schools and eliminated much of the popular vote, by extending residency requirements from six months to three years. These measures made the powerful, reactionary Catholic lobby disproportionately influential within the French body politic.[30]

The elected president, 'Prince' Louis-Napoleon, was outside the political party structure, but he spoke for nationalism, which was the only popular unifying force. The embittered Victor Hugo may have called this 'Little Napoleon' a 'bandit', 'ragman', and 'plucked owl', but he was able to gain widespread recognition on the part of both educated and uneducated society as the guarantor of social and financial stability *and* the best hope of the poor. He had only one four-year term that would expire in December 1852, and was properly suspected of wishing to restore his uncle's Empire. Conservative Europe did not want that, but desired French instability even less. The prince-president's tenuous position meant that French foreign policy would serve his domestic needs, which favoured stable relations with immediate neighbours, but did not preclude adventures further afield where the interests of his greatest supporters, commerce and Catholicism, converged.

The only major power with anything close to real democracy, at least for Caucasian men, was the United States, whose press was the most economically dynamic in the world.[31] The Americans relied upon 'free soil' in the West to provide a social safety valve for whites, and upon ethnic hostility and prejudice to control Amerindians, free and unfree Afro-Americans, and even the numerous European immigrants in the workforce. As in any democracy, disproportionate power lay with the rich, who operated here through the political machines and mass media in the North and the oligarchical county courthouses of the South. Policy was determined by shifting political alliances among the plantation élites, industrialists, bankers, merchants, patronage-wielding urban bosses and representatives of the freeholders, who could not be ignored, since they bore arms and knew how to shoot.

The absence of strong central administrative institutions and any traditional intellectual leadership threatened to leave the United States a headless dynamo, especially with the growing controversy over slavery. Much of northern capital was British, and most of southern capital was generated by the sale of cotton to Britain, but northern and southern capital could not ally effectively due to popular 'free soil' opposition to the spread of the 'peculiar institution' of the South. The deadlock between North and South created the strong possibility that a regional interest or a passing passion might commit the nation to an aggressive foreign policy or to sectional strife. Consequently, the English felt that American democracy and nationalism had to be coddled and managed, and French and Russian statesmen hoped to use the threat of America to exert leverage upon England.[32] It was, however, England that had the greatest leverage.

GOVERNANCE: THE EASTERN PART OF THE WEST

In 1850 Central and Eastern European governments did not pretend to be democratic or really liberal. The hereditary crowns controlled the very prestigious military, appointed ministers and had a decisive voice in legislation. Society was very much stratified, and, as in Britain and France, a handful of exclusive schools educated a large proportion of the élite.

Prussia, Austria and Germany as a whole were in a state of flux. A loose national Confederation of sovereign states, led by Austria, tried to impose uniform standards for law and order between 1819 and 1848 and ensure military cooperation against external aggression, but only Prussia and Austria really counted. Before 1848 both of these great powers were still absolute monarchies, with weak provincial legislatures organized on an unequal class basis favouring the nobilities as such, and strong, paternalistic central institutions balanced by respect for law and property. In both states the ministers were appointed by and responsible to the crown, which also controlled foreign policy.

In response to the revolutionary movements of 1848–49, the

Prussian government granted a constitution, which left the king with all of his former powers except control over legislation and taxation. These now were shared with a parliament, which was still elected in the older, inegalitarian manner. Prejudice in favour of the titled junker class kept the army and the bureaucracy aristocratic and monarchist in its leadership. Previously, the dynamic upper bourgeoisie had been able to influence state policy only indirectly via the ministerial mechanisms whereby the state promoted economic development. The new constitution now offered some possibilities for more influence from below. Prussia also had the most advanced civil service and public education system of any of the major powers, and Germany as a whole had a diverse press, due to many sovereign states with a variety of orientations.[33]

A basic problem for Prussia was the issue of orientation. Pure patriots were necessarily conservative, while liberals, not to say democrats, tended to be German nationalists willing to submerge Prussia in Germany. The royal court itself was split between reactionary and moderate factions, the latter supported by the heir-apparent or Prince of Prussia, the king's brother William. The romantic and sentimental Frederick William IV was cautious, though willing to try to expand in northern Germany if this could be done without international embarrassment. Due to the actual power and prestige of Russia and Austria, however, a Prussian Louis-Napoleon or Palmerston, who would dare to balance social conservatism, cautious domestic reform and an assertive foreign policy, was still a decade away from high office.

The Austrian monarchy faced a more difficult set of challenges, since nationalism threatened to explode the realm. The dominant German nationality did not even constitute one-fourth of the total population and had to contend with significant numbers of Hungarians, Italians, Czechs, Poles, Romanians, Slovaks, Ukrainians and South Slavs (Slovenes, Croats and Serbs), each of whom had national territories. Attempts at creating workable constitutional solutions in 1848–49 failed due chiefly to national rivalries and the ultimate cohesion of the Imperial army, composed of excellent raw material drawn from a variety of peoples.

The result was an attempt at bureaucratic centralization, with the use of the army, police, censorship and economic development policies to recreate a strong Austria. One of its most pressing tasks was to oversee the liquidation of the remnants of personal serfdom in most of the non-Alpine provinces. The seventeen-odd crown lands remained separate, but lost their autonomy. Power was now almost completely concentrated in Vienna: the court, the Council of Ministers, the Army High Command, and the upper echelons of the bureaucracy. The Catholic Church was very influential and promoted loyalty among the diverse peoples. The upper bourgeoisie lacked an institutional power base, but had some influence, since the state was in a financial crisis and needed to expand production and income.[34]

Most of the ethnic communities which populated the Habsburg Empire had close ties with ethno-linguistic brethren or cousins in neighbouring states. This ethnic overlap created a classic example of the *Primat der Innenpolitik* in the formulation of foreign policies. Austrian domestic security required stability next door and a conservative Russia that would resist the temptation to utilize Czech or South Slavic Panslavism for selfish purposes. Counter-revolutionary success in 1848–49 also presented the ambitious new Chancellor, Felix Schwarzenberg, with an occasion to reassert Austria's influence in Germany, Italy, Switzerland and the Balkans.

The Russian Empire, like Austria, was cosmopolitan at top and multinational below. The state had been attempting to introduce Western law for a century and a half, but the power of officials remained quite arbitrary. The bloated and underpaid bureaucracy was hopelessly inefficient and corrupt, with horrendous speculation at the top. Secure private property for nobles and townsmen was an institution less than ninety years old and not respected by the masses of peasants, who considered all of the land to be theirs under God and the Tsar. From 1801 on, the state, however, fully respected and even subsidized noble, serf-holding landowners and retired army officers, who aided the appointed governors in running the provinces and keeping the peasantry under control.[35]

The fundamental social and political unit was the strong peasant village, nominally under a landowner, his steward or state officials. It was just as much under its own peasant oligarchy of fathers and grandfathers, who redistributed arable lands to the able-bodied adults and benefited from noble or state granaries to cover for bad harvests. Truculent young men who did not wish to submit to such a regime in the village were shipped off to the army, essentially for life. In the eyes of Karl Marx, the foundations of Russian society were those of an Oriental despotism, which explained the nature of the state and the weak development of Russian capitalism.[36]

The reigning Tsar, Nicholas I, saw himself as the senior European aristocrat and conservative. At heart a fatalistic martinet, police chief and his own foreign minister, he tried personally to coordinate his family's devotional life and court activities, military training and naval development, administrative reform and cultural policies. He consulted with the Minister of War and Chief of the Third (Security Police) Section of His Majesty's Own Imperial Chancery virtually every day. Without obstruction from any channels he could initiate a police investigation, authorize the construction of battleships, set a rigid timetable for a major project, connive to partition a neighbouring state, or mobilize the army and navy. There was no real Cabinet system as in Austria, Prussia, or even Turkey.[37]

The understaffed Russian Orthodox Church, by far the most intolerant of official churches among the major powers, was also a department of the state, the ruling Holy Synod of metropolitan archbishops headed by a lay Procurator instead of a patriarch. The Church disseminated official proclamations, preached obedience, and cooperated with the state in the realm of primary education and censorship for the Russians, Ukrainians and Belarusians (the latter two not recognized as such), who together comprised about 80 per cent of the population. The Old Believers and other Russian sects that had sprung from Orthodoxy in the seventeenth and eighteenth centuries, and who attracted up to one-third of the Russians, were illegal. So was that hybrid product of the defunct Polish–Lithuanian Republic, the Uniat Church, made up of Ukrainians and Belarusians, whose rituals were Slavic Orthodox, but whose organization and loyalties were Catholic. Nicholas had allowed the Holy Synod to take over the Uniat Church inside the empire and all of its buildings and institutions in the late 1830s. Catholics, Armenians, Lutherans, other established Protestants and Muslims enjoyed freedom of worship, but proselytizing and apostasy from Orthodoxy were illegal. Jews, on the other hand, were subject to far more discrimination and disabilities in the Russian Empire than in other illiberal European countries. The religious policies of the state fostered the patronage of the Orthodox Church abroad, but also contributed to Russia's bad reputation in Europe and the Ottoman Empire, even among some Christians, as well as to discontent among some of the Tsar's subjects.[38]

The press and book importation were subject to harsh, if clumsy censorship, and after 1848 there may have been more Russians working for censorship organs than there were books published.[39] This created a curious anomaly. In the other major states, the press could influence policy and help create war scares. In Russia it could at times be patriotic and express the nationalists' hatred of Austria, fear of Prussia, anger towards France, envy toward England, and disgust with Turkey, but it could not incite hostilities by expressing

Table 1   Mid-century economic indicators[40]

	Steam power (1000 HP)		Pig iron (1000 tons)	Railways (miles)	Per capita GNP (1990 US $)
	1840	1850	1850	1850	1850
Great Britain	620	1290	2250	6635	2277
United States	?	?400	633	8683	2130
France	90	270	410	1994	1410
Germany (Prussia)	40	260	300	3717 (1573)	1320
Austria	20	100	?200	1008	1190
Russia	20	70	250	410	735
Belgium	40	70	140	528	1725
Netherlands	—	10			1653
Italy	10	40			1205
Spain	10	20			1303

Table 2   Mid-century foreign trade (1850)

	Total export	Total import	British Share export	British Share import	Share of British export	Share of British import
	million £		(percentage)		(percentage)	
Great Britain	71.3	100.4				
US	42.0	43.0	62.3	48.8	21.4	19.2
France	49.0	43.0	14.9	6.3	2.7	7.3
Zollverein (Germany)	34.8	36.1	17.1	19.9	7.2	5.9
Austria	10.7	14.1	4.0	5.0	1.1	0.5
Russia	14.0	14	44.0	27.6	5.4	5.6
Ottoman Empire	?12.0	?12.0	39.0	31.3	5.8	4.7
Holland	13.6	13.6	15.2	17.8	5.8	4.1
Belgium	9.0	10.0	17.9	16.7	1.6	1.5

private opinions on current official matters. The Russian foreign ministry could not offer the excuse of nonexistent constitutional liberties.

Like all autocrats (and Nicholas was far more of one than Louis-Napoleon ever could be in France), the Tsar depended upon the information his officials supplied, so their views counted, and these included both nationalism and, among certain circles, a variety of romantic conservative, liberal and socialist ideas. However, propagating radical reform projects from below was treated as illegal. Even partaking in a study group of intellectual dissidents could loand someone like the young Dostoyevsky a term in Siberia after 1848.[41] On the other hand, the state could not suppress the nationalist sentiment of army officers and soldiers, officials, writers, clergy and rank-and-file urbanites. Indeed the only safe outlets for some of the people in this realm which cried out for a domestic overhaul were nationalistic foreign policy enterprises and military action.

As a defensively assertive, conservative multinational empire with concern for the governance of minority nationals of neighbouring countries, post-1848 Russia was similar to both Austria and Turkey. As a nationalist state with devilish contradictions that invited resolution via assertiveness abroad, Russia resembled France, England, the United States and Prussia.

NOTES

1. Kuan I. Chen, *World Population Growth and Living Standards* (New Haven 1960), p. 64; Marcel Reinard, et al. *Histoire de la population mondiale* (Paris 1968), Annexe statistique; Kemal H. Karpat, *Ottoman Population, 1830–1914: Demographic and Social Characteristics* (Madison 1985), p. 116.
2. Paul Bairoch, 'International Industrialization Levels from 1750 to 1980', *Journal of European Economic History* 11 (1982): 290–6, as cited in Paul Kennedy, *The Rise and Fall of the Great Powers* (New York 1987/9), p. 149.
3. B.R. Mitchell, *British Historical Statistics* (Cambridge, UK 1968), pp. 535–6; Paul Bairoch, *Révolution industrielle et sous-développement* (Paris 1974), pp. 326–7; David Good, *The Economic Rise of the Habsburg Empire, 1750–1914* (Berkeley 1984), pp. 64–7.
4. Karl Dinklage, 'Die landwirtschaftliche Entwicklung', *HM* I: 401–14.
5. François Crouzet, *The Victorian Economy* (Anthony Forster, trans., New York 1982), p. 199; W.L. Blackwell, *The Beginnings of Russian Industrialization, 1800–1860* (Princeton 1968), p. 425.
6. Bernard Cook, 'Poverty', and 'Wages', *Victorian Britain. An Encyclopedia* (Sally Mitchell (ed.), New York 1988), pp. 623–4, 838–9; Peter H. Lindert, 'Reinterpreting Britain's Social Tables, 1688–1913', *Explorations in Economic History* 20 (1983): 90–104.
7. Dick Geary (ed.), *Labour and Social Movements in Europe before 1914* (Oxford 1989).
8. Board of Trade, Central Statistical Office, *Abstracts*, 1849–53, Abstract Tables, Nos 4–7; Frank Edgar Bailey, *British Policy and the Turkish Reform Movement. A Study in Anglo-Turkish Relations* (Cambridge MA 1942), p. 70; Paul Bairoch, 'Europe's Gross National Product', *Journal of European Economic History* (1976): 281; also Bernard Porter, *The Lion's Share. A Short History of British Imperialism, 1850–1970* (London 1983).
9. Albert H. Imlah, *Economic Elements in the Pax Britannica* (Cambridge MA

1958), pp. 42–81; Rondo Cameron, *France and the Economic Development of Europe, 1800–1914* (Princeton 1961), p. 79; Lane Davis et al., *American Economic Growth. An Economist's History of the United States* (New York 1972), pp. 34, 40, 316.

10. John Gallagher and Ronald Robinson, 'The Imperialism of Free Trade', *Economic History Review*, 2nd ser., VI.1 (1953): 1–15.

11. *GJ* (for 1848–55); Bailey, *British Policy and Turkish Reform*, pp. 102–6; Ugo Cova, 'Österreich(-Ungarn) und Italien', *HM* VI. 1: 630.

12. Cf. A.K. Weinberg, *Manifest Destiny: A Study in Nationalist Expansionism in American History* (Baltimore 1935), pp. 59–71; Bolkhovitinov: 49–58.

13. B.R. Mitchell, *European Historical Statistics, 1750–1975* (2nd rev. edn, New York 1980), p. 543; Thomas: 83–100; ZSAM HA, Rep. 50, E.I. No. 27 (from Brussels, 20 Jan. 1853).

14. Richard Charmatz, *Minister Freiherr von Bruck: Der Vorkämpfer Mitteleuropas* (Leipzig 1916), pp. 41–66; Paul W. Schroeder, 'Bruck vs. Buol: The Dispute over Austrian Eastern Policy, 1853–1855', *JMH* 40 (1968): 193; Herbert Matis, 'Leitlinien der österreichischen Wirtschaftpolitik', and Klaus Koch, 'Österreich und der deutsche Zollverein', *HM* I: 28–32, VI. 1: 537–45; Harry Hearder, *Italy in the Age of the Risorgimento, 1790–1870* (London 1983), pp. 40–1.

15. William Carr, *The Origins of the Wars of German Unification* (London 1991), pp. 104–11; Frank Coppa, *The Origins of the Wars of Italian Unification* (Harlow 1992).

16. See Table 2 and Paul Bairoch, 'Europe's Gross National Product, 1800–1975', p. 281.

17. Harold Ingle, *Nesselrode and the Russian Rapproachment with Britain, 1836–1844* (Berkley 1978). pp. 148–56.

18. Puryear *ERSQ*: 82–4, 122–3.

19. Pierre Vilar, *A History of Gold and Money, 1450–1920* (trans., Judith White, London 1976, first published Barcelona 1969), pp. 204–32; Ernest L. Bogart, *Economic History of Europe, 1760–1939* (London 1942), p. 190.

20. Charles P. Kindelberger, *A Financial History of Western Europe* (London 1984), pp. 75–122, *passim*; Crouzet, *Victorian Economy*, p. 333; Alan T. Peacock, *The Growth of Public Expenditure in the United Kingdom* (Princeton 1961), p. 37. Kennedy, *Rise of the Great Powers*, p. 176.

21. David Cresap Moore, *The Politics of Deference: A Study of the Mid-Nineteenth Century English Political System* (New York 1976), p. 282; B.R. Mitchell, *British Historical Statistics* (Cambridge UK 1988), p. 793.

22. Elizabeth Longford, *Queen Victoria: Born to Succeed* (New York 1964), p. 202.

23. Geoffrey Best, *Mid-Victorian Britain, 1851–1875* (London 1971), pp. 149–70.

24. Martin: 85–102; also Ivon Asquith, 'The structure, ownership and control of the press, 1780–1855', *Newspaper History from the Seventeenth Century to the Present Day* (Gordon Boyce, James Curran, Pauline Wingate (eds), London/Beverly Hills 1978), pp. 99–101; E.A. Smith, *A History of the Press* (London 1970), pp. 48–9.

25. Edward Royle and James Walvin, *English Radicals and Reformers, 1760–1848* (Lexington KY 1982), pp. 160–80; D.G. Wright, *Popular Radicalism. The Working-Class Experience, 1780–1880* (London 1988), pp. 138–55, 183–90.

26. J.B. Conacher, *The Peelites and the Party System, 1848–1852* (Plymouth/ Devon 1972).

27. Brian Connell, *Regina vs. Palmerston. The Correspondence between Queen Victoria and her Foreign and Prime Minister, 1837–1865* (Garden City NY 1961), pp. 163–75.

28. Roger Price, *The Second French Republic. A Social History* (London 1972), pp. 193–326; Stuart L. Campbell, *The Second Republic Revisited: A Study in French Historiography* (New Brunswick NJ 1978), pp. 1–26; Thomas R. Forstenzer, who uses the term 'permanent counter-revolution', *French Provincial Police and the Fall of the Second Republic. Social Fear and Counterrevolution* (Princeton 1981), pp. 3, 243; William H. Sewell, *Work and Revolution in France: The Language of Labor from the Old Regime to 1848* (Cambridge UK 1980), especially pp. 90–1, 162.

29. Robert David Anderson, *Education in France, 1848–1875* (Oxford 1975), pp. 39–70; Robert J. Smith, *The Ecole Normale Supérieure and the Third Republic* (Albany NY 1982), pp. 5–29.

30. Adrien Dansette, *Histoire religieuse de la France contemporaine: de la Révolution à la Troisième République* (rev. edn, 2 vols, Paris 1948–51), I: 233–375; Price, *Second Republic*, pp. 254–60.

31. Frank Luther Mott, *American Journalism. A History, 1690–1960* (New York 1962), p. 237; two New York papers, the *Sun* and the *Herald*, rivalled the London *Times* in circulation.

32. For example, Cln. to Crampton 1, 8 April 1853 (ClDp. c. 125).

33. Theodore S. Hamerow, *Restoration, Revolution, Reaction. Economics and Politics in Germany, 1815–1871* (Princeton 1958), pp. 173–237.

34. Dinklage, 'Die landwirtschaftliche Entwicklung', and Herbert Matis, 'Leitlinien der österreichischen Wirtschaftpolitik', *HM* I: 33–4, 403–15.

35. Don Karl Rowney and Walter Pinter (eds), *Russian Officialdom: The Bureaucratization of Russian Society from the Seventeenth to the Twentieth Century* (Chapel Hill 1960), pp. 190–249; W. Bruce Lincoln, *In the Vanguard of Reform: Russia's Enlightened Bureaucrats, 1825–1861* (DeKalb 1982), pp. 1–40; Marc Raeff, *Understanding Imperial Russia* (Arthur Goldhammer, trans., New York 1984), pp. 147–68.

36. Jerome Blum, *Lord and Peasant in Russia from the Ninth to the Nineteenth Century* (Princeton 1961), pp. 414–74; Steven Hoch, *Serfdom and Social Control in Russia: Petrovskoe, A Village in Tambov* (Chicago 1986), pp. 133–90; Karl Marx, 'On Land Relations in Russia' (first published 1875), Karl Marx and Frederick Engels, *Select Works in Two Volumes* (Moscow 1956), pp. 49–61.

37. Nicholas Riasanovsky, *Nicholas I and Official Nationality in Russia, 1825–1855* (Berkeley/Los Angeles 1969), pp. 1–35, 184–234; Sydney Monas, *The Third Section. Police and Society in Russia under Nicholas I* (Cambridge MA 1961), pp. 1–21; Anatole Mazour, *The First Russian Revolution, 1825; the Decembrist Movement* (Berkeley 1937), pp. 203–21.

38. Igor Smolitsch, *Geschichte der russischen Kirche, 1700–1917* (Leiden 1964), pp. 287–99, 591–633; Derek Hopwood, *The Russian Presence in Syria and Palestine, 1843–1914: Church and Politics in the Near East* (Oxford 1969), pp. 33–45; David W. Edwards, 'The System of Nicholas I in Church–State Relations', *Russian Orthodoxy under the Old Regime*, ed. Robert Nichols and Theodore Stavrou. (Minneapolis 1978), pp. 154–69.

The documents in TsGIA 796/1661 indicate a very limited role of the Synod in foreign policy regarding Orthodox Churches.

39. Monas, *Third Section*, pp. 132–96, 230–9; W. Bruce Lincoln, *Nicholas I. Emperor and Autocrat of All the Russias* (Bloomington 1978), p. 320.

40. For Tables 1 and 2, the relative figures are probably closer to reality than the estimated absolute numbers. In addition to works cited in the text: *EB* (1911 and 1947 edns), *GJ* (for 1848–53), David S. Landes, *The Unbound Prometheus: Technological Change and Industrial Development in Western Europe from 1750 to the Present* (Cambridge UK 1969); Richard L. Rudolph, 'The Pattern of Austrian Industrial Growth from the Eighteenth to the Early Twentieth Century', *AHY* XI (1975): 10; Ernest Bogart, *Economic History of Europe, 1760–1939*, p. 164; *Sbornik svedenii po istorii i statistike vneshnei torgovli Rossii* (St Petersburg 1902).

41. Joseph Frank, *Dostoevsky. The Seeds of Revolt, 1821–1849* (Princeton 1976), pp. 239–91.

CHAPTER TWO

Western Questions – The Projection of Power

FORMALITIES

The ultimate decisions concerning war, peace and major policy matters differed according to state structures. In England Parliament decided, which in practice meant the Cabinet or its core members. In the United States policy was under the president, declarations of war belonged to both Houses of Congress and peace treaties had to be ratified by the Senate. By 1852 President Louis-Napoleon could make foreign policy decisions, but his political instincts led him to treat public opinion very seriously. In theory only did the crowned heads of Austria, Prussia, Russia and Turkey control foreign policy. In Austria the Chancellor (Metternich, Schwarzenberg, Buol) was usually decisive, if somewhat weakened after 1852. In Prussia the irresolute king vacillated between court and ministerial factions. Sultan Abdülmecid conceded this power to the regular Council of Ministers or the Grand Council. Nicholas I of Russia, however, was free to initiate an act of armed diplomacy and continue on a course unchecked. He consulted a great deal, but made all important decisions in whatever manner he so chose.

Outside of decision-making, the five European Great Powers organized diplomacy in a similar fashion, with foreign offices or ministries responsible either to the Cabinet as a whole or to the chief of state, professional staffs, and regular diplomatic and consular services. London's Under-Secretary of State for Foreign Affairs, H.H. Addington, France's Chief of the Political Directorate Eduard Thouvenel, and Russia's Assistant Foreign Minister and head of the Asiatic Department, Lev G. Seniavin, all contributed stability to policy. A foreign ministry was normally a premier service, attracting talented people who could move in high social circles.[1]

Heads of foreign missions all had perfect command of French, were usually sympathetic to the country where posted, and tended to share a common European conservative culture with diplomats and high society throughout Europe. Russia's Minister in London, Baron Philipp Brunnow since 1839 was on intimate terms with Lord (George Hamilton Gordon) Aberdeen, a leading Whig, who had been Foreign Secretary under Peel (1841–46). Britain's Minister in Vienna as of 1851, John Fane, Earl of Westmorland, had been British Military Commissioner to the allied armies under Karl Philip Schwarzenberg in 1813–14 and also composed martial music. The gallophile Joseph Alexander Freiherr von Hübner of Austria, having begun his diplomatic career as attaché to Paris in 1837, returned there as ambassador in 1849. Baron Christian Karl Josias von Bunsen, Prussian Minister in London since 1841, was a popular anglophile. Austria's Chancellor Count Karl Ferdinand von Buol-Schauenstein, a former ambassador to both St Petersburg (1848–50) and London (1850–52), was the brother-in-law of Baron Peter Meyendorff, russia's minister in Vienna as of 1850. Nicholas I apparently used his close friend, General Theodor Rochus Freiherr von Rochow, the Prussian envoy as of 1845, to communicate to some top Russian officials.[2]

The semi-parvenu Louis-Napoleon utilized this system. An anglophile himself, in 1851 he sent to London his like-minded, Polish-born, illegitimate first cousin, Count Alexandre Walewski, a natural son of the great Napoleon. The prince-president also dispatched to St Petersburg in 1849 the Marquis de Castelbajac, a personal friend, general, veteran of 1812 and an admirer of Nicholas I.[3] Certainly the necessary personal contacts existed to resolve conflicts and manage crises within Europe.

The methods of diplomacy of the European great powers were quite similar. There were well-worked-out norms for appointments and presentation of credentials by envoys, with uniform rankings within a country's diplomatic service: ambassador, minister, chargé d'affaires, and first secretary of the legation, which allowed for relative standings of the envoys within the entire diplomatic corps accredited to a given court or chief of state. And there were similar procedures for the transmission in both directions of ostensible, reserved, confidential and secret dispatches, all carefully numbered. Communication among capitals and legations or between a country's legations, either directly or via the foreign office at home, proceeded with regularity.

Diplomats often had access to the ostensible dispatches of other countries, so that in the working out of policy, statesmen could assume that their counterparts had a pool of common facts about all the major states. They also regularly used each others' couriers. Loose talk, mistrust, bribery, disinformation and spying were also part of the game. So were special verbal communications, which are impossible for the historian to trace in the liminal realm of open diplomacy, where intrigues were launched and deals suggested. Disinformation and the misuse of verbal communications played a key role in exacerbating the triangular Russian–Turkish–French relationship in 1852.

The ambassador's ostensible dispatch could become an important state document with the official version that committed a state to a certain version of events, unless a regime reversed a policy and backed down without losing face by blaming an envoy for exceeding his instructions. An envoy could be recalled at a pinch. A politic way of attacking another state's policy was to attack the envoy instead, but this could backfire, if the home government, leaning on public opinion, supported him.

Envoys often tried to be major figures in international relations, and they are often portrayed as such in scholarship. In fact, when they were not adhering precisely to their instructions from home, they were usually representing the interest of their legation or an influential faction in the country where they were posted. Home governments made the key policy decisions, and the envoy's opinion was simply one voice. Moreover, in Western Europe the press, with *ad hoc* couriers, telegraphs and fast steamers, was often ahead of the regular diplomatic service, sometimes with incorrect information which then influenced public opinion.

THE TERRESTRIAL BALANCE

In the middle of the nineteenth century the pen was indeed mighty, but political power still required swords as well as ploughshares to back it up. This meant, among other things, to organize some of the adventurous and some of the dregs of society as soldiers to follow orders, kill and die, and to recruit some of the seasoned troops and social élite as officers to lead these other men into battle. Every one of the Great Powers had to do this, and most statesmen respected the trained armies and up-to-date weapons of all the Great Powers.

Their armies and navies, like their foreign ministries and diplomatic corps, were structured in rather similar fashion and shared the same technologies, though at different rates of application. Everywhere officers were officers with similar educations, men were men, horse and foot were different species, artillery and engineering were the premier branches commanding special resources and talent, staffs tried to manage and record everything. Standard ships-of-the-line with eighty to 120 guns took precedent over frigates with forty to seventy and smaller craft. New technologies were only beginning to change the calculus of war.

The significant differences among the armies and navies of the Great Powers were due to national conditions and strategic needs. The West Europeans and Americans, followed by the Germans and Austrians, manufactured the best small arms and artillery. It did not matter who pioneered a weapon. A Swede (von Wahrendorff) and a Sardinian (Cavalli) developed breech-loading, rifled artillery; but the British, when they chose, gained the immediate lead in manufacture, and the French were not far behind. The Prussians secretly manufactured 45,000 needle rifles during 1841–47 and then increased production, but quality and quantity were below the French Minié model. By 1850, the French could arm most of their soldiers with rifles, while the Austrians had about twenty-seven rifle battalions (totalling maybe 15,000–16,000) of *Jägers* and *Feldjägers*, and the Russians barely had 6,200 rifles and a mere 1.3 muskets per soldier, and lacked the wealth to make up the shortfall with imports.[4]

Using manpower to compensate for technological lag, the Russian army conscripted about 80,000 men each year for a twenty-five-year term. There were also military colonies, where peasant-soldiers farmed, trained and begot more soldiers – a scheme devised during the Napoleonic wars to meet the new manpower requirements. A system of trained reserves was only in its infancy. In 1850 the army totalled about 1.1 million regulars, 118,000 irregulars (mostly Cossacks) and 730,000 reserves in military settlements, not all of whom could be called up. Over a million recruits had disappeared since 1828 as a result of harsh training, disease, desertion, the campaigns against Turkey (1828–29), Polish insurgents (1830–31), and Austria's Hungarian rebels (1849), the continuous fighting against the Muslim tribesmen of the Caucasus, and a few Central Asian adventures; the supply of cannon fodder seemed limitless. The typical Russian soldier was tough, but neither his weaponry nor training were up to European standards: Russian officers tending to prefer the bayonet to firearms. Staff work was at a miserable level as maps were considered a state secret. Nevertheless, on paper, Russia did have about 500,000 troops near her Western frontiers from the Baltic to the Black Sea. The French estimated in late 1852 that Russia could deploy 700,000 troops in European operations alone.[5]

On Russia's defensive side the lessons of 1812 were still clear. No one in his right mind would dream of invading the interior, but still Russia might have to face the hostility of most of continental Europe, as in 1809–12, or a combined land and sea attack on the Baltic coast. The Tsar's strategic thinking in this case far outran economic capabilities. With less railway than Belgium, he dreamed of a North–South system along the western frontier to enable the rapid deployment of overwhelming numbers at any sector.[6]

The Austrian army still used the Serb and Croat peasant-soldiers settled in the Military Frontier, but was less than one-third the size of Russia's. Units were deployed around the realm, with regiments in Hungary, Lombardy, Bohemia and Galicia to deal with domestic as well as international eventualities. Austrian staff work and artillery then were excellent and use of railways more effective than Prussia's. The biggest weaknesses were multi-ethnicity and limited human and financial resources in comparison to Russia and France respectively.[7]

The French army, with some seasoned troops in North Africa, had increased from 240,000 in 1847 to 450,000 due to the insecurities of the Revolution of 1848. It had a workable reserve system, was the best armed in the world, and was stationed chiefly in the north and east. Prussia, with only 130,000–200,000 regular soldiers, had an excellent staff and developed a superb reserve system to muster 430,000 in order to counter virtual encirclement by three larger major powers.[8]

England had only about 100,000 troops outside India. Many were stationed in colonies in the West Indies, Canada and Africa, or in Ireland, thus leaving very few for any European campaign or defence against the chimera of a French landing. The Indian Army was a peculiar hybrid, numbering a little more than 35,000 Europeans and 350,000 natives, each component, however, with the same amount of artillery pieces. The greatest force in Asia, its purpose was to defend and expand British India, not to supply reserves for England's European needs.[9] The United States army barely had 10,000 regulars, many guarding frontier posts against Plains Indians, and did not count at all in Great Power calculations.

The force structures created their own balance. The refurbished and feared French *Armée de terre* could march into Belgium and the Rhineland, or into North Italy as Piedmont-Sardinia's ally, and might even attempt a surprise landing in Britain. The Prussian and Austrian armies were expected to spearhead a German response to any French attack in Europe or any hostile Russian move into Central Europe. Russia's ability to overrun the Balkans was balanced by the Austria and Turkish armies and the British and French navies. Inside Germany, Austria and the smaller states together were more than a match for Prussia.

The uneven acquisition of newer technologies only started to have some effects by 1850. Awe of Russia's quantity more than compensated for disdain for her overall quality. Neither the French advantage in rifles nor the Russian advantage in numbers tempted them to commence an aggressive war in Europe. On the other hand, Prussian worries about lack of rifles for their reserves and inexperience with their railroads helps to explain Prussia's retreats in the international arena in 1848–50. Curiously, it appears as if the myth of French military prowess, as much as its reality, worked to France's advantage in dealings with Austria, Prussia and England, and this contributed to the fear of a France led by the nephew of Napoleon I.

For now, however, the relative weakness of the railroad systems of even Western and Central Europe decreased the possibility of a Great Power war. They had yet to show that they could move men and *matériel* in sufficient numbers and with requisite speed for strategists to think in terms of the decisive battles and one-campaign victories that would justify initiating a land war.[10] No leaders sought a repetition of the drawn-out carnage of 1792–1815.

THE MARITIME IMBALANCE

On the high seas things were different. The wide range of industrial advancement made for the crucial differential among Great Power fleets, where quantity could not transform itself into quality. It was England, France and Russia, in clear order, with the United States playing the role of a wildcard with advanced technology.

The general adoption after 1837 of explosive artillery shell signalled the coming end of the era of the purely wooden warship. Functional ironclad naval armour against heavy shells existed more on paper than reality, so what mattered was the number of first-class ships equipped with the biggest and best guns and with the most effective shot. The paddle-wheel war steamer was not a tactical improvement over sail, but the development of screw propulsion threatened to replace seafaring prowess with industrial progress as the measure of maritime power. England still had the corner on both markets, but this could change since America and France had pioneered the new war steamer. One Yankee even sought a naval contract in the 1840s to build a ship with a super gun to decimate an entire enemy line. However, the French, who began a new arms race with their screw-propelled battleships, had to order high-quality coal from England, whose navy soon had far more of these craft too. The belated Russian entry into this race assumed British engines, which also powered the steamers in Austria's small squadron.[11]

The huge British numerical advantage on the high seas meant that the smaller French, American, Dutch and other fleets were virtual auxiliaries to the British around the coasts of the non-Western world, and dependent upon British naval stations. Theoretically, the French, and especially the Russians, might buy enough ships and guns from America or even Europe to make up for native backwardness, but this nightmare for the Admiralty never materialized. On the contrary, the British could bottle up the Russians or Prussians at the Danish Sound and Belts, the Austrians at the mouth of the Adriatic, or the French or even Americans, as well as everyone else, at their ports. Still, the British found themselves hustling to improve the defences of their home bases in the late 1840s and early 1850s.[12]

The French fleet was divided between Cherbourg and Toulon, which made it locally very impressive. Russia's navy, the second largest in the world, was also divided. The slightly larger fleet was in the Baltic, which also had new fortifications at Bomarsund – one of the Åland Islands between Finland and Sweden – and seemingly impregnable defences, including the latest Paixhans cannon at Kronstadt off St Petersburg. Russia's Black Sea fleet had better ships and crews, but a potentially vulnerable base at Sevastopol. These units assured Russian dominance of the Baltic and Black Seas, unless the British, or French with British backing, chose to mount a direct challenge. In that case, the Russians, with only two or three screw frigates, would most likely take a defensive stance.[13]

The Austrian Adriatic fleet was that of a second-rate Italian power, not yet a match for Naples or Piedmont, and much smaller than Turkey's. All the same, Vienna unrealistically dreamed in 1850 of creating the fourth greatest navy in the world. Prussia at this time had a limited amount of coast and hardly any navy at all. The Americans, for their part, simply did not bother to have more than local parity with the British, total American naval ordnance being no greater than Holland's or Sweden's. Nevertheless, American naval potential and penchant for privateering were factors in Great Power thinking.[14]

In the case of the Baltic, the Danes theoretically controlled the Sound and the Belts, but had learned in 1800 and 1807, at the cost of two fleets and many fine Copenhagen buildings, not to oppose the British when they were determined to enter. The Swedish fleet, with about one half the ordnance of the two Russian Baltic squadrons, was barely a credible defensive force against Russia and certainly could not defend Norway (under Sweden's crown since 1814) from British attacks. The Scandinavian states, in their own interest, could at best be benevolently neutral towards Britain in any crisis.[15]

The Black Sea was different. The Turks really did control their Straits, the key to Russia's house, as Tsar Alexander I put it, and thereby hangs an important part of this tale. Since the early 1800s the Russians had feared a Franco-Turkish or Anglo-Turkish attack on Odessa or Sevastopol. On the other hand, Western experts assumed that the Russian fleet could land 16,000 troops at the poorly fortified Bosphorus in forty-eight hours, before any help from outside the Dardanelles could sail upwind and up-current. The Turkish navy was half the size of the Russian Black Sea fleet and of poorer quality. France, however, had two new, huge, untested screw battleships, the *Charlemagne* and the *Napoleon*, names signalling imperial and Mediterranean ambitions. Maintenance and coaling proved to be serious problems, but this was not suspected, and it looked as if the Toulon squadron – maybe by itself, definitely if combined with the Turkish fleet – would best the Russians. The Turks were also contemplating buying three screw battleships, which could grant them parity with Russia in the Black Sea, but bind them more to their Western supplier.[16]

Turkey's normal alignment with a Western power presented a peculiar potential danger to Russia's southern exports and Black Sea establishments. As of the 1830s, Russian and British naval planning considered seizing one or both Straits as a preventive measure. Some British and French thought about a preemptive strike into the Black Sea against Sevastopol as well.[17]

THE DOUBLE STANDARD OF IMPERIALISM

Whatever their real or apparent weaknesses, any Great Power army or navy with moderately modern weapons and proper preparations and staffing could make mincemeat out of the forces of a more backward country armed with obsolete ordnance, muskets, and wooden ships and fortresses that were firetraps. The Russians showed this against the Persians and the Turks, especially on the Transcaucasian front, in 1826–29. The British were continuously demonstrating this principle in India; they did so too in southern China in 1840–42 and in Burma in 1826 and 1852. The Americans levied a mere 20,000 and relieved the Mexicans of more than half of their territory in 1846–48, even though the latter had purchased a couple of iron warships from England and pretended to organize armies on European models. Redoubtable local leaders, such as Abd-al-Qadir in Algeria and Shamyl in the Caucasus might hold the French and Russians respectively at bay for years, but eventually had to submit, as did the Sikhs in India.[18] The last time that a European power had lost ground to a non-European one was in 1739, when the overextended Austrians retroceded to Turkey their Balkan conquests of 1718.

With all of this unchecked force at their disposal, the Great Powers could force the rest of the world to follow accepted European diplomatic practice, including unequal *de jure* Western treatment of non-Western polities. The smaller European states fitted into the European system without any difficulty, as did the Latin Americans, given the European culture of their élites. Nevertheless, such common culture did not prevent the Great Powers from intervening in the domestic affairs of an unstable European or Latin American state, even one so eminent as Spain.[19] As for the rest of the world, the Great Powers took the moral high ground, considered only Western practices to be civilized and exacted reparations and juridical extraterritoriality at the barrel of the gun.

The most spectacular example of how the advanced states of Europe and North America dealt with the non-Western world is the origin of the First Anglo-Chinese War in 1839 over Chinese attempts to outlaw traffic in narcotics. Heeding the people directly involved in the China trade and even in smuggling opium, Foreign Secretary Palmerston felt that force was necessary so that 'our future relations with China be placed on a secure footing'. He authorized military measures and then informed Parliament. Actual encounters were few and Anglo-Indian battle casualties meagre. The war itself was no more than protracted and costly gunboat diplomacy, against some concrete fortifications and primitive firearms, to obtain the lease of Hong Kong and the opening of five treaty ports.[20] One more such 'Opium' War at the end of the 1850s, and the land of Confucius would learn the hard way how to conduct relations with the West.

THE EUROPEAN SYSTEM

In Europe, on the other hand, a peculiarly stable structure of interstate relations held after 1818, when post-Napoleonic France was admitted as an equal member to the Concert of Europe. As usual, some powers were 'more equal' than others. England and Russia made up a big two within the five; at some point in the later 1820s, France replaced Austria as the third; Prussia was always fifth. After 1848, France, with a Bonaparte at the top, was ready to bid to become number two or one.

The fundamental goal of this system was to provide for order, though this was interpreted one way in London and Paris, where liberalizing changes were generally welcome, and another in Vienna and St Petersburg, where such developments were anathema. Each of the five great European powers had a particular place within Europe's balance of power.[21] The British needed to prevent any single power, usually Russia, from gaining too much influence on the continent or a hostile maritime combination from being formed between the French and either the Russians or Americans. A strong France represented everybody's insurance against British, Russian, or some kind of German hegemony, while the other four shared a basic, conservative commitment to prevent the recrudescence of an expansionist France. Austrian dominance of the German Confederation and Italy was tolerated by the other four precisely because this supremacy was loose, and Austria lacked the dynamism to threaten the other great powers. At the same time the totality of Germany still balanced France and Russia defensively. The United States, like France, had to learn to live with permanent British maritime supremacy and with the prevalence of conservative monarchism in Europe, and then served as a reserve, either to help limit British maritime hegemony or strengthen Britain against a continental combination.

In actual practice, Russia had helped restore France's Great Power status as a check on the Anglo-Austrian combination of 1814–15. A threat in 1823–24 that France and Russia together would restore the Spanish Empire in the New World led to temporary Anglo-American cooperation, yielding the non-operational, programmatic Monroe Doctrine for American hegemony in the New World. The moderate French Revolution of 1830 and French support of Belgium's liberal revolt against Dutch rule created something of an East–West political split in Europe. Russia, Austria and Prussia were already linked as co-partitioners of Poland, whose Tsarist section attempted armed rebellion in 1830–31. The recrudescence of Anglo-French rivalry in the Mediterranean in 1838–41 led to a new shift of alignments, with both Russia and Austria aiming to see that France did not lose too badly and become revolutionary or aggressive on the rebound.

The revolutions of 1848 reawakened Prussia's dynamism and assertiveness for the first time since 1817, set Piedmont and Italian nationalists against Austria, and also resulted in a Bonaparte as France's president, elected by universal male suffrage, and an implicitly more dynamic and assertive France. Moreover, the popular movements threatened to render Austria asunder and reorganize Central and East-Central Europe according to national principles, which found favour in British and French public opinion. In their own turn, Austria and Russia became aggressively counter-revolutionary. The dynamics of the balance of power were still the same, but the Concert was more fragile.

On the other hand, the new technologies created a different set of parameters within the maritime imbalance of power. France faced the danger that England might find an excuse to make a preventive strike in order to pre-empt the bogeyman of a French landing. French policy was clever enough to avoid such a strike by making it more feasible and hence utterly unnecessary – an implicit guarantee under normal circumstances of policies consistent with London's interests. Louis-Napoleon decreased expenditures and concentrated on the Mediterranean squadron at the expense of the Atlantic, while in 1852 and 1853 alone the British launched eleven new screw battleships and large frigates with a total of 927 guns.[22]

The danger for Russia lay in increased qualitative lag resulting from

Table 3   Major and minor armies and navies *c*.1853[23]

	'Line' ships (steamers in parentheses)	Frigates (steamers in parentheses)	Naval 'guns'	Soldiers (thousands of regulars)
Great Britain	81 (15)	114 (26)	13391	103
British India				386
Russia	42 (0/1)	32 (14)	6008	1100
France	29 (4)	57 (20)	5200?	450?
Austria	0	6 (?)		350?
Prussia	0	?		200?
United States	11 (?)	17(5)	2039	12
Turkey	6	16 (6)	1500	220
Holland	5 (?)	17 (?)	2175	
Sweden	10	6	2000+	

The Origins of the Crimean War

the post-1840 Anglo-French naval arms race. Under certain conditions both might combine against her and test their overwhelming maritime superiority in local theatres outside the European core, while in Europe proper the terrestrial balance of power still held. Russian diplomacy proved clumsy enough to allow this – whereby hangs the greater part of this tale, and leads us from the West over to the Eastern Question.

NOTES

1. Cf. Lynn M. Case. *Edouard Thouvenel et la diplomatie du Second Empire* (Paris 1976), pp. 17–33; W. Bruce Lincoln, *In the Vanguard of Reform*, p. 15; Helmut Rumpler, 'Die rechtlich-organisatorischen und sozialen Rahmenbedingungen für die Aussenpolitik der Hapsburgermonarchie 1848–1918', *HM* VI. 1: 15.
2. Schiemann IV: 421–3 (citing Seym. to Mlm. 4. Dec. 1852).
3. Monnier: 9–10, 46.
4. Gunther Rothenberg, *The Army of Francis Joseph* (West Lafayette 1976), p. 43; John Shelton Curtiss, *The Russian Army under Nicholas I, 1825–1855* (Durham NC 1965), p. 126.
5. A.L. Beskrovnyi, *Russkaia armiia i flot v XIX veke* (Moscow 1973), pp. 19–34; John L.H. Keep, *Soldiers of the Tsar. Army and Society in Russia 1462–1874* (Oxford 1985), pp. 323–50; Fuller: 238–43; AAT Russie, Mém. et doc., 1831–1852, pp. 360–6 (16 Oct. 1852).
6. Fuller: 252–60; Richard M. Haywood, personal communication, June 1990.
7. Dennis E. Showalter, *Railroads and Rifles: Soldiers, Technology and the Unification of Germany* (Hamden CT 1975), p. 36; *GJ*, 1843–53; Walter Wagner, Die k.(u.)k. 'Armee – Gliederung und Aufgabenstellung', HM V: 300.
8. Manfred Messerschmidt, 'Die politische Geschichte der preussisch-deutschen Armee', *Handbuch zur Deutschen Militärgeschichte, 1648–1939* (2 vols, Gerhard Papke and Wolfgang Petter (eds), Munich 1979), II: 18; Ludovic Jablonsky, *L'armée française à travers les âges* (Paris n.d.); Showalter, *Railroads and Rifles: Soldiers, Technology and the Unification of Germany*, pp. 91–6.
9. Hew Strachan, *Wellington's Legacy: The Reform of the British Army, 1830–1854* (Manchester UK 1984), pp. 180–99; *EB* 1911 II: 615.
10. Hajo Holborn, 'The Prusso-German School: Moltke and the Rise of the General Staff', *Makers of Modern Strategy From Machiavelli to the Nuclear Age*, ed. Peter Paret, Gordon Craig, Felix Gilbert, (2nd edn, Princeton 1986), p. 287.
11. James Phinney Baxter, *The Introduction of the Ironclad Warship* (Cambridge MA 1933), p. 52; cf. Edward L. Beach, *The United States Navy, 200 Years* (New York 1986), pp. 196–22; Beskrovnyi, *Russkaia armiia i flot v XIX veke*, p. 496; Lawrence Sondhaus, *The Habsburg Empire*

and the Sea. *Austrian Naval Policy, 1797–1866* (West Lafayette IND 1989), pp. 149, 163.

12. Strachan, *Wellington's Legacy: The Reform of the British Army, 1830–1854*, pp. 196–211; C.I. Hamilton, 'The Diplomatic and Naval Effects of Prince de Joinville's *Notes sur des forces navales de France* of 1844', *HJ* 32.3 (1989): 686–7.

13. ZP I.192, 196, 201, 211 (Russian Admiralty reports, 1853).

14. Sondhaus, *The Hapsburg Empire and the Sea,* pp. 149–64; *GJ* for 1848–55; C.I. Hamilton 'The Royal Navy, *La Royale*, and the Militarization of Naval Warfare, 1840–1870', *Journal of Strategic Studies* VI (1983): 183–94.

15. Halicz: 22; R.C. Anderson, *Naval Wars in the Baltic, 1522–1850* (2nd edn, Robert Stockwell, 1969), pp. 350–1.

16. AAT, Russie, Mém. et doc., 1831–1852, p. 357 (dated Nov. 1852); Rose to Mlm., 28 Dec. 1852 (PRO FO 78/895); Lambert *CW*: 4.

17. Art Crawley, 'Anglo-Russian Relations, 1815–1840', *CHJ* 3 (1929): 61; Puryear *ERSQ*: 110–15; Ingle: 102.

18. John F. Baddeley, *The Russian Conquest of the Caucasus* (London 1908), pp. 152–482; W.A.J. Archbold, 'The Conquest of Sind and the Panjab', and G.E. Harvey, 'Burma, 1782–1852', *The Cambridge History of India*, vol. V. *British India*, ed. H.H. Dodwell (Cambridge UK 1929), pp. 522–62, *passim*; Baxter, *The Introduction of the Ironclad Warship* p. 34; Russell F. Weigley, *The American Way of War. A History of United States Military Strategy and Policy* (London 1973), pp. 71–6; John Ruedy, *Modern Algeria. The Origin and Development of a Nation* (Bloomington IN 1992), pp. 58–64.

19. Webster, *Palmerston* I: 416–78.

20. Graham, *The China Station. War and Diplomacy, 1830–1860*, pp. 102–229; Hsin Pao Chang *Commissioner Lin and the Opium War* (Cambridge MA 1964), pp. 141–60, 194.

21. See, *inter alia*, Gordon Craig, 'The System of Alliances and the Balance of Power', *The New Cambridge Modern History* 14 vols, ed. J.T.B. Bury et al. (Cambridge UK 1957–70), X: 248–260; also see Paul W. Schroeder, Enno E. Kraehe, Robert Jervis, and Wolf D. Gruner, 'AHR Forum', *AHR* 97.3 (June 1992): 683–733, for a recent discussion of the applicability of 'balance of power' and 'Great Power hegemony' at this time.

22. C.J. Bartlett, *Great Britain and Sea Power* (Oxford 1963), p. 342.

23. In addition to sources listed so far, Const. Memos, 17/29 Jan. 1853–26 Feb./10 Mar. 1854 (TsGAVMF 224/1/241); Mnsh. to Nes. No. 34, 14/26 April 1853 (AVPR K 19); Lac. to Dr., 5 June, 4 Nov. 1853, AMAE CP Turq. 313, 316; M.A. Ubicini, *Izobrazhenie sovremmenago sostava Turtsii* (St Petersburg 1854).

CHAPTER THREE

The Eastern Question

FOUNDATIONS

According to the famous Eleventh Edition of the *Encyclopedia Britannica* (published in 1910–11), 'the Eastern Question is the expression in diplomacy from about the time of the Congress of Verona [1822] to comprehend the international problems involved in the decay of the Turkish Empire and its supposed impending dissolution'.[1] Behind this problem lay five phenomena: the fourth-century division of the Roman Empire into Western and Eastern halves, with capitals in Rome and Constantinople (Byzantium); the growing separation of the Latin (Catholic) and Greek (Orthodox) Churches, which spread to different parts of Europe; the Ottoman Turkish conquest of Constantinople, the Balkans, the Holy Land, and most of the rest of the Arab world, by the early sixteenth century; the rise of both Western Europe and Russia as threats to that empire in the course of the eighteenth century; and the strategic location of Constantinople on the Bosphorus at the entrance to the Black Sea.

So long as the Ottoman Empire was a successful Great Power, the Sultan's Orthodox subjects enjoyed a *modus vivendi* with him. The Ecumenical Patriarch became the administrative chief of the Orthodox. Wealthy 'Phanariot' (Lighthouse District) Greeks became tax-farmers and part of the Ottoman élite. The Serbs, and the Romanians even more so, enjoyed a great deal of ecclesiastical autonomy from the Greek Patriarchate. Some Ottoman Christians dreamed of liberation by Russia, but for most of them the Sultan was the secular protector of their Church. In the eighteenth century, however, the nationality question among the Ottoman Orthodox Christians became a serious factor. The growing European orientation of educated Ottoman Christians, moreover, produced the anomaly that a very large subordinate minority was becoming more advanced than the ruling Turks and the other Muslims, and just as likely to look to Europe as to Russia for support.

When the Turks took over Byzantine territory they confirmed the commercial privileges of the Europeans or 'Franks', who already resided in Galata, across the Golden Horn directly north of Constantinople, where the European legations would eventually be located. The first Franco-Turkish treaty or 'capitulations' (literally, titles, chapters or articles) of 1535 also confirmed judicial autonomy and special procedures for the Grand Vizier or someone else of high rank to handle problems between French and Turks. The articles did not create onerous conditions for the Ottomans or give the foreign powers any rights to interfere in Ottoman affairs. For example, the Turks expressly denied Louis XIV the right he sought to protect the Catholics who were Ottoman subjects. The French did obtain in 1740 some new promises concerning the older, vague rights of the Catholic missions and possessions in the Holy Land, but no more.[2]

As Ottoman power waned in the face of European progress, the Turks had to make concessions to some Europeans in order to obtain protection against others. The net result was the broadening of the use of the capitulations and the weakening of Ottoman commercial monopolies and also sovereignty, as European embassies started granting passports to Ottoman subjects. There are no certain statistics, but some historians believe that by the mid-nineteenth century as many as one million inhabitants of the Sultan's realm were using the protective powers of the European legations to escape the full authority of Ottoman magistrates.[3]

THE GREAT POWER BREAKTHROUGH AGAINST TURKEY (1767–1821)

It was Russian military power from the north-east, not Austria's from the north-west or the commercial and naval prowess of France or England, that broke the Ottoman monopoly on Black Sea trade, dating from the late fifteenth century, and initiated the abuses of the passport system. Catherine the Great's First Turkish War (1767–74) resulted in Russia's gaining territory at the mouth of the River Dnieper and the right to sail commercial vessels in the Black Sea and through the Turkish Straits into the Aegean and the Mediterranean

Seas. Other Europeans demanded similar rights for their ships to pass the Straits and navigate the Black Sea. Russia developed her Black Sea commerce by granting passports to Christian Ottoman subjects to sail under the Russian flag, and as the trade grew, so did the number of Russian consuls in Ottoman Greece and the Balkans. The commerce and number of consuls of other European states grew there too.[4]

The Treaty of Kuchuk-Kainarji (Kücük-Kainarca), which ended the war, contained another set of clauses concerning the protection of Ottoman Christians and constituted a potential time bomb. The Sublime Porte (as the Ottoman government was called) absolutely rejected Russia's original demand during the negotiations that all Ottoman (Orthodox) Christians be placed under Russian protection. However, the Turks did grant an amnesty to Christians who sided with Russia, promised future protection to the Church, and allowed the Russian envoy to the Porte the crucial (and abusable) right to petition on behalf of the Romanian Principalities and of an Orthodox Church that the Russians could build near their mission in Pera (in the hills north of Galata).[5] The Turks certainly displayed no 'imbecility' in these negotiations, as has been claimed,[6] but the strategic implications of Russian rights regarding overwhelmingly Orthodox Moldavia and Wallachia were immense. The Polish–Russian Treaty of 1686 had mentioned the respect for the Orthodox cult and its property within the Ukrainian and Belarus regions of the Polish realm, as well as reciprocally for the Catholics in provinces recently ceded by Poland to Russia. Subsequent Russian diplomacy used this clause as a pretext to intervene in Poland,[7] setting the stage for the eventual partition of that ill-fated realm, starting in 1772.

Catherine the Great did not stop with her 1772–74 gains, but devised her 'Greek Project', or plan to create a separate kingdom of Dacia out of Moldavia and Wallachia and, if Turkey collapsed, a new Byzantine Empire. She also schemed with the Austrian Emperor, Joseph II, to partition Turkey. France, which was losing its commercial hegemony in the Mediterranean to Britain, was envisioned as the maritime partner. News of such talk contributed to the increasingly expansionist reputation that Russia under Catherine had acquired.[8]

Meanwhile the Turks were forced to accept Russia's annexation of the Crimea in 1783, while Russia also proclaimed a protectorate over the Orthodox Kingdom of Georgia, located in nominally Persian central Transcaucasia and having historic claims to the Turkish-controlled eastern coast of the Black Sea. The Porte then pre-empted Catherine by launching a war of revenge under favourable diplomatic conditions in 1787. The English Cabinet toyed with the idea of sending a fleet to help the Turks in the Black Sea, but Parliament would not go along with that, so the Russians were victorious once more. Distracted by other problems in Europe, the Russians limited their peace terms to recognition of the annexation of the Crimea, the cession of a small part of coastal 'Bessarabia', from the Dnieper to the Dniester, and a reconfirmation of Kuchuk-Kainarji. Soon afterwards, Catherine engineered the final partitioning of Poland with Prussia and Austria.[9] Among other results, now virtually all of the Russian, Ukrainian and Belarus Orthodox and Uniates lived under the Russian rule – a vivid example of how legal 'protection' of foreign Orthodox Christians by Russia was followed by annexation within 110 years.

The French Revolution complicated matters immensely by challenging the entire European order based on monarchy and aristocracy. Russia, in particular, now faced a real danger from the fact that the thrust of her Balkan policies eroded Ottoman authority, but the disorders that might result could undermine the prevailing system at home. The Austrians grasped far better their reciprocal dependency upon the Turks for regional stability and had an Oriental Academy (founded in 1754) for training interpreters and diplomats for service in the Ottoman Empire.[10] Simultaneously, Ottoman rule in the Balkans and Ottoman–Phanariot rule in the Principalities had become more brutal, rapacious and disorderly than usual, with provincial warlordism and a 'civil war within the establishment' compounding the abuses of tax-farming.[11] Hence some foreign intervention in domestic Ottoman affairs was inevitable.

The international complications engendered by the French Revolution led to shifting alliances and set several precedents. At various times France, Russia and England were either allied to or at war with Turkey, the French trying to take Egypt and the British and Russians opposing a later Franco-Turkish alliance. The Russians at one point negotiated as an ally with Turkey and at the same time tried to interest the British in partitioning Turkey.[12] The British actually forced the Dardanelles in 1807, but then made a treaty in 1809 that upheld the 'ancient' principle of keeping the Straits closed to all foreign warships and secretly allied with Turkey.[13] Henceforth, Britain would treat this agreement as the foundation of a policy that implicitly linked support of the Turks with their excluding the warships of other states. Similarly the Russo-Turkish alliances of 1799 and 1805 mandated open Straits for Russian ships during the war against France, the latter treaty demanding strict closure to the warships of all other states. A separate agreement of 1802 required Russian approval of the appointed Hospodars of Moldavia and Wallachia.[14]

On the other hand, the Russo-Turkish War of 1806–12 was preceded by a Russian occupation of Moldavia in an unsuccessful attempt to exert diplomatic pressure on the Porte.

Curiously, as Napoleon prepared to invade Russia in 1812, a twenty-five-year-old English chargé d'affaires, Stratford Canning, helped arrange the compromise Treaty of Bucharest, which, however, left a few ticklish issues unresolved. The Turks ceded Bessarabia (eastern Moldavia) and Anapa in Kuban (east of the Crimea); promised amnesty and autonomy for rebellious Serbia, which Russia had been forced to abandon, and for the Principalities, which Russia had occupied for over five years; and pledged to cease harassing Russian commerce through the Straits. Secret clauses, never ratified by the Porte, gave the Russians several forts on the eastern end of the Black Sea. This treaty was also a compromise between Russian and British imperialism, since it implicitly renewed the 1805 alliance, while England still had her 1809 agreement. However, the Congress of Vienna in 1815, which ended the Napoleonic Wars, did not touch the Eastern Question, in part because the Turks would not grant more commercial concessions to the British and other Europeans in return for the general guarantee that everybody else desired to replace Russia's exclusive pretensions.[15]

RUSSIA'S FURTHER ASCENT (1821–33)

A Greek revolt in 1821 against the Ottomans set off a twelve-year crisis. The Russians found quickly that neither Britain nor Austria would allow them to invoke their alleged rights under Kuchuk-Kainarji and that no one, not even the Greeks, favoured Tsar Alexander's so-called 'Greek solution' of six autonomous Greek and Balkan Christian principalities under the Sultan. A swing of British opinion in favour of the Greeks, though, enabled the Russians to extract unilateral concessions from the Turks in their bilateral relations and in conjunction with Britain and France to broker a settlement of the rebellion. The unplanned Anglo-French–Russian sinking of a Turko-Egyptian naval squadron in Greek waters in 1827 led the angry Turks, who hoped for British support, to denounce their recent agreement with Russia.[16]

The new Tsar Nicholas I declared war in 1828, but then, advised by special ministerial council, was careful not to try a march on Constantinople or to exceed his assurances to the other powers in his peace demands. The upshot was the 1829 Treaty of Adrianople, whereby the earlier political and commercial agreements and Russian acquisitions in Transcaucasia were confirmed and Russia obtained more rights in the Black Sea and lower Danube. Now Moldavia, Wallachia and Serbia had genuinely guaranteed autonomy, and so did Greece, which, as a result of a British initiative, was about to become independent. The Hospodars were to be Romanians appointed for life by the Sultan with Russian approval and have full power within the confines of established treaties and charters – an elastic provision that opened the door further to direct Russian interference and for Romanian resistance.[17]

The Turks only agreed to recognize Greek independence because of the threat of a French-backed Egyptian rebellion that aimed to establish a separate realm that included Greater Syria (Syria, Lebanon and Palestine). By December 1832 the Egyptians had occupied Syria and taken Konya in central Anatolia, thereby threatening Constantinople. The English did not act, but Tsar Nicholas took a defensive, interventionist attitude, due to the recent Polish uprising, and backed the Sultan on the grounds that the combination of *emigré* Poles in Constantinople and French-backed Egyptians were actually a threat to Russia. Rejecting the suggestion that he ask for a fortress on the Bosphorus, Nicholas proffered military and naval support, which the Turkish ministers were reluctant to accept, but, as the Sultan allegedly said: 'A drowning man clings to a serpent.'[18] The British and French had no formal grounds to oppose the Russians, whose troops the Sultan had invited in order to save his throne. Ten thousand of them, led by Count Alexander Orlov, passed the Bosphorus in May 1833 and landed in a northern suburb, safe from the fanatically anti-Russian Turks of Constantinople.

By then the British had recovered their decisiveness; Palmerston dispatched the anti-Russian John Ponsonby as ambassador to the Porte, and both Western powers sent fleets to the Aegean and induced the Turks to compromise with both the Egyptians and the Russians. The British did not pass the Dardanelles this time, but the arrangements were worked out, and the Russian regiments packed up in July and went home, thus ending the possibility of an Anglo–French–Russian clash of arms.

The English did not like either deal. The Egyptian Pasha obtained the lifetime governance of Syria as well as hereditary rule in Egypt and was in a position to bid for the allegiance of the Sultan's other Arab subjects and thus threaten British land communications to India via the Persian Gulf.[19] The Russo-Turkish Treaty of Unkiar-Skelessi

(Hünkâr-Iskelesi) provided for an eight-year defensive alliance, Russia pledging openly to grant military aid upon request, and the Turks promising in an officially but not effectively secret article to render their help when needed by closing the Dardanelles to foreign warships.[20] Essentially this clause gave the Russian alliance legal primacy over any other arrangement Turkey might make. However, due to Russian attempts to control Turkish interpretation of the treaty, the British immediately suspected that the Russians had obtained the right to close the Straits to others and open them for themselves. The Russians never officially and explicitly said that they had obtained such a right, though many of them believed that they had.[21]

Palmerston did not want the Turks to ratify the Russian treaty because of its political implications, but was not ready to start a war, as Napoleon I had been in 1805–06, when he urged the Turks to duck out of an agreement with Russia. The immediate crisis blew over, but genuine russophobia began to develop in certain British circles.[22]

Meanwhile, Nicholas, the Austrian Emperor Francis I, and the Prussian Crown Prince William met on the Tsar's initiative for ten days at Münchengrätz (in Bohemia). Earlier that year Nicholas had tried to interest the Austrians in a hypothetical disposition of European Turkey. Now, by a special convention, Austria and Russia pledged to uphold the integrity of the Ottoman Empire under its present dynasty and, in the secret articles, keep the Egyptian pasha out of European Turkey and to act in concert in case Turkey collapsed.[23] Metternich was also rightly concerned that the Russians would use their new influence in the Romanian Principalities and their control of the mouth of the Danube to obstruct Austria's commercial outlet to the Black Sea, but he could not interest Palmerston in an anti-Russian combination.

ENGLAND'S LEAP FORWARD (1833–41)

The British made a three-pronged response to Unkiar-Skelessi and Münchengrätz. They actively fostered a Turkish resurgence in the Black Sea; they demanded commercial concessions from Turkey; and they pressed for domestic reform that would undercut Russian claims that the native Christians needed protection.

The dangerous Black Sea moves came first, since Ponsonby, under the influence of his deputy, David Urquhart – a fiery russophobe – and some Polish patriots, began helping the Turks ship munitions to the

Muslim Circassian, Daghestani and other opponents of Russian rule in the Caucasus. At one point the Russians captured the *Vixen*, a British vessel that ostensibly carried salt, but also delivered arms to the insurgent tribesmen. Ponsonby then wished to call up the English fleet and risk hostilities with the Russians over the vessel, while Nicholas was ready, in turn, to launch an expedition to the Bosphorus.[24] Back at home, some French and English were frightened by the heavily fortified Russian naval base at Sevastopol. Although they themselves were hardly innocent of aggressive schemes, they had reason to be worried. The Naval Minister, Prince Alexander Menshikov, wished to send two battleships from the Baltic fleet through the Straits in order to reinforce the Black Sea squadron, while the Russian Admiral M.P. Lazarev had already drawn up an operational plan for a 10,000-man surprise landing at the Bosphorus.[25] The Russians also essentially violated their 1809 treaty with Sweden, by which Finland and the Åland Islands were transferred to Russia, by starting to fortify Bomarsund. In the last analysis, it was the moderates on both sides who prevented an Anglo-Russian war. Neither the Russian Tsar nor the majority of British cabinet ministers were ready to push things that far in the 1830s.[26]

Britain's commercial and reformative prongs were more serious because of their lasting consequences. By 1835, against Russian opposition, Britain obtained permission to develop steamship traffic on the Euphrates to facilitate communications with India. Then in 1838, when it was apparent that the Egyptians planned to break away completely from the Sultan, the British were able to extort from the Porte the commercial convention that ended a series of Ottoman monopolies and reduced the duties that British merchants had paid.[27] After some striking Egyptian successes on the battlefield the next year, the brilliant young Ottoman official, Mustapha Reshid, bidding for a British alliance, induced the new Sultan, Abdülmecid, to grant the Hatt-i Sherif of Gülhane (Gulhané), a solemn programmatic declaration of the intention to create a legislative council and the rule of law on an equal basis for all of his subjects. Thus were launched the celebrated Turkish Tanzimat reforms.

Reshid never got his alliance with London, but rather an agreement among England, Austria and Russia to support the Sultan against the Egyptians, England and Russia each having the right to send warships temporarily into the Straits to defend Turkey. Common opposition to France's Egyptian policy induced Nicholas and Palmerston to agree that Russia would relinquish Unkiar-Skelessi in exchange for Great Power support of the Sultan and a general guarantee of the closure of the Straits to foreign warships. The Anglo-Russian combination created a diplomatic showdown, leading to a humiliating French retreat, while a British–Austrian–Turkish force drove the Egyptians from Syria, thereby securing the Sultan's power. A four-power agreement, made in London in the summer of 1840, was reworked into the five-power Straits Convention of 1841, which generalized the British and Russian treaties of 1809 and 1833 by removing the bilateral alliances with Turkey. Its preamble asserted the ambiguous goal of strengthening the Ottoman Empire,[28] which could be seen as a guarantee of its integrity or just empty rhetoric.

Following the 1841 agreement there were still several problems. French national pride was hurt, and the naval arms race with England on the basis of the new steam technologies picked up. Russian nationalists, who had already written off Turkey and were in the process of dismissing Austria as well, thought that the Tsar had conceded too much. Few people anywhere, apart from a faction of Englishmen, believed that Turkey was reformable. Certainly no Russians and not many Turks believed that the Tanzimat could work, and most saw it as destructive modernization. The Ottomans themselves were more interested in improving their army and navy than in changing anything else.[29] Perhaps the English belief in Ottoman reform was no more than a useful myth for keeping the Russians and their Kuchuk-Kainarji out and establishing a British-led European protectorate in the interest of commerce.

THE WIDER CONTEXT: THE ANGLO-RUSSIAN 'GREAT GAME' (TO 1847)

The Anglo-Russian rivalry in the Ottoman Empire was part of a 'Great Game' that pitted the world's richest, most industrialized and greatest maritime power against the biggest and strongest land power on the globe after the defeat of Napoleon. It was a rivalry which by the 1840s stretched from the boundaries of the Russian–American and Hudson Bay Companies (Alaska and Canada) in North America to eastern China, and from Central Asia to Persia and Turkey and across Europe to the Baltic and Sweden. It was a rivalry based on the fact that British commercial and imperial expansion, with two loci of power, England and India, as well as commerce with the Americas as a logistical reserve, threatened to carry British influence to most of Russia's borders. And it was a rivalry based on the fact that after the fall of Napoleon, only Russia could conceivably threaten British power in India. Although Constantinople was within Russia's reach, and India was not, it was fear for Britain's position in India more than anything else that animated the rise of British russophobia on the part of colonial officials, diplomats, members of the Board of Control in London that oversaw Indian affairs until 1858, and their publicists.[30]

The British also had two not so little games: one with France, the other with the United States, each possessing advanced industrial and maritime technologies and no more prepared than Russia to let London determine who expanded where, when, and under what conditions. The Anglo-French rivalry stretched from the Low Countries and Spain through the Mediterranean, North Africa and the Middle East, reappearing in the South Pacific. An Anglo-American rivalry persisted in the Western Hemisphere and northern Pacific. The British thus had no particular reason to seek out a conflict with Russia. For most of the 1840s, especially, France and the United States appeared to Britain as more dangerous rivals.[31]

The British imperialists desired the impossible from Russia – a Russian Empire that would not attempt to expand into the backward territories and political vacuums that lay to Russia's south, and would content itself with its assigned role of supporting the status quo in Europe, while Britain pursued commercial ascendancy in many distant lands including Russia. Russian imperialists, on the other hand, accepted the British Empire and commercial and maritime supremacy as a fact of life, but saw themselves as the natural masters or protecting power in the Balkans, the entire basins of the Black and Caspian Seas and Central Asia. Except for a mad statesman such as Tsar Paul (1796–1801) or a few poetic dreamers, a Russian thrust toward India was a diplomatic card to be used to counter England's maritime supremacy, rather than a programme for expansion.[32]

The English, for their part, defined a vast expanse of territory as vital for the security of India and communications between India and England: north-eastern Anatolia, Syria, Egypt, Iraq and coastal Arabia, all nominally under the Sultan, and also coastal Persia, as well as Afghanistan. This explains rival British and French attitudes toward Egypt, British fears of a Russian takeover of the Turkish Straits and Russian expansion towards the historic overland trade routes linking the Persian Gulf to the Mediterranean or Black Sea, and the guarded British support of the anti-Russian rebels in the Caucasus.[33]

The Anglo-Russian competition produced some tense moments in the 1820s and 1830s. British agents had prompted Persia to go to war with Russia in both 1804 and 1826, resulting in Russia's annexation of what are now the Republics of Azerbaijan and Armenia. Thereupon Russian nationalists aimed to increase Russian influence in the Central Asian khanates and compensate Teheran by backing a Persian conquest of the Khanate of Herat in western Afghanistan and the anti-British factions in the other Afghan khanates, Kabul and Kandahar. Russia's anglophobic minister in Teheran, Colonel A.S. Simonich, actually directed the siege of Herat in 1837–38.[34] Meanwhile, Governor-General Perovsky of Orenberg hoped to time the siege of Herat with an expedition from Orenberg to Khiva. Palmerston thus knew what he was doing when he asked the Russian ambassador if Foreign Minister Nesselrode, with his assurances, or Simonich represented official Russian policy.

Thinking in terms of Alexander the Great and Tamerlane, the British feared that the Russians could sail up the Amu Darya (Oxus) from Khiva and then march along the Kabul River in Afghanistan and down through the Hindu Kush into the Indus Valley. London's new envoy to Persia, Sir John McNeill, was a russophobic mirror-image of Simonich, and persuaded the Earl of Auckland, Governor-General of India, to dispatch a fleet from India to the Persian Gulf. The British also occupied the island of Kharg in the Persian Gulf and Aden on the Arabian Peninsula at the mouth of the Red Sea to secure the overland connection. Nesselrode meanwhile induced the Tsar to replace Simonich with a less fiery envoy and to appoint a more moderate head of the Asiatic Department. Without Russian support, the Persian Shah had to call off the siege of Herat the next year. Palmerston's plain-speaking had worked.[35]

As a sequel to the Herat crisis, both sides overextended themselves and lost badly. Auckland sent an Anglo-Indian expeditionary force to Afghanistan in 1838 and installed protégés in Kandahar and Kabul. To counter this, the Tsar sent Perovsky and 5,000 men in November to bring Khiva to heel. Few Russians and even fewer English made it back alive.[36]

Nicholas's decision in 1839 to cooperate with Britain against France and Egypt meant that the British imperialists' nightmare – a coalition of Russia, Persia, Afghan princes, and French-backed Egypt to take over the Middle East and threaten India – never materialized. On the other hand, he did engineer a sequel to the 1841 Straits Convention at Turkey's expense, perhaps as a result of serious differences over the governance of Serbia. From late 1843 through late 1844, Nicholas tried in vain to interest the Austrians in a partition scheme allowing Austria to be 'heir to European Turkey', while Constantinople became a free city, Russia gaining a stretch of territory down to the Bosphorus.[37]

The Tsar also obtained an invitation to visit Britain, where he was lavishly fêted. He and Orlov held several discussions with the Prime Minister, Foreign Secretary and Commander-in-Chief – Peel, Aberdeen, and Wellington – and tried for an Anglo-Russian agreement at French expense regarding Turkey. Nicholas promised to uphold that realm and consult Britain in case it collapsed, but also warned of a powerful faction that advocated a French alliance and predicted a future Russo-British war. Nothing concrete resulted from his efforts. Nesselrode's follow-up visit to England that year, where Aberdeen recorded a non-binding personal agreement to consult in any future Ottoman crisis, did not dispel British misgivings. Nicholas, for his part, never seems to have understood that he had not obtained a serious agreement from these three British statesmen.[38]

The 'Great Game' between England and Russia, however, was not dormant anywhere. In 1842 Stratford Canning returned to Constantinople, wholeheartedly supported Reshid's reforms, and encountered the opposition of the Russian legation. On the other hand, in 1843 the Russian Black Sea squadron obtained five war steamers, and Nicholas threatened to send 20,000 troops to Serbia to uphold a reasonably friendly regime there.[39] The Russians, however, could not get what they wanted in cultural matters or even control administrative developments where they had protectorate rights. They could not block Western secular and religious influences that came into the Romanian Principalities, Serbia and the Ottoman Bulgarian provinces, where American Protestant missionaries promoted native-language bibles. Serbs from Habsburg territory and with an essentially German education developed the educational and scientific infrastructure of the Belgrade regime right under the nose of the Russian consul. Young educated Romanians gravitated toward Paris and pursued a consciously Latin orientation, negating the political significance of their Orthodoxy – their only emotional tie to Russia.[40]

In East Asia, though, the Russians responded to the Anglo-Indian victory over China by consolidating their North Pacific holdings, the Russian America Company abandoning Fort Ross in California and any claims to North American territory below Alaska.[41] Moreover, Rear Admiral E.V. Putiatin started in 1843 to exert pressure in St Petersburg for a military thrust south of the Russo-Chinese border, which had been established in 1689. He wanted to take over the River

Amur in order to counter the British advance in South China, and this lobbying paid off. In 1847 the Tsar appointed another experienced great gamesman, N.N. Muraviev, to be Governor-General of Eastern Siberia, with instructions to implement Putiatin's plan.[42]

The British, too, were not sleeping after 1842, but rather taking over the Indus valley. Aberdeen may have adopted a different line to Palmerston; nevertheless, in 1843 he annexed Sind. And Stratford bought a little insurance at the Straits in 1846 by prearranging the requisite authorization for English warships to enter the Dardanelles quickly.[43]

The period of 1842–47, however, drew to a close without any special Anglo-Russian or Eastern crisis. British russophobia had peaked, as had the Russian naval budget. The Russians and English had learned to tolerate each other's influence in the Ottoman Empire. Neither the Russell–Palmerston duo that dominated the London Cabinet as of 1846 nor the Nicholas–Nesselrode pair who managed Russian diplomacy were seeking a scrape. Their ministers plenipotentiary at the all-important post on the Bosphorus, Stratford Canning and Vladimir Titov, got on quite well. The British were bickering with both the French and the Americans over a series of overseas interests. But no one could control the domestic forces that shape human affairs.

NOTES

1.   *EB* 1911 VIII: 831.
2.   Philip Marshall Brown, *Foreigners in Turkey. Their Juridical Status* (Princeton/London 1914), pp. 3–37; G. Pélisse du Rausas, *Le régime des capitulations dans l'Empire Ottoman* (Paris 1902), p. 70; Testa I: 15–21, (1535 Fr.–Turk. Treaty), trans. *MENA* I.1; *CTS* XXXVI (Fr.–Turk. Tr. 28 May 1740).
3.   S. Rosenthal, *The Politics of Dependence. Contributions in Comparative Colonial Studies* 3 (Westport CN 1980), pp. 6–7, 103–5; Sheremet: 103.
4.   E.I. Druzhinina, *Kuchuk-Kainardzhiiskii mir 1774 goda (eë podgotovka i zakliuchenie)* (Moscow 1955), pp. 294–5; Norman Saul, *Russia and the Mediterranean, 1797–1807* (Chicago 1970), pp. 1–21.
5.   *CTS* XLV (Italian, French Texts), trans., *MENA* I.32.
6.   Druzhinina, *Kuchuk-Kainardzhiiskii mir*, pp. 217–21, 295–301; PRO SP 97–50, No. 18: 147–8 (from Constantinople, 17 Aug. 1774); for the standard view, Albert Sorel, *La question orientale au XVIII siècle* (Paris 1878), p. 291, and Marriott: 137; cf. Roderick Davison, '"Turkish Imbecility and Russian Skill?" The Treaty of Kuchuk-Kainardji Reconsidered', *Slavic Review* 35.3 (Sept. 1976): 463–83.

7. *CTS* XVII 491–504, especially art 9: with divergent Russian/Latin and Polish/French versions; also Herbert H. Kaplan, *The First Partition of Poland* (New York 1962), pp. 7–12, 50–82, 147–73.

8. B.A. Georgiev, N.S. Kiniapina, M.T. Panchencko, V.I. Sheremet, *Vostochnyi vopros vo vneshnei politike Rossii konets XVIII-nachalo XX v.* (Moscow 1978), pp. 42–4; O.P. Markova, 'O proiskhozhdenii tak nazyvaemogo grecheskogo proekta (80-e gody XVIII v.)', *Problemy metologii i istochnikovedeniia istorii vneshnei politiki Rossii*, ed. A.L. Narochnitskii (Moscow 1986), pp. 7–18.

9. Isabel De Madariaga, *Russia in the Age of Catherine the Great* (New Haven/London 1981), pp. 416–26; R.H. Lord, *The Second Partition of Poland* (Cambridge MA 1915), pp. 377–505; 'The Third Partition of Poland', *SR/SEER* III.9 (March 1925): 483–98.

10. Heinrich Pfusterschmid-Hardtenstein, 'Von der Orientalishen Akademie zur k. u. k. Konsularakademie. Ein mariatheresianische Institution und ihre Bedeutung für den Auswärtigen Dienst der Österreichisch-ungarischen Monarchie', *HM* VI.1: 137–43.

11. Sugar, *Southeastern Europe under Ottoman Rule, 1354–1804* (Seattle/London 1977), pp. 140–1, 238–47.

12. Alexander I to Novosil'tsev, 11/23 Nov. 1804 (*VPR* I.II).

13. Nouradounghian II.27 (Ang.–Turk. Tr., 6 Jan. 1809), especially art. 11, trans. *MENA* I.52.

14. *CTS* LIV, LVII (Russ.–Turk. Trs., et al., 23. Dec. 1798/3 Jan. 1799, 9/21 Nov. 1805), trans. *MENA* I.40, 48; cf. J.C. Hurewitz, 'Russia and the Turkish Straits: a Reevaluation of the Origin of the Problem', *World Politics* XIV (1961–62): 609–29; *VPR* I: 713–5.

15. Temperley *ENEC*: 30–1; Lane-Poole I: 149–76; *CTS* LXII (Russ.–Turk Tr., 16/28 May 1812), trans. *MENA* I.54. *VPR* I.8:652n129.

16. Charles and Barbara Jelavich, *The Establishment of Balkan National States, 1804–1920* (Seattle/London 1977), pp. 38–44; Paul W. Schroeder, *Metternich's Diplomacy at Its Zenith, 1820–1823* (Austin 1962), pp. 123–4, 164–87; Lane-Poole I: 324; Harold Temperley, *The Foreign Policy of Canning, 1822–1827: England, the Neo-Holy Alliance, and the New World* (London 1925, repr. Hamden CN 1966), pp. 329–55; Patricia Kennedy Grimsted, *The Foreign Ministers of Alexander I. Political Attitudes and the Conduct of Russian Diplomacy, 1801–1825* (Berkeley/Los Angeles 1969), pp. 284–5; Schiemann II: 126–42; *CTS* LXXVI (Russ.–Turk. Conv., 25 Sept./7 Oct. 1826), trans. Hertslet I.131.

17. Schiemann II: 367; *CTS* LXXX (Russ.–Turk Tr., 2/14 Sept. 1829), trans. Hertslet II.145; Radu Florescu, *The Struggle against Russia in the Roumanian Principalities, 1821–1854* (Munich 1962), pp. 135–60.

18. Barbara Jelavich, *St. Petersburg and Moscow: Tsarist and Soviet Foreign Policy, 1814–1974* (Bloomington IN 1974), p. 85.

19. Martens IV: 442–5. Schiemann III: 208–22; G.H. Bolsover, 'Lord Ponsonby and the Eastern Question (1833–1839)', *SR/SEER* XIII (July 1934): 98–102; Webster, *Palmerston* I: 303; Maria Todorova, 'Russian Policy in Constantinople: the Treaty of Unkiar-Skelessi, 1833' (Manuscript, Oct. 1989).

20. Nouradounghian, II.27, *CTS* LVII (Russ.–Turk. Tr., 26 June/8 July 1833); trans., Hertslet II.168, *MENA* I.72.

21. Bolsover, 'Lord Ponsonby and the Eastern Question (1833–1839)', pp. 102–6; Todorova, 'Russian Policy', pp. 3–8; S.M. Gorianov, *Le Bosphore et les Dardanelles* (Paris: 1910).
22. *MENA* I.73 (Ponsonby to Subl. Porte, 26 Aug. 1833); Webster, *Palmerston* I: 306; V.N. Vinogradov, *Velikobritaniia i Balkany*, pp. 158–60; John H. Gleason, *The Genesis of Russophobia in Great Britain* (Cambridge MA 1950).
23. G.H. Bolsover, 'Nicholas I and the Partition of Turkey', *SR/SEER* XXVIII (1948): 116–23; *CTS* LXXXIV, also ZP I.14 (Conv. of Münchengrätz, 6/18 Sept. 1833), trans. *MENA* I.74.
24. C.W. Crawley, 'Anglo-Russian Relations, 1815–1840', *CHJ* 3 (1930): 60–1; Puryear *ERSQ*: 30, note 69; Sir Charles Webster, 'Urquhart, Ponsonby, and Palmerston', *EHR* 62 (1947): 327–51. In 1833 Urquhart published his programmatic *Turkey and Its Resources* and *England, France, Russia, and Turkey*.
25. Mnsh. to Nes., Nes. to Nich. I, 4/16, 18/30 Jan. 1838 (*MENA* I.79); Ingle: 97–8; Lazarev memo, 1835 (TsGAVMF 19/4/92); cf. Col. A.A. Samarov (ed.), *M.L. Lazarev. Dokumenty* (3 vols, Moscow 1952–1961) II.149–73; Puryear *ERSQ*: 30–1.
26. Paul Knaplund, 'Finnmark in British Diplomacy, 1836–1855', *AHR* 30 (1925): 479–90; Bolsover, 'Lord Ponsonby and the Eastern Question, (1833–1839)', pp. 111–12; Webster, *Palmerston* I: 318–19, II: 558–81; Ingle: 65–72, 156–7.
27. Vinogradov, *Velikobritaniia i Balkany*, pp. 185–7; Sheremet: 86–7; *CTS* LXXXVIII (Conv. of Balta Liman, 16 Aug. 1838), trans. *MENA* I.80.
28. Webster, *Palmerston* II: 644–64; Ingle: 101–47; Temperley *ENEC*: 119–130; *CTS* XLII (London Conv., 13 July 1841), trans. *MENA* I.87.
29. Ralston, *Importing the European Army*, pp. 54–64; L. Carl Brown, *The Tunisia of Ahmad Bey, 1837–1855* (Princeton 1974), pp. 6–7, 261–303.
30. David Gillard, *The Struggle for Asia, 1828–1914* (London 1977/80), pp. 27–42.
31. Kenneth Bourne, *Britain and the Balance of Power in North America, 1815–1908* (Berkeley/Los Angeles 1967), pp. 75–178.
32. E.L. Steinberg, 'Angliiskaia versiia o "russkoi ugroze" v XIX-XX vv.', *Problemy, metodologii i istochnikovedeniia istorii vneshnei politiki Rossi*, pp. 67–8.
33. Steinberg, 'Angliiskaia versiia o "russkoi ugroze"', pp. 59–69; Gillard, *The Struggle for Asia, 1828–1914*, pp. 18–82.
34. Ingle: 77–8.
35. Webster, *Palmerston* II: 742–51. In 1836 McNeill published his alarmist *Progress and Present Position of Russia in the East*.
36. M. Ivanin, *Opisanie zimniago pokhoda 1839–1840 g.* (St Petersburg: 1873); A. Lobanov-Rostovsky, *Russia and Asia* (Ann Arbor 1933, repr. 1951), pp. 153–4.
37. David MacKenzie, *Ilija Garašanin: Balkan Bismarck* (New York/Boulder, 1985), pp. 24–33; Bolsover, 'Nicholas and the Partition of Turkey', *SR/SEER* XXVIII (1948): 124–35.
38. Schiemann IV: 44–55; ZP I.15–23 (8/20 Aug. 1844 to '21' Jan. 1845

memos); *MENA* I.94 (Nes. memo, 16/28 Dec. 1844, trans.); for an alternative view, Puryear *ERSQ*: 1–73.

39. ZP I.189 (from *Morskoi sbornik*, 1880); Schiemann, IV: 34.
40. MacKenzie, *Ilija Garašanin*, pp. 24–38; Jelavich and Jelavich, *The Establishment of Balkan National States*, pp. 94–5.
41. Bolkhovitinov: 39–49.
42. Ingle: 152, 164; R.K. Quested, *The Expansion of Russia in East Asia, 1857–1860* (Kuala Lumpur 1968), pp. 30–58.
43. Gillard, *The Struggle for Asia, 1828–1914*, pp. 72–7; Puryear *ERSQ*: 155–6.

PART TWO
The Sparks

CHAPTER FOUR

Counter-revolution on the March (1848–1850)

THE CONTRADICTIONS OF 1848

A popular liberal revolution broke out in Palermo in January 1848. Before the reigning Bourbon king could get any outside help, he was forced to grant separate constitutions to Naples and to Sicily. This stimulated the simmering nationalist movements throughout the rest of Italy. A negotiated compromise between Italian nationalists and Austria was out of the question. By April, the Austrians had been driven by popular power from Venice and from all of Lombardy except the Quadrilateral of fortresses. Piedmont now had a liberal-monarchist constitution, and its king was leading a combined Italian army of 90,000–135,000 regulars and irregulars against the 115,000 trained men of the Austrian commander, General Joseph Wenzel Radetzky.[1]

Meanwhile, a new French Revolution erupted in Paris in February, sending King Louis-Philippe fleeing for his safety to England and creating misplaced fears throughout Europe's establishments of a new edition of the wars of 1792–1815. The Republicans who came to power promised to respect the borders of 1815, so long as there was no foreign intervention in France, but they also openly supported the principle of the 'reconstruction' of nationalities.[2] Thus encouraged, revolutionary fervour spread throughout Central Europe and was at the gates of Tsarist Poland. By the end of March, Metternich had resigned in Vienna, popular forces controlled Pest (right bank Buda-Pest), and the Prussian army had relinquished Berlin to democrats.

The Habsburg and Ottoman Empires, those seeming 'gaudy-birds made up of borrowed feathers', as the Prince of Serbia would call

Austria,[3] faced the supreme danger of disintegrating into national states. The Habsburg Croat–Serb movement incited passions among the Ottoman Serbs, Bosnians, Montenegrins, and Bulgarians. The Porte, partly out of fear of Russia, even took it upon itself to urge Vienna to take control of the situation. Moldavia and Wallachia were inspired by events in Paris, Budapest and the Habsburg Romanian lands. South Slavic strivings and Czech Panslavism, moreover, inspired anti-Tsarist feelings among Ukrainians and even some Russians, while Poles everywhere, including in St Petersburg, could stir up not only the mixed Polish, Lithuanian, Belarusian, Ukrainian and Jewish populations in all the lands Russia had acquired from Poland from 1772 to 1815 but also young Russians.

The incompatibility of nationalism and liberalism came right to the surface. A Prussian conflict with the Poles of Poznan (Prussian Poland) led the German Liberals to abandon the Polish cause as early as April 1848. The Danes forced their new king to grant a genuine constitution, but attempts to incorporate wholly German Holstein and mostly German Schleswig into the Danish state produced uprisings among the local populace with support throughout Germany. By early April Prussian and Danish regulars were fighting each other in Schleswig. In the Habsburg lands Hungarian and German revolution-aries tended to support each other, but would not compromise with the aspirations of most Slavs. Viennese radicals tried to prevent the separation of Croatia from Hungary in April, and Germans in Germany and Austria applauded the Imperial Army's suppression of Czech nationalists. Real civil war raged between Hungary's Magyars (ethnic Hungarians) and its Croats and Serbs.

Revolutionary sentiment and class interests also clashed. The French peasants would not pay for social programmes in the cities, and propertied elements supported the brutal suppression of insurgent Republicans and socialists in June. The German middle classes feared the social radicalism of some of the masses and generally preferred the traditional reactionary domestic alliance with the privileged classes that supported absolutism to a democratic domestic alignment with plebeians. The peasantry of the Habsburg lands returned to traditional political docility once the feudal dues were abolished in September 1848, and even the Hungarian nationalists would not fully support the extreme Viennese radicals. In France the one person who could best reconcile city and countryside, peasant and merchant, worker and capitalist, Republican and Catholic, revolution and order – Louis Napoleon – got himself elected president in December.[4]

GREAT POWER DILEMMAS AND URGES

The revolutionary movements and the Italian–Austrian and Prusso–Danish wars created peculiar dilemmas and opportunities for the new French Republic, for the Whig (Liberal) government in Britain, for the Russian autocracy, and even for Turkey.

The French had to prove that they did not represent a new edition of the First Republic, with a provocative set of foreign policies almost certain to lead to war, as in 1792. But they could not sit back and let Austria or any other state increase its power in Italy or elsewhere. The enemies of Russia, Austria and the counter-revolution in general, moreover, looked to France for help. All the same, domestic concerns kept France vigilant, but relatively inactive throughout 1848.[5]

Britain was a different matter. The court supported the German dynasts; public opinion backed liberalism and moderate nationalism; the bankers and merchants favoured stability; and the government did not want the political goals of the larger or smaller peoples to upset the balance of power and strategic relations on the Continent or in the Baltic and Black Seas. So long as France was quiet, Palmerston could afford to follow British public opinion, which was favourable to the Italian national cause, as toward the Greeks in the 1820s. He seems to have believed, cynically enough, that Austria, without the burden of Lombardy and Venetia, would constitute a better barrier against Russia. On the other hand, Swedish and Danish control over the Sound and the Belts between the North and Baltic Seas was not to be threatened by Prussia or Germany fighting for co-nationals in Holstein and Schleswig.[6]

Tsar Nicholas had much to fear besides the simple collapse of Austria and European Turkey. Theoretically, Russia could attempt to establish a bloc of small client states in East-Central Europe and the Balkans, but the road to such a happy outcome for the nationalist or Panslav was treacherous. Even if he kept the European revolution from spreading to Russia in the short term, the repercussions could be ominous. A victorious revolutionary Italy might ally with a revolutionary France in the Mediterranean and support either the Balkan nationalities or the Turks, or both. The French could do this on their own if they wished. A revived Hungary or a Wallachia or Moldavia free to give expression to Romanian nationalism were bound to be permanent magnets for Polish nationalists. On the other hand, either a reformed Prussia or a triumphant Austria could place herself at the head of German nationalism and destroy Russia's regional preponderance. Whatever the domestic outcome in Germany,

Russia had the same interest as Britain in preventing Prussia or the Confederation from taking Schleswig from Denmark. Ergo, Europe's senior monarch and aristocrat had to lead the counter-revolution or relinquish the international position he had acquired for himself and Russia since 1826.

The Tsar's immediate reaction was to act as if Russia herself were threatened at home and abroad and thus institute repressive policies toward dissidents, as well as to alert up to 400,000 troops. Attempting to mobilize the Prussian and Austrian governments, he worked out contingency plans for the German states and Russia to invade France, as if the events of 1813 or 1815 were about to be repeated.[7]

The French manifesto of 2 March, repudiating the conservatism but not the territorial settlement of 1815, satisfied London but not St Petersburg. Distraught at the unwillingness of the King of Prussia to use his army against rebel civilians, Nicholas responded with his own 14/26 March manifesto, where he stated: 'God is with us. Take heed O Nations and Submit.'[8] The diplomatic community in St Petersburg saw it as a warning to revolutionaries and to France. Devout Russians could recognize 'God is with us' (*s nami Bog*) as a common liturgical formula – which was also used as a patriotic rallying cry. Nesselrode, now Chancellor, soon had to announce that Russia did not intend to intervene unless threatened – a mirror image of the French disclaimers.

It was also understood that Nicholas was willing to send troops to wherever he was invited. He was serious about protecting Denmark and even worked out a plan for an invasion of Germany. Once more he thought in terms of 1813 and hoped that he would be able to make a special arrangement with one faction of the Prussian army, which would allow him to help restore a strong Prussian monarchy as the cornerstone of German order. He also made ready the Baltic fleet. As it turned out, combined Anglo-Russian pressure induced the Prussians to call off an invasion of Danish Jutland and make an armistice in July.

RESCUING THE OTTOMAN AND HABSBURG REALMS

Turkey and the Balkans were a different matter. The 'Big Three' of those days went to work on the Porte, each singing a variation of his old tune. Stratford pushed the realization of the Tanzimat, and with this a British loan – which would be the new vehicle of British influence, once the capitulations were replaced by a uniform rule of law. Titov pressed for a hard, reactionary line, and had the ear of the Sultan and the conservatives, who removed Reshid and his coterie from office. Titov and his consuls used all of their powers of persuasion to keep the Serbs and Montenegrins from helping the Habsburg Serbs and Croats. This also kept Turkey's Bosnians and Bulgarians quiet. The French Republic eventually sent a new envoy, General Jacques Aupick, to propose an outright alliance.[9]

The Principalities and especially Bucharest, the capital of Wallachia and centre of Romanian nationalism, posed a unique challenge to all. Ever since the Russians evacuated in 1834, there had been, by treaty, no foreign soldiers in either Principality. However, the Russians let the Turks know that Imperial troops would enter Moldavia if disturbances occurred,[10] and in fact helped nip a revolt in the bud there in April, as General Diugamel was given plenary powers. Then a radical Bucharest uprising in June, supported by peasants and favouring union with Moldavia, became the signal for part of the Fifth Corps (army of Bessarabia) to occupy Jassy, the Moldavian capital.

The Ottomans now sung a new version of their old imperial tune. The Turkish élite was split between those like the Sultan, who desired to cooperate with Russia in repressing the Romanians, and those like Reshid, who courted British and French support and were willing to compromise with the Romanian democrats. In both cases, the Ottoman authorities, like the Austrians, hoped to use the threat of revolution to strengthen the power of the centre at the expense of the provinces. The Porte found its own solution, namely to suppress the Bucharest radicals, but at the same time weaken Russian power in the Principalities by subverting the Organic Statutes of 1834 and introducing the Tanzimat reforms, a package that could attract anti-Russian Romanian moderates. Reshid returned to power as Grand Vizier. Omer Pasha was sent with 15,000 regulars to crush the insurgents, which he did in September. Fuad Effendi, a partisan – in theory at least – of sorely needed agrarian reforms in the Principalities, was sent to restructure them under Turkish auspices, but was liberal with repressive measures.[11]

Russian troops eventually entered Wallachia to assist the Turks. Palmerston wanted it clear that the occupation was only temporary. Fearing for a moment the possibility of war with Russia, the Turks started to mobilize 200,000 troops in July, half in the Balkans and half for the Asiatic frontier, where there had been serious action in the 1806–12 and 1828–29 wars. Now the Russians desired a counter-revolutionary alliance with Turkey. Nicholas himself had advised the Sultan and the Romanian Hospodars to follow the Russian policy of recalling all students who were abroad. The Turks instead sounded out London for an alliance, but Palmerston was not prepared for such a commitment.[12]

By November, Stratford, fearing the Russian navy, was urging Palmerston to send a British squadron, with or without French participation. Palmerston was less nervous and wished to compromise with the Russians. Nicholas sent General P.Kh. Grabbe as a special envoy to Constantinople to make a new arrangement for the Principalities. He was also to try to conclude a new alliance, get the Turks to contribute 10,000-odd troops to the intervention in Hungary, and allow for a prolonged occupation of the Principalities.[13] Had the Turks agreed, Nicholas would have obtained under his leadership the perfect reactionary Holy Alliance of Tsar, Kaiser and Sultan. The best Grabbe could extract, however, was the compromise Convention of Balta Liman, whereby the Moldavian and Wallachian assemblies lost some of their powers, the Hospodars were again to be appointed only for seven years, the Turks could oversee administrative reform, and both powers could send troops in case of disorders.[14]

Meanwhile, in Central Europe the Austrian and Prussian high commands regained their confidence. In June General Alfred Windischgrätz put down insurgent Czechs in Prague. In July Radetzky smashed the Italian army, drove it back to Piedmont, reoccupied Milan, and besieged Venice. The loyal Croat general, Josip Jelačić, gained ascendancy over the Croats and Serbs by supporting those who fought for the Empire in Italy and Hungary. In September he invaded ethnic Hungary in the name of their common sovereign, fought one indecisive battle, and retreated. Windischgrätz and Jelacic now turned to subdue rebellious Vienna, and held off a detachment of Hungarians coming to help the insurgents. This heartened the Prussian king, who authorized the army to take charge in Berlin in November.[15]

Windischgrätz's brother-in-law, Prince Felix Schwarzenberg, took charge in Austria, effected the abdication of the Emperor Ferdinand and his replacement by the young Francis Joseph II, and resolved to bring Hungary to heel. In December Windischgrätz invaded Hungary from the north and south-west with 120,000 troops against an equal number of Magyars, aided by some *emigré* Polish officers, including Henryk Dembinski, one of the heroes of the 1830–31 uprising against Russia. Windischgrätz took Budapest, but could not defeat the main

Hungarian army and needed reinforcements. In Transylvania, a foray by about 6,000 Russians under General Lüders failed against another *emigré* Polish general, Józef Bem.[16]

Italian affairs were complicated by the competing forces for revolution and order. Radicals and Republicans in Venice, Rome, Tuscany, and the south were allied as nationalists with the King of Piedmont. But he, as a force for stability, was socially allied with the Pope, the Austrians, and King of Naples, who had regained control of his state with some Spanish help. When Republicans took power in Rome in February 1849, the Pope appealed to four Catholic powers: Naples, Spain, Austria and France. Meanwhile, encouraged by Hungarian successes, the Piedmontese, under General Bernard Chrzanowski, a Polish *emigré* who had earlier served the Porte, tried to renew the war with Austria. This time Radetzky beat them even more badly at Novara in eastern Piedmont. Austrian arms now assured the restoration of the other North Italian dynasts, and this put the French on the spot: either they intervened in Rome, or the Austrians would. Joint Franco–Austrian action was another option, but President Louis Napoleon and the National Assembly decided in April just to send French troops to Rome in order to 'save liberty'. The Austrians moved into Ancona and Bologna in the north-eastern parts of the Papal States, and the Italians at Rome had to make terms with the French by July.[17]

In the meantime the Magyars reduced the Habsburgs to only three strongholds in Hungary proper. Schwarzenberg would have loved to be able to reduce Hungary single-handed and go on to dominate Germany and owe nothing to Russia, but in April the Magyars threatened Vienna again. Nicholas already had armies in Tsarist Poland, Volhynia and Wallachia to prevent the spread of revolution from Galicia, Hungary and Transylvania into his domains. In quick, tough negotiations, the Austrians accepted Russian terms regarding the aid. The King of Prussia obliged with the use of his Silesian railroads to help transport Russian troops. Russia eventually sent in 320,000 men, more than had crossed the borders in 1812–13 to chase Napoleon, but engaged in very little actual combat. Instead the Russian commanders accepted surrendering rebels with grace and mercy, while the Austrians, under General Haynau (recently called in from North Italy), did most of the necessary hard fighting. By early September it was all over.[18]

Up to this point 1849 had been an excellent year for imperialism and expansion. The Prussian army dispersed the German constitutionalists (who were meeting at Frankfurt) in the spring, and suppressed the popular movements in Baden, Saxony and the Palatinate (Rhenish Bavaria) in the autumn. Austria saved Lombardy and Venetia, invaded Tuscany, Modena and (papal) Romagna, while the French took Rome itself. The Russians kept the Principalities quiet and helped save Hungary for Austria, while the Americans were rushing to (formerly Mexican) California for gold. The British, besides keeping restless Ireland under control and suppressing a rebellion in the Ionian Islands, finished subjugating the Punjab without a word of protest from the Russians. The cynical Palmerston also had not wished to see Austria disintegrate or reduced to a Russian client-state, so telling Brunnow to 'do it quickly', did not help the Hungarians. Neither did Louis Napoleon, and he received his pay-off too. Nicholas recognized the French Republic, that temporary conquest of French democracy, the day his troops crossed the Hungarian frontier. This helps explain the 'unexpectedly calm' reaction of Paris and London to Russia's intervention in Hungary.[19]

Counter-revolutionary cooperation among the Great Powers could not and did not last. General Haynau's harsh reprisals in Hungary created a terrible press for Austria in the West. A stream of more than 5,000 Polish, Hungarian and Italian refugees into a sympathetic Turkey created a new diplomatic problem. Russia, Austria and Prussia were already physically mobilized. The French and British publics were spiritually mobilized. And the Turks, seeing how Austria had almost fallen apart and how poorly organized the Russian army in Hungary had been, exuded uncharacteristic confidence. All six powers were in a position, to quote Shakespeare: 'from ancient grudge [to] break to new mutiny'.[20] The question was: which mutiny or mutinies?

AVERTING A WAR OF GERMAN UNIFICATION

Neither the Danish nor the German issues had been resolved, when the last Hungarian units surrendered in August and September 1849. The Danes had renewed the war in Schleswig in February and defeated the native German troops from the Duchies. However, in May, Palmerston warned the Prussians that if they did not accept British good offices, they would have to face French and Russian mediation, and Nicholas wrote to the king that a Russian fleet was on the way to protect Jutland. He gave way, but it took another year before the Russian fleet convinced Berlin to accept a

British compromise that excluded a Prussian military presence from the Duchies.[21]

The renewal of the Austro-Prussian rivalry in Germany made the Prussian–Danish issue even more tense. Once the Italians, Hungarians and radical Germans were suppressed, Berlin and Vienna squared off against each other. One could forget about the dreams of a united, democratic Germany: it was 'Greater Prussia' vs 'Greater Austria'. On paper, Austria and her German allies had about 450,000 mobilized troops, but some of them were needed in Italy and Hungary. Prussia could levy up to 300,000 soldiers, so the position of the other German states and the outside powers was crucial. During the counter-revolutionary fighting in 1849, Prussia had secured the adherence of all of the north and central German states and Baden in the south-west to the federal Erfurt Union. With social peace established, however, Hanover and Saxony defected in October and joined with Bavaria and Württemburg to form the 'League of the Four Kings' in favour of the old Confederation. The Prussians were not so ready to abandon their goals, but Schwarzenberg cleverly promoted the reassertion of Confederation powers in Holstein. The Tsar's position was decisive. He activated his Baltic fleet and his armies in Poland as a signal to Prussia. Berlin gave way in late June 1851, allowing all the Great Powers and Sweden to work out a solution to the tricky questions of royal and ducal succession in Denmark and Schleswig-Holstein.

The Austro-Prussian rivalry now concentrated on the north German state of Electoral Hesse (Hesse-Cassel), which faced revolutionary upheavals and also possessed military roads vital for Prussia. The Tsar's insistence that Hesse also lay within the purview of the Confederation once more forced Prussia's hand. Berlin's remaining options were war or capitulation. The king would fight only if England would join as Prussia's ally, an impossibility over this issue. When Schwarzenberg pressed with an ultimatum, the king ordered a mobilization, but the conservative partisans of capitulation to the Tsar and subordination to Austria had no heart for such a fight. Austria's rapid concentration of 75,000 troops by rail to Bohemia convinced the king to back down. However, uncertain of what either the French or the British would do if Austria attempted to press its advantages in northern Germany to the hilt, Schwarzenberg agreed to see Prussia's Otto von Manteuffel at Olmütz. Nesselrode's friend Peter Meyendorff, the Russian minister in Berlin, came too and helped to reconcile the parties at the end of November.[22]

A war of German unification between Central Europe's two Great Powers was averted for three basic reasons: (1) the strategic considerations of Britain and France; (2) the attitude of Russia; and (3) the reluctance of the Prussian conservatives and king to break with the Tsar and the Habsburgs. The British and French would not support Prussia's expansion, but neither would they countenance her reduction by an Austro-Russian combination. Nicholas favoured the status quo *ante* of 1847 and saw Prussia as the aggressor over Schleswig-Holstein and the Erfurt Union. Prussia's own élite was too divided to carry out a credible mobilization, and without one, the king had to back down.

Neither Austria's small German allies nor France nor Russia favoured Schwarzenberg's plan to bring the entire Habsburg realm into the Confederation and create an 'Empire of Seventy Millions', which could be the most powerful state on the Continent. Consequently, he had to accept the next best deal from Prussia, a defensive alliance, covering all of Austrian territory for the first time, including Lombardy and Venetia.[23] This at least put Austria in a fine position to settle her outstanding issues in the Balkans. However, with the Danish and German problems moved to the negotiating table, Russia, Britain and also France felt free to press for their goals in the Near East.

THE REFUGEE CRISIS: DRESS REHEARSAL FOR 1853?

The immediate issue after the collapse of Hungary was that of the refugees, many of whom under General Bem joined Omer Pasha in Wallachia and talked of clearing the Principalities of Russian troops. St Petersburg wanted Omer to hand over all Poles who were originally the Tsar's subjects, especially four veteran revolutionary generals. The Austrians wanted the Russians to evacuate the Principalities, but wanted the Hungarian leader Kossuth even more and so joined the Russians in formally demanding extradition on 28–29 August. Both powers relied on extradition clauses found in the Treaties of Belgrade (1739) and Kuchuk-Kainarji (1774) that had ended the eighteenth-century wars.[24] International Law normally provided for extradition of criminals, but the Turks liked anti-Russian refugee soldiers and were prepared to counter with the right of political asylum, just as the liberal states of Western Europe had generally exempted political offenders since 1830.[25] The normal procedure in such cases was for the receiving government to reconcile the two principles by curbing the political activities of the refugees, as France did with some Poles after the 1830–31 revolt against Russia. On 30 August the Turkish Council, with strong Anglo-French support, decided in principle in favour of incarceration far from the Austrian and Russian frontiers of all refugees who did not become Muslims.[26]

Neither St Petersburg nor Vienna was pleased. Nicholas had already decided to dispatch Prince Michail Radziwill, a loyal Polish aristocrat, with an autograph letter urging the Sultan to respect the demand of his 'ally' and to ask for a categorical answer regarding extradition. Radziwill arrived on 4 September, and immediately he and the Austrian Internuncio (ambassador), Count Barthélemy Stürmer, stepped up the pressure with threats to break relations. The Russians, Austrians and Turks engaged in heated debates over whether the rebels were criminals, and the Turks relied on a Metternich memorandum to confound the Austrians. French and British support for resistance was very strong, so on the 17th, Stürmer and Titov submitted notes demanding a favourable response within forty-eight hours. Nothing of the sort materialized, so they officially suspended relations with the Porte, but remained in Constantinople nevertheless.[27]

This pressure was sufficient for Stratford to invite Admiral William Parker and the British Malta squadron to cruise in Greek waters. Stratford's appeal reached London about 1 October, the same time direct Turkish requests for material aid arrived in London and Paris. Palmerston immediately warned Brunnow that Britain considered Turkey to be guaranteed by the 1841 Convention and would help the Porte against an outside threat. Brunnow got the message and informed Nesselrode that the British might pass the Dardanelles. Word of this reached St Petersburg about 12 October, four days after Palmerston authorized Parker to sail to Besika Bay, just outside the Straits. Louis Napoleon jumped at the opportunity to please the British, bypassed his own Cabinet, and ordered a French squadron to accompany the British ships. The British and the French also urged both Vienna and St Petersburg to be moderate, and the Austrians quickly decided to separate their diplomatic pressure from Russia's.[28]

The Turks, however, did not wait for word from London, but rather dispatched Fuad to St Petersburg to work out a compromise outside of the treaties: a simple promise to keep the refugees far from the Russian border. By the time he arrived on 5 October, the Russians had worked out their compromise position that upheld the 'treaties'. According to Orlov, the Porte had the right to choose among extradition, expulsion and incarceration, but in this third case, Austria and Russia had the right by treaty to have a commissioner supervise the confinement. The Foreign Ministry's operational plan was to ascertain if Fuad had brought a satisfactory response. If not, the Tsar would refuse to see him. Then Titov would close down the mission except for the commercial section, announce that the army in Moldavia was being strengthened, and communicate these moves to Austria. On 1 October the Tsar approved and amended this plan to include a threat to remove the Principalities from Ottoman jurisdiction.[29]

Fuad saw Nesselrode on 8 October and presented the Sultan's letters, which Nesselrode saw as a refusal to execute the Russo-Turkish treaties. Fuad replied that he came with an explanation and that the right of asylum was sacred to Orientals, so Nesselrode reported to the Tsar that Fuad was trying to be conciliatory. At a second interview, Nesselrode suggested expelling Poles who would not embrace Islam and incarcerating those who would. Fuad promised to refer this to the Porte and then had a positive working session with Nesselrode's deputy, Seniavin, on the 15th and a satisfactory interview with Nicholas the next day. Two days later Fuad promised Seniavin not to allow any British involvement; rather the Russians and Turks 'would wash their dirty laundry *en famille*'. Then a deal worked out on the side by Titov and the Turks for relocation away from the borders arrived, and it met with the Tsar's approval. On the 19th he officially dropped the demand for extradition, but then immediately took up the issue of the British and French fleets. He ordered a powerful rejoinder to Palmerston's message, and urged Fuad to tell his government to send the fleets away.[30]

Despite the fears of the Austrian ambassador, Count Buol, Nicholas was eager for peace and was working out the timetable for the withdrawal of the troops from the Principalities when really alarming news from Constantinople arrived. Titov did not know all the details, but he knew enough. Stratford and Calvert, the British consul at the Dardanelles, had improvised a reading of the 1841 Treaty to allow Calvert and Parker to bring the fleet into the Dardanelles at their discretion, if the physical conditions in Besika Bay so dictated. Parker arrived on 27 October, discovered that 'the wind set in very strong', and entered on 1 November. Titov immediately complained to Stratford, who, soon learning of the impending Austro-Turkish settlement, wanted the squadron out too. So Stratford, like Palmerston, did not seek war, but interpreted the 1841 Treaty in a British sense, the implicit goal of protecting Turkey taking precedence over the explicit provision for Straits closure.[31]

Meanwhile, Nicholas said that he would not be intimidated and was not mollified by the news that the French fleet was being recalled. 'What is done is done', he wrote. While Brunnow was instructed to get Palmerston to disavow Parker, Titov was told to inform the Porte that Russia had the same rights regarding the Bosphorus as did Britain in the Dardanelles. This notion convinced Palmerston in January to apologize and reaffirm Britain's commitment to the 1841 Treaty.[32]

The Tsar could not hide his continued displeasure over this incident. Before Palmerston's apology arrived, Nicholas told the departing British envoy, Bloomfield:[33]

> I do not understand the conduct of Lord Palmerston. If he chooses to wage war against me, let him declare it freely and loyally. It will be a great misfortune for the two countries, but I am resigned to it and ready to accept it. But he should stop playing tricks on me right and left. Such policy is unworthy of a great power. If the Ottoman Empire still exists, this is due to me. If I pull back the hand that protects it and sustains it, it will collapse in an instant.

Nesselrode, for his part, was optimistic about Turkey's future cooperation with Russia and was satisfied with Palmerston's retreat. Relations with Turkey were restored at the end of the year, though not all the issues were settled. While Stratford thought that Russia wanted to keep up the dispute only in order to exert pressure for an alliance, the Tsar's attitude was not so simple. He was happy that the 'mauvaise affaire' with Turkey had ended, but not so hopeful. On 17 December he instructed Admiral Putiatin to prepare a plan for a pre-emptive, surprise attack on the Straits the next time a crisis erupted, to prevent another British entry. The plan, which was ready the next July, envisioned seizing the Dardanelles as well and forcing the Turks into a defensive alliance. It required eight new war steamers, four of which the Tsar authorized.[34]

Nicholas was not alone in his readiness to use his navy to secure an alliance with Britain in November 1849, and Stratford hoped thereby to obtain an open door for British commerce. The natural passing of Egypt's Mehmed Ali and his redoubtable son, Ibrahim, from the scene in 1848 had created conditions for opening up that land as well. Palmerston, however, rejected any fully-fledged alliance with such a fragile entity as Turkey, favouring instead a more cautious cooperation in building up the Ottoman fleet.[35] In either case Russia and Britain were engaged in a new, heated round of their competition over Turkey, while once more an Eastern crisis showed that Austria would not back Russia and that some Vienna statesmen looked upon Russian support as a Trojan horse.

Other explosive problems also loomed in the Near East. Schwarzenberg, while opposed to Russian tactics, refused until April 1850 to accept mere Austrian inspection of incarcerated Hungarians – and this agreement soon broke down. Meanwhile, the French legation in Constantinople had another ploy for increasing influence without simply trailing after the British. At the end of 1849, prompted by the French, the Latin Patriarch of Jerusalem went to Paris to ask for aid against the local Orthodox.[36]

A new chapter in the struggle of four of Europe's six great imperialisms for influence in the domains of the 'sickest' of their number was about to begin. The Turks, Austrians and French were more assertive, and England and Russia had probed a hostile armed diplomacy. Ideologies and interpretation of the 1841 Straits Convention differed. But nothing so far had occurred to make an armed showdown over Turkey or the Balkans inevitable. If the already fragile Concert of Europe was even more weakened by the events of 1848–49, the balance of power mechanisms that had helped to prevent war since 1815 were still in fine working order.

NOTES

1. Hearder, *Italy in the Age of the Risorgimento, 1790–1870* (London/New York 1983), pp. 142–203, *passim*; for the numbers, *EB* 1911 XV: 52–3.

2. Lawrence C. Jennings, *France and Europe in 1848. A Study of Foreign Affairs in Time of Crisis* (Oxford 1973), pp. 1–23.

3. Fonblanque to Rose No. 7, 29 Jan 1853 (PRO FO).

4. Cf. Barrington Moore, Jr, *Social Origins of Dictatorship and Democracy. Lord and Peasant in the Making of the Modern World* (Boston 1966); Karl Marx, 'The Class Struggles in France' (first published 1850), Marx and Engels, *Selected Works* I: 139–242.

5. Jennings, *France and Europe in 1848*, especially pp. 24–43, 251–3; cf. T.C.W. Blanning, *The Origins of the French Revolutionary Wars* (London/New York 1986), pp. 1–163.

6. Charles Sproxton, *Palmerston and the Hungarian Revolution* (Cambridge UK 1919), pp. 21–2; QV to Plm., 5 July 1848 (*LQV* II), seeing a contradiction in Palmerston's principles; on attitudes toward Germany, see W.E. Mosse, *The European Powers and the German Question, 1848–1871* (Cambridge UK 1958), p. 20.

7. For Russia in 1848, Schiemann, IV: 140–62; A.S. Nifontov, 'Rossiia i Revoliutsiia 1848 g.', *Revoliutsii 1848–1849 gg.* (2 vols, F. Potemkin and A.I. Moloka (eds), Moscow–Leningrad 1952), II: 272–3; A.S. Nifontov, *1848 god v Rossii: ocherki po istorii 40-kh godov* (Moscow/Leningrad 1931), pp. 155–61; Sydney Monas, *The Third Section*, pp. 238–42.

8. Schiemann IV: 143–4; A 'counter-revolutionary crusade' is discounted by Fuller: 232.

9. For Turkey and the Principalities in 1848–49, Sheremet: 125–52, supplemented by the reports of Blondeel van Cuelebroeck (AMAE Blg. Turq. II).

10. Nes. to Tit., 2/14. April 1848 (AVPR Pos. Konst. 204).

11. N.V. Berezniakov, 'Osvoboditel'skie dvizheniia v Moldavii i Valakhii v 1848 g.', Revoliutsii 1848–1849 gg., p. 367.

12. Nes. to Tit., 7/19 Feb. 1848 (AVPR GA-V2 518); Plm. to Brw., 21 Jul. 1848 (AVPR Pos. Konst. 204); Temperley ENEC: 260.

13. Sproxton, Palmerston and the Hungarian Revolution, p. 15; Florescu, The Struggle against Russia in the Roumanian Principalities, 1821–1854, pp. 212–13.

14. Nouradounghian II: 389–91, CTS CIII (Russ.–Turk. Conv., 19 April/ 1 May 1849), trans. Hertslet II.209.

15. Gordon Craig, The Politics of the Prussian Army, 1640–1945 (Oxford 1955), p. 119.

16. Kenneth W. Rock, 'Schwarzenberg vs Nicholas I, Round I: the Negotiations of the Habsburg–Romanov Alliance against Hungary in 1849', AHY VI–VII: 114–23.

17. Rothenberg, The Army of Francis Joseph, p. 34; Echard: 181; Hearder, Italy in the Age of the Risorgimento, 1790–1870, pp. 116–19.

18. Rock, 'Schwarzenberg vs Nicholas I, Round 1', pp. 124–41; CTS CIII (Aus.–Russ. Conv., 29 May/10 June 1849); Curtiss, The Russian Army under Nicholas I, 1825–1855, pp. 295–313.

19. Messerschmidt, Handbuch zur Deutschen Militärgeschichte, 1648–1939 II: 18–22; Lawrence Sondhaus 'Prince Felix zu Schwarzenberg and Italy', AHY XXII (1991): 65–6; Martens XII: 254; Sproxton, Palmerston and the Hungarian Revolution, p. 101; Heindl: 43.

20. William Shakespeare, Romeo and Juliet, Prologue.

21. Holger Hjelholt, British Mediation in the Danish-German Conflict, 1848– 1850. 2 Pts, Historisk-filosofisk Meddelelser (Det Konglige Danske Videnskabernes Selskab, Bind 41. nr. 1, Copenhagen, 1965–6) I: 103, 110, II: 242–6.

22. Schiemann IV: 156–62; Mosse, The European Powers and the German Question, 1848–1871, pp. 33–42; Craig, The Politics of the Prussian Army, 1640–1945, pp. 129–31; Manfred Messerschmidt, Handbuch zur deutschen Militärgeschichte II: 21–3; Rothenberg, The Army of Francis-Joseph, pp. 48–9; PM II: 347.

23. Joseph Wieskirchner, Die Dresdener Konferenzen, 1850/1851 (diss. phil., Vienna, 1928), pp. 260–3 (Aus.–Pruss. Tr., 16 May 1851), cited in AGK II:1: 331.

24. CTS XXXV (Aus.–Turk. Tr. of Belgrade, 18 Sept. 1739), art. XVIII; CTS LXV/MENA I.32 (Tr. of Kuchuk-Kainarji), art. II.

25. S. Prakash Sinha, Asylum and International Law (The Hague 1971), pp. 172–5.

26. Sheremet: 145–6.

27. BlC. to Hoffschmidt, 15, 19 Nov. 1849 (AMAE Blg. Turq. II); Lane-Poole II: 191–2; Bapst: 85–90.

28. Sheremet: 148; Temperley ENEC: 263–4; Martens XII: 258; Bapst: 96–8;

Heindl: 60–1; the Russian sources belie Heindl's claim that St Petersburg only demanded the four generals. The French Foreign Minister at this time was Alexis de Tocqueville of *Democracy in America* fame.

29. Orl. et al., memos, with Nich. I gloss dated 20 Sept./1 Oct. 1849 (AVPR K 469 204: 150–4, 168–9).

30. Orl. and anon., memos, with Nich. I gloss, 20 Sept./1 Oct. 1849; Nes. to Nich. I with some glosses, 26 Sept./8 Oct. 4/16, 6/18, 8/20, 12/24 Oct. 1849; memos of parleys with Fuad, undated; Sen. memo, 5/17 Oct. 1849 (AVPR K 204); cf. Mdf. to Nes., 2/14 Oct. 1849 (*PM* II); Temperley *ENEC*: 267–8.

31. Nes. to Nich. I, 24 Oct./5 Nov. 1849 (AVPR K 204); Heindl: 70–1; Temperley *ENEC*: 264–5; Puryear *ERSQ*: 170–1.

32. Nes. to Nich. I with glosses, 2/14, 3/15 Nov. 1849, to Brw., 19 Nov./1 Dec. 1849 (AVPR K 204); cf. Puryear *ERSQ*: 174–80.

33. Nes. to Brw., 8/20 Dec. 1849 (TsGADA, III/115).

34. Nes. to Nich. I with gloss, 19 Nov./1 Dec. 1849, 24 Dec. 1849/ 5 Jan. 1850 (AVPR K 204); Martens XII: 272; BlC. to Hoffschmidt, 25 Dec. 1849, 5 Jan. 1850 (AMAE Blg. Turq. II); Putiatin memo with Nich. I's gloss, 8/20 July 1850 (TsGAVMF) 19/1/276b).

35. Puryear *ERSQ*: 183–6; Temperley *ENEC*: 269; Sheremet: 151–2.

36. BlC. to Hoffschmidt, 5 May, 15 Dec. 1850 (AMAE Blg. Turq. II).

CHAPTER FIVE

Holy Places, Profane Litigation (May 1850–March 1852)

THE TENSE AFTERMATH OF THE REFUGEE CRISIS

The outcome of the refugee crisis heartened some Turks, but embittered Nicholas. However, the focus of European diplomacy shifted away from Constantinople to Germany, France and their neighbours. The nexus of problems associated with the German Question dominated throughout 1850 and part of 1851. The possibility that the Bonaparte prince-president might re-establish the French Empire and overthrow the settlement of 1815 loomed in the background and seemed highly likely in late 1851. Switzerland, Belgium and the Italian states were the political battleground for the conflicting interests of their Great Power neighbours. In the light of all of these matters the Eastern Question appeared somewhat secondary; however, it would not go away.

All of the major states, except for Prussia, added some fuel to the Ottoman fires. The Tsar continuously hoped that others might grasp, as he did, that the Ottoman Empire was on the verge of collapse and make a preliminary settlement providing for Russia's security needs; however, he made no disruptive moves in the Orient. His navy was trying on paper only to prepare strategically for the next Turkish crisis. Nevertheless, he remained touchy over what he perceived as Russia's political space.

Palmerston, already mobilized by the refugee crisis in late 1849 and hardly moved by criticism over the Dardanelles, pursued unilateral and stubborn gunboat diplomacy until July 1850 against the Greek government. His aim was to stop it from supporting Ionian–Greek patriots and to force it to compensate Don Pacifico, a Portuguese businessman with a British passport, whose property an Athens mob had looted. Brunnow tried mightily to embarrass Palmerston in his own backyard, but he would brook no Russian interference in the Mediterranean, and only reluctantly agreed to minimal French mediation.[1]

The Turks supported Britain in the Greek affair, continued to rebuff Austria over the refugee issue, and moved to strengthen their own hold over the Balkans. Omer Pasha, military governor of Bosnia as of May 1850, cynically employed Hungarian and Polish refugees in his armies to suppress native Balkan insurgents, who opposed both older and more modern forms of Ottoman administration. Schwarzenberg showed his chronic displeasure with the Porte by pensioning off the Internuncio Stürmer and leaving the Austrian mission under a chargé d'affaires – Eduard von Klezl. Austro-Turkish relations remained tense into early 1853, each side encroaching on the other's preferred political space in the Western Balkans and the lower Adriatic Sea.[2]

The French, having helped temper the Russians, Austrians and British, were angling to increase their own influence in Turkey and the Mediterranean. As the protecting power in the Vatican since April 1849, France sought to lead a bloc of Mediterranean powers in support of the Catholic renaissance in the Holy Land and the overthrow of the Orthodox or Greek domination of the Holy Places. A common conjecture is that Louis Napoleon raised this issue in order to provoke a crisis with Russia, destroy the 1815 settlement, break up the Austro–Russian alliance, and make one with England.[3] In other words, the new bully on the western end of the block was cleverly setting the stage for future fights with the established bullies to his east. Such a *post hoc* reading assumes that the prince-president could predict the Russian foolhardiness. In fact, Napoleon's outlook was much more defensive. He feared the recreation of the British–Austrian–Russian alignment that stymied France in 1839–41, and his Foreign Minister, La Hitte, told Aupick not to provoke a crisis.[4]

Contemporaries, including some Russians and Turks, assigned a more modest motive: Louis Napoleon's need to placate his Catholic supporters. His Foreign Ministry also harboured a few advocates of an aggressive Catholic policy in the Levant, but normally paid scant attention to this issue except when pressured by foreign powers. The astute French diplomats understood how seriously Russia took religious issues and saw to it that Paris compromised rather than face ostracism and isolation in Europe.[5] All the same, and despite this suppleness, any moves by Catholics to reassert their influence in the Holy Land had to evoke a Russian response.

The historian's mission is to determine whether this quarrel, among the others of 1848–53, was the chief issue that led to war, and if so, how and why. As we have noted, social conditions, material constraints and the operations of the balance of power prevented a land war at this time over German unification, the most powerful European problem connected to mainstream economic and intellectual developments. The balance of power also worked in a normal fashion in the quarrel over the Holy Places and provided guidelines for rational behaviour. This was true, even though most regimes were insecure at home, and the weakened Concert of Europe after 1848 reduced the impediments to unilateral, strident moves by the Great Powers or the Ottomans. The Sultan's government had the ultimate authority over the Holy Places, so any recourse to threats would involve Turkey's security and hence England, Austria and the entire Eastern Question. Neither France nor Russia could have any rational grounds for provoking a war against a coalition of the other powers. The Turks might gain something from a successful war against Russia, but the price would be more economic subordination to Western Europe.

Only an irrational impulse, one sufficiently powerful to override simple considerations of other states' interests and the correlation of forces, could set off a war under these circumstances. And maybe there were some such impulses. Even if rather puny material interests underlay the rival claims for the sanctuaries, their symbolic meaning was immense for the Orthodox and Catholic clerics in the Holy Land and their backers everywhere. There was a second symbolic issue as well. Nicholas I, as God's chosen and anointed leader of Holy Russia, was no more ready to admit the legitimacy of a Bonaparte proclaimed Emperor by the will of the people than to allow a Latin assault on the leading position of the true, Orthodox Church in Jerusalem and Bethlehem. Louis-Napoleon, on the other hand, could compromise with the Tsar over the Holy Land without losing power or prestige, but not over French domestic politics. Nicholas eventually gave way in both matters, but before he did, he set Russia on a disastrous diplomatic course that led to war.

RIVAL CHALLENGES TO THE STATUS QUO

A local conflict over the Christian sanctuaries in Judaea was about to erupt on the eve of the 1848 Revolutions. Confessional rivalry was on the increase. Catholics had never accepted as final the recent

Orthodox gains and Protestants were making their own inroads. In 1842 Anglicans installed a bishopric in Jerusalem, the same year that the Russians established their Palestine mission. Three years later the Greek Patriarch of Jerusalem moved his residence back from Constantinople to his see. This was followed in 1847 by Pius IX's sending of a Latin Patriarch to Jerusalem – an office that had been titular since the fall of the Crusader states in 1291. Meanwhile, French monks were repopulating the Latin cloisters of Palestine, and Vienna financed a local Franciscan printing press in 1846. Catholic propaganda even called for the expulsion of the Orthodox from common Christian shrines as a holy act. Hostility between Latin and Greek reached such a level that the Turks had to place soldiers inside and outside the Church of the Holy Sepulchre in Jerusalem to preserve order, though this did not prevent rival groups of monks from joining battle with candlesticks and crosses.[6]

The spark that ignited the conflict at the end of 1847 was the disappearance of a silver star with Latin inscriptions that was located over the place where Jesus was thought to have been born. This was in the Greek-owned sanctuary in the Church of the Nativity in Bethlehem. The Latins held title to an adjoining sanctuary, but, unlike the Greeks and Armenians, no longer possessed a set of symbolic keys to the main doors of the church, and so had to enter through a side door. Now the Latins used the 'theft' of the star as the pretext for demanding the restoration of all Greek 'usurpations', calling upon the French government for support. Deliberations over this matter in Paris were under way, when Louis-Philippe was overthrown in February 1848.[7]

The revolutionary situation of 1848–49 allowed the new French regime to try to combine support for the Catholics with opposition to Russia's Balkan policies, an approach consistent with Napoleon's desire to anchor French policy with a British *entente*. Early in 1849 his first Foreign Minister, Edouard Drouyn de Lhuys, instructed Aupick to combine a protest in the name of the 1841 Treaty against Russia's unilateral occupation of the Danubian Principalities with a demand for the restoration of the star and France's 'religious protection' that had declined since 1740.[8]

Once the refugee crisis abated, La Hitte instructed Aupick in January 1850 to seek a solution on the basis of France's 1740 Treaty that guaranteed the Latins the Holy Places which were then in their possession. The cleverness of this argument was that if the Turks could violate a formal treaty, then, implicitly, France could too – something which the other European powers wished to avoid. La

Hitte tried to mobilize France's fellow Catholic missions, which also had an interest in the Catholic cloisters and other institutions in the Holy Land. Belgium was at the forefront with its dominant Catholic party at home, commercial presence in the Orient, historical links to Europe's Crusades, and a very Catholic envoy, Blondeel van Cuelebroeck, an expert on the Near and Middle East. Piedmont, Naples, Spain and Portugal seconded French efforts. The Austrians, however, held off: though they claimed the need to examine the issue their reluctance was really due to the perception of the French as rivals and an unwillingness to annoy the Russians or the Turks.[9]

Blondeel pre-empted Aupick on 6 May 1850 with a separate request for the restoration of the tombs of Godfrey and Baldwin, the founders of the Flemish Jerusalem dynasty (1099–1187). Three weeks later Aupick demanded the restoration to the Catholics of the Holy Places allegedly in their exclusive possession in 1740. These were the Sanctuary of the Nativity in Bethlehem with the right to replace the star and the tapestry in the Grotto; the all-important right to repair the main cupola of the Church of the Holy Sepulchre in Jerusalem and restore the building to its pre-1808 condition; and the Tomb of the Virgin outside Jerusalem at Gethsemane. Aupick argued that compliance would be in keeping with the Porte's recent adoption of European attitudes toward the rule of law.

At the same time Cyrill, the Orthodox Patriarch of Jerusalem, made his own formal request for permission to repair the cupola of the Holy Sepulchre. Anyone who has seen an Orthodox cupola with the face of the Pankrator – the Omnipotent Christ staring down upon the human worshippers – can grasp the meaning of control over the iconography and inscriptions on this representative of 'heaven on earth'. The Orthodox had repaired this dome in 1808 and reputedly had substituted Greek iconography and inscriptions for Latin ones.[10]

The Russian minister Titov needed no special instructions to urge the French to leave matters alone and save the Turks from an embarrassing situation. In reporting the Belgian and French *démarches* he hit the bull's eye:[11] 'The litigation is as old as it is complicated; no attempt to resolve it has proved successful; the titles are obscure and contradictory.' The Porte knew this too and 'abstained from committing itself to either side without the maturest deliberation', as the well-informed Stratford urged privately on Grand Vizier Reshid.[12]

The Turks in fact did nothing, so in mid-August Aupick asked the Foreign Minister Aali Pasha if he would at least take the 1740

Treaty as the basis of negotiation. Aali temporized by referring to a Council of Ministers that would not reconvene until the holy days of Ramadan and Bairam passed. Meanwhile, Nesselrode told Titov to support Cyrill's request to repair the dome and also affirmed Russia's opposition to any alteration of the religious status quo, claiming this would stir up the Sultan's Orthodox subjects in Europe and Asia. This became a standard Russian line, and since each side held to its position, the French and Russians were heading for a clash.

The Porte tried to ignore both requests, seeing in Russia's warning of potential Orthodox unrest a threat 'to draw away the affection of the [Christian] rayahs from the Sultan's government'.[13] Consequently the Turks sought to satisfy their Orthodox subjects without the dreaded Russian official interference. Titov himself favoured an arrangement that affirmed the Sultan's authority and reduced the embarrassment to the Latins. According to a scheme which was acceptable to the Russians and some Greek notables and clergy, the Turks would repair the cupola to Orthodox liking and later be reimbursed by the Greeks.

The Ottomans, however, could not ignore Aupick, so they disputed his claim that the 1740 Treaty took absolute precedence over earlier and subsequent internal grants. Though willing to recognize charters from the pre-Ottoman, Mamluk sultans of Egypt to the Latins, they also produced a firman or charter to the Greeks, granted by Selim I (1512–21), the Ottoman conqueror of Palestine. Finally, they offered to establish a commission with a Greek, a Catholic and an Armenian to examine everyone's rights. Stratford, who was still trying to interest both London and the Porte in a long-term loan secured by Ottoman assets, favoured such a mixed body and tried to persuade Aupick to recognize any post-1740 firmans to the Greeks that did not blatantly contradict the 1740 Treaty. By early 1851 Titov was pleased with both the British and the Turks, but Aupick was not and sought fresh instructions from Paris.

The new word from France was quite explicit. A year had elapsed since Aupick was first told to raise the issue and no progress had been made, so he was to ascertain if the Turks still considered the 1740 Treaty valid. Meanwhile, the Russian government, neglecting Titov's attempts to work with Stratford, reacted strongly. Nesselrode fired off an unmistakable challenge on 21 January:[14]

> The day that the Emperor sees the cult or the Church persecuted or humiliated, be it in the Holy City or elsewhere, as the result of the suggestions of outsiders or with political aims in mind that we care not to fathom, His Majesty will not recoil before any consideration

or any sacrifice to take up with pride the defence of his co-religionists and to insist upon the maintenance of the immunities which they have enjoyed since time immemorial, and among which control over the Holy Sepulchre and precedence in the celebration of offices may not be assaulted without a dreadful injustice.

Eleven days later, Nesselrode instructed Titov to base Russia's claims on the vague terms of the 1837 *Hatt-i Sherif* of Mahmud II (1808–39) and the precedence of the post-1808 restoration. Titov then 'protested against all inquiry into the right possession and insisted, in the Emperor's name, on the actual state of occupation', while Aupick demanded 'to know purely and simply if the Porte considered itself bound still by the capitulations of 1740'.[15] Klezl tried to reconcile the two sides by affirming Vienna's theoretical support for Latin claims, but backed the Ottoman plan for a mixed commission. Aupick, however, vetoed it, leaving the deadlock intact.

THE ABORTED MIXED COMMISSION

This standoff created a dilemma in Paris and ended Aupick's tenure in Constantinople, but not, of course, Tsar Nicholas's in St Petersburg. Not seeking extra trouble, Nesselrode urged the Paris government to consider the ill effects of raising such a turbulent issue for the Ottoman regime, already rocked by ongoing disturbances among the Christians of the Levant. Similarly, the Russian representative in Paris, Count N.D. Kiselev concluded that the French did not know what they were doing and told the new Foreign Minister, Jules Baroche, that what was useful for obtaining Catholic votes in France was bad for Turkey and for the general peace. The Ottoman envoy, Prince Callimachi, also pleaded for moderation, but French newspapers clamoured for action. To mollify the clerical party, Napoleon appointed one of his friends, the Marquis Charles de la Valette, to replace Aupick and bring home a victory. To make a point, la Valette passed through Rome on his way to Constantinople and tried to rally the Vatican behind French leadership.[16]

La Valette did not have much luck in Rome, but he did have the initiative in Constantinople. A few months after he arrived in May, Baroche authorized a mixed French–Ottoman commission in return for the Porte's admitting the 1740 Treaty as the basis of negotiations, and the French chose as representatives their expert Consul in Jerusalem, P.E. Botta, and the embassy's First Dragoman or Interpreter, Ch. Schefer. Stratford expected the Turks to favour the Greek side and he was not far off the mark. They cleverly balanced their First Dragoman, Emin Effendi, with the Patriarchal Logothete or chief minister, Nicholas Aristarchi, whom even Nesselrode somewhat distrusted.[17]

The initial meeting took place without Aristarchi on Sunday 4 August at Emin's home. The participants established procedures and admitted as valid some Ottoman documents and the 1740 Treaty and its antecedents. The commission then met there again on nine successive Mondays with one break up to 28 October before the Turks suspended it. The Latins had on hand a set of detailed firmans and confirmations from the mid-sixteenth to the mid-eighteenth centuries, as well as stipulations from as late as 1811 refuting Greek pretences and precedents. Catholic scholars compiled another list alleging that almost all of the Holy Places were in Latin hands in 1740 and specifying which ones now excluded or discriminated against Latins. The Greeks and Turks, on the other hand, grounded the Orthodox case on a quasi-Donation of the Caliph Omar (634–44), who conquered Jerusalem in 636, and on confirmations and special firmans of more than half the Ottoman sultans since 1453. Bazili, Russian Consul in Syria, composed his own lengthy analysis of the conflicting rights.[18]

The first seven substantive meetings of the commission were devoted to establishing exactly what was actually stated in the firmans and judicial rulings from 1635 to 1757. At each session, the four commissioners duly signed the minutes of the previous conclave. Had only the documents discussed and recorded been recognized as valid, then the Latins would have taken control of the Churches of the Holy Sepulchre and the Nativity. But at the eighth session, on 21 October, Emin and Aristarchi began with Omar's 'Treaty'; Botta denied its validity; and the commission was deadlocked. Aristarchi conveniently missed the final meeting a week later, and the minutes of the last three sessions were never signed. Meanwhile, diplomatic pressure had overtaken the commission.[19]

The commission had actually laboured under competing guns from the start. Aristarchi aired his reservations before it met, and St Petersburg did not want it to meet at all, considering any official discussion to be a violation of the sacred status quo. Even before the sessions began, Nesselrode informed Titov that Russia was ready to counter French reliance on their 1740 Treaty with Kuchuk-Kainarji[20] – what no other country would consider applicable to this case. La Valette wanted a rubber stamp of French demands and did not even wait for the commission to finish all of the Catholic documents before asserting the half-truth: 'the Latin right is clearly established by the Committee of Investigation'. He further threatened: 'if the moderation of his Government in seeking only joint participation were not duly appreciated, the claim of undivided possession by the Latins would be urged with all the weight of a demand warranted by Treaty.' He thought that he had a private compromise arrangement with Aali Pasha to admit the Latins to all shrines claimed under the 1740 Treaty, without expelling the Greeks from any places where they were *de facto* in sole or joint possession. La Valette thus viewed the Porte's apparent intention not to satisfy the Catholics 'in very strong colours'. He talked of 'France being justified in a recourse to extreme measures' and boasted 'of her superior forces now in the Mediterranean'.[21]

The Russians did not wait either. In response to Titov's reports and perhaps to an appeal by Patriarch Cyrill of Jerusalem, the Tsar sent two letters to the Sultan towards the end of September. One was a friendly sovereign-to-sovereign greeting.[22] The other was a ministerial communication that spelled out Russia's position: namely that there should be no re-examination of 'a question that was clearly and positively resolved by solemn ordinances and sovereign *hatt-i sherifs*, some of which had been officially communicated to the Russian mission'. And there should be no 'unjust concessions regarding the religious establishments that have been possessed since time immemorial by the Greek Church and visited annually by thousands of my [Nicholas's] subjects by virtue of the treaties that fortunately exist between our countries and the intimate alliance [*sic*] that unites me with your majesty'.[23] In other words, any Turkish recourse to the 1740 Treaty with France at the expense of Russia's claims regarding the Holy Places was tantamount to violating Turkey's existing treaties with Russia and breaking the Sultan's alleged alliance with the Tsar. Nesselrode also informed Titov of Nicholas's intention to close down Russia's mission if the Ottomans persisted with their 'blunders'. It seems to have been this explicit threat, rather than just the Tsar's letters or la Valette's loose talk, that caused the Turks to suspend the commission's deliberations.[24]

Nicholas's direct intervention was one aspect of a policy that presupposed the imminent collapse of the Ottoman Empire. The Russell Cabinet with Palmerston in the Foreign Office had been on shaky grounds since the Don Pacifico imbroglio. Brunnow and others had been lobbying for a more conservative government and were hopeful. These facts explain why that August the Tsar summoned Brunnow back from London to consult and to compose some position papers, among them a detailed plan to initiate talks with Britain for the partition of Turkey.[25]

While Brunnow laboured, Nicholas journeyed to Moscow and back on the maiden voyage of the recently and hurriedly completed longest single railroad line in the world at that time. He left no written record of his strategic thinking at this moment, or what his new major construction project might be. Extension of the railroad network for strategic purposes, building up of Sevastopol as a 'Second Kronstadt', and launching some screw-propelled battleships of his own were all possibilities.

Nicholas also ordered Kiselev to try to arrange an *entente* with France in the Holy Land, but the Paris Cabinet refused to affirm most of Russia's pretensions in return for a few concessions. On the other hand, Nicholas rejected Napoleon's secret offer to curb the French mission in return for 'respect regarding his ambitions in France'.[26] Thus the impasse continued, and the stakes were getting higher.

THE ULEMA'S DEFT COMPROMISE AND THE SULTAN'S AMBIGUOUS PLEDGE

Some Turks sought to cut the knot by opening all the shrines to all believers, but Titov and la Valette would apply the principle of joint possession only to shrines in the hands of the other Church, and both badgered the Porte. Titov insisted that any further move against the status quo of the Holy Places would force him to make an official protest in the name of the Emperor. La Valette wanted to call the Mediterranean squadron, but lacked the authority to do so, and instead merely asked for new instructions. The Turks, though, aided by Stratford's embassy expert and friend, Charles Alison, persevered with their own notions of legality and equity and towards the end of the year appointed a commission of ulema (leading mullahs) to weigh the conflicting claims.

At this point French domestic politics helped the Turks. While Britain urged an embarrassed French government not to push so far as 'to lead to a diplomatic rupture', Bonaparte engineered his 2 December coup, which, besides setting off the last serious peasant disorders in French history, made the restoration of the French Empire more likely.[27] Consequently, it was politic for Napoleon to appear peaceful, and he promised the British to grant la Valette a leave. Although the latter continued to bluster and even boasted that Britain would do nothing if French warships bombarded the Dardanelles, his word now counted for less. Once Paris's call for moderation arrived in mid-December, Aali explicitly denied to Titov that la Valette had made any threats at all.[28]

The French retreat cleared the way for an Ottoman compromise proposal, with Stratford's and Titov's partial knowledge. The Catholics could have a set of keys to the Bethlehem Nativity doors and officiate at the Tomb of the Virgin, but had no exclusive rights to either. At the end of December the ulema produced their official report. Arguing with delicacy and hair-splitting finesse, these doctors of Islamic law rested their case on Mehmed IV's ruling from around 1686 against a Latin attempt to invalidate an earlier firman of Murad IV (1623–40). Since there was no subsequent invalidation of either decision, the Treaty of 1740 implicitly recognized Greek possessions as of 1686. The circle was thus squared, and the Ottomans, hopefully, could deny some Latin claims and still recognize the Treaty of 1740, without giving the Russians a pretext to mention Kuchuk-Kainarji.[29]

The Porte now hoped to satisfy the Greeks and Russians with 'new firmans, explaining and fixing the extent of the rights on both sides, with a due regard to the status quo',[30] that is, they tried to smuggle in the restoration to the Catholics of the Bethlehem keys as a status quo measure. The Turks were also willing to offer to the Orthodox a new privilege of officiating at the Chapel/Mosque of the Ascension on Mount Olivet as compensation. On 25 January the Ottoman Council formally recommended this package to the Sultan. A week later Titov complained, but the Greek Patriarchs of Constantinople and Jerusalem were willing to accept an exchange of concessions in the Tomb of the Virgin and the Ascension Chapel, provided that it also consolidated the status quo for the other sanctuaries. This soon became official Russian policy.

The Franco-Russian struggle now focused on the terms of the settlement, more precisely, how the Porte would interpret the status quo in Bethlehem and Jerusalem. Expecting that la Valette would accept *ad referendum* and hoping that Titov at least would not formally protest, the Turks prepared to issue four documents on 8–10 February: a new firman regulating the Holy Places, an official note for la Valette, a less official one for Titov, and a responsive letter in the name of the Sultan to the Tsar.[31]

This time la Valette's threat to depart worked in that it neutralized Titov's attempt to keep the Bethlehem keys out of any official

Turkish documents. But Titov's pressure also worked. The note to the French, faithful to the spirit of the ulema's report, stated that the Latins could obtain a replacement set of Bethlehem keys, but the similarly worded communiqué to Titov did not. The initial draft firman that Titov saw really clouded the issue by mixing tenses:[32]

> As earlier the Greeks, Latins, and Armenians were all given a key to the southeast and north portals of the Great Church and to the door of the Grotto, and that this measure was confirmed and ratified in the supreme firman granted to the Greek nation in the year 1170 of the Hegira (1756–1757), we shall continue this policy.

Thus the Porte cleverly promised nothing other than the logically impossible policy of continuing to have done something. Stratford, who was really aiming for greater influence in Egypt for Britain and the Foreign Office or Paris Embassy for himself, considered the solution 'equitable'. He thereby glossed over the contradiction between the two notes.

Titov and the Turks continued to clash over Russia's alleged right to give prior approval to any agreement, and with this came a fissure in the Ottoman Cabinet. Having failed to get changes in the note to the French, he immediately let the Turks know about their own 'lack of courtesy towards the Emperor'. Aali explained away the latest concessions to the Latins as due to recent French threats and Russia's lacking something comparable to France's 1740 Treaty. Reshid, however, blamed Aali for acting on his own and suggested the all-important restoration of the cupola as a reparation to the Orthodox.[33]

By late February Titov received St Petersburg's provisional acceptance of the Tomb–Chapel exchange, with the proviso that the status quo, meaning Orthodox control over cupola repair and no essential change in Bethlehem, be reaffirmed. He thereupon requested and obtained the draft of the Sultan's letter and the new firman. The letter, as the French recognized, was an evasive masterpiece. Formally responding to Nicholas I's letter of the previous autumn, the Sultan stated that the Tsar himself had to comprehend why a sovereign 'Padishah' must observe his predecessor's solemn engagements to another sovereign (i.e., King Louis XV of France in 1740). Noting the sole exceptions regarding the Tomb and the Chapel, but without mentioning the cupola or the keys, the Sultan gave a vague guarantee, which Nicholas himself marked with his characteristic 'NB':[34] 'Your Majesty will have learned from the reports of his representative that the salutary result of the scrupulous investigations that have been held concerning this question was that the present state of the sanctuaries is integrally preserved, confirmed, and consolidated.' On the contrary, His Imperial Majesty would have just learned from Titov that the Patriarch of Jerusalem considered the guarantees in the firman too loose and that Stratford agreed that 'the wrong was not on our [the Orthodox] side'. In fact, Nesselrode only needed an earlier report about the imminent Tomb–Chapel exchange to reply imperiously that the cupola was non-negotiable and to demand a special firman authorizing its repair. Furthermore, if a rupture ensued, the Emperor would *not* accept a special envoy to smooth out this difference, as in 1849.

The Greek community itself was divided over what to concede to the Latins, and Titov could not obtain all the changes he desired in the text of the new firman. The best he could manage before he took a leave on 20 March were some verbal assurances, which were rather unlikely to have come from an Ottoman official, and more indicative that bribery was at work:[35]

> Formal assurances contained in a document addressed to the Emperor and signed by the Sovereign of the country have virtually the value of a Treaty, and the Ministers of His Highness do not dissimulate that henceforth, by the very admission of their Padishah, Russia becomes the guardian of their fidelity to ward off any deviation from the status quo. The engagement is precise and the wisdom of the Imperial Cabinet will determine the best procedure to guarantee the future and to recompense the Sultan for his loyal courtesy.

FROM SLEIGHT OF HAND TO BLATANT FRAUD

In fact, what had been transacted was neither 'precise' nor an 'engagement', although the Porte tried to pretend that the 'arrangement . . . appears to satisfy the parties concerned'. The new version of the firman was backdated from mid-March to 10 February; it could satisfy Greek *amour propre* by refuting the Latins' old maximal claims, but was vague and contradictory concerning the keys. The Latins had the right, as in the past, to have a set of keys and 'not be prevented from officiating', but no one was to 'make any changes in the present state of the doors of the Church of Bethlehem'. The vizirial letter to the Pasha of Jerusalem also fudged the issue somewhat by stating that the award of the keys, together with the new arrangement for the Ascension Chapel, did not signify any changes in their traditional *ab antiquo* operations.[36]

Neither side would be pleased for long. The French were only ready to terminate the Holy Places dispute on the basis of the 8 February note, so long as the Russians did not force the Porte to enshrine the status quo. La Valette politely accepted the copies of the vizirial letters and firmans with reservations, just before he departed on 20 March, and enjoyed a gala send-off by the Turks.[37] Sabatier, the French chargé d'affaires, was more guarded and rightly nervous about the precise wording of all of these documents. Aali temporized and as late as 25 April would not show the French the text of the latest version of the 'February' firman.

The Russian chargé, Alexander Ozerov, for his part, finished Titov's work by making one more change in the copy of the 'February' firman that was communicated to St Petersburg on 5 April. A month later the gist of it ended up in Sabatier's hands in the form of another, different firman for Hafiz Ahmad to execute in Judaea. Now, as part of the status quo, the Latins were forbidden from officiating in the very Bethlehem church where they had just in principle reacquired a set of keys.[38]

The Holy Places dispute had finally reached a very serious impasse. La Valette, Botta and the Tsar had torpedoed the promising mixed commission. After the ulema made their ruling, Aali issued a note and a subsequent set of firmans and instructions that Stratford thought fair, but the Russians and, allegedly, Reshid opposed. Then the Russians got the Turks to introduce nuances into the concessions to the Latins, followed by a firman on behalf of the Greeks, which rendered the chief Catholic gain meaningless without expressly contradicting the note or firmans in favour of the Latins. The French were furious over this blatant fraud.

The Russians were furious too, chiefly over the cupola, and they hid behind several myths. One was that the note of 8 February had been a clever Turkish device to allow the French to retreat with honour. Another was that the Sultan's letter was a solid guarantee, as was the *hatt-i sherif*, or formal sanction, that encased the 'February' firman, even though this too was nothing but doublespeak and in no way denied the Latins a share of the Bethlehem services or the restoration of the cupola. Ozerov went further and suggested that a formal Cabinet communication be addressed to the Porte to insure that this firman be treated as an unalterable guarantee[39] – as if the Russians were the ultimate interpreters of Ottoman charters to Ottoman subjects. None of these notions were conducive to rational analysis.

The Russian legation was really angling, with generous offers of bribes, for a cupola–keys exchange. Accordingly, the iconography in Jerusalem and the actual precedence in officiating in Bethlehem would leave no doubt that the Orthodox had the upper hand in the Holy Places, due to Russian pressure and prestige. It was precisely this that the French were determined to oppose, and they had a few more assets in their portfolio. The next time la Valette appeared on the scene in Constantinople, it would be on board the newly commissioned, ninety gun, screw-propelled *Charlemagne*.

NOTES

1. For conflicting interpretations, see Lynn M. Case, *Edouard Thouvenel et la diplomatie de la Seconde Empire*, pp. 34–51; E. Driault, *Histoire diplomatique de la Grèce de 1821 à nos jours* (5 vols, Paris: 1925–26), II: 318–71; Martens XII: 261–6; Puryear *ERSQ*: 186–8; Sheremet: 151–2.

2. Unckel: 57–64.

3. Nes. to Nich. I, 13/25 Dec. 1852, 20 Dec. 1852/1 Jan. 1853 (ZP I. 96–7), followed by official Russian historiography; Kinglake, *Invasion of the Crimea* II: 57–65; Tarlé I: 128–33; Rich: 6–7, 21–2; more cautiously, Thouvenel: 1–2; Monnier: 25–6; Saab *OCA*: 9–11; and many, many more with varying degrees of certainty.

4. Saab *OCA*: 10.

5. *MQLS*: 288–9; Kis. to Nes., 16/28 April 1852 (AVPR Pos. Konst. 213); Echard: 26; Thouvenel: 1–2.

6. Colbi-Zander Ben-Arieh, *Jerusalem in the 19th Century* (2 vols, Jerusalem/New York 1984), I: 229–32; Hopwood, *The Russian Presence in Syria and Palestine, 1843–1914*, pp. 33–45; Temperley *ENEC*: 280–5; *Otchety Az. dep.*, 1850, *Dela dukh.* (AVPR K 38).

7. *MQLS*: 296–8; Monnier: 34.

8. Echard: 26–7.

9. Tit. to Nes., 4/16 Aug. 1851 (AVPR GA V-A2 521); cf. M.A. Volkov, 'Chto dovelo', 1856 (ZP I.30: 183), erroniously dating Aupick's *démarche* May 1849; the basic sources for these events of 1850–1 are Stratford's reports in *CORR* I; Titov's correspondence with St Petersburg in AVPR K, GA–V2, and Pos. Konst.; and Aupick's and La Valette's correspondence with Paris in AMAE CP Turq.; a straightforward, factual account of the dispute, based mainly on *CORR*, is found in Alyce E. Mange, *The Near Eastern Policy of Napoleon III* (Urbana 1940), pp. 18–23. Bapst and Saab use French sources.

10. Rose to Rus., 10 March 1853 (*CORR* I.198).

11. Tit. to Nes. No. 64, June 1850 (AVPR GA V–A2 520).

12. Str. to Plm., 20 May 1850 (*CORR* I.1).

13. E. Pisani to Str., 27 Dec. 1850 (*CORR* I.10).

14. Nes. to Tit., 9/21 Jan. 1851 (AVPR Pos. Konst. 213).

15. Aupick to Aali, Str. to Plm., Klezl to Aali, 23, 25 Jan., 3 Feb., 1851 (*CORR* I.14–15).

16. Nes. to Kis., Kis. to Nes., 13/25 March, 16/28 April 1851 (AVPR Pos. Konst. 213).
17. An Ottoman memorandum attributed to Fuad incorrectly states that the French proposed the commission: *MQLS*: 302.
18. Cf. Turkish Abstract of Charters to 1811 (Testa III: 313–20); Latin memo. (*CORR* I.28); Bazili memo (*NLP* X: 81–118).
19. Temperley and other historians, following Rose, mistook the commission as pro-Latin: cf. Protocols, 4 Aug.–21 Oct. 1851, to Mlm., 16 Dec. 1852 (*CORR* I.36, 86); *ENEC*: 288.
20. Nes. to Tit., 19/31 July 1851 (AVPR Pos. Konst. 213).
21. Str. to Plm., 17 Sept., 25 Oct., 4 Nov., 1851 (*CORR* I.22, 26, 28) cf. Bapst: 208–9.
22. Nich. I to Abdülmecid, 7/19 Nov. 1851 (ZP I.89); the questionable M.A. Volkov noted Cyrill's appeal, which I did not find in the archives: ZP I.30: 184.
23. Undated, but with Nes. to Tit., 13/25 Nov. 1851 (AVPR GA V–A2 521).
24. Nes. to Tit., 13/25 Sept. 1851 (AVPR Pos. Konst. 213); cf. *MQLS*: 302–3; M.S. Volkov (ZP I.30); Str. to Plm., 4 Nov. 1851 (*CORR* I.28); Lav. to Drn., 15 Jan. 1853 (AMAE CP Turq. 311); Bapst: 210–11.
25. Nes. to Br., 12/24 July 1851 (AVPR K 83; TsGADA, III/115); Brw. report, 16/28 Oct. 1851, read by Nich. I, Jan. 1853 (TsGADA III/120); cf. Martens XII: 274–6.
26. Martens XV: 250–1.
27. Normanby to Plm., 20 Nov. 1851 (*CORR* I.30); Ted W. Margadant, *The French Peasants in Revolt. The Insurrection of 1851* (Princeton 1979), pp. 334–5.
28. La Valette's later claim that Louis Napoleon ordered the Toulon squadron to Turkish waters in November and then called it back after the coup appears to be without foundation: *CORR* I.60 (Rose to Mlm., 18 Oct. 1852); cf. Temperley *ENEC*: 289.
29. Commission Report, by 31 Dec. 1851 (*CORR* I.44); cf. Saab *OCA*: 168, note 6, citing the Turkish scholar Baykal, that the ulema rejected the applicability of Kuchuk-Kainarji to the Holy Places dispute.
30. Str. to Plm., 7 Jan. 1852 (*CORR* I.46).
31. *CORR* I.51 dates the Note 18 Rabiul/9 Feb., while Testa III: 230–1 has 17 Rabiul/8 Feb.
32. AVPR GA V–A2 522: 90–4.
33. Tit. to Nes., 4/16 Feb. 1852 (AVPR GA V–A2 522).
34. Abdülmecid to Nich. I, dated 29 Jan./10 Feb. 1852, sent 4/16 March 1852 (AVPR GA V–A2 522: 113–15); *CORR* I.55 (sent 18 March 1852); and Turgot to Sabatier, 28 April 1852 (AMAE CP Turq. 308), correctly viewing the letter as justifying compromise.
35. Tit. to Nes., 4/16 March 1852 (AVPR GA V–A2 522).
36. 'February' Firman, English copy (*CORR* I.54, also ZP I.90); Porte to Hafiz, sent 19 March 1852 (AMAE CP Turq. 308).
37. Lav. to Aali, 19 March 1852 (AMAE CP Turq. 308).
38. Firman to Hafiz, sent 6 May 1852 (AMAE CP Turq. 308).
39. Oz. to Nes., 14/26 March 1852 (AVPR GA V–A2 522).

CHAPTER SIX

The Return to Armed Diplomacy (April–November 1852)

SERIOUS COMPLICATIONS

While the Russians and the Greeks appeared to have 'won' the initial struggle over the firman to Hafiz Ahmad, the French and the Catholics benefited from other aspects of the Eastern Question and European politics. Turkish opposition to Stratford's schemes to introduce the Tanzimat and railroads to Egypt and then use Egyptian assets to guarantee a loan to shore up the Turkish currency weakened Reshid. When Stratford left Constantinople in late June for what was assumed to be his final departure, his relations with the Porte were very chilly and local newspapers were attacking his 'utopian' concepts of reform and the practice of granting British passports to revolutionary refugees.[1]

Meanwhile Turkish–Austrian problems were intensifying. Schwarzenberg had feared that discontent in Bosnia and Herzegovina would spread across the border and that Omer's use of Hungarian and Polish exiles in his army might stimulate more unrest. The release of interned Hungarians against Austrian wishes in September 1851 added fuel to the fire. Schwarzenberg's death and Buol's succession in April changed nothing, as both saw the current Turkish moves to create a naval presence in the lower Adriatic and use brute force to disarm their Balkan subjects as provocative. Newly reported Turkish atrocities made things worse, as 4,000–5,000 refugees fled from Bosnia to Austrian territory in 1851–52. Omer's redeployment to Herzegovina then set the stage for a confrontation over Montenegro and wider Great Power, especially, Russian involvement.[2]

Russia had treated Montenegro as a historically sovereign entity since Peter the Great's second war with Turkey. In reality, for most of the sixteenth to eighteenth centuries Montenegro had been an effective buffer between Ottoman and Venetian domains, but had been ruled by prince-bishops or vladykas invested by an Ottoman subject, the Archbishop or Patriarch of Pec (Ipek). Vladyka Petar I (1782–1830), however, was invested in Austria by a refugee Patriarch. During the Russo-Turkish alliance of 1799–1805, Selim III had issued a firman recognizing that 'the Montenegrins have never been subject to our Sublime Porte', but the Turks did not treat this as binding. The Austrians also temporarily recognized the independence of Montenegro during their 1788–91 war with Turkey, but then hedged and simply treated it as *de facto* free but *de jure* under the Porte. Finally, Vladyka Petar II (1830–51) was ordained in St Petersburg at a time when the Turks were too weak to make serious objections.[3]

Petar II died in October 1851, and his designated successor Danilo and the local élite secularized the principality. In keeping with Austrian Balkan policy, Vienna supported this change in early 1852. The Turks then challenged Austria by supplying Omer via Suttorina, one of two tiny enclaves in the Bay of Cattaro in the southern Adriatic, which were Herzegovina's outlets to the sea and also facilitated Turkish maritime communications with the northern border of Montenegro. During the 1832–33 crisis, when the Porte desperately needed Russian aid, the Austrians claimed to be heirs to Venice's former control over the enclaves and wanted the Turks to cede them.[4]

In January 1851, just as Aupick was demanding of the Porte categorically whether the 1740 treaty was still valid, Schwarzenberg revived Austria's claims to Suttorina and the other enclave, Klek. The Turks, however, defiantly dispatched warships to the lower Adriatic. By the end of April 1852 Vienna in turn had empowered the local military and naval commanders in Dalmatia to act unilaterally to prevent Turkish landings. France stood to gain from all of this, since Russia was also bound to support Montenegro, and Stratford's relations with the Porte were shaky.

Bonapartism now enhanced France's position. Since the coup of 2 December 1851, St Petersburg and Vienna sought to contain France, Nesselrode fearing that Napoleon, having smashed 'the ideologues and the reds, would force upon us a *guerre de l'Empire*'.[5] Talk of revival of the Empire and a Franco-Belgian Customs Union was enough to involve all the other Great Powers in secret military feelers. Nicholas wanted a humiliating French disclaimer of aggressive intentions, and engineered an Austro-Russian *démarche* to dissuade Napoleon from reestablishing at least the dynasty. The Tsar also activated Russia's standing offer of 60,000 troops for such eventualities. Nesselrode was more discreet, sending a top assistant, Ksaverii Labenski, to make an on-the-spot report regarding Napoleon's external designs.[6] The French response to this posturing was to maintain good relations with the other powers, especially Britain, but they made it clear that France would brook no external meddling in domestic matters.

FRENCH NAVAL PERSUASION

The Mediterranean Sea and the Eastern Question were the perfect arena for the French to show their colours with impunity, if they did so intelligently. Apart from the Holy Places dispute, the Turkish Admiralty had invited the French in March 1852 to demonstrate at the Golden Horn the virtues of their latest model, and Sabatier had been working out the tricky details of the invitation that stretched the 1841 Treaty to its limits. By late April, the Smyrna and Constantinople newspapers were reporting the future visit of the *Charlemagne* and the impending departure of Omer and his army for Herzegovina. Stratford and Ozerov, however, invoked the 1841 Treaty to block the permission for the vessel to pass the Dardanelles.[7]

The news of this blow reached Paris in late May on the heels of Sabatier's reports concerning the altered firmans. Napoleon's reaction was angry, but calculated. He made it clear to the Turks that to follow through with this decision would destroy his affection for them. He convinced London and St Petersburg not to back Stratford and Ozerov to the hilt. And he sent la Valette back in the enhanced capacity of 'Ambassador' on the *Charlemagne* to make it harder for the Turks to decline, while signalling the greater ability of Western navies to plough the Sea of Marmora upwind and upstream. Sabatier for his part threatened to break relations over the insult if the Porte did not allow the warship to come. The Turks then reversed course again, but at the same time affirmed their commitment to the 1841 Convention, as also did the French.[8]

The brief stopover of the *Charlemagne* in early July was pulled off with great éclat, if not perfect harmony. The British in turn muscled their own passage of the Dardanelles by an eighteen-gun corvette. Ozerov had to be contented with Turkish gratitude for the infrequency of Russian naval stopovers at Turkish ports. He admitted that Russia's reputation for rancour at Constantinople kept him from protesting the *Charlemagne* too loudly – an indication of Russia's weak position. All Nesselrode could obtain was a meaningless admission by the British and other powers that the 1841 Treaty had been violated.[9]

The *Charlemagne* incident was not an isolated event. Napoleon's government had decided to use its Mediterranean squadron to settle outstanding problems with Ottoman provincial authorities. The French wished to obtain a reparation for an insult in Epirus, maintain autonomous Tunisia as a buffer between Algeria and Ottoman Tripoli (Libya), and get the pasha of Tripoli to relinquish two French deserters. A demonstration with six battleships and six frigates took place off Tripoli just as the Turks were about to depose Reshid and finalize their decision not to give the Russians what they wanted in Jerusalem and Bethlehem, moves that had been in the works even before the French resorted to naval diplomacy. Aali replaced Reshid as Grand Vizier, and the French-leaning Fuad became Foreign Minister. Ozerov, his English counterpart Colonel Hugh Henry Rose, and subsequent historians believed the Turks had bowed to French menaces.[10]

Meanwhile St Petersburg reached its own conclusions in July. Another Ozerov *demarche* to a frightened Aali would be fruitless, even though the French had no rights to the cupola. As soon as it became clear that the Turks were using delaying tactics, the Emperor himself would appeal directly to the Sultan – which probably meant a special mission of some sort, since the latest personal letters had been fruitless. Nevertheless, Ozerov was to continue to utilize Titov's unofficial channels, and the Tsar was preparing to send 25,000 silver roubles to grease the Ottoman wheels.[11]

Simultaneously Nicholas was both hostile and friendly to France. He intensified his efforts to create a united front with Vienna and Berlin against Bonapartism and to normalize relations with Belgium, the focal point of any action against France. On the other hand, he was friendly to Castelbajac and other Frenchmen and repeated his standard line concerning the collapse of Ottoman power. He did not want Constantinople for himself, but would not allow anyone else to occupy it.[12]

MOUNTING UNCERTAINTIES

Ozerov obtained a copy of the long-awaited instructions to Commissioner Afif Bey in August and was not pleased with the planned execution of the firman. The Greek, Latin and Armenian Patriarchs would all have to approve of the plans for the repair of the cupola, and the Latins would obtain keys to the big door of the Bethlehem Church.[13] In Russian eyes this was a violation of promises regarding both major sanctuaries. La Valette, however, was still insistent that the firman be altered to allow Latin services and use of the main portals in the Bethlehem church. He hinted that war with Turkey and/or Russia might ensue on the grounds of the 1740 Treaty and that France might blockade the Dardanelles and would certainly occupy them, if the Russians aided Turkey.

The British Mediterranean squadron now paid a surprise visit to Vourla, near Smyrna, and Rose, who ceded to no one when English interests were at stake, warned la Valette that France could also be on the receiving end of armed intimidation. Rose also told Ozerov that la Valette had grounds to complain and, grasping the heart of the issue, informed London that the Russian arguments were false: 'the general opinion here [is correct] that the Porte committed a breach of faith, and indeed an error in policy, in inserting into the Firman to the Greeks terms at variance with the understanding which had just before been come to between the Porte and the French Embassy'.[14]

French efforts resulted in a new Note to la Valette from the Porte on 7 September with a promise to execute the firman in such a way as to uphold the February promises and respect the 1740 treaty. Both Ozerov and Rose believed that the Porte had bowed to French threats, but Rose attributed the modest French success to patience.

The French did not, though, get away so easily with their gunboat diplomacy, and Napoleon took some heat for the Tripoli incident, once the British learned of it. The Turks themselves made no secret of their distaste for French muscling and instructed their envoy Callimachi in Paris to make a quiet protest. Callimachi and his British counterpart Cowley then joined forces to work on the French Cabinet in September, where Drouyn de Lhuys had resumed the portfolio of Foreign Affairs. Drouyn retreated by assuring the English that he would be satisfied with a Turkish declaration that the firman did not contradict earlier promises, but covered his position by telling Callimachi that the Turks ought to prefer France's friendship to Russia's.[15] The statement to Callimachi was more honest, since the Russians were not ready to compromise, and Paris could gain simply by curtailing the naval antics to please the British and the Turks, without curbing la Valette's minimal demands.

Positioning for British support, la Valette told a delighted Rose that France did *not* seek a general protectorate over the Sultan's Catholic subjects along with the religious protectorate at Jerusalem. Rose now hoped to extract a similar denial from Russia concerning the Ottoman Orthodox. For la Valette, however, the real issue for the moment remained the Catholics' use of a key to the main portal at Bethlehem for religious processions. Once more he threatened war in case Greek pressure were to prevail. The French squadron was expected to arrive off the coast of Judaea when Commissioner Afif arrived, but the Turks knew that the Russian consul Bazili was instructed to ensure that they did not retreat from their promises to Russia. Rose thus hit the nail on the head with his contemptuous and suggestive remark: 'The question will probably make its exit out of the Great Door.'[16]

Ozerov sought Turkish allies in building a case against the French and wanted to believe Reshid and the other Turks who cast the blame on French intimidation for 'annulling a part of the *hatt-i sherif*'. This would explain why they were reneging on Fuad's and Aali's earlier reassurances to Patriarch Cyrill against the Latins' obtaining new concessions. Actually, Ozerov's dispatches from early and mid October reveal that a genuine fog of diplomacy had set in for the Russian mission. Aristarchi reported that the 'solemn word' to the Emperor would be kept, while Aali said to the First Russian Dragoman, Emmanuel Argyropoulos, that the Porte wished to satisfy the French. Then the Sultan's anti-reformist brother-in-law, Mehmed Ali, replaced Aali as Grand Vizier and enticed Russia by blaming the concessions to the French on Aali and telling Argyropoulos that he (Mehmed) 'recognized no rival of Russia in the Orient',[17] whatever that meant.

A NEW 'GREEK PROJECT'?

Meanwhile, the international politics of the Balkans and the Black Sea were hotting up. In early July the Tsar agreed that Danilo of Montenegro could become a secular prince and appoint another bishop. The Turks concurred, so long as Danilo go to Constantinople for investiture. The Russians retorted that Russia was the sole protector of Montenegro.[18]

Buol now presented a package of Austrian demands to the Porte: an apology for the release of Kossuth and other Hungarian refugees, an end to the 'persecution' of Bosnian Christians, compensation for Austrian losses during the latest Turkish pacification campaign, and the authority to veto individual Turkish ships docking at Klek and Suttorina. The Porte was willing to talk, but not to accept diktats, and while Omar wished to subdue Montenegro by force, Fuad said that Ottoman policy would depend upon the Tsar's decision concerning investiture.

The answer came back rather quickly and was circulated to the other major Cabinets: the Porte had never exercised any sovereignty or investiture rights over Montenegro. This meant that unless the Porte backed off, two Turkish showdowns were in the works: *de jure* with Russia and *de facto* with Austria. The French cleverly alerted the British to the possible 'dangers' of Austria's demands, and neither Western power allowed their eager financial circles to dictate a loan-foisting policy that might drive the Turks into Russian and/or Austrian arms.

The Tsar was more interested in the Balkans than Western Europe, and, while renewing his pledges to a frightened Belgium, urged Brussels not to provoke France. On the other hand, he journeyed to Odessa and Sevastopol and back during 10 September–21 October, evoking shadows of Catherine II's expansionist policies of the 1780s. He had recently turned his attention to the development of Sevastopol as 'another Kronstadt', and to the commissioning of his own ninety-gun screw. On this trip he was accompanied by the Austrian ambassador Mensdorff, giving the impression of an Austro-Russian alliance that could only be directed against the Turks. In addition, the Tsar wished to receive the Hospodars of Moldavia and Wallachia as 'vassals render homage to a sovereign' en route. Unsubstantiated rumours of increased Russian armaments in the Black Sea reached as far as Paris and London.[19]

Under these conditions, European backing for Russia against France in the Near East could only result from a Bonapartist threat to the European status quo. Louis Napoleon's celebrated Bordeaux speech on 9 October, where he declared defiantly that 'the Empire means peace', was thus crucial in obtaining international support for his domestic plans. He favourably impressed several key elements of British public opinion which feared Russia and America, as well as French Bonapartism, screw steamers and Near Eastern policy. The logical response to Napoleon was to avoid provocative combinations and use the potential French threat to justify naval expansion, which only Britain could afford.[20]

THE LAW'S DELAY

The saga of the Holy Places continued to proceed at a snail's pace. Two months passed after the Tripoli incident, and nothing occurred inside or outside the Ottoman Empire to produce the decisive victory that the Greeks and the Latins each desired. When Afif Bey finally arrived in Jerusalem on 18 October, he summoned the Greek, Latin and Armenian patriarchs to the Holy Sepulchre and proceeded in the face of obstruction of the local clergies to execute his instructions. These satisfied no one. The Latin Star for Bethlehem did not materialize. The Orthodox prevented the Catholics from obtaining use of keys to officiate at the Church of the Nativity as they wished. Bazili had trouble convincing the Jerusalem Greeks even to allow the Latins to officiate in the Tomb of the Virgin on their own altar in order to facilitate the minimal Tomb–Chapel compromise.[21] On the other hand, the Turkish engineer, who was to determine how to repair the cupola under Greek supervision, had not arrived; but when he did, he would, as Ozerov had been forewarned, consult with a representative of each Patriarch, not just with Cyrill. And as for the firman, which would put the Latins in their place and secure the new status quo for the Greeks? Afif, upon questioning by Bazili, allegedly declared: 'I have no [official] knowledge of the firman . . . I only have [official] knowledge of my instructions, and it is not prescribed there either to execute the firman or to authorize its reading.'[22] The promised day of execution thus came and went, and the impasse still continued.

Mixed news concerning the non-execution and the instructions to the Turkish engineer kept St Petersburg in suspense. Ozerov's mid-November dispatch had to be both disturbing and enticing to the Tsar. The Turks admitted to having promised the French not to read the firman. Fuad haughtily dismissed the complaints of Patriarch Cyrill with: 'He is our raya; how dare he utilize an employee of a foreign mission!' On the other hand, Mehmed Ali had allowed that the Porte had been forced by the French to act as it did; moreover: 'to treat cheaply the solemn word of the Sultan given to a Sovereign who is our strongest and most generous ally . . . was a despicable act of treason'. Ozerov also admitted his own failure as well as his absolute lack of confidence in Fuad and his promises. At the same time la Valette reported his own frustration at the non-execution of what was promised him earlier by Aali, as well as Fuad's admission that Ottoman good faith toward the Prince-President was on the line.[23] Nevertheless, la Valette, and Ozerov to a lesser extent, were trying to cool local religious tempers; so each was working to control the situation and to effect the compromise solution that he felt was due.

The simultaneous rise of controlled Russian and French ire put the British mission in an excellent position to engage in fact-finding and unofficial action and to try to separate the Greeks from the Russians. Fuad told Rose that he foresaw the need for official British mediation, since Ozerov had said that Russia would accept a keys–cupola (*cum status quo*) exchange, but would otherwise break relations with Turkey. La Valette confided that France would, if necessary, accept such mediation, but first make a 'very lively' demonstration. Rose then told the Greek prelates that Louis Napoleon would accept British mediation.

To Rose, the Russian and French threats signified occupation of the Danubian Principalities (precisely what Russia eventually did) and an occupation of Jerusalem (precisely what France never dared). The prescient English chargé also understood Turkey's greater fears of Russia, as he saw the Tsar's September 1851 letter and Russia's view of the firman implying an inadmissible protectorate over the Sultan's Orthodox subjects. To Ozerov, however, Rose's unofficial intervention meant: 'the Greeks were profoundly alarmed because they could see that the Porte will bend before the united action of two big embassies'[24] – a convenient excuse for Russian failure.

Ozerov had an additional cause for complaint. The British legation *sub rosa* had prevented the selection by the Porte of Russia's candidate to be Patriarch of Constantinople. The Tsar let this pass for the moment without comment, but from his later actions it is clear that foreign influence over the patriarchate, as well as Turkish Balkan policies, contributed to his escalation of the latest round of armed diplomacy that France had initiated. However, it would be Ozerov's exaggerations regarding the Holy Places dispute that ignited the explosion.

NOTES

1. Oz. to Sen., 14/26 June 1852 (AVPR K 38).
2. Unckel: 57–62, and for Austro-Turkish relations, 1852–53.
3. Peter I, Manif., 3 March 1711; Mikhail Miloradovich., Manif., 16 April 1712, Catherine II, Procl., 20 Jan. 1769; Aus.–Mont. Conv., 1788; Tr. of Sistova, Art. I, 4 Aug. 1791; Paul I, Rescr., 11 Jan. 1799; Selim III, Firman, 1799 (Testa IX: 158, X: 297–302); *ES* 38.2: 620–2.
4. Oettenfels, Note, 13 Feb. 1833 (Testa IX: 202–5).
5. Nes. to Brw., 15/27 Jan. 1852 (TsGADA III/115).
6. Schwarzenberg to Lbz., memo, 15 Feb., 4 April 1852; Three-Power Prot., May 1852; Labenski to Nes., 2/14 May 1852 (ZP I.41, 45–7); Nes. to Brw., 5/17 Apr. 1852 (AVPR K 80); Martens XV: 255–6; Thomas: 114–18.

7. The main sources for Constantinople events, May-Nov. 1852, are the correspondence of Ozerov, Sabatier, and la Valette, AVPR K and GA–V2, and AMAE CP Turq., supplemented by Rose: *CORR* I, originals in PRO FO 78. Here, also Echard: 27–8.

8. Oz. to Sen., 16/28 June 1852 (AVPR K 38); Turgot to Wal., 1, 26 July 1852 (AMAE CP Angl. 686); Bapst: 258–61; cf. Temperley's different interpretation based on Cowley's reports: *ENEC*: 467.

9. Nes. to Brw., 12/24 July 1852 (AVPR K 80).

10. Temperley, using only British sources, was certain that Paris dispatched the Tripoli expedition to block the execution of the firmans as the Russians desired: *ENEC*: 293–4; cf. Rose to Mlm., 10 Aug 1852 (PRO FO 78/893, not in *CORR*).

11. Sen. to Oz., 10/22 July 1852 (AVPR GA V–A2 522). Some of the money was to go toward buying two 'harems', which were next to the Holy Sepulchre and which the French and Austrians were also attempting to purchase.

12. Bapst: 243; on Russia's Belgian policy in 1852, de Jonghe's correspondence with Hoffschmidt, AMAE Blg. CP Russ. I.

13. Porte to Afif by Aug. 1852 (AVPR GA V–A2 522).

14. Rose to Mlm. No. 55, 16 Aug. 1852 (PRO FO 78/893).

15. Cwl. to Mlm., 12 Sept. 1852 (*CORR* I.62).

16. Rose to Mlm., 1 Oct. 1852 (*CORR* I.71).

17. Oz. to Sen., 14/26 Sept., 4/16 Oct. 1852 (AVPR K 38).

18. Sources for this phase of the Balkan crisis include Ozerov's correspondence in AVPR K and GA–V2 and Unckel.

19. Const. to Nich. I., 17/29 Sept., 1/13 Oct. 1852 (TsGAVMF 224/2/317); de Jonghe to Hoffschmidt., 7, 10 Sept., 23 Oct. 1852 (AMAE Blg. Russ. I); Lav. to Drn. 25 Oct. 1852 (AMAE CP Turq. 310); Seym. to Mlm., 3 Oct. 1852 (*CORR* I.69); Bohl: 9–10.

20. Cf. La Gorce *HSE* I: 97–9; Bapst: 276–7; Case, *Edouard Thouvenel*, p. 56.

21. Oz. to Nes., 14/26 Oct. 1852 (AVPR GA V–2 522) is better than Finn to Mlm., 27 Oct. 1852 (*CORR* I.73).

22. Bazili to Oz., 7/19 Oct. 1852 (AVPR GA V–2 522); cf. *PHQSL*, whose slightly distorted account has entered scholarship: 'Afif-Bey responded, *that he had no knowledge of the firman* – and that his instructions made no mention of it' (ZP I.88).

23. Oz. to Nes., 4/16 Nov. 1852 (AVPR GA V–A2. 522); Lav. to Drn., 14 Nov. 1852 (AMAE CP Turq. 310).

24. Rose to Mlm., 23 Nov. 1852 (*CORR* I.76); Oz. to Nes., 15/27 Nov. 1852 (AVPR GA V–A2 522).

CHAPTER SEVEN

Nativity (December 1852)

MONTENEGRO'S PROVOCATION: THE FIRST SHOTS

The non-execution of the ('February') firman would have made for good opera buffa, had the sequel not been so serious. And it is possible that the Porte might have bobbed, weaved, feinted and weaseled its way out of the Holy Places dispute without a war, had not other issues increased the complications and the stakes of Russia's problems with France and the Ottoman Empire. But these problems crested toward the end of 1852, and upon the heels of a Turkish decision regarding the Bethlehem Church, a war crisis was born in the twelve days that separated the Catholic and Orthodox Christmases that year.

The Western Balkans were the first to explode, though not due to great power activity. Turkish repressions in Bosnia were continuing; Fuad challenged Buol by demanding full sovereignty over the approaches to the Adriatic enclaves; and Nesselrode instructed Ozerov to support Austria. La Valette thereupon warned Fuad that failure to stand up for the principle of freedom of the seas that France and Britain had supported would be a sign of bad faith. By latter November, however, all four interested Great Powers were trying to keep the Balkan cauldron from boiling over. Buol also told the Russians that the Austrians recognized Ottoman *de jure* sovereignty over Montenegro, though they scorned Ottoman pretensions to convert this into *de facto* control.[1]

Nevertheless, Montenegrin hotheads pre-empted the Jerusalem clerics, the Turks, the Great Powers and the diplomats, and initiated the first act of war. On 23 or 24 November, in defiance of Russian desires, a small band of mountaineers drove the Ottoman garrison from their ancient capital, the fortress of Zhabljak, which lay about 40 kilometres below Cetinje toward the sea. Ozerov accepted the Turkish explanation that the Montenegrins had acted on misintelligence concerning hated Albanian irregulars. Klezl was less positive, reporting Turkish intransigence toward Austria's demands and troop concentrations against Montenegro. By 7 December the Austrian Minister of the Interior, Alexander Bach, warned the Council of Ministers that the Turkish military alert threatened the internal security of Austria's border provinces.[2]

NAPOLEON 'III' ENTHRONED

The issue of the re-establishment of the French Empire was peculiarly problematic, due to the Tsar's gut reactions. He had hardly returned in late October from his trip to the Crimea when he learned of Napoleon's Bordeaux speech, a clear signal that the latter intended to assume his uncle's mantle. 'The Empire means peace' meant little to the Tsar, who had to be convinced that the re-establishment of the French Empire was in itself no grounds for war. In London, Brunnow had some influence over *The Times*, where a veritable press war raged over British policy. However, neither the mouthpiece of the Tory Cabinet (*Morning Herald*) nor that of Palmerston (*Morning Post*) would allow attacks on the French President. Still by early November, the politicking of Brunnow and assorted other anti-Bonapartists finally made some inroads. Much to the chagrin of the French, Foreign Secretary Malmesbury began to suggest a non-dynastic title, such as 'Louis-Napoleon I'.[3]

The French, however, were not to be intimidated. On 6 November a *Senatus consultus* declared the forthcoming restoration of the Empire, pending ratification by a referendum in two weeks. This would reflect the will of the French people and the desire to consolidate the 'conquests of 1789'. The Foreign Office then shot off to St Petersburg, Berlin and Vienna a hair-splitting, compromise memorandum, accepting French governmental changes as a domestic affair, but disputing the validity of the use of 'III' ('II' having been the 'King of Rome', Napoleon I's infant son) and demanding that the other four Great Powers cooperate to protect the 1815 settlement. Paris did not back off, but continued the line that the Empire really did 'mean peace', and proceeded on 15 November to circulate the announcement of the impending change, since ratification was assured.[4]

The French ambassador Walewski was willing to swallow his

Bonapartist pride and took a place of honour next to Prince Albert at the funeral of the Duke of Wellington, the victor of Waterloo. On the other hand, Walewski warned the indecisive Malmesbury about Brunnow's new intrigues and asserted that a four-power agreement which bypassed France could lead to a 'chilling', itself just a 'step from war', since 'distrust engenders distrust'.[5] By 27 November the British had agreed to recognize the 'III' but still not fully cave in to Paris. Rather, Brunnow obtained what turned out to be one of the last manifestations of the four-power coalition that had defeated Napoleon I and subsequently contained French revanchism. On 3 December, the day after the Second Empire was proclaimed, London signed on to a four-power agreement in London to preserve the territorial status quo in Europe.[6]

Meanwhile, Nesselrode had attempted a last-ditch appeal to the British to oppose the 'III', lest the entire 1815 settlement collapse. He also did what he could to reconcile the differences between Austria and Prussia and to block the recognition of the 'III'. Nicholas also made a belated and futile attempt via a personal letter to dissuade Napoleon, but it arrived well after the 20–21 November plebiscite that overwhelmingly approved of his imperial plan. Nicholas soon lamented the acquiescence of his conservative British friends as 'miserable' and 'cowardice', even though he considered the four-power arrangement to be 'very good'. Despite Britain's openly discussed plans to expand the army and navy chiefly due to uneasiness over French potential and intentions, the Tsar could not get it out of his head that the British were acting like 'frightened children'.[7]

The Austrians, however, had made it clear that they desired an accord with Britain over the title and announced a middle position that accepted the 'III', but denied that Napoleon was the *frère* ('brother') of Francis Joseph. But the French still had the Austrians over a barrel, since Francis I had recognized Napoleon I as *frère*, and Vienna dared not quarrel with France over a mere form. Nicholas, though, did not wish to cede, so diplomatic messages flew and crisscrossed in all directions. One thing is certain: the British Foreign Office had been right a month earlier in foreseeing that the key moment would be when the diplomats in Paris submitted new, official credentials to 'Emperor' Napoleon.

In the final analysis, the British called the shots, and no major faction in London wished to perpetuate the international insecurity of the popular regime of their powerful French neighbour. The Russian Emperor, however, while not consciously seeking trouble in the West to free his hands in the East, hardly minded that his policy toward Napoleon threatened his would-be British, Austrian and Prussian allies with French reprisals. At any rate, a European war with Turkish complications was not to be excluded until the credentials issue was solved.

THE NEW OTTOMAN RULING AND THE TSAR'S BLANK CHEQUE

By late November, with Ozerov and la Valette still deadlocked over the execution of the firman, the Holy Places conflict finally started to come to a head in both Constantinople and St Petersburg. On 25 November, the Turkish Council of Ministers decided provisionally to grant a single key to the Great Door of the Bethlehem Nativity to the Catholics and find a compromise mode of publishing the firman.[8] Ozerov then met with Mehmed Ali, who allegedly blamed Aali for the difficulties. Accordingly, Aali had secretly and without authorization altered the original words concerning the keys in the ('February') firman to the Latins. By this point who had lied to whom how many times on the Bosphorus over the past two years was immaterial. What Nicholas would read on 21 December was that Mehmed Ali called Aali a cheat who had defrauded the Sultan and the Tsar, when in fact Aali had swindled the French with Titov's, Ozerov's, Seniavin's, Nesselrode's and even the Tsar's connivance, and then reversed course.[9]

Ozerov also met with la Valette, who argued the priority of the 1740 Treaty over the firman and the Sultan's letter to the Tsar. La Valette did not officially report this meeting to Paris, but it must have been at this encounter that Ozerov raised the stakes of the game. According to Rose, Ozerov voiced the dangerous, if perennially subtextual, Treaty of Kuchuk-Kainarji argument: 'Russia protects the Orthodox, that is, the Greek religion in Turkey.' After la Valette leaked this to the Turks, Rose could report that 'the Porte has heard this assertion of Russian protection of the religious interest of ten or eleven millions of her subjects with unmingled dissatisfaction'.[10]

Dissatisfaction or no, the Turks proceeded with *their* compromise. The firman was read on 29 November in Jerusalem, but not in front of the Catholic leaders. La Valette did not object. More Council meetings on 2 or 3 December confirmed that the 1740 Treaty gave France a right to a key to the Great Door. Contrary to a popular view in historiography, the Turks did not 'concede everything the

French government had demanded'.[11] All the same, la Valette gloated that he had overcome a major Russian thrust and induced the Council to favour France's 'just claims' over the promise to Russia to adhere to a strict status quo. Ozerov reported this outcome differently. The ulema wished to keep their word to the Tsar, but their fear of the West (i.e., France) was greater than their fear of the North (i.e., Russia). Later Rose would elaborate the naval aspects of such thinking, as raised at the Ottoman Council. The *Charlemagne* could sail at eight and a half knots, and its sister the *Napoleon* at twelve – which meant that the French could defeat the combined Russo-Turkish fleets. Such arguments, which several eminent diplomatic historians have taken very seriously, and which certainly could only provoke the Tsar, overrated French naval *élan* and missed the crucial factor in any showdown: Great Britain. And the British were apt to look favourably upon another Turkish concept, which Ozerov placed in Fuad's mouth regarding the keys: the Sultan interprets his own *hatt-i sherifs*.[12]

Nesselrode was attempting measured reactions. Upon receiving the news of Fuad's attitudes and French threats, the Russian foreign ministry followed Ozerov's advice in the further instructions for him. He was to deal directly with Mehmed Ali and the Sultan, offer them military aid against a possible French attack, and promise to deliver the support of the Sultan's Orthodox subjects[13] – as if they were Russia's to deliver. Ozerov received these instructions much too late to utilize them, but they were incorporated into Russia's subsequent plans.

The Russian Emperor, however, did not wait for news of the award of the keys or for anything else beyond Ozerov's report of the probable award of a key to the Latins to internationalize his own threat to use violence. In relating Rose's attempts to mediate, Ozerov had made a provocative plea to Nesselrode:[14]

> I retain a calm appearance in the midst of the misfortunes that surround me, but I have, M. le Comte, a poignant fear inside my heart – that of not being able without powerful assistance to maintain faithfully my most important charge, that of defending with a clear and imposing firmness the rights that the magnanimous protection of the Emperor, our August Master, has assured of our co-religionists in Turkey.

Nicholas immediately resolved to do something. On 9 December, a day after this appeal arrived, Nesselrode wrote to Brunnow 'in darkest colours', lamenting the double complications of the 'number III' and 'the new cloud that begins to grow in the Orient'. The

Chancellor complained about 'the singular role that Colonel Rose had assumed in this question' and ended with an ominous warning that something extraordinary was in the works: 'You can expect a vigorous *démarche* on our part, if the next post does not report to us that the firman has been issued in Jerusalem. If Lord Derby wishes to prevent a serious conflagration in the Orient, he must order Rose to support us and not be the advocate of French pretensions.'[15]

This letter belies the near bankruptcy of Russia's war-threatening diplomacy in Constantinople. It did not occur to Nesselrode or Nicholas then or later that Russian-induced Ottoman bad faith in February and March 1852 had created the situation in which the Russian mission would see its British counterpart as the 'advocate of French pretensions'. Although Rose at this point was generally more anti-Russian than anti-French, he had adhered to Stratford's Turkish position regarding the sanctuaries. Nevertheless, Nicholas was already giving the English one of the strangest blank cheques in diplomatic history – to start a coalition war against the giver, in this case, the Anglo-French–Turkish war against Russia that had been avoided by mutual concessions in 1849. All the British had to do was to continue the policy of compromise in the Holy Places dispute.

TOWARDS A FATEFUL DECISION

Nesselrode might have spent less energy trying to manipulate the British, who tilted toward Russia on the issue of the cupola and the religious status quo, and more trying to curb the impulses of his 'August Master'. The net effect of Ozerov's next dispatches that arrived on 17 and 21 December was to confirm Nicholas in his conviction of the 'gravity' of the situation in the Near East. At the same time he was happily concluding from Brunnow's reports that the British were cowards and that this was excellent, since now Russia could proceed without them.[16] The Tsar does not seem to have put two and two together and realized that, even if the British really feared the new Napoleon across the Channel, they might not oppose him in the Near East.

Nicholas read things entirely incorrectly. Rose not only upheld the Turkish compromise of 25 January 1852, but also supported the Russian view that France should not be allowed to reopen the Holy Places question whenever she wished. Malmesbury, when he received Rose's first alarming reports on 11 December, complained to the French, not to Brunnow, and told Rose to abstain from direct intervention. In fact both Malmesbury and Thouvenel took the same line. Without bothering with details, they both blamed la Valette for raising the issue of the Holy Places again. To force a humiliating victory over Russia for the sake of a few keys was to threaten a Russian occupation and the end of the Ottoman Empire. Ergo France should give way a little more. Cowley even exceeded his instructions and elicited from Drouyn an admission that la Valette had acted without authorization, if he had indeed threatened violence.[17]

Rose's next alarming set of dispatches, reporting Turkish dismay over Ozerov's referral to Kuchuk-Kainarji, reached the Foreign Office on the 19th. This was just after Nesselrode's threatening complaint about Rose with the implicit blank cheque arrived in London. Here was a time, if there ever was one, for diplomats to nip a crisis in the bud. Brunnow, however, fed to the outgoing Derby and Malmesbury Russia's standard fiction that had become doctrine. French threats had forced the Turks to violate the Sultan's 'solemn word', enshrined 'in a firman that was itself issued as a *hatt-i sherif*', a view which many British then and many historians since have accepted.[18] Derby and Malmesbury appeared to concur, and Brunnow happily reported their warnings to the French and new instructions to Rose. Brunnow, however, refused to discuss the heart of the matter – how Russia envisioned the 1740 Treaty and Kuchik-Kainarji. Instead he composed his typical, doctored memorandum of a diplomatic dialogue, with the British statesmen seeing things more or less as he did.

On the other hand, Brunnow also attempted to advise the Tsar. Without contesting the official Russian line, Brunnow accused the French of having used gunboat diplomacy to trap Russia into over-responding, since any justified insistence that the Sultan honour his broken word to the Tsar would be seen by Britain as an attack on Turkey's independence. Russia's only way out would be to persuade the Porte that the French were menacing Turkey's internal and external peace, while Russia wished to defend both. The basic problem with Brunnow's plan was that the Turks knew from experience, and the British could learn from Rose, that the Russians had earlier forced the Porte to try to break its word to the French government. In the diplomatic parlance of the time, Brunnow's plan was 'false', even if the French had indeed been attempting to lure England into an entente to defend Turkey from Russia. Brunnow's report and memorandum reached St Petersburg on 27 December.[19]

As it turned out, neither Montenegro nor the enclaves (that is, neither a Slavic-Orthodox entity nor a strategic point), was the catalyst of the explosion. Rather, it was a new concatenation of words dispatched from the Russian legation on the Bosphorus. Ozerov wrote on 13 December that the Porte had preempted a collective *démarche* of the Orthodox clergy to the palace by forbidding any protests over the Holy Places ruling. He enclosed some super-emotional lamentations and appeals from the Patriarch of Constantinople to the Russian Holy Synod – as if the awarding of a set of Bethlehem keys was the equivalent of the sacking of St Sophia 399 years earlier or of the first Jewish Temple more than two millennia further back.[20] A few days later, on 16 December, Ozerov sent the news of the Adriatic blockade and some apocalyptic premonitions concerning the Turks' disregard for the Sultan's letter to the Emperor. Fuad allegedly remarked: 'I know I am taking a dangerous path, which will lead, perhaps to an abyss, but if there is still any future for Turkey, this is the only route that can save her.' The Sultan in his turn was reported as saying: 'The final hour of Turkey has thus struck, since I myself have been pushed to appoint an imbecile [Mehmed Ali] and a rogue [Fuad] as leaders, and I am reduced, due to other causes, to dare to play the desperate part, which they propose for me.'

In other words, Fuad was consciously playing the French card for the highest stakes: regeneration or collapse, while the Sultan would welcome some kind of a bale out. Moreover, according to Ozerov, Russian influence in Constantinople was nil, the Turks needed a real scare, and 'a heroic remedy was necessary'. These dispatches, with their improbable quotations and no word at all concerning the limited nature of the Latin victory, reached St Petersburg on 26 December.[21]

Meanwhile, Nesselrode had been busy since 9 December trying to concoct a solution that would avoid the predicted conflagration, since the 'next post' did not announce the execution of the firman. His own plan, which contained some thinking close to Brunnow's, was presented on 25 December at a normal Saturday-morning Nesselrode–Seniavin briefing session in the Imperial Cabinet in the Winter Palace in St Petersburg. It was attended by the Emperor and a suite of five of the top security officials in the Empire, including the diplomatically talented, if domestically paranoid Orlov. Nesselrode proposed to send an extraordinary ambassador to convince the Sultan that his betrayal of a sovereign-to-sovereign word was without precedent, and that the other Great Powers would support him against French threats. Nesselrode further banked on an alleged secret message from Reshid to Ozerov, not to be found in any of the latter's nearly complete set of surviving dispatches: 'to renovate and complete the clause of the Treaty of Kuchuk-Kainarji relative to the protection and the immunities that the Orthodox cult and its clergy must enjoy in the Ottoman domains'. In the form of a non-negotiable Russian demand, this became a fatal bone of contention leading to the outbreak of the Crimean War. Finally, fearing that war would finish off the Ottoman Empire, Nesselrode feebly attempted to outline the next stage in case the Sultan rebuffed the extraordinary envoy. The best solution he or his staff could manufacture, however, was to threaten to publish the firman, which would then lead to an uprising of the Ottoman Orthodox[22] – as if a critical mass of Greeks and Bulgarians or Christian Arabs really cared about the keys and the cupola. This notion was strange at best, since St Petersburg knew that the firman had already been printed in the local press in Turkey.[23] Any Russian threat to explode Ottoman domestic tranquillity would surely create the European coalition against Russia, not France, so long as France behaved reasonably. In addition, to send an extraordinary ambassador simply to publish an ambiguous charter issued by a crowned weakling could hardly have qualified as a 'vigorous *démarche*' in the eyes of the Commander-in-Chief of the world's largest army and only Black Sea fleet.

MOBILIZATION

Nesselrode's plan was dead the day after it was presented to the Emperor, as soon as Ozerov's 16 December packet reached the Emperor's desk. In reaction to the news about the silencing of Greek protests, the Patriarch's appeal, Fuad's gamble with destiny, and the Sultan's lament (but *not* the Turkish move on Montenegro), Nicholas pencilled: 'Here is the unexpected compliment. I foresaw this, and I directed all of our attention to it; there is nothing more to review, and we must immediately make our preparations. God will decide the rest; we can no longer stay where we are.'[24]

He meant what he said. At the celebrations of the centennial of the Naval Cadet Corps that day, Nicholas told Naval Minister Menshikov and Vice-Admiral V.I. Kornilov, Chief of Staff of the Black Sea squadron, that 'Turkish audacity is leading to a rupture . . . and we must prepare everything necessary for a Bosphorus expedition.'[25]

In fact more than a thought had already emerged, and Menshikov may well have known it, since military parleys had eclipsed the normal foreign policy briefings the previous week. The Emperor's will initiated serious planning. That same day (27 December) he set in motion the secret mobilization of the Fourth and Fifth corps, 37,201 of whose troops were needed for the expedition, and 91,261 troops for a simultaneous Balkan campaign.[26] In the next two days the Emperor consulted with his naval chiefs – his son Constantine, as well as Menshikov and Admiral Kornilov – concerning an attack on Constantinople and received various plans. The Austrian envoy Mensdorff knew something grave was in the works, since the Tsar's entourage talked of dismembering the Ottoman Empire, starting with the Principalities, but Nesselrode would not talk. On 30 December, though, he informed Brunnow in a secret dispatch of the decision to send an extraordinary ambassador to help Ozerov and alluded to the 'inevitable consequences', were the Porte not to yield. Kiselev was already warning Cowley that Russia was preparing to answer French naval threats in kind. By 5 January, Nicholas had received a comprehensive plan for the expedition.[27]

The *ad hoc* nature of the Tsar's orders is evident in the light of the unsettled and unsettling news from abroad. On 28 December Nicholas read that 'Viscount Canning' would be the Foreign Secretary in the new Aberdeen Cabinet. Two days later the word from London and Berlin was that the haughty and mercurial reformer Lord John Russell would occupy the Foreign Office instead, that another nemesis, Palmerston, would sit in the Home Office, and that the King of Prussia would address Napoleon III as 'brother'. 'The King's cowardice prevails', noted Nicholas. The French were clearly winning the day in the West, and Mensdorff offered no hope of an Austrian *carte blanche* to Russia in the Near East.[28] All Nicholas could reasonably hope for was some form of simultaneous Austrian pressure against Turkey over Montenegro and the Adriatic enclaves.

In fact, on 27–28 December, Francis Joseph alerted his Adriatic squadron and ordered more troops to be ferried to Dalmatia to strengthen the defences around Klek and Suttorina against the Turkish campaign. At the same time, however, Buol made it clear that he expected that Austria would have good relations with the new British Cabinet and that both would get on well with France[29] – an implicit veto over any isolation of France and hence a rebuff to Nicholas's diplomatic strategy.

The year 1852 thus began with the spectre of a Bonapartist restoration and a flawed settlement of the Holy Places dispute and ended with Turkey, Austria and Russia, as well as Montenegro, mobilized or mobilizing. Turkey and Austria faced off over concrete and limited territorial and strategic issues that could be negotiated. On the other hand, the Tsar, following the awarding of the keys, but before the more important cupola issue was resolved, moved towards a war footing against Turkey over religious symbols, an untenable concept of the status quo in a changing world, a manufactured insult, and foggy claims of tutelage over the Sultan's Orthodox subjects. Colonel Rose had been correct three months earlier: the question *was* 'making the exit out of the Great Door', for it was this mobilization which would escalate to war.

NOTES

1. For the Austro-Turkish embroglio, in addition to la Valette's, Ozerov's, and Rose's dispatches, Unckel: 64ff.
2. Also *POM* III.I.77 and p. 381, n. 2.
3. For this battle over Britain, Walewski's and Brunnow's dispatches, AMAE CP Angl. 686 and AVPR K 469/1852/79; cf. ZP I.56.
4. La Gorce *HSE* II: 100–2.
5. Wal. to Drn., 23 Nov. 1852 (AMAE CP Angl. 686).
6. Brw. to Nes., 22 Nov./4 Dec. 1853 (ZP I.73).
7. Nich. I's glosses on Brw. to Nes., 17/29 Nov., 22, 25 Nov./4, 7 Dec. 1852 (AVPR K 79); many pertinent Russian documents regarding the 'III' from Nov.–Dec. 1852 are found in ZP I; also useful were Nordin's reports to Stockholm (SRA KUB).
8. That the Greeks were also deprived of their key is a common misunderstanding in scholarship: for example, Gooch *CHOCW*: 35.
9. Oz. to Nes. with Nich. I's glosses, 4/16 May, 18/30 Nov. 1852 (AVPR GA–V2 181 522): in May Nicholas read a copy of the 8 February Note to the French and marked 'NB' twice on it.
10. Rose to Mlm., 5 Dec. 1852 (*CORR* I.79).
11. Cf. Rich: 22; Wetzel: 43.
12. Lav. to Drn., 5 Dec. 1852 (AMAE CP Turq. 310); Oz. to Nes., 6 Dec. 1852 (AVPR GA V–A2 181 522); Rose to Mlm., 28 Dec. 1852 (PRO FO 78/895, not in *CORR*); cf. Temperley *ENEC*: 495; Taylor, *Struggle for Mastery in Europe*, p. 49.
13. Nes. to Oz., 24 Nov./4 Dec. 1853 (AVPR GA V–A2 522: 833–42, two of three also in ZP I.92–3).
14. Oz. to Nes., 15/27 Nov. 1852, (AVPR GA V–A2 522).
15. Nes. to Brw., 27 Nov./9 Dec. 1852 (TsGADA III/120).
16. Oz. to Nes. with glosses, 18/30 Nov., 24 Nov./6 Dec., received 9/21, 5/17 Dec. 1852 (AVPR GA V–A2 522); Nich. I to Psk., 8/20 Dec. 1852: *PASK* VII: 41.
17. Mlm. to Rose, 14, 21 Dec. 1853, Cwl. to Mlm., 19 Dec. 1853 (*CORR* I.77, 81–2).
18. For example, *Hansard's Parliamentary Debates*, 3rd Ser. vol. 127 (London 1853), p. 657; Curtiss *RCW*: 44–8, a one-sided exposé of official Russian

views, taken from *PHQSL* and Jomini, themselves based selectively on the biased Russian dispatches.

19. Brw. to Nes., 8/20 Dec. 1853 (AVPR K 79); also ZP I.95; *CORR* I.83 (Extr. of Brw. memo.); Bohl: 10.
20. Germanos to Oz., Holy Synod, 29 Nov./11 Dec. 1852; Oz. to Nes., 1/13 Dec. 1852 (AVPR GA–V2 522: 665–82).
21. Oz. to Nes., 4/16 Dec. 1852 (AVPR GA V–A2 522); Cf. Valerga to Porte, 23 Dec. 1852 (*CORR* I.170).
22. *KfZh* 322:26; ZP I.96.
23. Oz. to Nes., 4/16 May 1852 (AVPR GA V–2 522).
24. AVPR GA V–A2 522: 691.
25. *DM* 14–15/26–27 Dec. 1852.
26. TsGVIA 1/1/7/20389–406: general order of Nich. I, broken down into parts for the Fourth and Fifth Corps, with Kornilov memo, 15/27–18/30 Dec. 1853: corrects Zaionchkovskii *VV* I: 728.
27. *KfZh*, 322:21–26, 46–47; *DM* 16–19/28–31 Dec. 1852; TsGAVMF 19/4/92: Mnsh. note, 16/28 Dec. 1853, between Adm. Lazarev's and Captain Shestakov's descent plans from the 1830s and 1850; Seym. to Mlm., 1 Jan. 1853 (PRO FO 65/424); Nes. to Brw., 18/30 Dec. (AVPR K 469 80); ZP I.213, TsGAVMF 19/1/276b: 1–20 (plans, dated 24 Dec. 1852/5 Jan. 1853).
28. Brw. to Nes., reg. and telegr., Budberg to Nes., with glosses, 8/20, 11/23 Dec. 1852 (AVPR K 79, 26), also ZP I.80.
29. *POM* III.I.76–7 (Protocols, 28, 30 Dec. 1852); Heindl: 108.

PART THREE
The Rupture

CHAPTER EIGHT

Preparations for Diplomatic Disaster (January–February 1853)

TURKEY'S STRONG MOVE AND LONDON'S STRONG HAND

As the year 1853 commenced, Tsar Nicholas was leading Russia into a trap which he and his Foreign Ministry officials had themselves set by trying to hold the Turks to promises which they had not really made. However, the main immediate issue was the fate of the Turkish expedition to subdue Montenegro. On 1 January Fuad announced that the Montenegrin constitutional changes represented an attack on Ottoman rights and a 'spiritual and temporal rebellion'.[1] If Omer's military campaign now succeeded, the Russians would have a perfect excuse to intervene, though no other power would like this.

Britain, as usual, held the most important cards, and most intelligent people saw this, even Nicholas I – but he did not wish to change his course. All the leading British favoured compromise in the Holy Land, since they needed France and Russia to balance each other and Austria to help balance both. They believed the French had a right to their Empire and to international security, but should not have singed Russian beards over the sanctuaries and ought to give way in Jerusalem. The Austrians had a right to have peace and stability next door in the Balkans, but not to abet Russian claims on Turkey, dispossess the Turks of the enclaves, or obstruct freedom of the seas. The Ottomans had a right to their 'sovereignty' and 'independence', that is, to keep their empire intact for the benefit of Great Britain and British India. Russia had a right to redress in the Holy Places dispute, but not to control the destinies of the Balkans or Constantinople. Only a few influential freetraders, such as Richard Cobden, believed

115

that partition of the Ottoman Empire and friendship with Russia would serve British commercial interests even more than containing Russia.[2]

Austria was in a potentially vulnerable position so long as the conflict with Turkey lasted and relations with England were not good – the aftermath of 1849 and the refugee crisis. The French could toy with a policy of friendship with Britain, Turkey, 'Italy', and even Prussia, and thereby threaten Austria with isolation or an isolated Austro-Russian combination, which was the last thing most Vienna statesmen desired. The Austrians therefore could not afford to alienate Paris or London too much and had to allow the Western powers a say in the Montenegrin and enclaves disputes. Nesselrode understood Austria's dilemma, but Nicholas I clearly did not[3] – or did not wish to.

Napoleon III for his part was not fooling when he said 'the Empire means peace', at least so far as Great Britain was concerned, since London also held the keys to any recreation of a hostile coalition. He thus swallowed his pride and allowed his half-brother Morny and Cowley to shepherd a compromise over credentials. Accordingly, the Austrian and Prussian envoys respectfully recognized Napoleon III as Francis Joseph's and Frederick William's 'brother' (*frère*), that is, a fellow legitimate monarch, while N. D. Kiselev represented Napoleon as merely the Tsar's 'good friend' (*bon ami*). The British also leveraged the French into adopting a slightly more conciliatory stance in St Petersburg over the Holy Places. The only French ploy left was to stand firm on their interpretation of the 'Note of 8 February' and the original firman and hope that Russia, with or without Austria, would act in such a way as to swing Britain over to the side of France.[4] Napoleon III remained fixed on securing domestic support for his new order, bolstered by an *entente* with Britain, rather than unilaterally maximizing gains in the Holy Places dispute. Nicholas I, on the other hand, remained in his self-contained box when it came to the Eastern Question.

THE TSAR'S HARE-BRAINED SCHEMES

The Tsar was most interested in action and moved quickly to select his special envoy. His first choice was P.D. Kiselev, the reforming Minister of State Domains, author of the Organic Statutes of Wallachia and Moldavia (1834) and, as Russia's proconsul there (1829–34), an experienced negotiator with the Porte. He declined. The impatient Tsar then turned to the perennially sarcastic, nationalist-minded, lackadaisical Minister of the Marine since 1830, Prince A.S. Menshikov, a man with questionable diplomatic credentials. His special mission to Teheran in 1826 failed to prevent war with Persia from erupting, while his suggestion to send battleships through the Straits into the Black Sea to beef up the squadron assumed an expanded and inadmissible interpretation of Unkiar-Skelessi. He provisionally accepted on 3 January, but Nesselrode worked behind the scenes for the appointment instead of the security chief Orlov, the formidable but more realistic negotiator of Unkiar-Skelessi in 1833. He had recommended a forward policy of ultimatum diplomacy during the 1849 refugee crisis, but he does not appear to have sought to undertake this impossible mission.[5]

'General-Admiral' Menshikov was an ideal choice from one standpoint only: Nicholas was interested in having someone in whom plenary military and naval powers could also be temporarily vested. The only problem here was that speed was essential to steal the jump on Britain as well as France, and Menshikov had been seriously ill since mid November. In the first five weeks of his ailments, he suffered from earaches, nosebleed, heavy cough, hoarseness, fever, insomnia, unbearable toothaches, splitting headaches, constipation, lesions and an abscessed sore throat. While he was recovering from gout, he suffered from more earaches and chills.[6] Either Nicholas was blind, or he lacked anyone else equally eminent and really qualified, or else he really wanted war.

The most telling contradiction in Russian policy at this time is that the news from Constantinople was becoming more favourable. La Valette and the local Catholics, much to their chagrin, now had to witness the Ottoman pendulum swing back in favour of the Orthodox and render the latest decision meaningless. Nesselrode could tell Menshikov that the Turks were 'willing to negotiate'. The Tsar even informed Seymour that the Turks were being more 'reasonable'. Nicholas himself, however, was not becoming more reasonable, but stayed his stubborn course. The other half of Nesselrode's message was: 'the mission shall proceed anyway'.[7]

The Russian Emperor appears to have been the prisoner of his own mobilization orders and the quixotic impulses which had constituted one of his father's fatal flaws. Determined to set something in motion right away, he considered the earliest plans for a *coup de main* on Constantinople that had been concocted already. Putiatin's 1850 plan to send 40,000 men in the first wave to force Turkey to join against the Western aggressor had to be set aside since only one of the required eight new war steamers had been added. Nicholas also rejected an alternative 1850 scheme to land 30,000 men at Sizopol on the Bulgarian coast with Russia's existing naval and merchant vessels, to be followed by a ten-day march to Constantinople. He readied instead by 19 January a variant of Admiral Lazarev's 1835 plan for a surprise descent on 'Tsargrad' (as the Russians still called the former Byzantine capital) in order to pre-empt both the British and the French with just 16,000 men with thirty two field guns. Nicholas thus heeded Menshikov's concern for surprise, lest the British Malta squadron, only two days' sail from the Dardanelles, should interfere. The Tsar also ordered a machine factory to be built in Sevastopol and hoped that some mechanics and workers could be brought in from England.[8]

This scheme however, was unrealistic from both the military and diplomatic standpoints. A surprise launch of a trained expeditionary force was beyond Russia's means at this time. The Tsar himself was distressed with the open enthusiasm and fanaticism of his patriotic officers during the initial phases of the mobilization, which could not remain a secret. His Foreign Minister of twenty-six years, Naval Minister of twenty-one years and most erudite ambassador (Brunnow) aired their worries about Britain, and Nicholas secretly shared them. Nevertheless, he proceeded as if the English would allow Russian forces to seize Constantinople and the Dardanelles, and his sceptical subalterns continued to execute his commands. He did not so much plan as hope that diplomacy would somehow preclude Aberdeen's England and Napoleon III's France from cooperating.[9]

Meanwhile Russia's all-important negotiations with Britain continued and took a new twist. The British were still demanding moderation and compromise from France and Russia over the Holy Places. Nicholas, however, had been contemplating raising the question of the imminent collapse of Turkey with Britain and Austria around the time he ordered the mobilization of the Fourth and Fifth Corps. Nesselrode tried to have this issue quashed, but failed, and even the better news from Constantinople did not help. Nicholas proceeded with his *idée fixe* as soon as he learned from Brunnow that the Aberdeen Cabinet had been installed, that Palmerston would keep to domestic affairs solely (which could only have been wishful thinking) and that Russell leaned to the Russian side in the Holy Places dispute (which was true).[10] At any rate, once the Tsar had mobilized against Turkey, he had nothing to lose by initiating secret feelers, since they might get Britain to convince the Turks to cede.

On 9 January, a day after Seymour had submitted a memorandum questioning the mobilization, Nicholas was in the midst of his serious war planning, but he interrupted his normal evening activities at the Winter Palace for a small dinner at the palace of the Grand Duchess Elena, who just happened to invite Sir Hamilton and Lady Seymour as well. Without mentioning the military moves, Nicholas confidentially raised the subject of his 1844 talks with Aberdeen, Peel and Wellington, and asserted that the British and Russian governments should be in complete accord over the Ottoman Empire, which was in danger of collapsing. In reporting this encounter, Seymour grasped the differences between the two governments perfectly: 'that England has to desire a close contact with Russia, with a view to preventing the downfall of Turkey – while Russia would be pleased that the concert should apply to the events by which this downfall is to be followed'.[11]

Three days later the Tsar met with Nesselrode and Seniavin for an inordinate three and a half hours. The latter two had prepared an official dispatch, which followed the Brunnow–Nesselrode line and adumbrated the position that Russia would take throughout the crisis: Russia mobilized in order to counter French naval demonstrations and to protect Turkey from France. Nesselrode summoned Seymour on the morrow and showed him the dispatch.

The following day Seymour visited Nicholas in his office. The Tsar elaborated on his earlier theme and offered 'as a gentleman' a direct *entente* with Britain to impose a solution to the Eastern Question upon the other Great Powers and Turkey. Intrigued by the possibility of binding the Tsar's policy to Britain, Seymour nevertheless pressed Nicholas on the dangers of his mobilization. It might cause a French counter demonstration and further uprisings of the Ottoman Christians against the financially weak Sultan. Nicholas answered with his own contrived response: 'a French expedition to the Sultan's dominions . . . would compel him to send his forces into Turkey without delay or hesitation, if the result of such an advance should prove to be the overthrow of the Great Turk, he (Nicholas) should regret the event'.[12]

Russian policy eventually played right into the hands of the French, who had no intention of invading Turkey. The British rejected both Rose's direct approach of supporting France as the lesser danger to Turkey over Russia, and Cowley's initial suggestion that France and Russia together impose a settlement on Turkey. The London Cabinet, or at least Russell, who was in contact with Stratford, preferred the latter's more subtle policy of support for the Russians on the Holy

Places issue, while the Porte remained the ultimate judge of any Franco-Russian compromise.[13] This would allow Great Britain to be the ultimate protector of Turkish 'sovereignty and independence' and ensure that, if Britain and France had to unite to curb Russia, they would be uniting to defend Britain's broad interests in the entire Ottoman Empire, not France's narrow ones in the Levant. At this point Russian actions were threatening – since the Tsar *was* trying to operationalize plans for a surprise attack on Constantinople and the Dardanelles – but Russian words were moderate. France needed something more to help sway England. In the event, Austria hoping to steal a march with impunity, and assured of Russian support, helped French policy along.

VIENNA'S GAMBLE: COUNT LEININGEN'S MISSION

As we noted at the end of the preceding chapter, Emperor Francis Joseph readied some of his land and naval forces at the same time as Nicholas did and in response to a more or less simultaneous Turkish decision. The Austrian alert was due to the Porte's projected campaign to subdue Montenegro and coincided with a new initiative on Buol's part to induce the Turks to grant Austria control over the Bay of Cattaro and to resolve other outstanding bilateral disputes. The Turks, however, held to their guns, officially informed the Great Powers of Montenegro's insubordination and offences and, now against ostensible French advice, prepared further for war. Klezl's menacing Note of 7 January to call off the offensive and concede to Austrian demands regarding the enclaves did not impress Fuad.[14]

The next day Vienna received confirmation of Turkish armaments and obstinacy. Within a week, the Austrian military men convinced their young Emperor to send an extraordinary ambassador, 'to place a fist under the nose of the Turks as Russia and England always do with success'. By this time Vienna knew of Nicholas's extreme irritation with the Turks, his mobilization, his offer to help in Montenegro and, most probably, his planned extraordinary mission. However, the Austrian move was made independently and aimed not to irritate Britain and France by backing Russia in the Holy Places dispute. Rather, Buol stood for compromise there, while seeking to induce the 'incompetent' and 'impotent' Turks to recognize a joint Austro-Russian protectorate over the Balkan Christians and gain for Vienna the upper hand in Montenegro.[15]

The selection of the extraordinary envoy fell upon one of the highest-ranking imperial aristocrats and officials, a step-cousin of Queen Victoria, Field Marshall Count Christian von Leiningen. His chief, non-negotiable aim was to terminate the Turkish military–naval campaign. He was also to try to obtain a satisfactory response to Austria's earlier demands: Austrian control over the enclaves, an apology for releasing Kossuth and other revolutionary refugees, dismissal of such persons serving in Omer's army, assurances concerning the Christians of Bosnia and Herzegovina and settlement of Austrian commercial claims. Since Vienna, unlike St Petersburg, also recognized the Porte's sovereignty over Montenegro and certainly did not wish to implode the Ottoman Empire, the Austrians were willing to compromise, just as they urged the French and Russians to do.[16]

Buol orchestrated Leiningen's embassy in hopes of pulling off a swift victory without the intervention of the other powers. Vienna first announced the mission and its goals to the Russian chargé Felix Fonton on 21 January. Within ten days Leiningen had arrived at Constantinople. St Petersburg, already anxious over Menshikov's illnesses and delays, learned of the mission only three days before Leiningen arrived. Nicholas approved of it, and immediately dispatched Colonel E.P. Kovalevsky as a special agent, ostensibly to assist the Austrians in curbing the Turks.[17]

The opportunistic French, armed with rumours that Austrian troops had actually entered Bosnia, pursued a three-pronged tactic. Drouyn urged moderation upon both the Austrians and the Turks, despite the request of the new Turkish ambassador, Veli Pasha, for outright support. The flip side of Drouyn's admonitions was to threaten Austria with a French occupation of Savoy and the Rhineland, Prussian domination of Germany, and an Anglo-Russian war for Constantinople. On the other hand, Drouyn demanded cooperation from the British to defend the Ottomans from the Austro-Russian combination, got Russell to disavow Malmesbury's earlier denial of Ottoman sovereignty over Montenegro, but held out the possibility of an Anglo-French division of the spoils, were Turkey to collapse.[18]

The British still would not fall into the French snare. However much Drouyn and the French chargé Charles Baudin might badger Cowley and Russell, the English feigned trust in Vienna's intentions and continued to press France on the Holy Places. But the British would not fall into the Russian trap either. Brunnow could urge and remonstrate with Aberdeen and Russell day and night and only obtain from them the instructions for Rose and Cowley that London desired. To wit, France and Russia should make an agreement concerning the

Holy Places that did not infringe upon Ottoman independence. In no way would Russell provoke France with a preliminary, preventive four-power arrangement, as Brunnow urged on several occasions. Moreover, Russell explicitly told Brunnow a week before Leiningen reached Constantinople that Britain did not wish the Montenegrin crisis to lead to a Russo-Turkish rupture. Foreshadowing Rose's obstructionist tactics toward Menshikov, Russell virtually destroyed Russia's diplomatic strategy. He insisted to Brunnow's friend and hope in the Cabinet, Aberdeen, that Britain could not support Russia without knowing what the latter's demands were.[19]

Leiningen, meanwhile, had his chance to work on the Turks. Arriving with little advance notice via a war steamer late on 31 January, he quickly saw the chief Turkish ministers, who consulted la Valette and Rose and were conciliatory concerning the refugees in the army and Austria's commercial claims, but adamant regarding Montenegro and the enclaves. Leiningen had no more luck with the Sultan on 3 February, and so presented an ultimatum, threatening to leave on the 9th, if Austrian demands were not met.

The Turkish power élite, emboldened by news of victory from the Montenegrin front, wished to offer full resistance. They were dissuaded by the improvising la Valette and especially Rose, who backed the Ottoman claim to the enclaves, and insisted upon open access to Turkish ports, but at the same time tried to get Klezl to restrain Leiningen. It appears that the Belgian minister Blondeel and his Prussian counterpart Colonel Ludwig von Wildenbruch prompted Klezl a few days later to assure everybody that Austria desired only the status quo.

The Turks, however, covered their bets by resolving their substantial outstanding debts to Western bankers, and initiating plans to deploy 40,000 more Ottoman soldiers and up to 40,000 Egyptian troops (an unrealistic number) in the Balkans. The Austrians were not bluffing either, but issued specific orders to the generals to enter Bosnia and occupy Sarajevo if the Turks crossed Austrian territory or used the enclaves. Peace or war in Europe seemed to hinge on where the Turkish naval squadron sailed, how far Omer's motley army marched, and how successful it was in Montenegro.

Still, in the absence of firm instructions to Rose and la Valette from London and Paris, Turkish fear of Russia was having its effects. Ozerov hinted that war might result from an unsatisfactory reply and on the night of 8 February convinced Fuad to negotiate with Leiningen. On the other hand, they all worked to get him to postpone his departure for three days. Fuad, then, aided by Rose and la Valette, who sometimes were stationed in adjoining rooms, had to convince a Turkish Grand Council and its ulema to modify the original Turkish response. The Turks were willing to listen to the British and French, but perhaps the deciding factor was the Austro-Russian difference over Montenegro's status. The Turks agreed to call off the Montenegrin campaign 'by a sovereign act emanating from the Sultan' and to continue to negotiate concerning the enclaves.[20] Austria's minimal demands were met, and on 15 February la Valette courier-wired Paris that the mission had ended with a peaceful resolution.

The crisis was not over and would not be until Vienna was certain that the Turks were withdrawing. As late as 25 February the Austrians were preparing diplomatically for armed intervention on 5 or 6 March. On the 26th, however, Leiningen telegraphed from Trieste that his mission was accomplished except for the specific arrangements regarding the enclaves. He failed to mention, however, that his mission had forced the Porte into a heightened state of mobilization and a greater willingness to entertain financial dependence upon the West in order to defend against Russian or Russian and Austrian encroachments.[21]

FRENCH POSITIONING AND OTHER MATTERS

The diplomatic fallout from the Leiningen mission and Austria's mobilization worked very much in France's favour. Turkey was even more committed to arming against Russia. The British finally were alarmed, and remained essentially more fearful of Russia than of Austria. At the same time a British press scare over a nonexistent French threat to launch an invasion of the home islands was a hot issue in England from mid-February to early March. This storm in a teacup, whose genesis is obscure, actually served the interests of the English military and naval men and their budgetary demands. The French Foreign Ministry welcomed this test of cross-Channel ties, in which the 'City', with its investments in France and natural fear of a destructive war, was a mollifying factor. The British government was also accepting French assurances in good faith.[22]

At the same time, due to London's continued lax policy toward revolutionary refugees, the French actually enjoyed better relations with Austria than did the British. Facing in February a nationalist-republican (Mazzinist) uprising in Milan and an assassination attempt by a Hungarian on the Emperor, Vienna was specifically annoyed with the English, Piedmontese and Swiss governments. Napoleon's regime was sympathetic, having its own problems with refugees across the border in Belgium. Insofar as good relations with Vienna were the key to any sound British or French policy that aimed to counter Russia at Constantinople without provoking a general European war, the French were well placed to take the diplomatic lead. But if the Austrians instead joined with Russia against Turkey, then the junior Napoleon, as the most important other ally of the British and the Turks, could start to recover for France what his uncle had lost. On the other hand, were Russia to prove conciliatory, then the French would still score a diplomatic victory, having posed as Turkey's champion and utilized gunboat diplomacy successfully. At least Napoleon III would have the prestige he desired. However, all of this depended upon what Russia did.

While the Austrians were dodging their own bullets in escalating a crisis and then deftly and fortuitously escaping unscathed, the Russians were digging a deeper pit for themselves. Even with the knowledge that the French were trying to make contingency arrangements with the British for a joint naval expedition to Turkish waters, Nicholas refused to use Napoleon's conciliatory ploy of blaming and recalling la Valette as the pretext for calling off Russia's mobilization.[23] St Petersburg also simply refused to accept the fundamental lessons from the Leiningen mission: that Britain and France would act together to protect Turkey from Russia; that the Turks would make a deal with Austria to avoid greater problems with Russia; that Austria would make a deal with the Turks in order to avoid being caught in a Western–Russian embroglio over Turkey; and that armed diplomacy can succeed only if one has either overwhelming force or diplomatic goals that other Great Powers will support or allow.

The Russian government continued the line adopted in 1852 and was oblivious even to events in Turkey. There the Greeks and Latins still continued to squabble over the Holy Places and showed thereby that nothing had really been settled in December. The Greeks tried to stop the Latins from officiating in the Church of the Nativity and to control the Latins' use of the Tomb of the Virgin. The Latin Patriarch Valerga complained about the French concessions and insisted that the Greeks should not obtain control over the repair of the cupola. On the other hand, news reached St Petersburg five days before Menshikov left that Aristarchi and Cyrill were ready to make their own deal with the Porte over the shrines. Rose meanwhile wanted the powerless Ozerov to accept some of the concessions to the Latins and suggested that a Turkish messenger convey to Russia a suitable 'reparation' for the Latin gains – an idea that reached St Petersburg five days after Menshikov left.[24] Compromise over the Holy Places was as close and as distant as ever.

To win over British and 'European' opinion, the French and Russians engaged in their own diplomatic dance, which initiated a public debate between foreign ministries that lasted on and off until the outbreak of war. The Tsar took such polemics very seriously and demanded that attacks be answered. Drouyn's dispatch of mid January to Castelbajac reasserted the French minimum claims, but pretended complete willingness otherwise to compromise and called for direct Franco-Russian negotiations. Nesselrode's response via Kiselev in early February was issued at a time when Menshikov's instructions were in the process of being completed. The Chancellor rejected such negotiations, as the French had fifteen months earlier, in favour of the fiction of bilateral parleys with Turkey. Instead he upbraided the French for their conduct and argued for the primacy of the 1757 firman, the precedence of the 1808 cupola reconstruction and the Sultan's 'autograph' letter and *hatt-i sherif* ('February' firman) of 1852. With British approval, Drouyn then sent a toned down request to Nesselrode to end recriminations in the interest of conciliation on the basis of each side's preferred firman, and the verbal storm abated for three months.[25]

BRITISH ADMONITIONS, RUSSIAN BLINDERS

This Franco-Russian war of words was no simple exercise in public diplomacy leading to an agreement. The French statement was an honest exposition of a real negotiating stance based on the Turkish promises and rulings of the previous year. The Russian statement, on the other hand, represented only a small part of a much larger package of unrealistic desiderata and demands that Nesselrode's office prepared for Menshikov and put in final form in the first nine days of February, while Leiningen was using ultimatum diplomacy in Constantinople.[26] Curiously, on 9 February, when Menshikov was departing, Seymour gave an already sceptical Russell a worst case view of the Tsar's intentions toward Turkey and pretty well guessed what the mission cum mobilizations were all about.[27]

Meanwhile Nicholas, Nesselrode and Brunnow continued to negotiate in London and St Petersburg as if an *entente* with Britain against Turkish perfidy and Bonapartist ambitions were in the works. In response, both Aberdeen and Russell, without blatantly asserting that England and France would cooperate against Russia were Turkey threatened, got Brunnow to concede that a Franco-Russian agreement followed logically from the Tsar's 'peaceful intentions'. Brunnow also spared no effort or subtleties to convince his master of Britain's strict neutrality and policy of the free hand. Aware of the gist of Nicholas's approaches to Seymour, Brunnow penned a special memorandum in early February. It analysed the vicissitudes of the Anglo-French *ententes* since 1833, emphasized once more London's unwillingness to enter into any preliminary agreements over the fate of other countries, and predicted that British policy would be fine for Russia so long as peace prevailed.[28]

At the same time Brunnow informed his superiors that the English were displeased with Austria's failure to continue to support the Ottoman Empire. In fact, Aberdeen and Russell together, pushed by public opinion, had convinced Stratford to return to his post in Constantinople, and he was planning to go via Vienna. English jitters over the implications of Austrian, Russian and French policies had immediately mandated sending the strong man back to the Bosphorus, where he had protected British interests so well in the past.[29]

A few days later Russell, who had taken the ideas of Seymour and Stratford to heart, sent off London's official response to Nicholas I's secret offer of an *entente* in the Near East. Any preliminary agreement between Russia and Britain concerning Turkey would have to be communicated to the other Great Powers, would thus become public knowledge, and would hasten Turkey's downfall. Were Turkey to collapse, any Russian possession of Constantinople, even temporary, was out of the question. The best Britain could promise was its own disinterestedness in controlling Constantinople and a pledge not to exclude Russia from any arrangement. Meanwhile, the wisest policy for all states to pursue was to avoid armed demonstrations and induce the Porte to continue on the road of legal and administrative reform. Russell slyly (and noncommittally) added: 'The more the Turkish government adopts the rules of impartial law and equal administration, the less will the Emperor of Russia find it necessary to apply that exceptional protection, which his Imperial Majesty has found so burthensome and inconvenient, though no doubt prescribed by duty and sanctioned by law.'

Nicholas I's marginal comments on the copy he received on 17 February or soon thereafter reveal his rather slipshod approach to a complex matter, as well as his fundamental divergence from British thinking. At the same time that Nesselrode was assuring Seymour that Montenegrin affairs were taking a turn for the better, the Tsar pencilled that Turkish actions in Montenegro 'could easily lead to war'. Accepting that the best he could obtain from England was a statement of what she did not desire in case Turkey fell, he wrote: 'This is a precious assurance, since it proves that perfect identity of interests exists between England and Russia.' Concerning Russell's desire for Ottoman legal and administrative reforms, Nicholas asserted with his sincere pessimism: 'This may be done, but futilely, and it is this which can lead to war and all of its consequences.'[30]

The Tsar proceeded to pursue his secret negotiations via Seymour and for this, apparently, studied not so much Brunnow's most recent, cautionary memorandum, as his equally guarded October 1851 position paper that outlined a partition settlement – but neither very well. Meeting Seymour once more at a Grand Duchess's on 20 February, Nicholas again tried to emphasize that the Ottoman Empire was really 'dying', that Her Majesty's ministers were mistaken if they thought otherwise, and that all he desired was a private preliminary understanding for a two-power diktat concerning what they did *not* desire from the corpse. The next day Nicholas and Seymour had a detailed tête-à-tête concerning Russell's dispatch. The Tsar asserted that he would use any Turkish atrocities against Montenegro as a signal for war. He felt that he had Austria in his pocket regarding the Ottoman Empire and that he could take Constantinople without opposition. If Turkey fell, he would have to intervene to prevent civil strife between Muslims and Christians and to prevent the establishment of a hostile or revolutionary state on the Bosphorus or in the Balkans. Forgetting what he had said the night before about simply agreeing about what each side did not want, he proceeded as well to outline a division of territories that almost outlined the settlement of 1878–80 and gave Egypt and Cyprus to Britain, while Bulgaria and Serbia attained the status he attributed to the Danubian Principalities, that is, 'an independent state under my protection'. What was missing from these conversations, and hence fatal for the Tsar, was any indication of Russian willingness to rescind or delay the mobilization or to deal with the French. If he really did believe that Austria would cooperate with him over Turkish affairs on any other basis than counter-revolutionary principles and the Convention of Münchengrätz – and it seems as if he did – then he was once more disregarding the manifest advice of his top diplomats. Seymour's report of this conversation that painted the Russian Emperor as both incompetent and dangerous reached the Foreign Office on 6 March, when Menshikov was already in Constantinople frightening the Turks.[31]

While Nicholas I was simultaneously wooing the British and dispatching Menshikov with demands that were bound to alienate London, the Russians also lost an opportunity to work something out with the Turks in England. In mid February the Turkish envoy Musurus asked Brunnow that the Holy Places issue be separated from Montenegro and told him confidentially that the Porte was willing to repudiate Fuad and grant Russia a reparation that was acceptable to the Patriarch of Jerusalem. In one of his last conversations as Foreign Secretary, Russell told Brunnow that Menshikov's demands and Musurus's suggestions to Constantinople ought to be reconcilable. Nicholas and Nesselrode could also learn by the end of February what the British Cabinet considered to be reasonable. Musurus hinted that his son-in-law, Stephanos Vogorides, a high Patriarchal official and the Ottoman Commissioner for Moldavia, could broker a settlement in Constantinople. However, a Musurus–Brunnow deal concluded in Palmerston's haunts was not what the Tsar envisioned. And Brunnow did not make it easy by telling Musurus to inform his government 'that the eleventh hour has struck for it'.[32]

As it turned out, the Russian refusal to negotiate directly with the Turks in London or with France anywhere played into British hands by precluding a settlement behind London's back. The future man of the hour, Viscount (since April 1852) Stratford de Redcliffe, understood perfectly the symmetry of the French and Russian positions, as he worked out Britain's future approach. He would go back to Constantinople and use the Russian, Austrian and French threats to force a British orientation in foreign policy and domestic reform upon the errant Turks.[33] Almost all of British diplomacy from February through to May 1853 reflected this thinking. If the other Great Powers were moderate, Britain could claim the credit. If not, Britain would be in a position to dominate the scene.

On the other hand, the anti-Bonapartist campaign was a perfect smoke screen for those who wished to fool themselves and forget what happened during the 1849 refugee crisis. Led in part by the ostensibly dovish, penny-pinching Lord of the Admiralty, Sir James Graham, with his quest for more naval credits from Parliament, the new invasion scare clouded Britain's necessary cooperation with the distrusted French, were Russia to threaten Turkey. Meanwhile, assuming that Russia would persist on a menacing path, Walewski was confident that the French could ignore Stratford's arrogance and difficult personality and win him over to an anti-Russian stance.

Walewski was right. The Russian and Austrian mobilizations had incited the Turks even more and put the British on edge. Nicholas's new, private initiatives for a partition had to be disturbing. The French, preparing for escalated Russian demands, were assertive but clever in posing as Turkey's and Britain's best friend. If Menshikov proceeded to follow his instructions, the French would obtain the desired British support and all the accompanying legitimization of the Bonapartist regime. No wonder the nervous and prescient Nesselrode wrote that he hoped that this dispute would end as 'well'[!] as the one over the title of the new Emperor of the French.[34]

NOTES

1. Unckel: 60.
2. For British attitudes, the despatches of Walewski and Baudin (AMAE CP Angl. 687); *CORR* I; also Puryear *ERSQ*: 76–7.
3. Nes. to Nich. I, 19/31 Dec. 1852 (ZP I.97).
4. Bapst: 296–306; Cwl. to Rus., 6 Jan. 1853 (*CORR* I.88); Kis. to Nes., 29 Dec./10 Jan. 1852/3 (AVPR K (1853) 111); Drn., Thv. to Ctb., 15 Jan. 1853 (*FR* I; Case, *Thouvenel*, 62); Drn. to Baudin., 17 Jan. 1853 (AMAE CP Angl. 688).
5. *DM* 22 Dec. 1852/11 1853; 2–3/14–15 Jan. 1853; Orl., Nes. to Mnsh., 23 Dec./4 Jan. 1852/3, 3/15 Jan. 1853 (TsGAVMF 19/3/217, 19/3/204); Nes. to Brw., 2/14 Jan. 1853 (TsGADA III/115); cf. Tarlé VIII: 156: the standard, unsubstantiated view, that Orlov was also asked before Menshikov.
6. *DM* 1/13 Nov.–1/13 Feb. 1852/3.
7. Lav. to Drn., 24 Dec., 5 Jan., 1852–53 (AMAE CP Turq. 310–11); Oz. to Nes., 14/26 Dec. 1852 (AVPR GA V–A2 522); *DM* 30 Dec./11 Jan. 1852/3.
8. Nich. I memo, 7/19 Jan. 1853 (ZP I.210); Lazarev, Putiatin, Shestakov memos, 1835–50; Volkov, Miller memos, 15/27, 19/31 Jan. 1853; Mnsh. to Nich. I, 16/28 Dec. 1852 (TsGAVMF 19/1/191, 19/1/276b, 19/4/92).
9. Du Plat (Warsaw) to Rus. (PRO FO 65/435); Nes. memo with gloss, 24 March/5 April 1853 (AVPR K 30).
10. Brw. to Nes, 12, 19/24, 31 Dec. 1852, received. 24, 27 Dec./5, 8 Jan. 1852/3 (AVPR K 1852 80); Nes. memos, 13/25 Dec., 20 Dec./1 Jan.1852/3: the later memo, not the earlier one, responded to Nicholas's queries concerning the partition issue: cf. Temperley *ENEC*: 301; Henderson: 243, only from British sources.
11. *KfZh* 321 (28–29 Dec./9–10 Jan. 1852/3); for Seymour's relations with Nicholas and Nesselrode, *CORR* I.91ff.; originals, PRO 65/424.
12. *KhZh* 322 (31 Dec./12 Jan. 1852/3); Seym. to Rus., 22 Jan. 1853 (*CORR* I.120).
13. Rus. to Rose, Cwl., 28–29 Jan. 1853 (*CORR* I.108–9).

14. For this phase of the Austro-Turkish crisis: *AGK* I.1–29; la Valette's and Ozerov's dispatches (AMAE CP Turq. 311, AVPR K 20, some copies in HHSA PA X 38), and Unckel: 60ff.; here also Klezl to Fuad, 7 Jan. 1853 (HHSA PA XII 46).
15. Unckel: 68; Buol to Mensdorff, 21 Jan. 1853 (HHSA PA XII 37); Baudin to Drn., 14 Jan. 1853 (AMAE CP Angl. 688).
16. Buol to Leiningen, 22 Jan. 1853 (*AGK* I.8).
17. Fnt. to Ness., 9/21 Jan., received 16/28 Jan. 1853 (AVPR K 145); Nes. to Fnt., Kovalevsky, 19/31 Jan. 1853 (HHSA PA X 38); *DM* 11–17/23–29 Jan. 1853.
18. Drn. to Baudin, 14, 27 Jan. 1853; Lav., 28–29 Jan. 1853 (AMAE CP Angl. 688, Turq. 311); Hüb. to Buol, 6 Feb. 1853 (*AGK* I.1.18).
19. For England, Baudin's, Walewski's, and Brunnow's correspondence (AMAE CP Angl. 686, AVPR K 73); also Rus. to Ab., Rose, Cwl., 27–29 Jan. (*AbC* X; *CORR* I.108–10).
20. Lav. to Drn., 14 Jan. 1853 (AMAE CP Turq. 311).
21. Also useful here are the Belgian, Dutch and Swedish reports.
22. Also Martin: 103–4; Lambert *PRW*: 17.
23. Martens XV: 271–2; Kis. to Nes., 13/25 Feb. 1852 (AVPR K 111).
24. Oz. to Nes., 14/26 Jan., 24 Jan./5 Feb., received 24 Jan./5 Feb., 4/16 Feb. 1853 (AVPR GA V–A2 523, K 20).
25. *FR* 1; *CORR* I.124; Cwl. to Cln., 10 March 1853 (*CORR* I.157).
26. Analysed below in Ch. 9., the first section.
27. Seym. to Rus., 9–10 Feb. 1852 (PRO 30/22/10; *CORR* I.140).
28. Brw., 'Politique générale', 24 Jan./5 Feb., received 2/14 Feb., 1853 (AVPR K 73).
29. Lane-Poole II: 234; to my knowledge, no one has elucidated precisely how Stratford was reappointed.
30. Rus. to Seym., 9 Feb. 1853, French trans., with Nich. I's glosses (ZP I.99).
31. Seym. to Rus., 21–22 Jan. 1853 (*CORR* I.155–6).
32. Brw. to Nes., 9/21, 13/25 Feb. (AVPR K 73); Howard's published extracts omit Brunnow's talks with Musurus and incorrectly paint Brunnow as not reporting Aberdeen's warnings: 'Brunnow's Reports on Aberdeen', *CHJ* 4 (1932–4): 313–21.
33. Cln. to Str., 25 Feb. 1853 (*CORR* I.146).
34. Nes. to Hélène Chreptowitch, 15/27 Feb. 1853 (*NLP* X).

CHAPTER NINE

Mission Impossible: I – Menshikov vs the Chargés (March 1853)

FATAL INSTRUCTIONS

The Turks had just agreed to call off the Montenegrin expedition and la Valette had barely skipped town when Menshikov arrived on 28 February 1853 at Constantinople on the *Thunderer*, a steam frigate with two eighty-four pounders (huge for those days) and eight lesser cannon. Accompanied by Nesselrode's son and a suite of high officers, he was greeted with fanfare by many of the local Orthodox population, some of whom acted as if a saviour had arrived. In fact, as hinted earlier, he came burdened with an impossible mission, and, as diplomatic rumour currently surmised, 'precise instructions'.[1] On paper these seemed logical enough, but they were totally divorced from political reality.

Menshikov was to demand nullification of any new concessions to the Latins, except the keys, and otherwise full execution of the February 1852 firman, as Russia understood it, with Greek-supervised repair of the cupola. Since the French would not allow a proper execution that would nullify the concession of the keys, Menshikov was to demand a reparation in the form of a formal convention or *sened*, which would enshrine the new status quo. But since France would probably also resist Greek control over the repair of the cupola, Menshikov was to offer a secret, defensive alliance to protect the Sultan's exercise of his 'sovereignty' in favour of his Orthodox subjects. And what could the Turks offer in return for Russian troops? The *sened* that was demanded as reparation for the keys. Circular logic at its best!

The draft *sened* prepared in St Petersburg went far beyond the original quarrel over the Holy Places. Not only did it confirm all former grants to the Greeks concerning the sanctuaries, the peculiar

131

rights of the Greek Patriarch of Jerusalem, and, as an extra, the permission to the Russians to construct a church and a hospice near Jerusalem under the control of their local Consul General. It also extended Russia's treaty rights protecting the Orthodox Churches of Moldavia, Wallachia and Serbia to all of the Ottoman Orthodox, confirmed all the existing privileges, and restored the ancient electoral principle for prelates, including life tenure for the patriarchs, which Byzantine Emperors as well as Turkish Sultans had often disregarded. Given the functioning of the Ottoman *millet* system, these reforms, if taken to their logical conclusion, would have created a Russian-protected network of ecclesiastical bailiwicks for civil matters and limited the application to the Orthodox population of the Tanzimat reforms. Reshid, who had initiated these reforms, could not possibly have envisioned the present set of Russian demands, if indeed he had suggested some amendments to the Treaty of Kuchuk-Kainarji to give Russia legal parity with the French and their 1740 document.

Operationally these instructions led to a rupture or a war in some fashion or other. Menshikov was to snub Fuad as the designated disloyal villain of the affair, next raise the demands concerning the Holy Places, and then find out from Mehmed Ali what modifications might have to be made in the draft *sened*. At the same time, having bribed the Dowager Sultana Validé and her circle who dominated the palace, Menshikov was to inform the Sultan during their first or second interview of Russia's full demands. It is nowhere clear how Menshikov was to coordinate negotiations with the Grand Vizier and the Sultan or prevent leaks. But if the Sultan's ministers vetoed an agreement (could Nesselrode have thought otherwise?) Menshikov was to depart, followed in three days by Ozerov and the rest of the legation, except for the Commercial Secretary, Viktor Balabin.

Curiously, although the Emperor empowered Menshikov to threaten the Turks with the independence of the Danubian Principalities, Nesselrode conceded that it was not so simple as in the past to employ force. A military shock would explode the Ottoman Empire, carry unforeseen political complications and compromise the desired religious solution. Nicholas, on the other hand, seems to have considered the diplomacy of the mission a charade and trusted only in military coercion;[2] he never grasped Leiningen's genuine compromise.

The instructions also outlined the settlement of a set of minor and not-so-minor problems, some of which might well have been left to lower-ranking diplomats to solve over an extended period. Two of these, however, touched upon Ottoman sovereignty, liberal principles and the rights of other Europeans. Menshikov was to demand an end to Turkish sufferance of heterodox Christian propaganda among the Balkan Orthodox Christians and to the progressive Garashanin ministry in Serbia. It seems as well that Menshikov was empowered to try to get the Turks to cede the East Anatolian border lands of Kars and Lazistan, including Batum, if not Trebizond.[3]

Menshikov's portfolio of instructions prepared him mentally and operationally not for negotiations, but for a diktat. The packet included a special historical sketch of the Holy Places dispute, which was supposed to enlighten Menshikov, but reflected entirely Titov's and Ozerov's one-sided dispatches, which had influenced the Tsar's decisions in the first place. The political analysis in the instructions simply assumed that British anti-Bonapartism and the persuasive words of Russian diplomacy in St Petersburg, London and Constantinople would serve to prevent combined Anglo-French opposition.[4]

Taken together, Menshikov's instructions were an elaborated version of the blank cheque explicit in the Tsar's December message via Brunnow to tell the British they must support Russia in Constantinople 'or face a general conflagration in the Orient'. The British could now write of three outcomes on this cheque: 'Turkey becomes a Russian satellite'; 'Turkey is partitioned', or, 'Turkey, aided by France and England, fights Russia.' Menshikov's diplomatic 'dilettantism', to use the expression of a contemporary Russian historian,[5] had little to do with the outcome of his mission. A better diplomat would have had to negotiate mainly with the Tsar to get him to change course. So long as Menshikov followed his instructions, Turkey, France and Britain would have to accept one of these choices, and the first two were wholly unacceptable. Reflective Russian Foreign Ministry officials hoped against hope that he could pull something off before Stratford and the new French ambassador arrived, and before the dichotomy between Russian assurances and reality became manifest.[6] British statesmen did not seek war with Russia in the first part of 1853 and therefore reacted with disbelief to the inner logic of Russian policy as long as possible. Even Palmerston and Stratford did. The entire diplomatic history of the Eastern Question for the next year followed from Menshikov's instructions and the reaction to them. They represented both the completion of Kuchuk-Kainarji and its death knell.

FOOLISH INTIMIDATION

Menshikov immediately tried scare tactics, though his suite of reconnoitring high military and naval officers might have been interpreted by others as show or bluff. Certainly the absence from their posts of Vice-Admiral Kornilov, Commander-in-Chief of the Black Sea squadron, and General Nepokoichitsky, Chief-of-Staff of the Fifth Corps, implied that no attack was imminent. But the appearance of a Russian fleet off the Bosphorus was as little as four days away from a rupture, so the Turks were now negotiating under the gun.[7]

Menshikov's first week was an ostensible success, but in fact a disaster. Two days after he arrived, he broke all diplomatic precedent by appearing at the Porte for his initial visit unexpectedly in civilian dress.[8] Refusing to see Fuad and threatening to close down the mission if he remained in office, Menshikov demanded, as a preliminary to negotiations, the appointment of a new Foreign Minister, 'who had the confidence of the Sultan'.[9] Within two days the Turks acquiesced. Menshikov had Argyropoulos interview Fuad's prospective successor, Rifaat Pasha, a former Foreign Minister and envoy to Vienna, who had ties to the Austrian legation. By 6 March, not without the influence of the Sultana, Rifaat was installed and ready to receive Menshikov the next day. Prince Alexander of Serbia, moreover, had fired Garashanin despite the opposition of the British and French consuls in Belgrade. Not bad for a first week of activity, except for the reactions of the French, the British, the Turks, and even the Serbs to Russian diplomatic tactics.[10]

The new French chargé, Vincent Benedetti, was ready under any circumstances to invoke France's standard claims and the 1841 Treaty against Russia. So was Rose, who assumed that Russian demands precluded any genuine settlement and told London that to invalidate the 1740 Franco-Turkish treaty would undercut the capitulations that constituted the legal basis of English influence in the Ottoman Empire. They were both ready to hold Menshikov to Russian assurances of peaceful intentions. If he and Ozerov could claim that London had promised to support Russian demands, Rose could counter that he needed to know what they were in order to help.[11] Thus all of Nesselrode's and Brunnow's laborious attempts to obtain Anglo-Russian cooperation in Constantinople simply served as a pretext for Rose to hound Menshikov, rather than for the Russian to hoodwink the British.

The Turks were not sleeping either. They knew how to turn

Russian assurances and the fiction of the alliance between the Sultan and the Tsar into ammunition to fire at Menshikov. The Porte prepared for him a splendid reception, attended by the native Greek élite, who had a stake in peace and would just as soon make their own deal with the French over the cupola. If Menshikov really came to settle the Holy Places dispute, the crisis could end, and Russian bribe money would make everybody happy.[12] Russia would achieve a resounding symbolic victory without offending the French; Ottoman ceremony would flatter Russia's self-esteem; they would concoct an acceptable status quo; and the Turks could continue to sandbag the *Tanzimat*. But if he had some tricks up his sleeve, such as the expected humiliation of the Sultan's foreign minister, then the Ottomans would seize the moral high ground, and the myth that Russia protected the Ottoman Orthodox would be exposed as a cynical bid for influence. There was only one danger: the Russians might launch an attack, and the British and French, for some reason or other (such as a strong adverse current in either the Turkish Straits or the London newspapers) might just sit back or join in the kill.

In the event, Menshikov's treatment of Fuad set off a flurry of activity in Constantinople and firmed up a *de facto* Anglo-French *entente* which Russian diplomacy had worked so hard to prevent. Thanks to the money and connections of some of the rich Ottoman Greeks, Rose and Benedetti were aware of the gist and implications of Menshikov's instructions. The two chargés immediately consulted and agreed that Menshikov's initial demand could lead to a new Unkiar-Skelessi and hence the abrogation of the 1841 Treaty, and on this basis urged the Porte to keep Fuad in office. Russell's belated, confidential instructions of 19 February to Rose to stay neutral if Menshikov sought Fuad's dismissal thus remained without any effect. The day after the snub of Fuad, Rose and Benedetti immediately sought out Menshikov, but he avoided them. Rose was especially persistent with his 'assault', to use Menshikov's term, in order to ascertain his instructions. At any rate Rose saw Ozerov no less than four times and told him that London's directives to help Russia to obtain an acceptable accord with the French were no secret. Therefore Menshikov should either be candid now or wait until Stratford returned.[13]

Benedetti and Rose did not limit themselves to containing Menshikov diplomatically. Rose especially was either a good actor or else he shared Turkish fears of a surprise attack. So Mehmed Ali, Mehmed-Rüshdi – the Seraskier or Minister of Defence, Benedetti, Rose and Captain Adolphus Slade – a Englishman serving in the Turkish navy, consulted about defensive measures, not so secretly as it turned out. The Turks were ready to dispatch Omer's army to Shumla, the central fortress in Eastern Bulgaria, and redeploy the Adriatic squadron near the Bosphorus. Slade and Borelace, another English captain, started to train Turkish gunners for defence of the capital. Menshikov dismissed these preparations as a lot of 'bravado', but still reported them.[14]

Mehmed Ali also asked the two chargés for concrete aid in the form of their Mediterranean naval squadrons. Rose, who seemed to Benedetti most eager to call up the fleets, officially replied that he could only refer the request to London. The Grand Vizier in turn officially insisted and used the old blackmail tactic of the weak: the Porte might be compelled to submit to Russian demands. Rose officially compromised. Admiral Dundas was due to leave Malta with the British squadron on 20 March and cruise first in the lower Adriatic and then come to Vourla. On the 8th Rose requested by fast steamer that the Admiral leave a week earlier and come immediately to his second destination, which was slightly closer than Sevastopol or Odessa to Constantinople in terms of distance, but effectively downstream. The civilian Benedetti let 'Colonel' Rose take the lead in these matters and simply sent word of the latter's request on to Paris.

Rose's action had far reaching consequences. In the short run, his request for the squadron, if immediately executed, would have limited Menshikov to less than two weeks to do something spectacular: force a rupture followed by a descent on the Bosphorus, or launch a totally secret attack. Dundas, however, followed his instructions and referred to London for orders. By heeding Rose, the British might have shattered the Tsar's illusions before he committed what could be seen as an act of war. The Russians, however, were not about to attack, and the British were not about to show pre-emptive resolve, so Rose's request was superfluous, except in one major respect. It provided the new Napoleon with an opportunity to call the question.

NAPOLEON'S REACTION – ROSE'S SWEET VICTORY

March may have come in like a lion in Constantinople, but European diplomacy was rather calm. There were post-mortems of the Leiningen mission and pre-game analyses of Menshikov's. The latter, of course, might prove tricky, but the new French ambassador would defend French interests, and Stratford would soon see that no harm came to Britain or Europe. Not Russia's mobilization, but the refugee question and Austria's diplomatic offensive against British policy, dominated the scene in London. The Home Secretary Palmerston, with the support of much of public opinion, was indulgent towards revolutionary exiles, while Aberdeen sympathized with the Continental conservatives and wished to meet them more than half way.[15] On the Continent, the impending exchange of high-level envoys between St Petersburg and Brussels was another capital event. King Leopold already got on well with every major monarch except for Napoleon, while the latter felt the projected modernization of the Antwerp fortifications looked like an invitation to foreign intervention in France.[16] The Bonapartists thus had concrete reasons to make the most in London of Russia's mobilization and Menshikov's scare tactics.

The first news of Menshikov's doings and Rose's summons to Dundas reached Paris on 16 March, and the French were ready. Drouyn wired Walewski and the next day sent him a sombre dispatch arguing that Menshikov was undoubtedly authorized to summon the Russian fleet and asking for some Anglo-French response in kind. The British temporized, waiting to learn what Dundas had done, but agreeing with Drouyn that Rose had called for the fleet in order to preserve the integrity of the Ottoman Empire, as per the 1841 Treaty. Official news via Dundas reached the new Foreign Secretary Lord Clarendon only on the 19th. By then, however, the French had already made up their minds. On the 18th or possibly the 19th Napoleon and some of his ministers and advisors decided that Rose's move was too good to be true and that they would force Britain's hand by dispatching their Mediterranean squadron from Toulon to Salamis near Athens. To pre-empt British objections, the French prepared an official announcement of the move for the *Le Moniteur* without consulting either Cowley or Clarendon.[17]

The events in London were equally dramatic. On the evening of the 18th Clarendon and Brunnow squared off at Buckingham Palace. Leaving his options open, Clarendon said to Brunnow: 'I hope that our fleet has not moved, but you should understand as well that such circumstances could arise, when the Porte would have to request our support.' Brunnow bluffed, but gave away the Russian game: 'The question will not be decided at sea. Ten battleships cannot save the Ottoman Empire from the consequences of its blindness, if it chooses to march to its perdition.' The next day he tried this line on Aberdeen too, who outwardly concurred, but also backed Graham's notion that the Malta squadron had to be beefed up to match the size of the French flotilla in order to keep an eye on it.[18]

Graham requested a meeting of the 'inner Cabinet' for 20 March at the Admiralty, and Clarendon demanded that Palmerston join the other four leading ministers. Russell for his part had an ambitious, ready answer for his more cautious colleagues in order to buy time for a showdown later. Let the Russians dare advance into Ottoman territory, even to Constantinople, and then not evacuate when so summoned, and they will have a war at the Dardanelles and the Baltic against Britain and France. The five ministers decided, however, not to dispatch the Malta squadron or threaten Russia with words, but officially to trust Nesselrode's assurances, hide behind Brunnow's argument about the ten battleships, and dissuade the French from escalating the strategic confrontation.[19]

This approach squared with London's outlook and present policy. The French were naughty children for initiating the scrape; Russia deserved a concession in Jerusalem; Stratford should be given a chance to guide everyone to a settlement; if the Russians really threatened Turkey, then the English, not the French, should lead; and, finally, mere chargés d'affaires do *not* call up fleets and decide matters of war and peace. On the other hand, the British did not repudiate Rose, but justified his request and the French response with reference to Menshikov's actions and to the Russian failure to be as candid with the French as with the British.

The French sensed Britain's inaction and disapproval from the start, so they peppered the pot by having Count Butenval, their representative in Brussels, declare that if Russian or Austro-Russian aggression toward Turkey led to war, the French would be freed from their treaty obligations too. Some analysts interpreted this move as a way to extort British support in the East, by showing how dangerous the French could be in the West.[20] In fact this was, under the conditions of Russian and Austrian mobilization, the logical extension and update of France's standing threat to treat the flouting of the 1740 Treaty as the signal to violate the 1815 settlement. The Anglo-French interpretation of the 1841 Treaty was Paris's hook.

The French may not have realized it, but they actually gave the Russians a splendid opportunity, which they did not seize, to back down with honour. Leopold immediately urged the Tsar, as 'Europe's arbiter', to exercise moderation in the East. Then on 25 March, Walewski showed France's hand by offering to renounce any designs on Belgian territory in return for an Anglo-French alliance. The British, though, played at reactivating their preventive *entente* with

Russia. The Tsar, however, did not believe that the British would 'be deceived [into allying with Napoleon] by such stupidity', and indeed they were not. The French instead apologized to London for unilaterally sending the squadron, which, however, could not be recalled without injury to their Emperor's prestige. They also quickly made it clear that they had been misunderstood concerning Belgium. On the diplomatic field of combat following Butenval's loose talk, not France, but England had prevailed.[21]

Diplomacy, of course, was not the only thing that counted – public opinion did too, and here Brunnow had to report that the British press was criticizing the government for not sending Dundas to join the French, and that patience might run out. Back in St Petersburg, meanwhile, Nesselrode needed only Menshikov's first reports about Rose's game with Ozerov, Mehmed Ali and Dundas to work out what was going on in Constantinople. Expressing his disbelief at the English envoy's being so 'French' and mixing German and French, Nesselrode exclaimed to Brunnow on 19 March: 'this Rose is a crude Englishman, who wishes to play a political role, for which Heaven did not create him'.[22]

The Russian Chancellor was wrong in both the long and the short run. 'Heaven' had prescribed for Rose a splendid future in the service of British imperialism, first in the Crimea, then India and finally Ireland. His work as chargé was his springboard, and his greatest aide was Menshikov. The two of them, in one week of March, overthrew a Turkish foreign minister, summoned the French fleet, brought Palmerston back into the thick of British foreign policy formation, and induced Russell to outline Britain's strategy for a two-front Anglo-French naval war against Russia.

Menshikov and Rose also stimulated Brunnow to develop a new political–legal concept to deny Turkey's sovereignty and pave the way for partition. He announced to the British that the Anglo-French fleets in Turkish waters, as in 1849, would both stiffen the Tsar's position and be the equivalent of a terrestrial occupation of Turkish provinces and hence of treating the Sultan like one of the Indian princes, whom Britain protects. Without revealing the meat of Menshikov's instructions, Brunnow also outlined Britain's three choices: Russia's clientization of Turkey, partition, or war. Small wonder that the periodically astute Queen Victoria wrote to Aberdeen on the 23rd: 'Everything appears to her [the queen] to depend upon the real nature of the demands made by Russia.' She was right, since they did, in English eyes, 'justify the reproach of . . . hostile ambition', despite her hopes.[23] So the real winners in March were the Roses, the Palmerstons and the Bonapartists, who started to operationalize the incipient Anglo-French alliance.

The stodgy political establishments pretended that the colonel-chargé had overstepped his bounds, that the fleets were unnecessary, as it so appeared for a while, and that the Tsar was a 'gentleman', but they did not neglect to arm themselves. The issue of when and where Dundas would sail remained a bone of contention in April among Brunnow, Walewski, Aberdeen and Graham. But when Menshikov finally laid his cards on the table in May, the British were ready with the Malta squadron, and Rose, whom the more politic Stratford despised, was back in London briefing Clarendon on the Turkish military.[24]

MENSHIKOV'S SOUND ADVICE

May was still almost two months away when Rifaat replaced Fuad and Menshikov could get down to business. He operated on three planes. Hoping, perhaps, that bribe money could produce an answer from the Sultan before the regular steamer left for Odessa on 16 March, Menshikov worked in vain on the palace to achieve the alliance and/or the convention. At the same time he went through normal channels, followed his formal instructions, and negotiated with Rifaat. He also continued reconnoitring, dispatching Kornilov and Nepokoichitsky on the 11th to inspect the Dardanelles and to visit Smyrna and Greece.[25] Nevertheless, the Turks became calmer, and Mehmed Ali told Rose on the 15th that the squadron was now not needed.

Benedetti and Rose had done their homework prior to Menshikov's negotations. Rose concluded that the original compromise of early 1852 was now unworkable. The Russians insisted on a clear decision from the Porte on the cupola, but for the French to allow this would be like having the 'squadron under sail with the broken treaty of 1740 on her mainmast-head, and Porte's unexecuted Notes of February and September on her fore and mizen masts'.[26] The best hope was a vague agreement with mental reservations on both sides.

Benedetti decided to get to the heart of the matter. On the 14th he asked Menshikov for a preliminary *entente*, but the latter could envision this only as a delaying tactic and had other plans. He would see Rifaat concerning the Holy Places, give him a few days to think it over, and then 'decide how to use more or less energetically' other means at Russia's disposal. On the 16th they had their first working session. Menshikov offered bribes, but submitted a haughty *note verbale* outlining a settlement for the Holy Places and demanding a 'sure and inviolable guarantee . . . which cannot be restricted to sterile and incomplete assurances that could be invalidated in the future'.[27] In other words, there was money to throw around, but no room for those vague formulas that often terminate sticky quarrels; and the threat of rupture or worse lurked in the background.

It was the early days of March all over again. As usual, someone leaked the essentials, but the Turks would not reveal the contents of the *note verbale* to the chargés. Benedetti thereupon thought the worst, and so exacted the standard Turkish promise from Rifaat not to make any engagement with Menshikov without first clearing it with the French legation. Rose 'pestered' Menshikov again, tried to 'interfere' with his mission, and once more started to sound the military alarm about a quick Russian seizure of the Dardanelles. And Rifaat, aware of the elasticity of the demand for the guarantee, came clean to Argyropoulos on the 19th: 'You know us well enough to know correctly what we can accept and what we cannot.'[28]

Knowing is one thing, doing is another. Menshikov had already concluded that it would be difficult to procure the *sened*, but he calculated that the Turks could not resist serious threats. He also had two unrealistic tricks up his sleeve. One was to concede a few more Holy Places in return for the *sened*, as if the French would double-cross both the Turks and the British over the keys and the cupola and ally with Russia. The other scheme was to engineer Reshid's return to office in order to have 'an Aberdeen in Turkey' as well as in Britain, as if the one could sign away Turkey's sovereignty over most of its Christians and keep his head, and the other could let this happen and remain Prime Minister of the world's premier power.[29]

Not to be daunted, Menshikov followed his design and proceeded to see Rifaat on the 22nd. First came detailed discussions concerning the Holy Places, where Rifaat upheld the 1740 Treaty and French concerns over the cupola. At the end Menshikov showed him the draft *sened* (convention) prepared in January by St Petersburg and stated that it represented 'no new privilege', but that without such a 'solid and durable basis', there could be no Russo-Turkish relations. Together the *note verbale* of the 16th and the draft *sened* constituted an open-ended ultimatum without an expiration date. Rifaat knew that such a demand might be coming, but may have been genuinely shocked that the Russians had the audacity to make this move in such an essentially take-it-or-leave-it fashion. At any rate he was sombre and speechless, and this had an effect on Menshikov and led to some serious parleys.[30]

The Turkish Cabinet authorized Rifaat to commence simultaneous negotiations with Benedetti and the Russians over the detailed draft, which the Russian legation had prepared to regulate the Holy Places. On 31 March Menshikov, Ozerov, Argyropoulos, Aristarchi, Rifaat and Arif Effendi – a mufti, an expert on the Christian sanctuaries and a member of the Turkish Council – met for five to seven hours and hammered out an Eight-Point draft. Once more Menshikov also asked for a convention and an alliance. To test French and British resolve, Rifaat resorted to the detested Turkish tactic of hinting acceptance of the other side's demands, even while assuring the chargés again that the Porte would not make an agreement with Russia without first checking with their legations.[31]

Benedetti immediately protested against four points that seemed to invalidate the 1740 Treaty: denial of Latin ownership of Nativity; failure to restore the pre-1808 status quo at the Holy Sepulchre; implied Greek precedence at the Virgin's Tomb; and the guarantee that would preclude future Catholic claims. Rose did not openly interfere, but fed useful information to the French. The advertised forthcoming arrival of the Toulon squadron – on 2 April – further undercut the already weak position of the pro-Russian Turks.[32]

Meanwhile, Kornilov and Nepokoichitsky had returned from their cruise, consulted with Menshikov, and concluded by the 24th that with eighteen Anglo-French–Turkish battleships in the vicinity to bolster Turkish defences, a *coup de main* by sea was impossible. They decided that the Tsar should direct his attention to Varna and Burgas on the Bulgarian coast and maybe use them as a decoy while attacking the capital. Menshikov, moreover, who earlier argued that a surprise attack would require a launch from a normal cruising pattern, soon lampooned Russia's open preparations and practising with assault ladders, which were the talk of the town. At home, meanwhile, Paskevich urged just an invasion of the Principalities and warned that Russia could not fight a Turkish war and a European war at the same time.[33] The Turks and their British supporters, however, still took Russia's preparations very seriously and even exaggerated the danger of the Burgas option. Raising as well the ephemeral spectre of Austria's joining Russia, Rose implored his superiors to send a squadron to Besika Bay to 'protect the keys . . .of the East'.[34]

Menshikov figured by now that without serious modifications of his demands he would have to force a rupture, as if this would result in the sought-after plenary talks and the guarantee. He thought, or was so led to believe by clever Turkish negotiators, that the main Ottoman objection was to the *form* of the convention/*sened* or treaty, not to its *content*, and he asked St Petersburg's permission to substitute a diplomatic note. He was also worried. On the day Stratford took over for Rose, Menshikov warned Nesselrode in a private letter, which was for the Tsar's eyes too, that the pressure necessary to obtain the guarantee might provoke the formation of a Turkish–Western alliance.[35]

Menshikov's most serious advice, though, went further than Paskevich's in the direction of common sense. Regarding the sequel to the rupture, which had to result from the demands as they stood, Menshikov suggested that Russia should seize not the Danubian Principalities but rather East Anatolian Kars or Bayazid or Batum on the Turkish Black Sea Littoral. Such a move would not threaten the interests of other Continental European powers or provoke the Turks to declare war.[36] The 'General-Admiral', who found, when he negotiated with an Ottoman minister, that 'there was only a mask, behind which one could perceive the end of a big mustache [Rose] and a fine nose [Benedetti]',[37] had come to a logical strategic conclusion. He was also admitting that even with two army corps and a naval squadron activated and with the maritime powers represented in Constantinople only by chargés d'affaires, an extraordinary ambassador of the Emperor of All the Russias could not cow the Turks. And, like most good advice that runs against the flow of current operations, it was barely acknowledged.[38] Menshikov himself continued to act as if he never warned against bullying the Turks.

NOTES

1. Travers to vH., 26 Feb., 3 March 1853 (NRA 2.05.01 BZ 2769 Const.); Nesselrode's various instructions and memos, dated 20–28 Jan./1–9 Feb. 1853, are published in ZP I.104–11.
2. *DM* 28 Jan/9 Feb. 1853 (oral instructions from the Emperor).
3. Nes. to Mnsh., 20 Jan./1 Feb. 1853 (AVPR GA V–A2 523:40–53, not in ZP I); also Arg. to Oz., 24 Aug./5 Sept. 1853 (AVPR K 20); cf. Rose to Cln., 6 March 1853 (*CORR* I.169); Dmitry Nesselrode to Longinov, 10/22 May 1853 (*NLP* X). The lesser issues concerned a disagreement concerning two villages on the Russo-Turkish frontier in Transcaucasia, the specifics of the contribution of non-native Orthodox Church properties to the state budgets of Moldavia and Wallachia, and

the establishment of a joint venture – a Russo–Turkish ferry service across the Bosphorus.

4. *PHQSL*; cf. Nes. to Mnsh., pr., 3/15, 13/25 Jan., 28 Jan./9 Feb. 1853 (TsGAVMF 10/3/204, TsGADA XI/1228, ZP I.109).

5. V. N. Vinogradov, 'The Responsibility of Nicholas I for the Crimean War', *The Traditions of Imperial Russian Foreign Policy* (ed. Hugh Ragsdale, forthcoming).

6. Longinov to Dmitry Nesselrode, 19/31 March 1853 (*NLP* X).

7. My basic sources for the Menshikov mission are first: Menshikov's official and private correspondence and diary, and the reports of Ozerov, Argyropoulos, and Aristarchi in AVPR, TsGADA, and TsGAVMF: second the correspondence of the French and English legations, with Stratford's private letters; third, dispatches of the Austrian, Belgian, Dutch and Swedish missions.

8. *DM* 18 Feb./2 March 1853: 'en frac': cf. Benedetti to Drn., Travers to vH., 4–5 March 1853 (AMAE CP Turq. 311; NRA 2.05.01 BZ 2769 Const.).

9. Travers to vH., 10 March 1853 (NRA 2.05.01 BZ 2769 Const.).

10. Also MacKenzie, *Ilija Garašanin*, pp. 129–35.

11. Rose to Rus., Benedetti to Drn., 6, 14 March 1853 (*CORR* I.170; AMAE CP Turquie 312).

12. Oz. to Sen., 5/17 March 1853 (AVPR GA V–A2 523); Aristarchi's 'current account' received 1,200 'half-imperials'.

13. *DM* 19 Feb./3 March 1853; Mnsh. to Nes. 25 Feb./9 March 1853 (AVPR K 19).

14. Mnsh. to Nes. 25 Feb./9 March 1953 (AVPR K 19/HHSA PA X 38); Rose to Rus., 8 March 1853 (PRO FO 78/390.78, not in *CORR*).

15. Leopold I to Ab., 2 March 1853 (*AbC* X); Wal.–Drn. correspondence, 4–11 March 1853 (AMAE CP Angl. 688); cf. Schroeder *AGBCW*: 36–7.

16. Leopold I to QV 25 Feb. 1853 (ARB VI I: 64251–55); de Jonghe–Bkr. correspondence, 24 Feb.–13 Apr. 1853 (AMAE Blg. Russ. I); cf. Thomas: 120–1.

17. Besides the regular Drouyn–Walewski and Clarendon–Cowley correspondence, Clarendon's private letters to Cowley (ClDp. c. 125); there is no reason to accept Fialin Persigny's self-serving account, that he alone convinced Napoleon, over Drouyn's caution, to send the squadron at a council meeting on 19 March, though this is normal in historiography: Bapst: 352–4; Wetzel: 73–4.

18. Brw. to Ab., Nes., 7/19, 11/23 March 1853 (*AbC* X, AVPR K 73).

19. Wal. to Drn., 19 March 1853 (AMAE CP Angl. 689); Cln. to Ab., Rus. to Cl., 20 March 1853 (AdMss 43188, Walpole II: 181); cf. Lambert *CW*: 17–8., Herbert C. F. Bell, *Lord Palmerston* (2 vols, London 1888) II: 85.

20. Puryear *ERSQ*: 242–9.

21. Bohl: 62–3; Brw. to Nes. with Nich. I gloss, 19/31 March 1853 (AVPR K 73); Howard (Brussels) to Cln., Apr. 1853 (PRO FO 10/173).

22. Brw. to Nes., with Nich. I 'NB', 19/31 March 1853; Nes to Brw., pr., 14/26 March 1853 (TsGADA III/115): '. . . dass der Rose ein

ungeschlachter Engländer ist, qui veut jouer un rôle politique pour lequel le Ciel ne l'a pas créé.'

23. *LQV* II.
24. *Inter alia*, Cln. to Str., 5 April 1853 (PRO 352/36/1).
25. *DM* 27 Feb./11 March 1853.
26. *CORR* I.200 (Rose to Rus., 10 March 1853).
27. *DM* 2/14 March 1853; Mnsh. to Rifaat, Nes., 4–5/16–17 March 1853; with Note Verbale (ZP I.113, AVPR, K 19).
28. Benedetti to Drn. 24 March 1853 (AMAE CP Turq. 311); *DM*, 4–6/16–18 March 1853; Rose to Cln., 21 March 1853 (*CORR* I.223); Arg. to Mnsh., 7/19 March 1853 (TsGADA XI/1234).
29. Mnsh. to Nes., pr., 7/19 March 1853 (TsGADA III/124).
30. Mnsh. to Nes., Rifaat, 10/22 March 1853 (AVPR K 19), partially also ZP I.115.
31. The reports of Menshikov, Benedetti and Rose's informants do not quite square with each other; also Saab's assertion that the Turks negotiated jointly with the French and Russians throughout April is not evident in their dispatches: *OCA*: 35.
32. Benedetti to Drn., 31 March, 5 April 1853 (AMAE CP Turq. 312).
33. Nepokoichitsky to Mnsh., 'March' 1853; Mnsh. memo, 12/24 March 1853 (TsGAVMF 19/2/72); Kornilov to Const., 19/31 March 1853, Nich. I, Psk., memos 22–23, 24 March/3–4, 5 Apr. 1853 (ZP I.210, 214–16).
34. Rose to Cln., 31 March, 11 April 1853 (*CORR* I.231, 261).
35. Mnsh. to Nes., reg. and pr., 24 March/5 April (AVPR K 19; TsGADA III/124).
36. Mnsh. to Nes., pr., 14/26 March 1853 (TsGADA III/124).
37. BlC. to Bkr., 25 March 1853 (AMAE Blg. Turq. V).
38. *DM* 22 May/3 June 1853.

CHAPTER TEN

Mission Impossible: II – Menshikov vs the Great Ambassador (April–May 1853)

THE 'REAL JOCKEY' TAKES CHARGE

Viscount Stratford (Canning) de Redcliffe arrived in Constantinople on 5 April and was given a regal welcome by the Turks, whose turn it was to act as if a saviour had arrived. More importantly, he came with his own political instructions to engineer a settlement, as well as to save Turkey by reforming her in the interest of the British Empire. In this he appeared to be different from Rose, who had shown a penchant for a French alliance against Russia and for negotiating with a friendly squadron or two only a day away by fast steamer. Stratford took the high moral ground, arguing that France, Austria and Russia should renounce their coercive diplomacy that had caused the crisis in the first place. Geography had allowed him to visit Paris and Vienna en route, where he had seen the two emperors, as well as Drouyn and Buol, and obtained commitments from them to support a peaceful resolution and the integrity of the Ottoman realm. Russia was the big question, since words and actions were not exactly squaring with each other, but Stratford displayed confidence in the Tsar's promises and Nesselrode's counsels.[1]

The new French ambassador, Edmond de la Cour, arrived the next day armed with instructions of a different nature. His bottom line was the Note of 8 February 1852, which could be reconciled with the 'February' firman, if Menshikov so desired. La Cour was to refer to Paris all new Turkish concessions to the Greeks, even if the cupola were involved or the Russians pushed the Turks to break previous engagements. In other words, la Valette had been bluffing, and France would not start a war with Turkey over the sanctuaries.

The meat of la Cour's instructions, however, concerned the deployment of the fleet after Menshikov's mission failed and Russia made a military move – which the French had to predict was likely to happen in order to justify their response to Rose's summons. Political Director Edouard Thouvenel, the author of these instructions, foresaw three possible Russian moves: (1) just the occupation of the Principalities; (2) the occupation plus a fleet against the Turks; (3) the use of that fleet to force the Bosphorus. In the first instance la Cour was to offer the French squadron to the Turks; if the Turks did not want it inside the Dardanelles, it should be close enough to deter an attack on Varna or Burgas. In the second instance, he was to obtain, with or without British help, permission to pass the Dardanelles. In the third instance, he was to pass the Dardanelles, secure the castles or fortresses there, and offer the remainder of his forces to the Turks. If the expected British help materialized, they each could defend a side of the Straits.[2]

The lack of a squadron actually was an asset for Stratford. La Cour was starting with the Menshikov-Benedetti impasse over the Holy Places, and both sides were armed and within striking distance of the Straits. The key for Stratford was not to associate with the French, as Rose had in March, but to pose as the true conciliator and cooperate with the Austrians and Prussians. La Cour and Menshikov could then fight it out over Bethlehem and Jerusalem, and the Russians and the Turks could battle over the guarantee. Stratford, meanwhile, could advise the Turks behind the scenes, force reform upon their empire and quietly send back military intelligence to boot.

The seasoned Englishman wasted little time. Within three days he had told first Menshikov that the 'status quo' included promises made to the French and then la Cour that he should concede as much as possible to Menshikov. Stratford also urged the Turks to give way to the Russians where feasible, while holding firm on matters of sovereignty and proceeding with the reforms. Mehmed Ali then tried the old idea of sending an extraordinary ambassador to St Petersburg, this time with a humble letter, but Menshikov rejected this compromise on the grounds that Russia already had an ambassador in Constantinople. Actually from the start Stratford had Menshikov cornered even more than Rose did, since the Turks now leaked everything to the British mission. Stratford would then level with at least Ozerov, so the Russians had to allow some unofficial mediation. It is no wonder that Clarendon, who complained of Rose's 'anti-Russian varnish', but had a similar inclination, reacted to Stratford's first dispatches with joy: 'We have a real jockey on our horse instead of a stable boy, and the odds are highest against the Czar.'[3]

Menshikov for his part soon wrote home that he envisioned a satisfactory solution to the issues of the Holy Places and the Russian church and hospice in Jerusalem. The Turks would resist the *sened* or convention, but the guarantee could be obtained by an exchange of notes with assurances. Even so, he would need to invoke Russia's military preparations and provoke a crisis, if Imperial legation were to regain its former influence. He went so far as to propose precise words to use in his final note in case of a rupture.[4]

All the same, for the next two weeks both Menshikov and la Cour talked with either each other, Rifaat, Mehmed Ali, or Stratford concerning the Holy Places at least every other day, and their subordinates were also busy. La Cour tried to avoid concessions, but the Turks held him off by demanding a firm military commitment. Then on 22 April at a three-power meeting concerning the Greco–Turkish frontier, Stratford took la Cour and Menshikov by the arms and got both to compromise over the cupola.[5] Thirteen more days were needed for the Porte and the diplomats to settle on a revised draft of the original firman of 'February' 1852 and a new one for the hitherto missing Holy Sepulchre.[6]

This near-solution to the Holy Places conflict only now made its entrance through the Great Door. La Cour accepted the posting of an Ottoman Greek porter at the Church of the Nativity who could not impede Latin passage, and there was no talk of ownership. The Greek Patriarch could not regulate Latin use of the Tomb of the Virgin, but the Latins had to accept only a ninety-minute daily service following the Greeks and Armenians and without special compensation. The Turks would reconstruct the cupola, and the Greek Patriarch of Jerusalem could make observations, but the Turks were not mandated to listen and the Latin Patriarch was not silenced. The vague compromise that Stratford had promoted for sixteen months had finally been enacted. Even here, Menshikov accepted only *ad referendum*, while la Cour made a few verbal observations. The Porte forlornly asked that these arrangements might serve as Russia's guarantee.[7]

THE 'PIG' WITHOUT A 'STRING'

The entrance to a greater door, however, was barred. Menshikov and Rifaat could not compromise over that guarantee. They toyed with a rupture over the draft *sened*, which the Turkish Council rejected on the 14 April. Both sides then retreated, but the draft remained formally on the table.[8] Menshikov's long-distance communications from St Petersburg turned out to be crucial. Nesselrode's further instructions and optimistic political commentary reflecting London's initial sweet talk started to arrive in late March. There were two basic messages: compromise with the French over the Holy Places, but first and foremost push vigorously for the guarantee. A third message came in mid-April and revealed only slightly more sober deliberations over British concerns and the dispatch of the French squadron. Now the Turkish alliance was no longer necessary, but some strengthening of Kuchuk-Kainarji still was. Stratford, in contact with both la Cour and the former Grand Vizier, Reshid, over the question of Ottoman reform, tried to talk Menshikov out of the *sened* altogether. The latter, however, was planning to make his concessions later. So he went ahead and on the 19th submitted another *note verbale*, restating the original demands of 16 March with the implicit threat to break relations if the Turks did not agree to the draft *sened*.[9]

The Turks by now were very fearful of a rupture. Their fleet of nine ships with 648 cannon was at the Golden Horn, and the Chief of the Arsenal, Naimik Pasha, even considered arming the entire Muslim population. They also continued their delaying tactics, while Rifaat tried to work something out with the two most important Greeks on the scene, Argyropoulos representing the Russian legation, and Aristarchi the Patriarchate. Rifaat had also been sounding out Austria's views of the draft *sened* and had some luck. By early May Buol too was worried about Russia's ulterior demands and about the difficulty of reconciling Nesselrode's assurances with Klezl's reports.[10] The Porte's good sense in compromising with Leiningen in February was obvious.

Menshikov, though, had come to the conclusion that Stratford and only Stratford was blocking the *sened*. However, precisely because the Russian legation did not take into consideration the foundations of British foreign policy, Menshikov believed that Stratford's animosity toward French and Catholic policies and his polite acceptance of Russia's assurances were signs that there would be no Anglo-French alliance. Curiously, Stratford did not yet believe that the Russians would be so foolish as to throw away what influence they still had in Constantinople by insisting upon the *sened*.[11]

He was mistaken. Back in St Petersburg, the Tsar was shaken but not moved by the sombre news from London about the responses to Rose's call for the fleet. 'Everything is uncertain and we must be ready for everything', Nicholas wrote on 5 April.[12] But his reaction on the

18th to the word of Turkish opposition to the draft *sened* and the advice about the Asian province was to adhere to his original scheme. He had no operational military plans yet. Still he did not even await the initial reports of Stratford's attitudes, but ordered Menshikov to commence the three-day ultimatum operation immediately, if the Turks had not yet agreed to the draft. When the plan for engineering the rupture arrived on the 18th by express courier, Nicholas treated it as already approved, and hardly bothered with the fine print. Menshikov asked about substituting a diplomatic *note* for the convention (*sened*), and Nicholas jotted: '*treaty* or *convention* are all the same to me'. The crucial matter was to restore Russian influence at the Porte, by whatever means it took – this, despite a polite word from Berlin indicating that Prussia, as well as Britain, did not want Menshikov to push things too far. [13]

Nesselrode, for his part, agreed with Menshikov on one crucial item and assumed from Ozerov's initial impressions that Stratford was dictating policy to the Ottoman ministers. If the Turks continued to procrastinate, then Stratford was preventing the Russians from re-establishing their influence via negotiation. Hence, Stratford alone (rather then Menshikov acting on instructions which Nesselrode helped compose) 'held war and peace in his hands'. [14] This argument could serve to throw the blame for Russian policy failures on the British ambassador, but actually revealed once more the blank cheque given to England to start a coalition war against Russia. Nesselrode's most bizarre logic was his mystification and cult of the Emperor in a dispatch that the latter approved. If others saw 'political aims', a 'new protectorate' and a 'new political transaction' in Russia's demands, that was because 'the true thinking of the Emperor . . . is of a higher order than one can comprehend in Constantinople and, perhaps, elsewhere . . . [since] His Majesty . . . obeys his conscience'. [15] This was the true believer, with his self-imposed mental black-out, heading for a showdown.

When these dispatches arrived in Constantinople toward the beginning of May, the diplomatic community, including the minor legations, were already awaiting Menshikov's next move and expecting some form of ultimatum. Menshikov by now seems to have lost interest in the course of normal diplomacy and was just awaiting the Porte's official firmans and notes regarding the Holy Places, before he moved on to the next phase of his mission. His only real hope was that court politics still might work, since now 'all of Europe', that is, the other important legations, opposed the *sened*. He was ready to try the note format next, but he also wrote to Brunnow to prepare Britain for the approaching Russo–Turkish rupture.[16]

Stratford himself wished that he could somehow bring Russia to compromise on the basis of the 1841 Treaty, but could not find a handle. On 5 May, the day the Porte issued the awaited firmans and notes, he bared his inner thoughts to Clarendon: 'The Turk is very much like a pig on a string. You may get him to market at last, but his bolts and zigzags by the way are sadly puzzling. The Russian has also a spit of this pig, but where is the string by which to guide him?'[17]

There was none. Nesselrode tried to be optimistic when Menshikov's reports of the Holy Places deal and his intentions to issue the ultimatum arrived. The Tsar, though, was characteristically fatalistic, as if the course of events were completely out of his control: 'Let us hope so, but not be too quick to believe in success; with this Redcliffe, there is everything to fear.'[18]

THE FIRST ULTIMATUM

On 5 May Menshikov responded to the settlement of the Holy Places dispute by submitting an ultimatum, threatening a rupture on 10 May, if the Turks did not sign a revised *sened*, prepared by Ozerov, as a guarantee for the future. The new draft contained two concessions, one retraction of them and one new requirement. These were: (1) no mention of Kuchuk–Kainarji; (2) no mention of the patriarchs' life tenure; but (3) a new Article I affirming the strict status quo of the 'rights, privileges and immunities, that the churches, pious institutions, and Orthodox clergies possess *ad antiquo*'; and (4) a new Article II granting automatically to the Ottoman Orthodox 'cult' any 'rights and advantages conceded by the Ottoman government in the past or in the future to other Christian cults by means of treaties, conventions, or particular dispositions'.[19] The legal tricks in Article I were two-fold, as Menshikov explained to Nesselrode but concealed from Klezl. One was to use the language of the Austrian treaties with Turkey concerning the Ottoman Catholics. The other was to introduce the words "status quo of the clergy", since its practical application "would be extendable to the entire ecclesiastical hierarchy". Article II, moreover, could be interpreted as giving the Ottoman Orthodox Church under Russian protection the same rights that native and foreign Catholics enjoyed under French and Austrian protection, even if Menshikov's accompanying note indicated that only other native cults were envisioned. Nobody was fooled, least of all the Turks, but they used the recent death of the Sultana Validé as an excuse to delay the response.[20]

Stratford obtained a copy of the draft *sened* the next day and was in a quandary, since he did not trust the French to keep secrets. On the other hand, he was more worried about the alleged '30 sail' at Sevastopol, the Russian legation's preparations to pack up, and Prussian and Austrian ignorance of Menshikov's true intentions. So forced by circumstances, Stratford saw to it that Rifaat supplied la Cour with copies of the *sened* and most of the other Russian notes and projects. On the following day, the two ambassadors finally consulted seriously about urging the Turks to resist, but Stratford also had a plan to promote British interests. Rifaat would refuse Menshikov with a note that could appeal to European public opinion, while the Porte enacted more domestic reforms. La Cour was persuaded, and he followed in Stratford's wake, which meant that the Turks were not going to get any *carte blanche* from the Western powers.[21]

Each ambassador saw Menshikov on 7 May and tried to talk him out of the *sened*, Klezl also weighed in that day and tried on Rifaat's behalf to work something out with Menshikov that bypassed la Cour and Stratford. But the Austrian chargé dared not be blunt about the two new articles. The best he could elicit from Menshikov was a repetition of Russia's standard line that no serious interference in domestic Ottoman affairs was intended and a vague promise to be generous with the Turks, if they became friendlier to Russia. This was not enough, and by the 9th Klezl was predicting a Russian occupation of the Principalities and war. Blondeel, the Belgian envoy who had contacts and sympathies with the Ottoman traditionalists, thought that the Turks might cede, but he appears to have been an exception. The sharper Stratford saw that the Russians were setting him up as their scapegoat, and so turned to public diplomacy and composed a 'confidential' letter to Menshikov, which the latter immediately answered.[22] It was also rumoured that Menshikov offered to abandon the *sened*, in return for an offensive–defensive alliance, though this does not appear in the Russian sources and smells like a new leak of an older story.

The nervous Turks, meanwhile, divided into parties of resistance and capitulation. The resisters themselves split between those who looked for Anglo-French military support and perhaps a war with

Russia, and those who favoured four-power mediation. Rifaat, as if forgetting which century it was or who was a great power these days, even revealed the essence of the demands to the Swedish envoy and tried to gain him 'for the party of resistance'.[23] More to the point, Mehmed Ali and Rifaat put their cards on the table and demanded to know at what point they could count on the Anglo-French squadrons. La Cour, however, found a way to reconcile his instructions with Stratford's intentions and told Rifaat that to agree to the *sened* would be a breach of the 1740 Treaty. In other words, the Turks had to resist to prove that they were sovereign and independent, while only if the Russians then attacked could la Cour summon the squadron. Stratford simply hid behind his instructions, but gave some opinions in writing. He did not explicitly say to Rifaat: 'Do not agree to the draft', but conveyed that message nonetheless – precisely what the Foreign Office expected.[24] Stratford's bottom line was that a *sened* concerning only the Holy Places and the Russian church and hospice in Jerusalem was permissible as a last resort. He also saw the Sultan on the 9th, hinted that the Malta squadron was available, and firmed up the latter's courage. Resistance prevailed. Menshikov soon learned that 'all the legations' opposed Russia,[25] and Rifaat wrote to the Turkish missions in Paris and London that the Porte would not sign the *sened*.[26]

In general, the events of 5–9 May were crucial for breaking the Gordian knot of British and 'European' trust of Russia and for making the Anglo-French alliance, which was Napoleon III's dream. By the time the ultimatum played itself out, London and Paris were ready with similar and virtually coordinated responses. The man in the centre of these events in Constantinople articulated the situation perfectly and revealed his inner thoughts again to Clarendon: 'Either I am dreaming . . . or Russia has regularly bamboozled us.'[27] Both, in fact, were true. Stratford and most of Europe's upper echelons had been dreaming that Russian disclaimers were accurate, while the Russian leaders and diplomats had been fooling most statesmen with their recent diplomacy and themselves to boot with their political mythology . Now some chickens were coming home to roost. But Stratford had his own special gripe: he thought he had convinced Menshikov to take out the clauses concerning Kuchuk–Kainarji and the Patriarchs from the draft *sened*, and Menshikov had pulled a double-cross with the new articles. As a result, the imperialism of free trade had to ally with the imperialism of Mediterranean Catholicism against the imperialism of Kuchuk–Kainarji. At least that is, more or less, what Stratford was telling a mistrustful la Cour.[28]

The British and French attitudes conditioned Rifaat's amicably worded answer to Menshikov on 10 May, which was approved by the Turkish Council. The Porte would negotiate a written arrangement, but only concerning the Jerusalem hospice and church, since the fundamental rights and privileges of the Ottoman Greek Church emanated from the sovereign will of the Sultans. Such a line had been implicit in almost everything the Turks had been saying from before Menshikov arrived and would continue to be the core of all Ottoman proposals and responses. This note was thus the first version of the many, many drafts, which embassies and foreign ministries would produce over the next six months to try to reconcile the irreconcilable.[29]

THE RETURN OF RESHID PASHA

The Russian legation did not immediately pack up and go, but rather sought another ministerial change and engaged in court politics and waiting-boat diplomacy, Menshikov abandoning his land quarters on and off for his war steamer, *The Thunderer*. On this dangerous turf he was dealing with a clever Ottoman Greek and an even cleverer Turk, who understood local politics much better than did Ozerov & Co. Fearful of leaving his Church without *any* Russian protection, Aristarchi hoped to engineer a Russo–Turkish reconciliation. Reshid sought to return to power, better with than without the reconciliation. Both were playing double games. Aristarchi was working with Reshid and trying as well to broker a workable response from the current Ottoman ministers. Reshid appeared to the Russians as their best hope, and to some extent was, while to others he was a leading member of the resistance party.[30]

Menshikov's formal response on 11 May to Rifaat's 'Anglofrench' note, as Aristarchi called it, was to extend the term of the ultimatum to the 14th to obtain the *sened* with a different type of guarantee. The Turkish Council, now in session daily, had two proposals on the table, representing imperialist alternatives: extend the Tanzimat reforms to satisfy the British or accept the *sened* or an equivalent to placate the Russians. Both legations were virtually lobbying for votes, as if this were eighteenth-century Poland or Sweden, and a parliament, half for sale, were in session. Mehmed Ali and the Turkish war party, lacking either British or French support, were temporarily marginalized. So the Turks made serious moves to satisfy some of their Orthodox with new, spontaneous grants of immunities, while some pro-Russian Greeks were preparing to skip town, if necessary.[31]

Reshid, meanwhile, furnished Aristarchi with string to lead Menshikov. Accordingly the Turks believed the ultimatum was making Russia appear as aggressive and predatory as under Catherine II, while the removal of Mehmed Ali would clear the way for the *sened*. Menshikov's best chance would be the private interview with the Sultan, which Aristarchi arranged for midday on the 13th. The night before, Aristarchi even provided a script prepared by Reshid, whereby Menshikov was to combine his insistence upon 'a formal act of a splendid guarantee', with the disclaimer that 'our propositions are innocent and completely religious'. In other words, Menshikov would demand something akin to the type of flowery and vapid document that the Porte was so brilliant at composing. The Sultan, presumably, would then turn to Reshid to engineer a harmless and 'completely religious' guarantee.[32] It is important to note that Reshid was not committing himself to the *sened*, just to negotiations.

Aristarchi almost did a brilliant job of prompting. The day of the interview, he provided Menshikov with some important information: the Turks resolved to resist independently of Stratford, and Musurus reported from London that Clarendon assumed that only the Holy Places were at stake. The Logothete, however, shot himself in the foot, by passing on some enticing news: the lack of a firm Anglo-French military commitment to the Turks was increasing the odds for the *sened*, and at least one influential minister, Fehti-Ahmad, favoured capitulation. Up to the last minute, moreover, Ozerov was still arguing for the *sened*, which would surely precipitate the rupture, and this countered Argyropoulos's arguments for a note, which might not.[33] Ozerov also found some way to implicate Argyropoulos in a 'mistake' in his dealings with Reshid, and this weakened the Russian legation moderates.[34] Actually a trio of reported conversations at this time showed that the Russian legation's basic goal was in fact the same as the nationalists' at home: to restore Russia's diminished influence at Constantinople.[35]

At the crucial meeting Menshikov used Reshid's draft only as a starting point, and then gave the Sultan two hypothetical choices: Turkey could be reduced to a Greece, Switzerland, or Belgium that was legally subject by treaty to the interference of several great powers, or Turkey could have bilateral relations with Russia. Menshikov also insisted on a quick response, which is precisely why the Ottomans preferred a five-power or four-power arrangement to a bilateral one. The Sultan was evasive and mendacious: 'You would have had it already, had not the retirement of the Grand Vizier at his request deprived me this moment of my principal adviser.'[36]

The naive Menshikov, trying to act like the power-broker that he certainly was not, cancelled his appointment with Mehmed Ali and sent the news over to Reshid, as if the latter needed to be informed by the Russian legation about what was coming. When the mist of court intrigue was lifted later that day, the Ottoman élite had made room for Reshid to return as Foreign Minister, but otherwise had only played musical chairs, shifting Mehmed Ali to Defence and Rifaat to the Council presidency and making Mustapha, a respected moderate, Grand Vizier.[37] What did not change at all was basic opposition towards Russia's maximum demands, but Reshid was ready to probe for modulations.

THE NEW TEAM IN ACTION

The return of Reshid to power on 13 May brought all of the pressing issues to a head and was decisive for the future. He and Stratford, first separately and then together, easily got the best of Aristarchi and Menshikov. The Russians may have learned from diplomatic scuttlebutt that the dismissal of Mehmed Ali shocked Stratford into 'fury approaching insanity',[38] but he never acted as if he were demented. He was in communication that night with Reshid, as well as with other Turkish ministers. The next day, the extended expiration date of the ultimatum, Reshid received first Menshikov and then Stratford.[39]

At the first meeting, Reshid, who had been forewarned by Ozerov and Argyropoulos of what was coming, used the 'nice cop/mean cop' routine by pointing out the rejectionist view of his colleagues and quickly disabused Menshikov of the idea of an easy victory. Menshikov in turn used 'severe language' and referred to 'recent' instructions calling for an immediate rupture in case of Turkish non-compliance. He then demanded a 'clear and precise response' with 'the briefest possible delay'. In other words, the moderate Menshikov of Reshid's script had disappeared. Soon afterwards Menshikov presented to some Turks Brunnow's earlier argument to Aberdeen, that 'a maritime occupation legitimized a territorial occupation',[40] a position that implicitly denied both Anglo-French freedom of the seas outside the Straits and Ottoman sovereignty. The battle for the moral and legal high ground in the realm of threat escalation was on again, this time in Constantinople, and Russia was taking on two maritime powers as well as Turkey.

Stratford, meanwhile, was ready for his meeting with a brief memorandum for Reshid, which expanded on Rifaat's note of 10 May, but reduced the guarantee to a solemn communication of the new firmans to all five Great Powers. This became Reshid's alternative to the draft *sened* of 5 May and would serve as his legal guide in dealing with Russia's demands over the next four months. With Stratford's coaching and the Council's approval, Reshid asked Menshikov for an additional five or six days for the new ministry, which was really seeking certain Western military support, were war to break out. The allegedly furious Stratford thus put in a good day's work on the 14th, regained his trust in Reshid, and had every reason to be hopeful.[41]

Menshikov obtained the Porte's formal request for a postponement right after the Council met on the 15th. He had little faith in the new ministry which he had helped bring to power, but had to grant the delay or he would appear especially unreasonable before he sailed off with nothing. His compromise was to declare relations officially broken, but delay his departure to allow for more negotiations, using now a new legation fiction, namely that Reshid had promised the desired *sened*.[42]

The real Reshid was now brokering between the Ottoman élite and the foreign legations. While the French still insisted on equality in the Holy Land, but would give no firm military commitment,[43] Reshid gave the Russians another chance for a back-door compromise, sending his son to see Menshikov on the 16th. The junior Reshid floated the old idea of dispatching a special Turkish emissary to St Petersburg, but old Menshikov in turn insisted on the justice of Russia's demands. Employing his recent legal invention, that Russia was merely asking for the same treaty rights enjoyed by Austria, he retorted: 'Only after the acceptance of our propositions will the Emperor receive an ambassador.'[44] Russia would hold to all of these positions until the war began.

Reshid and the Turks did not waste any time. A Turkish Grand Council of ministers, ex-ministers, provincial governors and ulema met for the next two days to consider Menshikov's demands, the governance of the Christians, and the possibility of war. Aristarchi personally saw most of the members on the 16th and deluded himself that Reshid's insinuations regarding Stratford meant that the Council would decide for Russian imperialism over British imperialism.[45] There was next to no support for Russia, only three votes, and a few hawks even entertained the offer of a military alliance from Piedmont-Sardinia. The real debates were between two anti-Russian camps. Mehmed Ali's group, representing majority Ottoman sentiment, wished to stonewall Stratford on reform and call the Anglo-French bluff by courting war with Russia. Reshid's minority, which gained the majority of votes, was willing to placate the West with domestic measures, at least on paper, as much out of opportunism as conviction.[46]

The Grand Council's compromise decision on the 17th was to authorize Reshid to offer Menshikov an official note containing the Sultan's reaffirmation of the rights of the Ottoman Orthodox, a promise of no future changes in the status of the sanctuaries without prior Russian *and French* approval, and a *sened* covering the Russian church and hospice in Jerusalem. Thus la Cour and Stratford, not Menshikov, got what they wanted from the Turks.[47] Aristarchi now hoped that he and Reshid could work something out and warned Menshikov that Stratford thought that the Russians 'were kicking up a row' and would not dare declare war, since all of Europe would favour the Turks.[48]

THE FINAL EXCHANGE: STRATFORD'S REAL VICTORY

Menshikov, however, hardly heeded Aristarchi any more and rejected the Turkish proposals without seeing the actual documents, when he met with Reshid on the 18th. Instead, while the Council was still in session, Menshikov sent over his rejection with an announcement that his government would 'seek means within its own power', that he was evacuating the entire embassy except for the commercial section, and that any assault on the status quo of the Orthodox Church would be seen as a hostile act.[49] The Council then finished its business by authorizing Reshid's note anyway and ordering a general mobilization over a period of three months, while protecting the Christian populations and Russian commerce. The note was published the following day in the *Journal de Constantinople*[50].

Now everybody got into the act simultaneously. Ozerov, fearful of Aristarchi's private agenda, opposed Reshid's note outright, while Aristarchi and Klezl suggested further use of one of Reshid's sons as the intermediary.[51] La Cour, having secured French interests and hoping Menshikov would retreat, was ready to work individually with him or to follow Stratford's plan for a four-power *démarche* to the Russian legation. So was Klezl, who now assumed the role of the delegate of the four powers and thereby showed Austria's dilemma, since the stronger two, Britain and France, saw no reason for Turkey to make further concessions, while Vienna was afraid that this stance would alienate Russia. Stratford met with Wildenbruch, Klezl and la Cour again on the 19 May to authorize Klezl's appeal, and both Klezl and la Cour saw Menshikov on the 20th.[52]

Menshikov, meanwhile without any help from the four powers, finally pulled out his draft of a Turkish note to be addressed to himself, and sent it over to the Turks. He later claimed this was a response on the 20th to Reshid's and Klezl's calls for more negotiations, but Ozerov had been working on such a piece for a week.[53] At any rate, the younger Reshid came once more on the evening of the 20th with a draft from his father, which was no more than a minor variation of the note from the 18th. Menshikov in turn pointed to *his* draft, said it would suffice, and officially communicated it. This one was also nothing other than the old wine in a new bottle. All the objectionable linkage was alive and well – the bilateral Sultan–Tsar alliance, the 'sense of the articles of former treaties . . . touching religious questions', the 'forever' guarantee, and the automatic extension to the entire Orthodox Church, generally in the Empire and specifically in Jerusalem–Bethlehem, of any rights that other Christian cults obtained by treaty.[54] Reshid and Menshikov were thus talking past each other, not to each other.

Since the Turks had just published Reshid's note of the 18th, they could not possibly accept Menshikov's of the 20th. Curiously, early in this century one leading French scholar deemed the Turkish opposition to the note 'silly', while in our time an eminent American historian found it 'difficult', and another 'impossible' to discover in it 'any threat to the independence and sovereignty of the Sultan'.[55] However, historical scholarship has not been aware of Menshikov's private letter to Nesselrode outlining how the revised draft *sened* would assure Russian influence over the Orthodox Church. This was proof that the Turks knew what they were doing in seeing precisely such a threat in the draft note, whose first article carried over the pertinent, objectionable stipulations from the draft *seneds*. Besides St Petersburg would consider it to be 'an obligatory note'.[56] Stratford was thus correct in viewing it as having, in Russian eyes, 'the force of a Treaty', without the specific reservations concerning the 'spiritual' rights of the Greek clergy that the Turks desired to insert.[57]

Here is the relevant text of Menshikov's note:

> The Eastern Orthodox cult, its clergy, its churches, and its possessions, as well as its religious establishments, *shall enjoy in the future without any harm*, under the aegis of His Majesty the Sultan, *the privileges and immunities that have been assured to them ab antiquo*, and which have been granted to them at different occasions by imperial favour, and by the principle of complete equity, *will participate in the advantages accorded to the other Christian rites, as well as to the foreign legations accredited at the Sublime Porte, by convention or by particular disposition* [my italics].

None of the Turkish leaders would make such a *bilateral* and hence dangerous pledge to Russia concerning the future of their Orthodox Church unless compelled by military defeat or combined Great Power pressure.

Reshid now expected the four-power support and got some. When Stratford reconvened the other envoys, they agreed that the Turks were the best judges of their sovereign rights, a position that effectively delivered the Porte from Menshikov, even if it did not go so far as Reshid or Stratford may have wished. Stratford also wanted Reshid to try once more to negotiate on the basis of the latest Turkish note and the four-power statement, but there was no time for this.[58] All the same, Stratford and Reshid would pick up from this point in the future, and Stratford would follow such a tack until war erupted. Menshikov, for his part, privately considered Reshid's latest proposals to be 'unusual (insolites)', and thereby showed that he had not paid much serious attention to the Turks all along. All he wished to understand was: 'Lord Redcliffe prevents the Porte from accepting my last demands'. If Menshikov had substituted the words 'capitulate to' for 'accept', he would not have been completely wrong.[59]

The next day, prompted by Ozerov, Menshikov warned the Porte again about any act that might 'invalidate the other rights, privileges, and immunities', of the Orthodox Church, lifted anchor, and steamed away. By then Stratford had checked out the Ottoman defences and made sure that the squadron was 'in readiness in Malta'.[60] In Constantinople it would be full steam ahead for the extension of the rights of the various Christian communities under Stratford's auspices, if not for full Muslim-Christian equality. The imperialism of 'commerce' had just won a resounding victory.

NOTES

1. Cln. to Str., 25 Feb. 1853 (*CORR* I.146); Str. to Cln., pr., 15 March 1853 (PRO FO 352/36/6); Wal. to Thv., pr., 11 March 1853 (AMAE PA PT 20); Arnim to Mnt., pr., 26 March 1853 (*PAP* II).
2. Drn. to Lac., 22 March 1853 (AMAE CP Turq. 312).
3. Cln. to Cwl., pr., 15, 29 April 1853 (ClDp. c. 125).
4. *DM* 25–27 March/6–8 April 1853; Mnsh. to Nes. 29 March/10 April 1853 (ZP I.120–1).
5. *DM* 10/22 April 1853.
6. Copies in *CORR* I.301; analysis in Lac. to Drn., 19 April, 7 May 1853 (AMAE CP Turq. 312), less so in Mnsh. to Nes., 24 April./6 May 1853 (AVPR K 19).
7. Arg. to Mnsh., 13/25 April 1853 (TsGADA XI/1234).
8. *DM* 2/24 April 1853; Arg. to Mnsh, 3/15 April 1853 (TsGADA XI/1234); cf. Str. to Cl., 15 April 1853 (*CORR* I.276).
9. Nes. to Mnsh., 3/15, 10/22, 19/31 March 1853 (AVPR K 20); Mensh. to Nes., pr., 4/16 April 1853, with Nich. I gloss, Note verbale, 7/19 Apr. 1853 (TsGADA III/124, ZP I.123).
10. Klezl to Buol, 31 March 18, 21 April 1853; Buol to Klezl, Lbz., 2, 6 May 1853 (*AGK* I.1 41, 47–50).
11. Arg. to Mnsh., 3/15, 6/18, 10/22 April 1853 (TsGADA XI/1234); Mnsh. to Nes., 14/26 April 1853 (AVPR K 19).
12. Gloss on Nes. memo. (AVPR K 1853 30).
13. Nes. to Mnsh., 31 March/12 April 1853; Mnsh. to Nes., 29 March/10 April 1853, with Nich. I gloss (AVPR K 19–20); Mnt. to Henckel, 22 March 1853 (*AGK* II.1.9).
14. Nes. to Brw., pr., 9/21 April 1853 (TsGADA III/115).
15. Nes. to Mnsh., draft, with Nich. I's 'so be it', 11/23 April 1853 (ZP I.124).
16. Mnsh. to Brw., 20 April/2 May 1853 (TsGADA III/124).
17. ClDp. c. 10.
18. Nes. to Nich. I, with gloss., 26 April/8 May 1853 (AVPR K 30).
19. Mnsh. to Rifaat with draft *sened*, 23 April/5 May 1853 (ZP I.126–7); cf. Oz. to Mnsh., 15/27 April 1853 (TsGAVMF 19/3/214).
20. Mnsh. to Nes., pr., 24 April/6 May 1853 (TsGADA III/124); Klezl to Buol, 9 May 1853 (*AGK* I.1).
21. Str. to Cln., one pr., 6 May 1853 (ClDp. c. 10, *CORR* I.300); Lac. to Drn., 9 May 1853 (AMAE CP Turq. 312).
22. Str.–Mnsh. exchange, 8–9 May 1853 (*CORR* I.305, 338).
23. SRA KUB Konst. Dép. (8 May 1853).
24. Str. to Rifaat, 9 May 1853 (*CORR* I.336); Wal. to Thv., pr., 19 May 1853 (AMAE PA PT 20).

25. Arg., Oz. to Mnsh., 26–27 April/8–9 May 1853 (TsGADA XI/1234, TsGAVMF 19/3/214): according to Russian intelligence, Stratford was upset that he could not call up the British squadron.
26. Cwl. to Cln. 23 May 1853 (*CORR* I.312); cf. Saab *OCA*: 38–9.
27. Str. to Cln., pr., 9 May 1853 (ClDp. c. 10).
28. Lac. to Drn., 7 May 1853 (AMAE CP Turq. 312): 'What you have accomplished with treaties in the interest of the Catholic Church, we have done for commerce.'
29. *CORR* I.331, ZP I.135 (English, French trans.).
30. Cf. BlC to Bkr., 9 May 1853 (AMAE Blg. Turq. V); Temperley *SROCW* I: 617.
31. Here also SRA KUB Konst. Dep. 1853 (12 May 1853).
32. Rsh., draft speech, French trans. by Aristarchi, 'Wednesday', i.e., 29 April/11 May 1853 (TsGAVMF 19/3/6).
33. Aristarchi, Oz. to Mnsh., late 30 April/12 May 1853, received early 1/13 May 1853, (TsGAVMF 19/3/16, 214).
34. Oz. to Mnsh. 2/14 May 1853 (TsGAVMF 19/3/214); Mehmed Ali's later, self-serving, fantastic tale of 'Levantine intrigue' surrounding Argyropoulos's momentary eclipse made its way into standard historiography via Thouvenel's memoirs: Thouvenel: 145–54; cf. Émile Bourgeois, *Manuel* III: 373–7; Temperley *SROCW* I: 613–17, which is more cautious; also Saab *OCA*: 40–3, Curtiss *RCW*: 128–30.
35. BlC. to Bkr., 12 May 1853; BlC–Balabin–Dmitry Nesselrode (AMAE Blg. Turq. V); Mollerus to vH., 16 May 1853: Mollerus–Mnsh. (NRA 2.05.01 BZ 2679 Const. Dep.); Str. to Cln., pr., 25 May 1853: Balabin-Oz. (PRO 352/36/6); cf. Temperley *ENEC*: 320–1.
36. Mnsh. to Nes., 4/16 May 1853 (ZP I.138); cf. Lac. to Dnr., 15 May 1853 (AMAE CP Turq. 313), with no indication that Menshikov 'was as violent as ever', as Temperley abstracted from private British correspondence: *ENEC*: 323–4, note. 490.
37. Cf. Saab *OCA*: 43.
38. Oz. to Mnsh., Mnsh. to Nes., pr., 3–4/15–16 May 1853 (TsGAVMF 19/3/214, ZP I.141).
39. *DM* 2–3/14–15 May 1853; Str. to Cln. 14 May 1853 (*CORR* I.337, orign., PRO FO 78/932); and Lac. to Drn., 15 May 1853 (AMAE CP Turq. 313) correct Mnsh. to Ness., 4/16 May 1853 (ZP I.139), that moved Reshid's first communications to the 14th and the meetings to the 15th, as in Temperley (*ENEC*: 324–5) and Curtiss (*RCW*: 131).
40. Mnsh. to Nes., pr., 4/16 May 1853 (ZP I.141).
41. Str. to Rsh., Cln., 14 May 1853; Resh. to Mnsh., 15 May 1853 (*CORR* I.321–322, 339); Str. to Cln., pr., 15 May 1853 (ClDp c. 10).
42. Mnsh. to Rsh., 3/15 May to Ness 4/16 May 1853 (ZP I.138–140): the Menshikov files in TsGAVMF or TsGADA give no indication of his source for this most unlikely story.
43. Drn. to Lac., 3 May 1853, rec. by 13 May (AMAE CP Turq. 312).
44. *DM* 4/16 May 1853.
45. Aristarchi to Mnsh., 5/17 May 1853 (TsGAVMF 19/3/16).
46. Saab *OCA*: 46–7.
47. Mnsh. to Nes., 9/21 May 1853 (ZP I.142): Menshikov wrote that an English dragoman observed the Council and that Stratford was waiting

in a small boat outside, a statement perhaps based on Ozerov's similar report from the 14th (TsGAVMF 19/3/214).

48. Aristarchi to Mnsh., 17 May 1853, 4:00pm (TsGAVMF 19/3/16).
49. Mnsh. to Sublime Porte., 6/18 May 1853 (ZP I.145).
50. Rsh. to Mnsh., dated 18 May 1853, Lac. to Drn., 19 May 1853 (AMAE CP Turq. 313); cf. *CORR* I.381, Saab *OCA*: 47.
51. Oz., Aristarchi to Mnsh., 7–8/19–20 May 1853 (TsGAVMF 19/3/214, 16).
52. Str. to Cln., 20 May 1853 (*CORR* I.343); Lac to Drn., 17, 24 May 1853 (AMAE CP Turq. 313); *DM* 7–8/19–20 May 1853; Saab *OCA*: 47–8.
53. *DM* 7/19 May 1853; Oz. to Mnsh. 2–3/14–15 May 1853 (TsGAVMF 19/3/214); Mnsh. to Nes. No. 47, 9/21 May 1853 (AVPR K 19).
54. Rsh., Mnsh., draft notes, dated 8/20 May 1853 (ZP I.144, 147).
55. Bapst: 377–8; Curtiss *RCW*: 136–7; Rich: 56.
56. ZP I.124; Saab *OCA*: 48.
57. Str. to Cln., 20 May 1853 (*CORR* I.343).
58. Str. et al., memo, 20 May 1853; Str. to Cln., 20, 22 May 1853 (*CORR* I.343–4).
59. *DM* 6/18, 9/21 May 1853; cf. Mnsh. to Nes., 9/21 May 1853 (ZP I.143, 146).
60. Oz. to Mnsh., Mnsh. to Rsh., 7, 9/19, 21 May 1853 (TsGAVMF 19/3/214, ZP I.148); Str. to Cln., pr., 20 May 1853 (ClDp. c. 10).

PART FOUR
The Twilight Zone

CHAPTER ELEVEN

Giant Steps (May–June 1853)

THE LOGIC OF THE SITUATION

The Russians had insisted upon negotiations that would be bilateral and would take place in Constantinople only. These negotiations had failed. Now military considerations were at the forefront of everybody's thinking. Russia was already almost on a local war footing, ready to send an army into the undefended Principalities, and maybe a fleet, with or without a landing force, into the Black Sea. The Turks were moving to a war footing too, but desired at least a guarantee against the certain Russian victory that would result from a one-to-one military contest. The British and French were morally committed and eager to protect Turkey, but neither government sought war at this time. Vienna fervently desired a peaceful settlement between her two traditionally hostile allies, but her Foreign Ministry 'Oriental Section' experts concluded that Russian demands regarding Ottoman Greek clergy represented a threat to Austria.[1]

The negotiations between Russia and Turkey thus continued, but now with the active participation of the other Great Powers and also without any real coordination. This was because Turkey and the three strongest states were negotiating for peace and for war simultaneously, and everybody hoped to mobilize a coalition behind specific national goals. The best linkages were between Paris and London to prepare to defend Turkey, and between Vienna and Berlin to keep Germany out of any Eastern embroglio. Vienna got on well with Paris and St Petersburg, but not with London, whose ambassador remained the most influential figure in Constantinople. Curiously, the Russians and the Turks understood each other very well.

Russia, virtually isolated, had a problem that was simple to diagnose, but impossible to solve, unless someone could engineer a diplomatic settlement. Otherwise a prolonged occupation of the Principalities would deliver Austria over to the Western powers. Even before Menshikov departed, Buol had told the Turkish representative in Vienna, Ahmad Arif Pasha, that the Porte was the proper judge of what it could concede.[2] If Austria, pressured by Britain and France, stuck to this position, then either Russia had to back down, or the Turks could commit the British and French to a coalition war against Russia. The minute the first Russian soldier crossed the Bessarabian–Moldavian frontier, the blank cheque that Nicholas had sent to Malmesbury in early December 1852 would be transferred to the Porte. The Tsar, thereby, to use Walewski's conceited and incorrect vision of his own influence, would deliver England 'hog–tied' to an alliance with France.[3] The Belgian issue simply faded into the background, even though Butenval once more asserted that the partition of Turkey would free France from any obligations.[4]

The above considerations explain a good deal: why the issue of the Anglo-French fleets was immediately topical; why the Great Powers, but not Turkey, urged the Russians not to occupy the Principalities; why, once the Russians went ahead and occupied them, the Great Powers urged Turkey not to declare war; why these powers tried time and again to find the elusive formula that would satisfy the two opponents who talked past each other; why the Turks could veto any four-power proposal that did not conform to their Notes of 10, 18 and 20 May, representing Ottoman concepts of the Porte's sovereign rights; and why Russia was reduced to desperate diplomatic strategies of trying to make the London Cabinet disavow Stratford, orchestrate favourable Austrian and British policies, or pull off a deal based on a French double-cross of England and Turkey.

The Russians were still caught in the contradictory cul de sac into which their mendacious diplomacy of 1852 had led them. Now they were trying to prove opposites: that their demands were really not an attack on Ottoman sovereignty, but that nobody else respected Ottoman sovereignty either.[5] It was a cul de sac with variants of the same three possible exits that had been around since December: a four-power diktat satisfying Russia; a five-power diktat for partition; or a war, which Turkey would lose to her opponents or to her stronger and richer allies. Russia, though, would at least win the argument, if not the contest, since, as Clarendon told Walewski: 'hostilities with Russia will not promote Turkish independence'.[6]

If nothing else, the invisible hand of capitalist imperialism was in full working order.

TAKING STOCK

The news of Menshikov's first ultimatum reached London and Paris on the evening of 16 May, and both Cabinets were ready. Clarendon immediately wrote to Seymour that Stratford's comportment matched his instructions and that the French had been correct in predicting that Menshikov's mission would come down to the demand for the protectorate. Napoleon was polite to Kiselev, extracted a copy of the earlier draft *sened* from him, and then informed him that it infringed on Ottoman sovereignty. The French promised the British not to act alone, but immediately went public with a critique of Menshikov's demands in *Le Moniteur*. Then the cross-Channel cat-and-mouse game continued, the French pressing for a genuine commitment and Clarendon holding back, but already calculating how to make Russia initiate hostilities.[7]

Aberdeen had already told Brunnow that the other British leaders agreed with Stratford's interpretation of the original draft *sened*. As more alarming news from Constantinople arrived, Aberdeen concocted draft modifications to safeguard Ottoman sovereignty, and Brunnow composed a letter on Russian policy for the British Cabinet. Russell, however, insisted upon trusting Stratford's judgements and associated with Palmerston and Walewski in favour of vigorous action.[8]

The Russians had no reason to be surprised with the British, since Menshikov had given a good indication of what Stratford would report, and Brunnow had been telling Aberdeen the truth about Menshikov's basic demands in order to quell even more damaging rumours. Brunnow himself was visibly shaken by the British response to Stratford's first dispatches and support of his views. By the end of April Nesselrode knew from Brunnow that Aberdeen opposed the draft *sened* and that Russell, Palmerston, and the majority of both Houses opposed any bilateral Russo-Turkish transaction. Soon word reached St Petersburg that Brunnow expected Aberdeen to cede to anti-Russian public opinion. Similar critical reports came in from a variety of quarters, and this led to unpleasant conversations between Nesselrode and the leading foreign diplomats.[9]

Some Russians, indeed, were worried. Baron Peter Meyendorff, Buol's brother-in-law who was on leave from the Russian embassy in Vienna, criticized Menshikov's initial showmanship and Nicholas's policy of mobilizing '150,000' men on the Danube, as detrimental to Russia's position in Europe. The Foreign Ministry official, Dmitrii Longinov, lamented the prevalent mood among those who 'distrust the rest of us', and he decried the irrational drive for 'a total protectorate, the appointment of the Patriarch, territorial concessions, monetary indemnities, and finally . . . a something, an idea, a fiction, a shadow, or a vapour without form . . . that X which is the basis and goal of Prince Menshikov's mission'.[10]

ESCALATIONS: RUSSIA

The Tsar, true to form, paid serious attention only to the military side of affairs. As early as 20 April he served notice to Francis Joseph that without the desired guarantee from Turkey Russia would resort to arms. On 28 May Nicholas received Menshikov's final reports from 'the fatal courier' and met with Nesselrode, Seniavin, War Minister Dolgorukov and the ever present Minister of the Court, Adlerberg. By the next day the Tsar had resolved upon a three-stage plan: (1) to give the Porte another chance to accept the 'Treaty' or immediately occupy the Principalities; (2) in the event of the Turks refusing to accept, to block the Bosphorous and maybe recognize the independence of the Principalities; (3) if the Turks continue to be stubborn, then either Austria occupies Serbia and Herzegovina or Russia proclaims them and the Principalities independent too. This plan envisioned requesting at least Francis Joseph's moral support and offering him chunks of the Western Balkans and reciprocity in the protection of Catholics and Orthodox in the other's sphere of influence.[11] Nicholas assumed French opposition and Austrian compliance, and only worried that London might not repudiate Stratford, when the truth (according to Menshikov's reports) was known. In that case: 'it would be the greatest breach of faith. But even this would not stop me. I shall march along my own path on the strength of my convictions, as Russia's dignity demands.'[12]

The immediate task now was to set into motion the logical sequel to Menshikov's departure, a final ultimatum from St Petersburg itself to Constantinople. This took the form of a letter from Nesselrode to Reshid, which announced a forthcoming occupation of the Principalities – as a material pledge, but not an act of war – if the Porte did not accept Menshikov's final draft note within eight days of receipt of the letter. [13]

Nesselrode, well aware that with British backing the Turks might choose to fight rather than to submit, and certain that Stratford held the key cards, played at enlisting Seymour's aid in the interest of peace by having him request an interview with the Tsar to delay the marching orders. The latter may have felt that by letting the partition initiatives drop, by retreating from the original draft *sened* to Menshikov's final note, and by postponing a declaration of war and an attack on the Bosphorus, he had taken British sensitivities sufficiently into account. Nicholas certainly acted as if these measures should have sufficed. In his meeting with Seymour on 30 May, however, Nicholas stonewalled, evaded and bluffed. He attacked Stratford's conduct and alleged breach of instructions, but dared not formally ask London to account for his behaviour. The Tsar referred to rights granted by Kuchuk-Kainarji, but would not be pinned down over chapter and verse. He brushed off Seymour's warnings that only Stratford's reports would carry weight in London and that an irresolute government there would fall. As for a delay, the Tsar retorted that London had received enough reports of his conversations to know his thinking, as if to say that he would not allow the British to deflect his orders. Could the draft note be altered to make it more palatable to the Porte? Not at all! The eight-day ultimatum would be dispatched on the morrow. And if war between Russia and Britain (and, presumably, her allies) were the likely result, and this was general war that lasted a quarter of a century? Nicholas was so certain of his right that he would fight 'as long as there should be a rouble in the Treasury, or a man in the country'. [14]

ESCALATIONS: TURKEY

The Turks did not sit by passively, waiting for the next Russian move. The military intelligence reaching Constantinople after Menshikov left was that the Russian forces of the Fourth and Fifth Corps would be poised to march by 6 June, about a week and a half before the earliest time envisioned by the Tsar. Under Stratford's guidance, the Ottoman government directed Turkish resentment and bellicosity in fruitful directions. One was to resume the intensive military preparations, which Rose had first encouraged, but Stratford had later tempered. These included shoring up the Bosphorus batteries and Balkan defences at the expense of the fortifications at the Dardanelles, calling up the irregular *redifs* in order to free all regular soldiers for duties in the Balkans or north-eastern Anatolia, applying to the Sultan's Egyptian vassals for extra troops and ships, and asking the British and French for war steamers.[15]

On the domestic front, Stratford followed his own script, as per the instructions he had authored, and induced the Porte to issue new *firmans* to all the non-Moslem communities and to communicate these charters to all the great powers so as to gain further favour for Turkey in European eyes. His not-so-hidden goal was to undercut the Treaties of Kuchuk-Kainarji and Adrianople and establish *de facto* a general European protectorate over all Ottoman Christians. The timing was perfect, since Russia was on the verge of invalidating these bilateral treaties by means of an act of war, the invasion of the Principalities.[16]

The public diplomacy of mobilization linked these measures. Reshid issued memoranda to the local diplomats and his envoys abroad to explain that Menshikov's demands and threats had necessitated countermeasures, to assure the safety of the native Christians, and to appeal for support on the basis of the 1841 Convention.[17] All of this meant that whatever Russia did the Porte was prepared.

Turkish policies after Menshikov left represented a great victory, not only for Stratford personally, but also for British-led European imperialism in the Ottoman Empire. There was only one sound way for the Turks to finance mobilization against Russia in 1853 – from abroad. The Sultan's government, having just authorized the creation of a new Ottoman bank in late May, applied for a short-term loan of £450,000, and the bank had to turn to British backers. Neither the loan nor the bank worked out as planned, and Turkish finances remained a mess and the troops' pay in arrears, but Nicholas's threats and armed diplomacy forced the previously reluctant Ottoman Empire to begin in earnest to open their doors to British and West European moneymen.[18]

ESCALATIONS: BRITAIN

The British Cabinet this time, however, was less concerned with the distant prospects of finance imperialism in the Near East, but rather felt the heat of the press and various MPs and peers, who were plainly worried about Russian designs on Turkey. Queen Victoria herself was 'shocked and grieved' over Russia's policies. The pressure mounted, partially due to Drouyn's transmission of la Cour's telegraphic dispatch of 19 May announcing the Russo-Turkish rupture. Parliament debated the Eastern Question on the 27th, and Lord Malmesbury presented an interpellation, castigating the Cabinet for inaction. Clarendon and Russell had to hold off demands in both Houses to reveal the diplomatic correspondence. Then that evening, just before the 'fatal courier' arrived in St Petersburg, the Foreign Office learned by telegram from Vienna that Menshikov had lifted anchor.[19]

Meanwhile Drouyn instructed Walewski to hector Clarendon about a joint plan to help the Turks protect the Dardanelles and Constantinople. Thereupon Walewski stepped up his pressure for a commitment and found Russell and Palmerston more than willing takers. The Cabinet doves resisted, since Aberdeen and Graham still feared the French more than the Russians. Clarendon did his best at first to temporize, calling for parallel British and French demands of an explanation from St Petersburg. He quickly produced a detailed memorandum for Seymour, a virtual indictment of the contradictions between St Petersburg's assurances to Europe and actual policies towards Turkey. This pre-empted Nesselrode's simultaneous dispatch to Brunnow justifying Russian conduct and the impending ultimatum. However, there was no Cabinet dissent about the essential question, even for Aberdeen. Rather, 'if his [Nicholas I's] whole conduct should have been a cheat, the case is altered', and Stratford would have to be empowered to call up the fleet.[20]

As it turned out, after the news of Menshikov's departure arrived, but before Stratford's explanations did, public opinion, French pressure, and Palmerston's arguments convinced Clarendon and Graham that Dundas should be dispatched to Besika Bay, and placed under Stratford's command if war erupted between Russia and Turkey. Drouyn's telegram that Russia's Fourth Corps was already marching toward Moldavia added to the pressure on the British Cabinet to tarry no longer in giving Dundas his sailing orders.[21] These were sent off on 3 June. The next day Napoleon authorized instructions to Admiral de la Suisse to bring the French squadron to Besika Bay and cooperate with the more experienced British there. However, even after news of St Petersburg's ultimatum arrived on 7 June, the British Cabinet still insisted on proceeding slowly and not entering the Dardanelles if the Russians did no more than occupy the Principalities, but Clarendon finally authorized Cowley in Paris to seek 'unity of action' with the French.[22]

SITTING PRETTY: NAPOLEON

The French government at this moment had every reason to congratulate itself. It had compromised over the Holy Places and watched Russia replace France as the odd man out among Europe's Big Five. The earlier predictions regarding Russian demands and armaments proved to be true. Dispatching the Toulon squadron in March when Rose sounded the alarm meant that the instructions to la Cour and la Suisse in late March would set the stage for French and British thinking in late May and June. Whatever the Russians might attempt with their army or fleet, the French were ready with a response and could see that the British had to join them.

For London the real question was where was the best place to send the squadrons in order aid diplomacy, rather than how to avoid provoking the Tsar. Palmerston himself told Brunnow outright that the combined Western fleets outside the Straits would in no way justify a Russian army crossing the Pruth.[23] The French leadership and Palmerston wanted the warships at the Bosphorus, though at least one experienced naval expert, Captain Baldwin Walker, vastly overestimating Russian ability to move troops overland, feared for the safety of the Dardarnelles and hence entrapment. The *capo di capi* among the doves, Aberdeen, actually argued that if the fleets were necessary to protect Constantinople, their best location would be inside the Black Sea. Clarendon's and Graham's winning argument in favour of Besika Bay was that this represented a measured response to Russia's ultimatum, did not violate any treaty, and would place the onus on Russia for such an infraction, were the troops to enter the Principalities. As long as Russian forces did not pass the Danube into Bulgaria, or the Black Sea fleet was not activated, the Anglo-French squadrons could afford to remain in Besika Bay, as Musurus and Brunnow reported to their home governments.[24]

At any rate, the Bonapartists finally had their *entente* with England and could proceed now with diplomacy to restore Paris as the centre of European politics. The key here was to take the lead in promoting a peaceful denouement, if this were possible, and at the same time continue to be Turkey's most loyal and consistent military ally. The main diplomatic broker, if there were to be one, would be Austria, and the French were ready here as well to take the lead on behalf of the Anglo-French-Turkish side to promote a settlement. The problem, however, remained as Stratford had posed it in late April: the 'string' was still missing, with which to lead the 'pig'. But if it could not be found, the French, with their superior understanding of Vienna's needs and less complex and ambitious agenda for the Near East, would be at the centre of the war alliance and the peace efforts.

NOTES

1. Heindl: 111.
2. Buol to Klezl, 23 May 1853 (*AGK* I.1).
3. Wal. to Thv., 15 April 1853 (AMAE PA PT 20).
4. Cf. Wal. to Drn., Thv., 19 May 1853 (AMAE CP Angl. 689, PA PT 20): in the former, Belgium is not mentioned; in the latter (private), Clarendon replied to Walewski: 'That's too strong.'
5. Nes. to Fnt., 4/16 May 1853 (HHSA X 36:64–72); Seym. to Cln., 27 May 1853 (*CORR* I.333).
6. Wal. to Drn., 20 May 1853 (AMAE CP Angl. 689).
7. Cln. to Ab., Seym., Str. pr.; Wal. to Drn., 17–26 May 1853 (ClDp. c. 125, AdMss 43188, PRO 352/36/1, AMAE CP Angl. 689); Kis. to Nes., 16/28 May 1853 (AVPR K 111).
8. Brw. to Ness., 13/25 May 1853 (AVPR K 74); Brw., Cln., Rus. to Ab., Ab. to Rus., 21–22 May 1853 (*AbC* X; PRO 30/22/11A); Wal. to Drn. 26 May 1853 (AMAE CP 689); Conacher *AC*: 147; also BHSA OA IV (from London, 21 May 1853).
9. Budberg, Fnt., to Nes. 25 Apr./7 May, 9/21 May 1853 (AVPR K 11, 145); Hatzfeld to Mnt., 26 May 1853; Buol-Lbz. correspondence., 6, 26 May 1853 (*AGK* I; HHSA PA XII 36); Seym. to Cln., 27 May 1853 (PRO 65/427, also *EP* I.195).
10. Mdf. to Nes., Longinov to Dmitry Nesselrode, 7/19, 10/22 May 1853 (*PM* III.424; *NLP* X).
11. Nich. I to FJ, 8/20, 18/30 May 1853 (HHSA PA KA GA 8); *KfZh* 327, p. 33 (16/28 May 1853), memo and to Psk., 17/29 May 1853 (AVPR K 1853 30, ZP I.150); Schroeder appears to confuse the old and new style dates for these decisions: *AGBCW*: 41; Conacher's claim that on 27 May Nicholas made the decision or gave the order to occupy the Principalities 'until full satisfaction had been received from the Porte' is also imprecise: *AC*: 148, 564; cf. *AGK* I.1: 195, with a different reading of the 18/30 May letter.
12. Nich. I to Psk., 17/29 May 1853 (ZP I.150).
13. Nes. to Rsh., 19/31 May 1853 (ZP I.152).
14. Seym. to Cln., 31 May 1853 (*CORR* I.367–8); cf. Nes. to Brw. pr., 20 May/1 June 1853 (TsGADA III/115).
15. Besides Str. and Lac. (*CORR* I, AMAE CP Turq. 313), Balabin to Oz., 24 May/5 June 1853 (AVPR K 19).

16. Str. to Cln., 30 May–18 June (*CORR* I.423, 470; II.7, 34).
17. Rsh. to Musurus, Four Legations, 26 May 1853 (*CORR* I.388, 395).
18. Lac. to Drn., 21 May, 16 June 1853 (AMAE CP Turq. 313); Str. to Cln., 30 May 1853 (*CORR* I.422); cf. Rodkey: 350–1; also Olive Anderson, 'The Beginning of the Ottoman Public Debt, 1854–1855', *HJ* VII.1 (1964): 52.
19. *Inter alia*, QV to Ab., 23 May 1853 (*AbC* X); Cln. to Seym., Str. pr. 24, 26 May 1853 (ClDp. c. 125; PRO 352/36/1); Wst. to Cln., teleg., 27 May 1853 (ClDp. c. 10).
20. Drn.–Wal. correspondence, 26–29 May 1853 (AMAE CP Angl. 689); Ab. to Cln., Grm.; Plm. to Grm. 29–31 May 1853 (*AbC* X); Cln. to Seym., Nes. to Brw., 31 May, 1 June 1854 (*CORR* I.324, 378); Conacher *AC*: 148–9; Lambert *CW*: 20–1.
21. Cln. to Ab., Str., pr., Admiralty, 30–31 May, 2 June 1853 (*AbC* X; ClDp. c. 125, *CORR* I.329).
22. Wal. to Drn., 1–3, 8 June 1853; Cln. to Cwl., 8 June 1853; Dr. to Lac., Ducos to La Suisse, 3–4 June 1853 (AMAE CP Angl. 689, Turq. 313).
23. Plm to Grm., 29 May 1853 (*AbC* X).
24. Saab *OCA*: 71–2; AVPR K 74 (8/20 June 1853); cf. Conacher *AC*: 149–50 and Lambert *CW*: 19–22, for the various opinions, if not the same interpretation.

CHAPTER TWELVE
Floating Projects (June–July 1853)

IMPERATIVES FOR PEACE AND WAR

The Anglo-French naval *entente* at the Straits was the chief result of the news of Menshikov's ultimatum diplomacy, and the Turks were now assured of defensive support. On the other hand, most Western leaders saw no reason to promote a war, if Russia could be induced to back down without one. Armed conflict against Russia in defence of Turkey might last a very long time with unforeseen effects. It could interrupt commerce, stimulate a fresh round of revolutionary outbreaks, and end up willy-nilly by destroying Turkey-in-Europe and toppling the regimes that started the wars.[1] Moreover, English conservatives and naval men had no desire to weaken Russia and strengthen Bonapartism. French nationalists had no desire to fight for British commerce and the security of India. Therefore, at the very moment when Clarendon, Walewski, Drouyn and Cowley were hammering out the minimum basis for naval cooperation, both foreign ministries were also at work conceiving compromise proposals.

These proposals were all of a kind. The trick here was to find a device whereby the Sultan would affirm the recent Holy Places settlement and promise the Tsar to protect the Orthodox Church so as to satisfy both Russian and Turkish *amour propre* and interpretations of the Treaties of Kuchuk-Kainarji and Adrianople. Presumably European diplomats and statesmen could do a better job in their own capitals than in Constantinople.

Such schemes would be worth very little, however, were actual fighting to erupt. Therefore the other Great Powers promoted the idea that a Russian occupation of the Principalities, despite the violation of Ottoman territory and resultant *casus belli*, should not be followed by an

177

immediate Turkish declaration of war.[2] Such a move also made strategic sense for all sides, but for varying reasons. Russia was militarily stronger at this moment, but diplomatically isolated. Turkey and the Anglo-French were diplomatically strong, but as yet unprepared militarily. Russia needed at least Austria's moral support in order to obtain an acceptable settlement without a war. The Anglo-French needed at least Austria's benevolent neutrality in order to obtain a cheap diplomatic or military victory. Most Austrian leaders wanted to avoid a war that promised them nothing but more problems. In early June only some Turkish and Russian hotheads, such as the Sultan's brother-in-law Mehmed Ali, who now ran the Turkish army, and the Tsar's son Constantine, who now headed the Russian navy, desired war. The former was politically neutralized by Stratford's and la Cour's diplomacy, the latter forced to wait by his father's timetable.[3]

On the other hand, among the Bonapartists Walewski was ecstatic about the orders to Dundas and felt that a coalition war with Britain as an ally against Russia would be 'a gift inspired by Providence which evidently protects the imperial dynasty'. His basic argument, which prevailed in the British Cabinet as well, was that if a protest against the Russian occupation did not work, then Turkey should be encouraged to resist by arms. This was no secret in diplomatic circles.[4]

The actual proposals are quite revealing of the mentalities prevailing in the various capitals. The general tendency was to discount some of the reports of Turkish sentiment from Constantinople and to create solutions based on direct dealings with the other great courts, including that of Russia. This placed Stratford, la Cour and the new Austrian Internuncio, Baron Karl Ludwig Freiherr von Bruck, in the anomalous position of trying to reconcile the irreconcilable. They were to combine standing instructions to support Ottoman independence with general orders to find a formula that Russia would accept or support a specific draft that had been worked out by one or more Great Powers somewhere else. No one, however, could alter the basic fact that both the Russians and the Turks were essentially interested in victory and continuously tried to duck genuine compromise proposals and force a solution in their own favour.

LONDON: THE ENGLISH 'CONVENTION'

Work on such compromises began on the basis of Menshikov's original draft *sened* even before his mission ended, and Clarendon was arguing with Brunnow and asking that Stratford and la Cour be allowed to make a few alterations. Aberdeen suggested limiting the articles to stipulations concerning the Holy Places only, placing all statements designed to satisfy Russia's *amour propre* in the preamble, and, most importantly, respecting Turkish objections. Clarendon played at assuming that St Petersburg did not understand the full significance (*portée*) of the draft *sened* and inferred from Brunnow's latest memorandum that Nicholas did not think that he had violated any promises.[5] Of course, all of this optimism that a revised convention was an option assumed that Nicholas would 'not act on his first impulse and order the Turks to be churned up by the Cossacks'.[6]

Brunnow was imaginative but cautious, concealing from the Tsar Palmerston's blunt warnings that Russia deserved from Turkey only redress over the Holy Places and that Western fleets outside the Straits did not justify Russian troops inside the Principalities. Trusting that the Tsar would respect Aberdeen's 'private opinions', Brunnow hoped that first he and Aberdeen and then Nesselrode and Seymour could broker a direct Anglo-Russian settlement, climaxed by England's sending a special ambassador to St Petersburg. However, as soon as news of Nesselrode's ultimatum reached London, Clarendon recoiled from this idea, as did Nesselrode, who arrogantly dreamed instead of Britain's replacing Stratford and even speculated on specific candidates.[7]

Aberdeen also pursued the notion that after Russia occupied the Principalities the four powers would have the right to intervene and a modified Russo-Turkish convention could result. With Brunnow's encouragement, the Prime Minister developed a scheme, whereby the Anglo-French squadrons in Besika Bay would provide armed reciprocity with Russia's troops in the Principalities. Then London and St Petersburg could come to a direct understanding over Stratford's head whereby the Porte would grant the Tsar his 'reparation', Russia would withdraw from the Principalities, and the squadrons would return.

Such thinking about a direct Anglo-Russian understanding disregarded the French as anything but English auxiliaries and accepted the fiction that Stratford was the sole cause of unwarranted Ottoman obstinacy and should be replaced. Nesselrode's son-in-law, Count Michael Khreptovich, Russia's new (and first) minister to Brussels, successfully fed this political myth to Aberdeen via King Leopold, who simply disregarded the reports of his own minister Blondeel.[8] Aberdeen, however, was either playing a double game (as the

Soviet historian Tarlé suspected), or he was seriously incompetent in assessing the issues at stake, or he simply hoped that a disavowal of Stratford coupled with the application of Stratford's suggestions could solve the problem. At any rate Aberdeen also told Clarendon that he approved of Stratford's principles – the very ones which had become the basis of Reshid Pasha's draft Notes.[9]

Clarendon tried two tactics. One was to call an *ad hoc* four-power conference in London to interpret the preamble to the 1841 Treaty as justifying four-power mediation in Turkish favour. Lacking instructions from Vienna and Berlin, the envoys Colloredo and Bunsen had to decline. Clarendon's other gambit was to promote a compromise, revised convention. Brunnow, whose thinking here was not so far from Stratford's 'pig on a string' metaphor, urged Nesselrode to seize this 'puerile' idea as the 'Ariadne's thread to conduct us happily out of this Oriental labyrinth'.[10]

By late June Clarendon had a draft of a convention which would define and delimit the religious stipulations of the Treaties of Kuchuk-Kainarji and Adrianople. Perhaps originating with Kiselev and Cowley in Paris and then supported by Brunnow, this 'English' project became Aberdeen's favourite, but he frankly doubted that either the French or the Turks would agree to it, and he was right. The French objected that it actually expanded upon the stipulations of the Russo-Turkish treaties, and the Foreign Office professionals advised against it.[11] So Clarendon revised it to contain a mere confirmation of the two treaties and the Turkish version of the most-favoured confession clause that applied to the Ottoman Orthodox only what was granted to other Christian 'subjects of the Sublime Porte'. In this manner Clarendon's and Aberdeen's original attempt to satisfy Russia ended up as more of a genuine compromise, which neither Aberdeen nor Walewski reckoned that Nicholas would accept. Palmerston thought it was merely 'all very well for the effect', that is, for the future 'Blue Book'.[12]

However, the more important debate that ranged in England was how to react to the imminent Russian occupation of the Principalities. Palmerston argued that the Western powers and Turkey had nothing to fear from a war with Russia, that the Anglo-French fleets needed to be inside the Dardanelles if not at the Bosphorus, and that the Four Powers should convene in London to coordinate diplomacy. But these ideas made no headway with the London Cabinet as yet, not even with Russell, who was willing to allow the Russians to negotiate for peace so long as they did not advance beyond the Principalities.[13] On the other hand, the British also started their precautionary naval moves in the North Sea, as did the Russians in the Baltic, though they tried to present them as counter-measures.[14]

PARIS: THE DROUYN 'NOTE'

From the start Drouyn and Thouvenel, who were under the influence of neither a Brunnow nor a conservative court, criticized Menshikov's revised draft *sened* more seriously than did Clarendon and Aberdeen. French sensitivities were hardly assuaged by Musurus's passing statement to Clarendon that the foundations of the French Capitulations were not a bilateral treaty (i.e., 1740), but, rather, declarations.[15] For their part, Thouvenel and Drouyn worked out the following formula, which reflected Stratford's thinking and advice to the Porte: 'For Russian subjects, treaties or conventions; for Greek subjects of Turkey, firmans announced or accompanied by notes that do not form bilateral engagements.'[16] Clarendon, who always ostensibly approved of Stratford's conduct, did not wish to be pinned down by such a formula, even after being cornered by Walewski into examining the text of Kuchuk-Kainarji together. The French, however, persisted, and, as already noted, blocked Clarendon's and Aberdeen's first attempt at a draft convention.

French logic was just as relentless concerning the application of the 1841 Treaty to the Russo-Turkish dispute, an approach which also suited Stratford and the Porte, since it would bind Austria and Prussia. By the end of May the French were pressing a very reluctant Buol to host a four-power conference in Vienna and this pressure continued throughout June. Drouyn argued that Austria and Prussia were obligated by that treaty to defend the integrity and independence of the Ottoman Empire. The French stepped up the pressure, first eliciting from Austria a denial of any plans to join Russia in a partition of the Balkans, and then initiating secret parleys to ensure that any Austrian military moves were directed against Russia. The French also sent military advisers to Turkey, who arrived at the time the combined fleets reached Besika Bay in mid June.[17]

In the course of that month, the French Foreign Ministry developed what became the most promising of the compromise proposals, a fusion of Reshid's and Menshikov's draft notes and parts of both draft *seneds*, for the Sultan's special ambassador to deliver to the Tsar. In fact this project avoided everything that had been objectionable from the Turkish standpoint with two exceptions, one general and one specific. First, the draft was a supplementary bilateral engagement with Russia concerning the Orthodox. Second, it did not specify 'subjects of the Porte' in the all-important clause that granted the Orthodox whatever privileges other Christians enjoyed.[18]

Initial reactions in London were mixed. Clarendon's subaltern Addington saw this project as offering a loophole for Russia to claim expanded rights. Aberdeen and most of the Cabinet were worried that it did not offer Russia enough. Walewski and Brunnow agreed with both of these positions.[19]

As it turned out, by 9 July the British and French decided to support both drafts, the French note as originally conceived, and the English convention as altered under the pressure of the French, Palmerston and Addington. However, by the time this was accomplished, Paris and London had received the text of the Russian manifesto announcing the upcoming occupation of the Principalities, and the two Western governments were now discussing how to protest, when the squadrons should pass the Dardanelles, and whether to offer Turkey a more formal guarantee of her independence and integrity.[20]

VIENNA: THE BOURQUENEY 'EXPEDIENT'

The Austrian government was the most energetic and persistent in pursuing peace initiatives as soon as the Menshikov Mission started to collapse, and had the support of the French representative, François-Adolphe Bourqueney. By the end of May, Buol had asked for modifications of Menshikov's demands and for a five-power solution, if the direct Russo-Turkish negotiations failed. At the same time Buol did what he could to avoid being manoeuvred by the British or French on the basis of the 1841 Treaty. Rather he urged first Turkey and Russia to compromise, then Turkey not to let the Anglo-French squadrons pass the Straits, next Russia not to enter the Principalities, then Turkey again not to go to war if Russian troops did cross the Pruth, and finally England and France not to enter the Dardanelles and to be ready to pull back the naval squadrons, if Russia withdrew from the Principalities after entering them. Buol's policies were guided by the simple considerations that Turkey was weak, Austria vulnerable, Russia strong, England and France stronger still, all the Great Powers the guarantors of the status quo from the Bosphorus and the Balkans to Berlin and Brussels, and peace more important than the actual words of a settlement. Thus he could both agree that Menshikov's demands were theoretically an infringement of the Sultan's sovereignty and ask the Porte to accept most of them.[21]

Buol's waffling reflected Austria's position and her disunity at the top. He himself shrank from putting into an ostensible dispatch that Austria could not counsel the Porte to accept the Menshikov Note 'without any variants', as Russia's ultimatum required. On the other hand, he did level with Meyendorff about this and the futility of occupying the Principalities as a means of pressuring Turkey. Nevertheless, the Austrian top brass as a whole, meaning the Kaiser and the military chiefs, as well as the Foreign Ministry, did not press Nicholas to remain on his side of the Pruth until much too late – not that the Tsar would have listened. This lack of decisiveness is hardly surprising, since some Austrian generals wished to march with the Russians into the Balkans, even if 'prudence' prevailed in Vienna.[22] The Kaiser's gambit was to send one of his leading generals, Count Francis Gyulai, as personal emissary to the Tsar – to affirm Austrian loyalty, to consult concerning eventualities, and to convince him that Austria was bound to oppose a permanent Russian presence in the Principalities. A careful reading of Buol's instructions to his chargé Lebzeltern and to Gyulai shows that Austria was announcing the possibility of her own defensive occupation of them.[23]

Austria's precarious position also required that Buol seek a peace formula, and he got by with a little help from his friends. Soon after Meyendorff returned to Vienna in early June, some combination of the Meyendorff–Buol–Bourqueney trio concocted the so-called 'Bourqueney expedient'. The Turks were to sign the last Menshikov Note, and the Russians would promise that they intended no violation of the Sultan's rights. Menshikov had already tried this approach in early May with his revised *sened* and failed, but such facts did not concern these three grand diplomats.

Buol's most serious ostensible *démarche* at this time was to instruct Bruck on 9 June to guide the Turks toward a fusion of Menshikov's and Reshid's final draft notes.[24] The other powers understood this approach and in general approved. It now appeared as if Vienna were playing its proper, intermediary role in such a crisis. However, this did not stop either the Tsar or the Porte from continuing to play the traditional game of 'Russians and Turks' or the Anglo-French and the Russians from tugging at Austria to come over to their respective sides.

ST PETERSBURG AND CONSTANTINOPLE: THE
SECOND ULTIMATUM

At this time the most serious decisions concerning war and peace were being made in St Petersburg and Constantinople. The Tsar's resolutions of 28–29 May set the stage for the events of June and early July, since he would not budge from the demand 'that the Porte accept our note, purely and simply'.[25] The Turks had to reject the ultimatum, unless the British and French renounced both their promises and their interests, and neither had any reason to do so. The Tsar then had to proceed with the occupation of the Principalities, lest he appear the fool in the face of the Turks and the Ottoman Orthodox, Europe and also, so he thought, his subjects.

The Russian government first acted as if it desired peace. To justify the Menshikov Note and the ultimatum, the Foreign Ministry published a major circular, dated 11 June, which repeated the charges of Ottoman perfidy regarding the Holy Places in 1852, but was otherwise free from invective.[26] However, when Balabin returned to Constantinople with Nesselrode's ultimatum of 9 June, Argyropoulos handed it to Reshid with a threatening reference to Russia's military and naval preponderance. Reshid then told Stratford even before the Turkish Grand Council met that it would be rejected and asked him to draw up the reply. Reshid also saw la Cour, Klezl and Wildenbruch, who all agreed that the ultimatum could not be accepted. On 13 and 14 June the British and French naval squadrons arrived at Besika Bay, making the Turks now much more secure. Balabin's attempt to work out a side deal with Benedetti was thus superfluous.

Both la Cour and Stratford helped Reshid compose his response, which was delivered to Balabin on 16 June. It was firm, polite, and ostensibly conciliatory, as in the past, but also threatening in turn. The latest firmans to the Orthodox Church sufficed; an engagement with Russia to this effect would violate Ottoman sovereignty; an occupation of the Principalities was intolerable; but the Porte was ready to send an ambassador to St Petersburg to renew the negotiations.[27] As expected, Balabin set off the next day for Odessa with the mission archives, as well as Reshid's letter that essentially dared the Russians to cross the Pruth. This left Argyropoulos with only his wits as Russia's sole diplomatic representative in Constantinople.

Just before Balabin departed, Bruck arrived with a set of contradictory instructions that reflected Austria's 'false' position. He was to support the Porte's reforms and assertion of sovereignty, to reduce the British influence which lay behind these policies, and to urge the Turks to send an ambassador to Russia – as if Russia would accept one without a signed and sealed Menshikov Note that nullified that sovereignty in Turkish eyes.[28] Immediately communicating Buol's wishes to Reshid, Bruck futilely attempted to delay Balabin's departure.

Ten days after Balabin closed down the Russian mission, the Tsar dispatched his final orders to troops that had already been alerted after Balabin arrived in Odessa, and the Foreign Ministry escalated its rhetoric. The published Russian manifesto of 26 June, which was read in the local Orthodox churches, protested a desire for peace, but announced the forthcoming occupation of the Principalities by Russian troops until 'the Ottoman Porte binds itself solemnly to observe the inviolability of the Orthodox Church'.[29] 'Calling God to our aid', and promising to seek both peace and the honour of the Orthodox Church, it calmed many of the faithful, even if it did not convince native minorities or radicals, not to say the diplomats on the spot and in the West, who saw an escalation, not a desire for a settlement.[30]

Nesselrode's circular of 2 July justifying the advance of the troops added the accusation that the Anglo-French, by taking the initiative in sending their fleets to Besika Bay, had made it impossible for Russia to alter its resolutions. Clarendon was willing to respond with just a simple dispatch to Seymour, even if British public opinion was aroused. Thouvenel and the French, on the other hand, pounced with their own circular published in *Le Moniteur*.[31] The Russian manifesto and the circular thus had the effect of assuaging some Russians, but further alarming much of Europe and allowing the French Foreign Ministry to play up to the sensitivities of the British public.

The anomaly of Russia's potentially inflammatory material was that the Tsar's forces were already taking an essentially defensive stance at the time the occupation began. There was no equipment, reserves, or real plans for an advance. This made a mockery out of the Tsar's boast to Castelbajac that the Anglo-French fleets, even if they destroyed the Russian Black Sea squadron, could not stop a Russian move on Constantinople. The Army of the Caucasus, moreover, far from preparing an offensive into Eastern Anatolia, was negotiating with the War Ministry for reinforcements to help control the Circassians and Shamyl's Daghestanis and Chechens, who were expected to acquire active help from the Turks. Such reinforcements could only come from the Thirteenth Division of the Fifth Corps – troops the Tsar had intended earlier for the descent force.[32]

THE EMBRYO OF THE PEACE TREATY

The Tsar really needed Austrian cooperation to protect his flank as his troops were preparing to enter the Principalities, but this could only come within the framework of a diplomatic compromise. In principle, Nicholas and Nesselrode were quite friendly to both the 'Bourqueney expedient' and the English convention project, even if Clarendon's draft in their eyes required modifications. Nesselrode doubted, however, that the Porte, bolstered as it was by the combined fleets and Stratford's ego, would accept such solutions, but on 23 June authorized Meyendorff to encourage the 'expedient'.[33] Ostensibly Nesselrode hoped that a Turkish acceptance would forestall the occupation, but the manifesto was ready to be printed. Seymour's last minute 'most private' correspondence with a contemptuous and unappreciative Nesselrode was passed on to the Emperor and changed nothing.[34]

Buol, meanwhile, had anticipated Nesselrode, but was clumsy. Bruck's instructions of 9 June arrived only on the 21st. This meant a senseless delay of a precious week, if the Austrians really hoped to postpone or deflect the advance of the Russian troops. The next day Bruck communicated Buol's fusion plan to Reshid and demanded an immediate reply, and they both consulted the other ambassadors. Reshid quickly disabused Bruck of any idea that the Porte would accept the Menshikov Note sweetened with a parallel Russian disclaimer suited to Turkish tastes.[35] This was confirmation that anything like the 'expedient' which was fusion in the form of reciprocal notes would also not work.

Stratford, for his part, quickly seized the upper hand again and diverted this offshoot of Vienna diplomacy in the direction he was trying to move British policy. La Cour and Reshid had just agreed that Austria should only be a collective instrument, and not an independent mediator, and that the response to the Russian advance should be an expanded 1841 Treaty to protect Ottoman integrity. Stratford now hosted another four-power meeting at his residence. The four envoys concurred that the Sultan could not cede to Russia, but should continue to improve the status of his Christian subjects and attempt to devise a compromise note that satisfied Russia without violating his rights as the Turks understood them. This reformist approach was consistent with Palmerston's advice to Musurus,[36] though Stratford openly carped that the proposal as it stood 'was commendable less for its chances of success than for the lofty utility of its goal'.[37]

The original 'Bourqueney Expedient' then died a miserable death in Paris and London, where Clarendon immediately suspected Meyendorff's creative hand, a hunch that both Bourqueney himself and diplomatic gossip in St Petersburg corroborated.[38] In early July Kiselev announced that Russia approved of the scheme, but Drouyn feigned ignorance and merely promised to investigate. Then while he urged Bourqueney to pursue the plan in Vienna, the real mastermind of French policy, Thouvenel, stipulated the basic contents of a letter that Nesselrode would have to send to Constantinople *before* the Porte would sign the Menshikov Note. As both Brunnow and Walewski noted, such modulations destroyed the 'expedient' as a workable plan.[39]

All of these projects for compromise conventions, notes, fusions and expedients emanating from Paris, London, Vienna and elsewhere suffered from the same basic defect. This was their incompatibility with what the British and French were committed to uphold in Constantinople – an Ottoman definition of what constituted the Sultan's sovereignty over his Christian subjects. The logic of these projects was that they promoted the pipe dream that Russo-Turkish compromise and hence peace was possible at a time when the British and the French did not desire war, and Nicholas was ready to be satisfied with his 'reparation' in the form of a diplomatic victory.

Another expedient, however, was definitely on the rise. The proposal to revise the five-power 1841 Treaty in the interest of Ottoman sovereignty and security was now out in the open as a natural response to Russia's invasion of Ottoman territory in the name of 'sacred' bilateral treaties. Little did any one know then that three years later such a treaty would be signed in Paris, ending the war that erupted as a result of that invasion.

NOTES

1. Cf. FJ to Nich. I, 15 June 1853 (*AGK* I.1); Cln. to Str., 18 June 1853 and draft (*CORR* I.435, 489, Incl.).
2. Cln. to Str. pr., 8 June 1853 (PRO 352/36/1); Buol to Lbz., Brk., Hüb/Colloredo, Thun, 9–14 June 1853 (*AGK* I.1); Drn. to Lac., 8 July 1853 (AMAE CP Turq. 313).

3. Tarlé I: 237.
4. Wal. to Thv. pr., 2 June 1853 (AMAE PA PT 20); Hüb. to Buol, 16 June 1853 (*AGK* I.1).
5. Brw. to Nes., 13/25 May 20 May/1 June 1853, to Cln., 14/26 May 1853 (AVPR K 74, *CORR* I.319); Cln. to Seym., 17, 24 May 1853 (ClDp. c. 125).
6. Cln. to Cwl., 28 May 1853 (ClDp. c. 125).
7. Brw. to Ab., 29 May 1853, Nes., 20 May/1 June, 26 May/7 June 1853 (*AbC* X, AVPR K 74); Nes. to Brw. pr., 3/15 June 1853 (TsGADA III/115); Cf. Wal. to Drn., telegr., 7 June (AMAE CP Angl. 690).
8. Howard to Cln., 1 June 1853 (PRO FO 10/173); Lpd. to Ab., QV, 1–10 June 1853 (*AbC* X; ARB 64314–27 – copies from Windsor Archive); Khreptovich to Nes., pr., 2–11 June 1853 (TsGADA III/122).
9. Tarlé I: 203–13; Abn. to Cl., 7 June 1853 (*AbC* X).
10. Wal. to Drn., Brw. to Nes. pr., 11, 2/14 June 1853 (AMAE CP Angl. 690; HHSA PA X 38).
11. Cwl.–Cln. correspondence., 13–28 June 1853 (*CORR* I.406, 489, 506, with drafts); Addington to Cln., 28 June 1853 (ClDp c. 10); Wal. to Drn., Brw. to Nes., 29 June (AMAE CP Angl. 690; AVPR K 74).
12. Wal. to Thv., 27 June, 7 July 1853, Cl. to Wal., 5 July 1853 (AMAE PA PT 20, PW); Cln. to Str., 9 July 1853 with draft (*CORR* II.508); Plm. to Rus., 7 July 1853 (PRO 30/22/11A).
13. Rus., Plm. memos, 19–20 June 1853 (PRO 30/22/11A), also Conacher *AC*: 156–61, and somewhat differently, Lambert *CW*: 43. Schroeder (*AGBCW*: 46–7) says that Russell was willing to let Russia keep the Principalities, but the manuscript and published version of his 19 June memo indicate only that he would not treat the occupation as an immediate *casus belli*: also Walpole II: 181–2.
14. Brw. to Nes., Nordins to Stierneld, Seym. to Cln., 8/20 June, 9, 11 July 1853 (AVPR K 74; SRA KUB Pet. Dep.; *CORR* I.434).
15. See Wal. to Drn., 6 June 1853, with gloss (AMAE CP Angl. 689).
16. Drn. to Wal., 20 June 1853 (AMAE CP Angl. 689).
17. Drn. to Brq., 12 June 1853 (*FR* 12); Buol.–Hüb. correspondence, 31 May–30 June 1853 (*AGK* I.1); Lac. to Drn., Balabin to Mnsh., 14, 16 June 1853 (AMAE CP Turq. 314; AVPR K 19).
18. Wal. to Cln., 27 June 1853 (*CORR* I.502); an initial draft, worked up by a certain M. Drouard on the basis of Menshikov's draft *seneds* and texts published in the British newspapers, was ready by 6 June and sent to La Cour two days later (AMAE CP Turq. 313).
19. Addington to Cln., Brw. to Nes., Wal. to Drn., 28 June–7 July 1853 (ClDp c. 10; AVPR K 74; AMAE CP Angl. 690).
20. Drn.–Wal. correspondence, 1–9 July 1853 (AMAE CP Angl. 690).
21. Buol's dispatches, 24 May–2 July 1853 (*AGK* I.1); Fnt., Mdf. to Ness, 12/24, 16/28 May, 26 May/7 June 1853 (AVPR K 145; *PM* III.433).
22. Mdf. to Nes., 18/30 June 1853 (AVPR K 146).
23. Buol to Lbz., FJ to Gyulai, 30 June 1853 (*AGK* I.1; also p. 182, note 1).
24. Buol to Brk., 9 June 1853 (*AGK* I.1).
25. Fnt., Mdf. to Nes., Nes. to Nich. I with glosses, 21, 27 May/2, 8 June – received 27 May/8 June 1/13, 6/18 June 1853 (AVPR K 145, 30).

26. *CORR* I.454.
27. *CORR* I.520.
28. Buol to Brk., 31 May, 6 June 1853 (*AGK* I.1).
29. *CORR* II.20
30. Third Section Reports, starting 16/28 June 1853 (TsGAOR III/109/353.1); cf. Lbz. to Buol, 5 June 1855 (HHSA PA X 36 39A); AMAE CCC Moscou 2 (from Moscow, 30 June 1853); Nordins to Stierneld, 1 July 1853 (SRA KUB Pet.).
31. *CORR* II.50, 85; cf. Wal. to Drn., 13 July 1853 (AMAE CP Angl. 690).
32. Mnsh.–Vorontsov correspondence, 1–3/13–15 July 1853 (TsGAVMF 19/2/51).
33. Nes. to Nich I. with glosses, 5/17 June, 22 June/4 July, 10/22, 18/28 July 1853; (AVPR K 30), to Brw., Mdf., 10–11/22–23 June 1853 (TsGADA III/115; HHSA X 38).
34. Lbz. to Buol, 25 June 1853 (HHSA PA XII 36.39B); Seym. to Cln., Nes.; Nes. to Seym., 18–26 June 1853 (*CORR* I.511, 513, II.24); Nesselrode had the temerity to mock 'Seymour's misfortune – his mania for writing' in a letter to Brunnow, whose 'mania' of this sort was many times greater (24 June/6 July 1853: TsGADA III/115).
35. Buol. to Brk., Brk. to Buol., 9, 23 June 1853 (*AGK* I.1); cf. Str. to Cln., 24 June 1853 (*CORR* II.30).
36. Saab *OCA*: 71.
37. Str. to E. Pisani, 25 June 1853 (*CORR* II.72).
38. Cwl. to Cln., Nordins to Stierneld, 11, 15 July 1853 (*CORR* II.60; SRA KUB Pet.).
39. Dr.–Brq. correspondence, 8–9 July 1853; Wal. to Thv., 7, 13 July 1853 (AMAE CP Aut. 451, PA PT 20); Brw. to Nes., 1/13 July 1853 (AVPR K 74).

CHAPTER THIRTEEN
Sour Notes (July–August 1853)

THE OCCUPATION OF THE PRINCIPALITIES AND EUROPE'S CONSERVATIVES

Two drastic and calculated Russian moves connected with the Tsar's timetable of late May loomed behind the diplomacy from early July to September: the occupation of the Principalities commencing 2 July and the order to the Hospodars to sever relations with the Porte and turn the tribute moneys over to the Russian authorities. The first, though expected, immediately made a 'bad impression', to use Meyendorff's euphemism, and Austria began to activate several regiments (up to 25,000 troops) on its southern frontiers.[1] News of the second measure did not break immediately, reaching Stratford only on 17 July and la Cour and Bruck maybe one or two days later.[2] It then caused a serious stir in Vienna, Paris and London, since Russia now appeared as an invader, living off the land, and planning to stay there and/or to go to war. The Tsar hoped to convert the Austrian move into combined pressure on Turkey if not partition. The Kaiser, however, who had mobilized as much as anything to cow his own Serbs and prevent revolution at home, made it clear that there would be no joint Austro-Russian action in the Balkans or Constantinople unless the Ottoman Empire totally collapsed.[3]

Most of Europe's top statesmen and diplomats were already fearful, anxious and frustrated. They considered the Holy Places to have been a stupid pretext for an international crisis, but blamed Nicholas for escalating it and the Turks for not ceding. Both sides seemed incomprehensible, since Russia was becoming more and more isolated, but the Turks could not possibly win a war. Of the French, Castelbajac actively strove for a peaceful outcome; Drouyn, Thouvenel and Bourqueney worked to ensure that France would be first in peace or war; and even Walewski was not single-mindedly in favour of the latter. The same could be said for Stratford, whose memorandum *No. 132* of early July placed the option of war on the Cabinet élite's debating agenda, and also Palmerston, for whom experience taught that the only fruitful conferences took place in London with a British squadron outside the Dardanelles. Russell and Clarendon had contempt for the Turks, while Graham, Aberdeen and Seymour still harboured hopes for the Tsar's moderation or Nesselrode's influence. Buol, of course, was most eager for a settlement and was backed by all of his ambassadors, who tried to tone down their host countries' bellicosity. Nesselrode, Meyendorff and Brunnow were no different in these respects, disdaining the Eastern Question, and wishing the other powers to curb the Turks because no one could curb Nicholas.

The Nesselrode clique was joined by Napoleon's half-brother Morny, Princess Dorothea Lieven (a friend of Aberdeen and former mistress of both Metternich and Guizot, now an unofficial Russian representative in Paris who had an active salon), King Leopold, Prince Albert, Albin Seebach (Nesselrode's son-in-law and Saxon envoy to Paris), the Mollerus brothers (Dutch envoys to Constantinople and St Petersburg) and other aristocratic conservatives, whose dream world, if not whose well being, ultimately lay in the alliance between London and the three 'Northern Courts'. For most of these people, some of whom considered public opinion and the telegraph, not to say 'parliamentary debates, Blue Books', and other democratic forces, to represent the decline and fall of civilization, Stratford was the best whipping-boy. Get him out of Constantinople, or at least bypass him, and all would be fine. The English would listen to Brunnow, the French would follow Buol via Bourqueney, and the Turks would be forced to heed Bruck. The best *modus operandi* would be a Vienna-led concert, since Austria was the most powerful and most concerned neutral. Russia, of course, was part of the concert; Turkey was not. If either the Tsar or the Sultan must be slighted, let it be the Sultan. Only end the conflict as fast as possible, in order to get the Russians out of the Principalities before someone starts shooting or Vienna bows to French threats, German opinion and its own strategic considerations, and abandons strict neutrality for a pro-Turkish stance.

THE PORTE'S REACTION: THE UNFORESEEN 'ULTIMATUM'

According to Nesselrode's and Buol's fantasies, Bruck was supposed to seize the commanding heights of diplomacy on the shores of the Bosphorus. He did no such thing. In fact, he complicated matters for himself by getting into a scrape with the Porte over a Hungarian radical, Michael Coszta, who carried an American passport and was being protected by an American naval captain and his brig from the Austrian consul in Smyrna.[4] While la Cour gave Bruck a helping hand against the Yankees, Stratford made another major move.

Her Majesty's Ambassador saw his chance to smash the Treaties of Kuchuk-Kainarji and Adrianople and was hopeful that London would envision this as an opportunity to open the Ottoman Empire to further economic penetration. So he worked in tandem with Reshid to combine a protest at the occupation of the Principalities with the formal response to the Bruck initiative. These were ready and almost approved before the news of the entry of the Russian troops reached Constantinople on 7 July, coinciding with the end of the Ramadan fast and the commencement of the Bairam celebrations. General Gorchakov's official announcement included the ominous assertion that Nicholas would avoid war 'so long as his dignity and the interests of his Empire permitted'.[5] An irritated Mehmed Ali then took advantage of a tipsy Sultan and engineered the dismissal of the Mustapha-Reshid team and its replacement by hawkish Mehmed Rüshdi and the anti-Austrian Aali. This might have led to increased French influence, but a nervous la Cour joined Stratford and Bruck to obtain the reinstatement of Mustapha and Reshid in two days' time. Stratford's private claim that he 'went bang down to the Padischah and put them back again' may be a colourful exaggeration of his personal role.[6]

A new diplomatic scramble over Ottoman policy ensued. Wildenbruch tried foisting what was a variant of the 'Bourqueney Expedient' on the Porte. Bruck, armed with more instructions from Vienna, still pressed for a new Turkish note that Vienna could transmit to St Petersburg. La Cour, on the other hand, urged Reshid to take advantage of the illegal occupation to declare Turkey free from any obligations toward Russia. Stratford, who personally saw most of the Turkish ministers, cautioned a slower pace, but made it clear that he desired a resounding diplomatic defeat for Russia, if not a military one, were Nicholas to push too far. And Argyropoulos talked to Reshid, Mustafa, Rifaat and Mehmed Ali in search of a direct, back-door arrangement and heard from all of them that Russia was still demanding too much.[7]

The majority of leading Turks really wanted to fight, but when the Grand Council met on 12 July and focused on the details of preparations, it determined that the right time was still three to four weeks in the future. Reshid thus had the green light to proceed with his diplomacy.[8] His first move was to issue the official protest against the occupation on 14 July and have it published in the *Journal de Constantinople*. Appealing to the other four powers as signatories of the 1841 Treaty, he charged that Russia had just violated the 1849 Convention of Balta-Liman and affirmed that Turkey now stood armed for defence. So much for Nesselrode's claim that the Porte, by rejecting the Menshikov Note, was not upholding Kuchuk-Kainarji. Moreover, to ward off any possible four-power diktat to Turkey, Reshid asserted that the Porte would accept no project until the responses to his forthcoming protest against the occupation of the Principalities arrived. Russian political and financial policies there, being breaches of General Gorchakov's original promises, added fuel to the fires of Ottoman resistance.[9]

The four envoys still insisted that the Porte send some project of its own along with the protest to Vienna and met almost daily between 16 and 23 July to hurry the process along. Reshid, for his part, shuttled back and forth between the envoys and his Council. Bruck now played into Stratford's hands by taking the lead in supporting a Turkish note that safeguarded the Sultan's rights and allowing a four-power memorandum in support of the Turks to accompany this note. He did not even oppose Stratford's scheme whereby he and la Cour would send directly to Seymour and Castelbajac in St Petersburg explanations of Reshid's proposals and offers of mutual withdrawal of the Anglo-French squadrons and the Russian troops.[10]

Obtaining the assent of the Turkish ministers was not easy, but on 20 July Reshid dispatched his protest, an accompanying letter to Nesselrode and the four-power memorandum of 17 July, which mentioned the forthcoming Note project to Arif Effendi in Vienna.[11] Three days later a slightly revised version of a laconic, draft Turkish note that Stratford had prepared was ready, along with another four-power memorandum. The new project in essence hardly differed from Stratford's earlier memoranda to Rifaat and Reshid. It reasserted the Sultan's rights, promised the Orthodox the same rights enjoyed by other Ottoman Christians, and expressed confidence 'that the assurance grounded on the above-mentioned firmans, which have inspired confidence everywhere, will give satisfaction to Russia too'. The memorandum of 23 July reiterated the Turkish assertion that this was as far as the Porte could go and that a war to defend Ottoman independence might follow, a fact that both la Cour and Bruck conceded.[12] Consequently, the package of three Turkish communiqués and two four-power memoranda constituted a mild ultimatum to the Russians to withdraw from the Principalities.

Needless to say, any Turkish threat to Russia had to be backed up by Anglo-French military might and maybe Austrian diplomatic support to be genuine and workable, and Reshid knew what he was doing. Therefore the *Turkish Ultimatum*, as this package come to be called, was open-ended, giving the other powers a chance to work out a non-violent solution until the Western powers were ready to go to war if they chose to do so.

THE CABINET'S TENTATIVE SOLUTION: THE VIENNA PROJECT

What would have happened had Bruck been able to deliver Buol's 9 June instructions on time, a full two weeks before the Russians crossed the Pruth, is an interesting question. A milder *Turkish Ultimatum* might have reached Vienna, Paris and London on the heels of the news of the Russian action and pre-empted any four-power attempt at a pro-Russian settlement. But the Austrian courier delayed, the Turkish war party became daring, Ramadan ended, the Sultan got drunk, Gorchakov cut off the Moldo-Wallachian tribute, and the Reshid–Stratford projects did not reach Vienna until 26–28 July. This delay gave Buol the opening that Stratford's enemies and critics, from then to today, have considered the best and maybe only real chance for peace.

Cabinet politics now had their chance. The 'Bourqueney Expedient' had already been derailed in Paris. The English convention project had a different fate. Nesselrode and Nicholas treated it as a reserve anchor, to be utilized with modifications, if no other solution worked, and Brunnow continued to talk about it with an earnest Clarendon into August. The Turks, for their part, were less delicate and made it clear that anything other than Reshid's draft note of 23 July was unacceptable, especially something like Clarendon's piece, a bilateral engagement reaffirming Kuchuk-Kainarji.[13]

The French fusion project had a totally different fate. Drouyn and Thouvenel acted as if they planned to bind first England, then Austria, and finally Turkey to it in order to present it as an ultimatum to Russia. Obtaining British support for the draft note in return for the modified draft convention was an essential first step. Secretly showing the draft note to Nesselrode in early July and then formally allowing Buol to offer it to Russia were the essential second and third steps. This last move meant that Bourqueney, more than a match for the listless Westmorland, would control the Western side of the negotiations with Buol and Meyendorff. The London Cabinet was quite willing to give this process a chance to work and still held back regarding common, 'precise' instructions to the ambassadors and admirals to give St Petersburg more time to respond.[14]

Buol for his part, less 'devoted' to Bourqueney than the latter thought, wished to give the Russians every possible chance to withdraw with honour, and did not fall for the French offer to trade support for Austrian policy in Italy and Switzerland for backing of France in the Eastern Question. By 13 July Buol was ready to make his move. Ostensibly giving up on Bruck's diplomacy in Constantinople as futile, Buol proposed to Meyendorff a combination of the English and French projects, which Russia already supported in principle. Fortified by word that Nesselrode would allow a few changes in the Menshikov Note, Buol instructed Bruck on the 18th to press the French Note upon the Turks.[15]

Meanwhile Nesselrode seized upon the French project and forwarded concrete suggestions to Vienna for modifications, insisting that Reshid's implicit nullification of Kuchuk-Kainarji required a reaffirmation of that treaty in any draft note. Meyendorff received this instruction on 21 July and within two days had worked out a quasi-deal whereby Buol would amend the French draft and treat it as an eight-day ultimatum to the Porte, with the threat of withdrawing Austria's 'good offices' if the Turks did not accede. The English project, Nesselrode's instructions, and, perhaps, Meyendorff's direct participation, all played a role in Buol's draft.[16]

On 24 July Buol convened Westmorland, Bourqueney and the Prussian chargé, Canitz, and let the French envoy play a stellar role. Either by design or coincidence, Bourqueney convinced the others that they should force this project on the Turks, so that Russia would look bad if the Tsar rejected it. Drouyn immediately agreed in principle and wired Walewski to obtain a similar move from London.[17]

The situation in London was more complex. Stratford's *No. 132*, advocating a war-risking policy to eliminate Russia's 'protectorate', had recently arrived and was circulating within the inner cabinet along with Clarendon's draft response that turned Stratford's arguments into 'an injunction for peace'. If the *Turkish Ultimatum* dovetailed perfectly with *No. 132*, then Buol's project offered a more flexible means of ending the occupation and limiting Russia's 'protectorate' without a war. Clarendon was sceptical concerning the Vienna initiative, and Russell was pessimistic about Turkey's demands for guarantees, but they seconded Drouyn. Palmerston clairvoyantly advised that the four powers should prepare a protocol spelling out how precisely they understood the project, lest disagreements arise later. He also agreed completely with *No. 132* and the prospects for increased Western influence in Turkey. And he insisted that the Porte should not be forced to choose between swallowing what Russia would permit or resisting without Anglo-French aid.[18]

Meanwhile, on the evening of 26 July Buol received advance news of the Porte's 20 July letter and protest. When they arrived on the 28th, however, he prevailed upon the other members of the Vienna Conference, as Buol and the three envoys came to be known, to lay these and the letters to Castelbajac and Seymour aside as counterproductive. Rather, on 27 July, having obtained authorization from their respective chiefs, Bourqueney, Westmorland and Canitz agreed upon Buol's text.[19]

Napoleon III immediately accepted it and Walewski again urged it upon the British. Once more Clarendon provisionally agreed, this time pending Cabinet approval. It came two days later with only minute changes inspired by Palmerston, conceived to strengthen the Sultan's claim to protection of the Orthodox Church prior to and independently of the treaties with Russia.[20] Russell and Aberdeen were ready to press the project on the Porte, and the latter had high hopes for it. The Cabinet, however, would not force Turkey, and Palmerston criticized Buol for routing the project through Russia before obtaining London's definitive assent.[21]

The final text of the Vienna Note was a composite document that included (1) professions of the Sultan's good will toward the Tsar and affirmations of both sides' concern for the well-being of the Ottoman Orthodox; (2) a promise that 'the Sultan will remain faithful to the letter and the spirit of the stipulations of the Treaties of Kuchuk-Kainarji and Adrianople relative to the protection of the Christian religion'; (3) a promise 'to cause the Greek rite to share in the advantages conceded to other Christian rites by convention or special disposition'; (4) a reaffirmation of the recent settlement of the Holy Places with a promise to make no changes 'without prior understanding with the Government of France and Russia and without any prejudice to the different Christian communities'; and (5) the grant to the Russians of the right to build the church and hospice in Jerusalem under the protection of their consul-general. While (4) and (5) more or less confirmed what Reshid had been ready to allow earlier, only the addition of 'spiritual' to qualify the 'privileges' that the Porte promised to maintain represented a concession to one of his specific earlier demands. On the other hand (1) implied a bilateral Russo-Turkish agreement that the Porte wanted to avoid; (3) lacked the limiting 'subjects of the Porte' clause that Reshid had demanded; and (2), a Buol–Meyendorff addition, harked back to the original draft *sened* of Menshikov's instructions.[22]

Drouyn's scheme to corner Russia thus ended up as a project that Nesselrode and Meyendorff had helped to draft.

STRATEGIES IN CONFLICT

Nicholas I responded favourably to the draft of 28 July, along with Meyendorff's explanations of Buol's intentions, when they reached the imperial summer quarters five days later. For him, the plan to coerce the Turks was 'the most important' aspect of the Vienna project. 'I find this ultimatum to be perfect, and I do not hesitate to accept it immediately', pencilled the Tsar, which meant 'pure and simple without modifications'. Nicholas also intuited that he was gambling, since Stratford remained in Constantinople, and 'it still would be necessary to reckon with the arguments of that ambassador'.[23]

Nesselrode was delighted that the Vienna Note had pre-empted any project that might be concocted in Constantinople, but still feared that Bruck could not master the situation. On the other hand, Nesselrode hoped that the evacuation could be effected simultaneously with the withdrawal of the fleets, if done without diplomatic fanfare. Here Castelbajac and especially Seymour pressed Nesselrode, but Nicholas chose to await the Turkish response to the *ultimatum* and leave his options open. He did so despite Brunnow's warnings that Aberdeen was politically vulnerable for being soft on the occupation, and despite the direct Anglo-French threat that the 'winds' of Besika Bay (still three months in the future, DG) would soon force the squadrons to pass the Straits.[24]

In the light of continued British reticence, the question of the

Western naval squadrons and the Russian army of occupation were on hold until the Porte responded to the Vienna Project. Buol, hoping to soothe Nicholas after he reacted so strongly to Austria's initial protests, held off from joining Britain and France in demanding speedy evacuation. Buol limited himself to asking for the retreat to accompany Ottoman acceptance, and asked Britain and France on 10 August to agree to withdraw from Besika Bay simultaneously in order to hasten a Russian commitment.[25] The Russian Foreign Ministry thus had a false sense of diplomatic security in August, despite Brunnow's warnings about British public opinion, specifically its desire to station England's fleet inside the Straits and its fear that Nicholas planned to prolong the occupation and march southward in the spring. Rather Nesselrode's chancery continued the public debate with Paris with a major mid-month circular that argued that Russia as a Great Power was acting no differently from others in pursuing its interests and sovereign rights within the bounds of existing treaties, including that of 1841.[26]

The French acted very eager for the Vienna project to work, though they also pressed the British to plan for contingencies of Russian non-evacuation and to agree to enter the Dardanelles. As soon as the draft was ready, Drouyn wanted Stratford's new instructions to mandate efficacious pressure upon the Porte. Of course the French and British foreign policy professionals were pursuing international Cabinet politics, since they knew that the Porte had rejected the original French project that underlay the Vienna Note. However, once word reached Paris of the Russian acceptance, Drouyn took the position that Russia had automatically agreed to evacuate as soon as the Turks adhered. Therefore la Cour and Stratford could virtually guarantee Russian withdrawal once Turkey accepted – which hopefully would be sufficient to overcome the Porte's resistance.[27]

The British were openly more cautious. The Cabinet at first instructed Stratford to push the Vienna project only if nothing else had been worked out at Constantinople. After the Vienna Conference adopted the English amendments, Clarendon recommended to Stratford that the Turks accept 'with perfect safety' what the 'allies of the Sultan unanimously concur in recommending for his adoption'. His apparent fear was that the Turks were willing to go to war, and that Nicholas would not back down after Russia had already twice issued ultimata concerning the Menshikov Note. Hence the next communication to Stratford was less an apology for the Vienna Note than a warning that Turkey would collapse under the weight of war if she did not accept.[28]

The British Cabinet was also concerned abut forthcoming parliamentary debates and needed to justify why the fleets were still outside the Straits and why Clarendon did not reply to Nesselrode's circulars publicly in the French manner. Clarendon at least made it clear in Parliament that evacuation of the Principalities was the *sine qua non* of any four-power project, and the Tsar soon knew this.[29] At the same time the British and French were finally talking to each other about the procedure for rewriting the 1841 Treaty once the Vienna project was accepted, but London would not satisfy Turkish requests to specify when the three powers should employ their own armed diplomacy.

In fact, in order to cajole the Turks into signing the Vienna Note, Drouyn was telling la Cour that Turkey enjoyed no specific rights in this case under the 1841 Treaty and even had to make restitution for Russia's grievance, as determined by the four powers, before obtaining their support. Only then would the French and British find a way to bring Turkey under the protection of 'European public law'. Paris asked this of the Turks without offering in return a firm guarantee even of the evacuation of the Principalities, and simply told the Porte to trust the four powers to continue to serve Ottoman interests.[30] That was a little too much to swallow for the Sultan's ministers, who saw things otherwise and acted otherwise.

THE TURKS DIG IN

Actually the gentlemen in charge of the Porte, feeling the anger of their own bellicose Muslim public opinion, did not stop their work with the *ultimatum* package of 20–23 July. They considered and dropped the idea of a fifteen-day ultimatum to Gorchakov to quit the Principalities, which corresponded to their earlier, overly optimistic timetable for war preparations.[31] They also had few doubts about their self-proclaimed European friends and allies and the solutions they were concocting. Aware of the nature of the diplomacy in Vienna and the projects the Great Powers were passing by Nesselrode, Reshid correctly second-guessed the Russian strategy of choosing the European project that would be least palatable to Turkey.

The shaky Reshid–Mehmed Ali coalition, therefore, did not remain passive. Instead they pre-empted the Vienna Conference with a manifesto of the Sultan dated the 27th and signed by a collective or Grand Council of sixty-two leading Ottomans, the same people who approved the *ultimatum*.[32] The manifesto was duly published in the *Journal de Constantinople* and hence committed the present Turkish government to rejecting any engagements with foreign powers concerning Ottoman subjects. Rather, the Orthodox privileges stemmed from the Sultan's sovereign will since the fifteenth century. This was a clever ploy, with all the marks of Stratford's foresight, to kill the Convention project before he formally submitted it and anything else like it. Consequently, the Turks were also declaring the Vienna Note an unconstitutional engagement with Russia before they saw the Meyendorff–Buol alterations to the original French project.

This was not the only Turkish move at the end of July. Simultaneously the Porte ordered the Hospodars to leave the Principalities or resign, and Stratford and la Cour recalled their consuls from Bucharest and Jassy. Meanwhile, caught between Russian and Turkish claims and the conflicting pressures of the Austrian, French and British representatives, many élite Romanians were trying to manoeuvre for independence. Such an idea, which the Polish Emigration also promoted for its own purposes, attracted not only Prince Stirbey of Wallachia, but also la Cour, who talked of recreating the traditional French 'barrier' to Russia.

The Turks, though, were adamantly opposed to the notion of an independent Romania and were also nervous about Serbia. By 30 July 1853, news arrived in Constantinople of an Austrian threat to occupy Serbia in case of disorders, of the action of the British and French consuls to moderate the local protest, and of Prince Alexander's desire for 5,000 French rifles and for Turkish troops on Serbia's southern frontier. Reshid protested to Bruck on 2 August about Austrian statements and troop movements and, with Stratford's and la Cour's help, worked out a firm but restrained response. Turkey would send a special commissioner to Belgrade and deploy troops near Serbia, but avoid any military provocation of the Russians along the Danube near western Wallachia. These measures were in place by 8 August, but the Turks also threatened to fire on any Russian naval vessels that sailed up the Danube beyond the confluence with the Pruth. The Porte, ever wary of *de facto* Austro-Russian collusion, thus used the Western powers in an attempt to assert its sovereignty over both Serbia and the Romanian Principalities.

The Turks were clearly in no mood to capitulate in the face of a Vienna diktat. After the Russian occupation of the Principalities, anti-reformist, bellicose hardliners had almost seized power in Constantinople, but Stratford, backed by la Cour and Bruck, had restored the shaky Reshid–Mehmed Ali coalition. The English Ambassador had then continued to work with Reshid in order to steal the march on European Cabinet diplomacy by producing the *Turkish Ultimatum* and rejecting out of hand any draft convention, note, or other such expedient that contained the objectionable clauses in Menshikov's original projects.

The Vienna mediation process, on the other hand, was an attempt on the part of French, Austrian and Russian diplomats to remove the negotiating process from Constantinople and Stratford's influence. Vienna had the advantage that Buol and the three ambassadors were operating with instructions from their home governments and were only a day or less away by telegraph and only three days from St Petersburg by wire and fast courier. If the Great Powers including, unofficially, Russia could agree in Vienna, they could impose a solution on the Turks. However, the British and French would have to concur with the Russian view that the Vienna Note was an unalterable 'Austrian Ultimatum'. And with Stratford in Constantinople, Palmerston in London, Napoleon III's prestige on the line, and a lot of people upset over the Russian troops in Moldavia and Wallachia, neither the British nor the French were likely to use such ultimatum tactics against the power they had just sent their fleets to protect.[33]

NOTES

1. Mdf. to Nes., 25 June/7 July 1853 (AVPR K 146); ASMAE Cart. LXXX 640 (from Vienna, 11 July 1853).
2. *CORR* II.150–1 (Str. and incls); cf. Saab *OCA*: 58.
3. Mdf., to Nes. pr., 12/24 July 1853 (*PM* III); FJ to Nich. I, Grünne to Gyulai, 21 July 1853 (*AGK* I.1).
4. Lac. to Drn., Swedish report, 30 June 1853 (AMAE CP Turq. 313; SRA KUB Konst).
5. Str. to Cln. 4 (*No. 132*), 9 July 1853 (*CORR* II.107, 111).
6. Str. to LStr., 9 July 1853 (Lane-Poole II: 84–5); cf. Lac. to Drn., 10 July 1853 (AMAE CP Turq. 313); Saab believes that Mehmed Ali may have been encouraged by Musurus's report that a Turkish declaration of war would automatically result in the ambassadors summoning the fleets (*OCA*: 72), but it is not clear whether Reshid shared diplomatic dispatches with his rival colleagues.
7. *Inter alia*, Arg. to Oz. in Odessa, 4/16, 6/18, 7/19 July 1853 (AVPR K 20).
8. Saab *OCA*: 56–7.
9. Rsh. memo, E. Pisani to Str., Str. to Cln., 14–17 July 1853 (*CORR* II.149–50).

10. Str. to Cln., Seym.; Lac to Drn., Ctb., 16–20 July 1853 (*CORR* II.147, 155–6; AMAE CP Turq. 314). Lambert (*CW*: 43–4) feels that the offer of mutual withdrawal was a strategic mistake that stiffened Russian resistance, but there is no such evidence in Russian sources.

11. *CORR* II.156; cf. Saab *OCA*: 58.

12. *CORR* II.183–4: the Turkish Draft Note is mistakenly entitled 'Projet de Convention'. The only difference between the two drafts is that the Ottoman version added 'in perpetuity' to the promise contained in the firmans.

13. Nes. to Nich. I with gloss, 10/22, 16/28 July 1853; Brw. to Nes., 15/27 July 27 July/8 Aug. 1853 (AVPR K 30, 74). Although Stratford did not formally show Clarendon's text to Reshid until it had officially arrived, more than a week late on 31 July, Bruck's dispatches of the 23rd indicated that Reshid had already rejected it: Mdf. to Nes., 19/31 July 1853 (AVPR K 146); cf. Str. to Wst., Cwl. pr., 4, 28 Aug. 1853 (PRO 352/36/6, 2) for a condescending opinion of Clarendon's sincerity.

14. Drn.–Wal. correspondence, 15–24 July 1853 (AMAE CP Angl. 690); Nes. to Mdf. pr., 27 June/9 July 1853 (*NLP* X).

15. Lbz., Hüb. to Buol; Buol to Brk., 9, 12, 18 July 1853 (HHSA PA XII 36.44A; *AGK* I.1); Brq. to Thv. pr., 16 July 1853 (AMAE PA PT 5); Mdf. to Nes., 1/13, 2/14, 8/20 July 1853 (AVPR K 146).

16. Mdf. to Nes., 9/21, 12–13/24–25 July 1853 (HHSA PA X 38: 626; AVPR K 146, especially pp. 294–7: 'Bases d'une Note').

17. Brq–Drn., Drn.–Wal. telegrams., 24–25 July 1853 (AMAE CP Autr. 451, Angl. 690); Hüb. to Buol., 25 July 1853 (*AGK* I.1).

18. Str. to Cln., 4 July, received 20 July, Cln. to Str., 28 July 1853 (*CORR* II.107, 138); Cln to Ab., Wal., Thv., 24–25 July 1853 (*AbC* X, AMAE PA PW 14, CP Angl. 690); Rus., Plm. to Cln., 26–28 July 1853 (ClDp. c.3).

19. Mdf. to Nes., Wst. to Cln., Brq. to Drn., 27, 30 July 1853 (AVPR K 146; *CORR* II.162; AMAE CP Autr. 451).

20. Drn.–Wal. correspondence, 28–30 July 1853 (AMAE CP Angl. 690); Cln. to Wst., 29 July 1853 (*CORR* II.176).

21. Cln. to Wal.; Ab. to Cln., QV; Plm. to Cln., 28 July–1 Aug. 1853 (AMAE CP Angl. 690; AdMSS 43188; *AbC* X; ClDp. c. 3).

22. Buol, draft note, 27 July with Drn. original (*CORR* II.162). Cf. Buol's text of 1 Aug. 1853, misleadingly backdated, 27 July 1853, without an indication of the changes requested by Clarendon – *restera* before and *que sa Majesté* after 'fidèle à la lettre . . . culte chrétien et' (*AGK* I.1.130). There was no virtual 'joint Franco-Russian protectorate over the Sultan's Christian subjects', as Alan Palmer and others have claimed, but rather a joint Franco-Russo-Turkish protectorate over the Holy Places: *BB*: 21.

23. Mdf. to Nes., Nes. to Nich. I with glosses, 12, 16/24, 28 July, received 21, 23 July/2, 4 Aug. 1853 (AVPR K 146, 30).

24. Nes. to Mdf., Br. 15/27 July, 25 July/6 Aug. 1853 (HHSA PA X 38; *NLP* X; TsGADA III/115); Brw. to Nes., 15/27 July, received 22 July/3 Aug. 1853 (AVPR K 74); de Jonghe to Bkr., Seym. to Cln., Lbz. to Buol, 4, 5, 11 Aug. 1853 (AMAE Blg. Rus. I; *CORR* II.218; HHSA PA 36 51G).

25. Brq.to Drn., Mdf. to Nes., Buol to Hüb./Colloredo, 1 Aug., 27 July/ 8 Aug., 10 Aug. 1853 (AMAE CP Autr. 451; AVPR K 1853 46; *AGK* I.1).
26. Nes. to Brw. pr., Brw./Kis., 1/13 July 1853 (TsGADA III/115; *CORR* II.271).
27. Drn. to Wal., 28 July–6 Aug., to Lac., 8 Aug. 1853 (AMAE CP Angl. 690, Turq. 314).
28. Cln. to Wal., 28 July, 7 Aug., to Str., 2, 3, 9 Aug. 1853 (AMAE CP Angl. 690, PA PW 14; *CORR* II.177; PRO 352/36/1.
29. Conacher *AC*: 167; Brw. to Nes., 5/17 Aug. 1853 (AVPR K 75).
30. Drn. to Lac., 8, 18 Aug. 1853 (AMAE CP Turq. 314).
31. Here see also (Black Sea Commercial Ship Captain) Pezzer, report, 14/26 July 1853 (TsGADA III/124). For the events of August and September in Constantinople, the regular British, French, Austrian, Dutch, Belgian, Swedish, and Danish reports; also Argyropoulos.
32. Str. to Cln., 31 July, 4 Aug. 1853 (*CORR* II. 240, 246).
33. Curtiss, using older Russian sources erroneously states, that 'the other cabinets' accepted Russia's view of the Note: *RCW*: 156.

CHAPTER FOURTEEN

Cutting Loose
(August–September 1853)

TURKEY: MASTERFUL MODIFICATIONS

Few of the informed statesmen, Nesselrode included, expected the Porte to accept the Vienna Note, after Reshid's package of 20–23 July was known. Those who favoured it, for example, Buol, Drouyn, Bourqueney, Walewski, and Aberdeen and Russell, saw coercion of Turkey as the only road to success, especially without a Russian commitment to evacuate the Principalities. Clarendon hoped that the Turks would 'behave wisely and accept quickly', but he had his 'doubts about these fatheads'.[1]

His intuition was right on the mark. By 4 August Stratford had learned of the Vienna Conference, was calling its aim of 'fusion . . . nothing more nor less than moonshine', and still wanted the (Turkish) 'ultimatum', a position that paralleled Ottoman policy.[2] Five days later, however, telegraphic instructions arrived from Vienna to the three ambassadors with the word that the Turkish package had been completely set aside in favour of Buol's scheme. Reshid was taciturn; Stratford hid behind the 'unless another arrangement has been made' escape clause, and both he and la Cour awaited the *Caradoc*, England's fast steamer, which was expected in a few days. Turkish spirits were bolstered by the arrival of Egypt's Alexandria Division of 10,000–11,000 troops, who camped outside Constantinople. By 11 August Stratford could confidently predict the Porte's polite refusal of the Vienna project, and la Cour knew that Reshid would demand modifications and sent this information to Vienna.

Both a courier with the news of the Russian adhesion 'without variants' and the *Caradoc* arrived on 12 August. No sooner had Stratford and la Cour executed their instructions – Stratford with undisguised reserve, la Cour with hypocritical gusto – than Reshid devised his alterations as the only possible vehicle for recommendation of the note to the Turkish Council. The Council's initial opinions on 14 August were three for a modified Vienna Note, eight against and seven abstentions. Reshid was ridiculed for even presenting the project, while Bruck's desperate lobbying on behalf of the Note was futile, Ann Pottinger Saab is thus correct in noting that the real question for the historian is not why the Turks rejected the original Vienna Note, but how they came to accept it at all.[3] As good an answer as any lies in their incomplete war preparations. Their official position a little later was that they would sign only under compulsion.

Reshid was still in a strong position between Stratford and the Turkish war party. The la Cour who counselled acceptance of the Vienna Note cancelled out the la Cour who offered the French fleet immediately and hence played into the hands of Reshid. Bruck was marginalized, hamstrung by his instructions and forced *de facto* to accept and even support the Modifications as the best expedient. Argyropoulos, who kept abreast of developments, was irrelevant at this time and not a party to any serious negotiations when the crucial decisions were made.[4]

The Porte's decision, a compromise between Stratford and the Turkish hawks, was affirmed on 17 or 18 August by a Grand Council vote of seventy-six to nine – the nine simply favouring immediate war. The Turks agreed to a modified Vienna Note with two reservations: the Russian order to evacuate was to precede the departure of the Turkish ambassador for St Petersburg, and the four powers were to guarantee that Russia never invade the Principalities again for diplomatic purposes. This second demand, an escalation of the Reshid's 20–23 July *Ultimatum*, flew in the face of Stratford's objections on practical grounds.

The actual Modifications, consistent with the manifesto of late July, were virtually the same that Reshid had proposed on the 14th – a rewording of the Vienna Note back toward the spirit of his final note to Menshikov, which had inspired the original French draft. The changes specified the Sultans' historic, spontaneous grants of religious privileges independently of any Russian influence; changed 'letter and spirit' of Kuchuk-Kainarji to 'stipulations'; and, as in Reshid's draft notes of 20 May and 20 July, restored 'subjects of the Porte' to the all-important clause that gave the Orthodox the same rights that other Christian cults enjoyed. The lone Turkish concession was to allow the mention of Kuchuk-Kainarji and Adrianople at all.[5]

La Cour and Stratford positively supported the alterations. Bruck, as well as other envoys, their regrets notwithstanding, accepted at face value that this was the most that could be extracted from the Porte in the direction of conciliation. If Norman Rich is also correct that the changes made a 'farce' of the Vienna Note, then what does this say for the Note, its framers, its backers and their disregard of their colleagues on the shore of the Bosphorus? The ambassadors in Constantinople had followed their instructions in supporting Reshid against Menshikov back in May, and the Modifications were a restatement of standard Turkish positions.[6]

Fuad Effendi, who remained out of office and behind the scenes, got back at Menshikov by publishing the modifications and an article in the *Journal de Constantinople* that bragged of a Turkish diplomatic victory over Russia. Bolstered by the Egyptian troops and a revival of Islamic self-confidence, the Turkish war party's weight continued to grow.[7] Stratford's influence was on the wane again, since he had not yet delivered any direct British military support.

Diplomatic activity in Constantinople then died down as the Russian reaction to the Modifications was awaited, with one major exception. Argyropoulos started talking again with Mehmed Rüshdi and Mehmed Ali, as well as with Reshid and Rifaat, and this needlessly frightened the Western legations. The two Mehmeds, Turkey's leading anti-Western hawks, offered a direct deal if the mighty Tsar would be truly 'magnanimous' and drop the Vienna Note, which no Turk would sign, regardless of Stratford. Argyropoulos, however, anticipating St Petersburg's decision, disallowed the guarantees and the third modification with the all-important 'subjects of the Porte' clause.[8]

EUROPE: ANXIOUS ANTICIPATIONS

The Modifications, travelling by fast courier and telegram, reached Vienna, London and Paris on 25–26 August and St Petersburg late on the 28th or on the 29th. Word of Reshid's initial 'consternation' with the Vienna proceedings and Stratford's reserve had already been received everywhere by the 20th, so there should have been no great surprises. On the contrary, the rumours that Stratford opposed the Vienna Note and even threatened to quit if his superiors insisted on it, created a momentary political bubble in London over his possible resignation or replacement – that is, until his dispatches arrived on the 31st. Within the 'inner Cabinet', Russell, Palmerston and – when the chips were down – Clarendon stuck by their controversial ambassador, while Aberdeen wavered, and only the generally mistrustful Graham blamed Stratford for the mess.

On the other hand, Austria's Lebzeltern and Britain's Seymour had been hectoring Nesselrode about the occupation, and the diplomat-generals, France's Castelbajac, Prussia's Rochow and Austria's Gyulai, were able to talk to Nicholas, as he was involved chiefly in summer manoeuvres at this time. There were some optimistic rumours about his intentions, but no confirmation until the end of August, by which time the *Journal de St Pétersbourg* had also claimed that Russia possessed as much sovereignty over the Principalities as Turkey did.[9] Herein lay one problem.

The other was the Modifications themselves. Just as no one really expected the Porte to accept the Vienna Note, nor did anyone really expect the Tsar to accept these amendments. Clarendon placed odds at two to one against. Lots of people, including Buol and Napoleon III, were also angry over the Turks flaunting a European decision. Had Buol been offered a cast-iron guarantee concerning the evacuation in exchange for a 'pure and simple' acceptance, he might have been able to assuage the British and French, if not the Turks, with verbal assurances, but that cupboard was still bare. Buol and Meyendorff could privately treat the Modifications as an 'asinine' product of 'the Rhetors of the Divan', but precisely because the changes were trivial, if regrettable, they did not merit Austria's withdrawing her good offices. Thus Buol sat between two stools again, urging the Russians to accept the changes and the Turks to rescind them. So much for the 'Austrian Ultimatum' as the Russians understood it. Buol also transmitted Reshid's memorandum to St Petersburg, which it might have been wiser to ignore in the interest of the vaguely worded compromise Vienna promoted.

Napoleon and Drouyn were angry over the Modifications, but would not withdraw their fleet so long as the Russians remained in the Principalities. In fact, Thouvenel's argument that the squadrons must enter the Dardanelles by 1 October, if the Russians were still there, became France's working policy.[10] Hence there was an implicit 'French Ultimatum' to Russia, not Turkey.

The English, on the other hand, were divided over the changes when the first telegraphic news arrived, but only the free-trader Cobden and his likes would assert that Russian rule in the Balkans was preferable to Turkish control and would not harm commerce.[11] The fundamental problem that the Cabinet addressed was what to do if the Tsar did not accept the Modifications or did not withdraw his troops. Aberdeen, in touch with Brunnow as always, urged Clarendon and Russell to abandon the Turks to face Russia alone if they would not sign the Vienna Note, but would not pull back the naval squadron without Russian evacuation, so his position was untenable. Palmerston, on the other hand, now renewed his criticism of the Vienna Conference for failing to clear the Note with the Turks first. He wanted Russia to accept the changes, but saw no technical reason to be rash and cave in to uninformed French pressure, since the fleets could remain outside the Straits into November or even December. Clarendon criticized the Porte's provocative and pre-emptive demand for a guarantee, but saw no chance of getting the Turks to accept the unaltered note, even if he argued: 'we are to decide for them'. Rather the Austrians should press the Modifications on the Tsar – a policy that would bind Vienna to the British and French in case the Russians refused. Russell also moved quickly from condemning the Modifications to backing Turkey. Stratford, meanwhile, was ready to challenge the Cabinet to deny that his recommendations were inconsistent with solving 'the Great Eastern Question' on 'fair and durable grounds'.[12]

The force of Stratford's dispatches and Palmerston's cool soon prevailed over Brunnow's protests that the Tsar could not accept the amendments. On 3 September, at an inner Cabinet of five, Clarendon, Russell and Lansdowne all leaned to the French position concerning the fleets, and were even 'more warlike' than Palmerston. Russell argued that if Nicholas did not accept the amendments, Britain should back Turkey, since Russia's demands were those of a military victor. Within two days Palmerston agreed with Russell that if the Tsar demurred, he should be summoned to explain his grounds. But since Palmerston simultaneously determined that the Russians had no legitimate grounds for doing so, he was asking them to provide London with an explicit pretext – what Clarendon would later call a 'violent interpretation' of the Vienna Note – to back Turkish counterforce.[13] Walewski soon warned Castelbajac outright that the Russians had better not refuse the modified Vienna Note and explain their reasoning, or the Western Powers could no longer press the original on the Turks.[14] Brunnow and Aberdeen simply despaired of the operational logic of the Porte's diplomatic manoeuvres. These had now produced an implicit 'British Ultimatum' too.

Nevertheless, Clarendon still ostensibly hoped for a peaceful resolution, but would not be cornered into telling the Turks to accept the note 'purely and simply' or face Russia alone. He composed a lengthy memorandum, his *No. 184*, to Stratford in response to Reshid's dispatch of 19 August. The Porte had had its chance in late June and early July to produce a compromise note first; the Modifications were essentially superfluous, since Clarendon's last-minute changes in the Vienna Note safeguarded the Sultan's rights; the evacuation was implicit in the signing. This much the four powers could assure, but the demand for a guarantee for the future was to be unrealistic and even incompatible with Ottoman sovereignty.[15] On the other hand, already expecting a Russian refusal of the Modifications and holding the balance between the Aberdeen–Graham and Palmerston–Russell factions in the 'Inner Cabinet', Clarendon was also going on record with a pro-Turkish interpretation of the Note and desired Russian adherence.

RUSSIA: RESOLUTE REJECTION

Russian policy continued to show some flexibility toward Austria and began to resolve the annoying Sulina Channel shipping bottleneck at the mouth of the Danube. Then, on 22 August the Tsar promised to uncouple the retreat of the combined fleets from the evacuation. Six days later he prepared a contingent order to recross the Pruth, but the issue of the Modifications remained.[16]

History with its surfeit of errors now repeated itself. Once more Nicholas and Nesselrode did not await the British reaction before making a key decision. Nesselrode let Gyulai know on 30 August, when telegraphic news of the Modifications arrived, that the 'subjects of the Porte' clause was the chief stumbling block.[17] When the full reports were in, Nicholas refused to renounce future occupations of the Principalities. Moreover, he agreed with Nesselrode that Reshid's grounds for demanding the Modifications 'compel us to reject them'.[18] There was no thought of modifying the Modifications in order to protect the Greek Church in Palestine from the Catholic missions, where Nesselrode could and did raise a serious objection to the 'subjects of the Porte' clause. According to the line fed to the foreign diplomats on 7 September, the Tsar had 'returned to conciliatory dispositions', but Nesselrode, Berg, Seniavin, Kiselev and Orlov, that is, the relevant 'Germans and Russians' in the Tsar's entourage, concurred that it was beneath Russia's dignity to accept any changes. Operationally, however, these 'conciliatory dispositions' signified only evacuation in return for the unaltered note.[19]

In the light of the parallel evolution of British Cabinet thinking, the fate of the Vienna peace process now depended upon the nature of the refusal. Once more the Russians played into the hands of the Turkish hawks and aggressive Anglo-French imperialism. Under a general illusion that Russia was still in a strong position, and unwilling under any circumstances to admit a change of line, Nesselrode had his redactor-in-chief, Ksaveri Labenski, quickly prepare an *Examen* or analysis of the Modifications. Nesselrode's essential goal was to demonstrate that these denied a legitimate basis for the entire Menshikov Mission, which had aimed to reaffirm the privileges and immunities of the Greek Church and Russia's rights stemming from the Treaty of Kuchuk-Kainarji.[20] Despite Anglo-French hostility to Russia's recent circulars with similar arguments, he hoped that the *Examen* would be persuasive in London and Paris, or so he wrote, even though it misrepresented what the Sultan actually was supposed to pledge.[21] Jomini's claim that it was written only for the Tsar and then inadvertently leaked is more than myth, it was an outright lie the day it was written by a Foreign Ministry official who had access to all the Russian diplomatic documents which this author has seen.[22]

The Tsar approved of the drafts on 6 September. Nesselrode announced the refusal and dispatched the *Examen* to Vienna on the next day.[23] Nicholas clearly feared losing face. For example, in response to Meyendorff's practical suggestion that acceptance of the Modifications would isolate Stratford and the Turkish war party and lead to military disengagement, Nicholas scoffed: 'Never!' and assumed that Europe would ridicule rather than applaud him.[24] Moreover, in framing policy, he and Nesselrode also only heeded favourable news concerning the readiness of the other Great Powers to lean on Turkey, not the hints that Clarendon would pay attention to Stratford's dispatches or public opinion. The Tsar in fact was banking on his upcoming trip to Olmütz in late September to attend Austrian manoeuvres and see the young Kaiser and was still thinking very much in terms of diplomatic or military victory.[25] And there is no evidence from the Russian sources or from the immediate reports of diplomats who saw the Tsar to support the myth that he was ready to accept the Modifications until dissuaded by Nesselrode.[26]

Nesselrode actually was depressed. He, unlike his 'August Master', could see the writing on the wall: a pattern of Anglo-French pressure on Vienna to force concessions upon Russia and the eventual Anglo-French displacement of the 'alliance of the three courts' (Russian–Austria–Prussia) as the preponderant factor in European politics.[27]

BRITAIN: VIOLENT INTERPRETATIONS

The news of the Russian rejection with an explanation reached London by telegraph on 13 September, and Palmerston returned from the country the next day to confer with Clarendon and Aberdeen, the only two Cabinet ministers in town. Clarendon now offered Stratford's compromise plan. The four powers would assert to the Porte that in recommending the Vienna Note, 'they do not consider that . . . [it] . . . confers to the Emperor of Russia any right of interference . . . and they shall adhere forever to this interpretation'.[28] The French hurried with this scheme as if they seriously hoped to pre-empt a rash Turkish reaction. And Buol, though not happy with the weak tenor of the British draft, supported it as the only means of binding London to a peace process.

Clarendon and Aberdeen, however, conceived of their assurances in the same way that the Porte understood the modified Vienna Note – a four-power *démarche* to constrain Russia. Moreover, an irate Russell, who did not take part in these discussions, was ready for war to stop Russia's alleged expansion at the Danube rather than the Indus, unless Nicholas's grounds for rejection implied 'virtual acceptance' of the Modifications.[29] In addition, once the Russian rejection was known, *The Times* – the chief remaining bastion of dovish opinion – focused its criticism on Russia.[30] This removed the last major societal obstacle to more resolute British action.

Meanwhile, Kiselev and Brunnow showed copies of the *Examen* to Drouyn and Clarendon on 15 and 16 September. The initial French response was to demand that the Vienna Conference refute the Russian interpretation, but Napoleon III and Drouyn then came around to the Austrian notion that the *Examen* could be treated as unofficial. Drouyn, however, had to admit that the most generous reading of Nesselrode's analysis would restrict the Porte's liberties regarding foreign religious missions in the future.[31]

Clarendon's immediate reaction was two-fold: he was pessimistic regarding the peace process and satisfied that Russia was now 'inferior' to Turkey in their dispute, especially regarding the 'subjects of the Porte' issue. On Sunday 18 September Clarendon spent a day in the country and was in contact with Russell, who had just made a scathing attack on the plan to couple a four-power assurance to Turkey with the unaltered note.[32] Then Stratford's latest dispatches arrived, reiterating further Turkish war preparations and continued unwillingness to sign the unaltered note, as well as his fears that Western pressures could result in either a fanatical Ottoman government or a defeatist one. In turn, Clarendon started to argue that Russia's interpretation made it impossible for the four powers to pressure the Porte to sign the Vienna Note, for themselves to guarantee its harmlessness, or for any Russian declaration at Olmütz to rescue it. He was ready to summon the Russians to declare what their pretensions were, but temporized and instead instructed Westmorland to show *No. 184* to Nesselrode at Olmütz and ask the Tsar to accept the modified note.[33]

Aberdeen was still willing in private to propose a new, more explicit Vienna Note and to threaten Turkey with non-support to 'bring her to reason'. However, he warned Brunnow that the only hope for peace rested in the upcoming personal negotiations at Olmütz and told him on 19 September that in the light of Russia's interpretation of the Vienna Note, for Britain to impose it on Turkey would be 'to inflict violence'.[34]

The next day Clarendon informed Colloredo that Britain could no longer support the original project, wired this message to Vienna and turned to two new matters. One was a French proposal to authorize summoning two French and two British warships to Constantinople. The other was a plan for a new Vienna protocol to serve as the basis of a new settlement in the sense of the Turkish Modifications. This could at least also tie the German powers in some form or another to the Anglo-French commitment to render Turkey material aid, if war broke out and Turkey was in need. Napoleon scrutinized the *Examen*, avoided Russia's Kiselev, hedged when Austria's Hübner tried to maintain the French commitment to the original Vienna Note, and allowed Drouyn to follow élite French opinion, which was in tune with the English press and Clarendon. Palmerston, re-experiencing the refugee crisis of late 1849, was already advocating revolutionary war against any Russian–Austrian alliance to partition European Turkey.[35]

OBSERVATIONS ON THE RISE AND FALL OF THE VIENNA NOTE

There was something strange, even archaic, about the Vienna peace process, with the juxtaposition of honorific concepts with hairsplitting over words in a world where telegraphs, railroads and steamships were starting to replace couriers, carriages, and sailboats. It is also interesting that when the diplomatic crunch came, the concerned Catholic and Orthodox powers, France, Austria and Russia – lands where clerical authority normally overruled Scripture – were willing to play lighter with words than Protestant England and Muslim Turkey, which were more grounded in the prophetic traditions of the Word of God. *Pace* Paul Schroeder and his brilliant scholarship, the 'precise language' of the various texts did matter, especially to the Turks, and they were the ones being asked to sign something as a reparation for a fictional offence or suffer humiliation and the occupation and possible loss of two rich provinces.[36]

Another way of looking at the fate of the Vienna Note is from a spatial perspective. The note was at heart a project of the French–German centre, with Paris representing the views of London and Constantinople, and Vienna standing in for St Petersburg. Then, in turn, the Russians, the Turks and the British weighed in with their own riders. Russia demanded 'pure and simple' adherence without any other conditions. Turkey insisted upon modifications with a prior Russian commitment to evacuate and a four-power guarantee thrown in to boot. Neither would give way except under compulsion. The British statesmen in their own minds required that Russia agree to the sense of the modifications, that is, repudiate what they had said for three months, or the note was useless. In this manner, the more bellicose periphery sabotaged the solution of the centre – a proposal which was certainly poorly conceived and even more poorly executed, but not an impossible starting point for further negotiations.

Had the Austrians really wanted the note to succeed – and they had more need of its success than the French who were in better financial and strategic shape – Buol should not have dismissed Reshid's *Turkish Ultimatum* when advance news of it arrived on 26 July, a day before the Note was approved. It was a clear message that the Vienna Note was in trouble, if not doomed in Constantinople. Bourqueney's original scheme to compel the Porte to accede in order to put moral pressure on the Tsar reveals the bankruptcy of the entire project, since the French were simultaneously aiding the Turks militarily. In fact, Buol should never have allowed Russia's *Austrian Ultimatum* and 'pure and simple' notions to get off the ground, if he really believed in the chances of his project, since the British and French were bound to support a reasonable Turkish counter-offer.

Buol, however, was fundamentally and properly concerned with

Austrian interests, and these required localizing any Russo–Turkish or Anglo–French–Russian war that might break out. To do this, Austria had to avoid petty bickering with Russia, keep its army in reserve, and continue to promote more versions of Drouyn's compromise note and Bourqueney's explicative expedient.[37] The Vienna project thus served the purpose of buying time for all concerned.

Had the Tsar really been alert and wanted to avoid war, he would have accepted the Modifications with a few reservations as a personal favour to the young Kaiser, declared victory, evacuated the Principalities and waited for the uneasy Anglo–French *entente* at Constantinople to collapse. But the Tsar was neither very alert nor all that interested in avoiding war, and still thought in terms of military–diplomatic victory over Turkey. Nesselrode, as is evident from a comparison of his and Meyendorff's letters, was totally a company man, completely committed to the line that his ministry had promoted all year. Boxed in by the nationalists in his own office, in the military, and at court, Nesselrode was unwilling to develop and present Meyendorff's arguments for using the Modifications as a means of retreating with honour. 'Je suis in very low spirits [*sic*!]', wrote Nesselrode to Brunnow on 3 September,[38] and proceeded to edit and dispatch the *Examen*, which finished off the Vienna Note.

British policy in September 1853 is still controversial. Several scholars have decried Clarendon's concept of 'violent interpretation' as applied to the *Examen*.[39] Professor Schroeder, for example, has focused on the three-day lag between Clarendon's reception of the *Examen* and his dropping of even a collectively guaranteed Vienna Note. Schroeder's conclusion is that Clarendon was motivated solely by domestic political considerations, especially Russell's threat to torpedo the Cabinet. However, Schroeder did not refer at all to Clarendon's prolix *No. 184*, whose arguments in favour of the Vienna Note were undercut by the *Examen*, or to his immediate dispatch to Cowley (16 September), that described the *Examen* as the death-knell of Russo–Turkish reconciliation.[40] Furthermore, it was not Clarendon, but Aberdeen, who is known first to have placed the words 'violence' and 'interpretation' side by side in characterizing the Russian dispatch. And if Aberdeen, of all people, could tell Brunnow that it was violent, then operationally, in the context of September 1853, it *was* violent.

At any rate, Russia's rejection of the Modifications and, more importantly, continued occupation of the Principalities constituted the most 'violent' of all interpretations of the Vienna Note.[41] Turkey's next ultimatum would carry a declaration of war.

NOTES

1. Nes. to Brw., 25 July/6 Aug. 1853 (TsGADA III/120); Cln. to Wal., 7 Aug. 1853 (AMAE PW 14).
2. Str. to Wst., 4 Aug. 1853 (PRO 352/36/6).
3. Saab *OCA*: 67–71: Saab's hypothesis that Musurus's exaggerations of British support for Turkey contributed to Ottoman resistence is an interesting mirror image of the old thesis that Brunnow's alleged underestimations hardened the Tsar in his position. Her own account and the Russian sources indicate that the Vienna Note had next to no chance of being accepted by the Turkish leaders.
4. Arg. to Oz., 4/16, 14/26 Aug. 1853 (AVPR K 20).
5. *CORR* II.276, Incl. 3; 283, Incl.2.
6. Rich: 80. Rich never once mentions *the* central issue in the draft notes for the Turks and the Russians, namely Turkey's desire to insert 'subjects of the Porte' in the pledge to grant equivalent privileges to the Ottoman Orthodox, lest Russia demand the same for the Ottoman Greeks as for foreign missions, as stipulated by treaty.
7. SRA KUB Dep. Konst. 1853 (25 Aug.)
8. Arg. to Oz., 24 Aug./5 Sept. 3/15 Sept. 1853 (AVPR K 20); Lac. to Drn., 5 Sept. 1853 (AMAE CP Turq. 315).
9. *Die Zeit*, 16 Aug. 1853 (as in *CORR* II.296).
10. Drn.–Wal. correspondence, 19–20 Aug. 1853 (*FR* 19, AMAE CP Angl. 691).
11. Seton-Watson *BE*: 314–15.
12. In addition to the Ab.–Cln.–Rus.–Plm. exchanges of 26–29 Aug. (*AbC* X, ClDp. c. 3, PRo 30/22/11A), Str. to LStr., LStr. to Str., 31 Aug., 6 Sept. 1853 (Lane-Poole II: 299, 303).
13. Cf. the brilliant insights of Schroeder *AGBCW*: 64–5.
14. Wal. to Ctb., 7 Sept. 1853 (AMAE PA PC 2).
15. Cln. to Str., 10 Sept. 1853 (*CORR* II.328).
16. Nes. to Mdf., draft; to Nich. I, 25 Aug/6 Sept. 1853 (AVPR K 148).
17. Lbz. to Buol, 1 Sept. 1853 (HHSA PA X 36).
18. '. . . doivent nous engager à les refuser': Nes. to Nich. I, Nich. I gloss, 24 Aug./5 Sept. 1853 (AVPR K 30).
19. Ctb., Brq. to Drn., 7, 13 Sept. 1853 (AMAE CP Rus. 210, Aut. 451)., Lbz. to Buol, 19 Sept 1853 (HHSA PA X 36).
20. ZP II.18.
21. Nes. to Brw., pr., 22 Aug./3 Sept., 29 Aug./ 10 Sept. 1853 (TsGADA III/115); it omits the crucial word *spiritual*, where the Sultan promises to uphold the immunities of the Orthodox Church.
22. Jomini: 214–17; cf. Curtiss *RCW*: 163–4, Schiemann IV: 298. Monnier figured that Nesselrode foresaw when he dispatched the *Examen* that

it would torpedo the Vienna peace process and/or was trying to avoid disgrace, but real evidence for either contention is lacking:p. 98.

23. AVPR K 469 (1853) 148.
24. Mdf. to Nes., Nich. I gloss, 20 Aug./1 Sept., 26 Aug./7 Sept. 1853 (AVPR K 148).
25. Nes. to Mdf., 20 Aug./1 Sept., 29 Aug./10 Sept. 1853 (*NLP* X).
26. Rumours to this effect circulated as early as 23 September: PRO FO 65/435 (Du Plat, from Warsaw, to Cln.). Walker (pp. 231–3) cites Greville and Beust, but the former's memoires do not mention any such advice on Nesselrode's part, and the latter is confusing. Accordingly Nesselrode stated much later he had convinced Nicholas not to accept 'die Wiener Propositionen' – a term never used by contemporaries for the Turkish Modifications: Friedrich Ferdinand Graf von Beust, *Aus Drei Viertel-Jarhhunderten* (2 vols, Stuttgart 1887), I: 196.
27. Nes. to Brw., Mdf., 22 Aug./3 Sept., 29 Aug./10 Sept. 1853 (TsGADA III/115, *NLP* X).
28. Wal. to Drn., 14 Sept. 1853 (AMAE CP Angl. 691).
29. Rus. to Ab., 15 Sept. 1853 (*AbC* X).
30. On 3 September *The Times* agreed with the French public criticism of the Turks on account of the Modifications with one caveat: 'unless' the differences between Russia and Turkey 'are greater than we think'. On the 14th and 15th *The Times* lambasted the Tsar for his 'unscrupulous policy', masked by 'an appeal to the transcendental rights of superior power', and claimed that both sides had the right to make modifications.
31. Hatzfeld to Mnt., 21 Sept. 1853 (*AGK* II.1).
32. Cln. to Cwl., Str., 16–17 Sept. 1853 (ClDp. c. 126); Schroeder *AGBCW*: 70–1.
33. Wal. to Drn., Thv., 19–20 Sept. 1853 (AMAE CP Angl. 691, PA PT 20); Cln. to Wst., 20 Sept. 1853 (*CORR* II.352).
34. Brw. to Nes., 9/21 Sept. 1853 (AVPR K 75).
35. Plm. to Cln., 21 Sept. 1853 (ClDp. c. 3).
36. Schroeder *AGBCW*: 53.
37. Buol. to Lbz., Brk., 15, 19 Sept. 1853 (*AGK* I.1); cf. Schroeder *AGBCW*: 41–7.
38. TsGADA III/115.
39. Schroeder *AGBCW*: 69–72; Curtiss *RCW*: 163–6; Rich: 78–80.
40. ClDp. c. 126.
41. Cf. Plm. to Herbert, 21 Sept. 1853 (Ashley II: 37–40).

PART FIVE

The Passage to Arms

CHAPTER FIFTEEN

The Outbreak of the Ninth Russo-Turkish War (September–October 1853)

OLMÜTZ: THE TSAR FEIGNS RETREAT

In late September and early October 1853, the normal time of year for Russian, Austrian and Prussian autumn manoeuvres, Nicholas I made his last visits to Austria and Prussia, their sovereigns paid their last calls on him. He also made his final attempt at personal diplomacy to bind Vienna and Berlin to his brand of conservatism in Europe and his policies regarding Turkey. The Tsar, two of his sons and Orlov left St Petersburg for Moscow on 13 September, stopped off at Warsaw, where Nesselrode and Field-Marshall Paskevich joined them, and then picked up Meyendorff en route to Olmütz to be Francis Joseph's guests from the 24th or 26th to the 28th. Next Nicholas hosted the Kaiser and Frederick William IV at Warsaw on 4 October. Finally, as an uninvited visitor, the Tsar followed the Prussian king back to Berlin before returning to St Petersburg on the 13th.[1]

Twenty years earlier at Münchengrätz and Berlin, at the pinnacle of his prestige, Nicholas had linked his Turkish alliance within the Treaty of Unkiar-Skelessi to the Holy Alliance. He started out on this voyage full of confident bluster, but in the end he and Nesselrode were struggling to preserve the treaties of Kuchuk-Kainarji and Adrianople in the face of a Turkish resurgence, backed by the Western powers and much of Central European public opinion. The Autocrat of all the Russias thus found himself an itinerant odd man out precisely when his continued occupation of the Principalities produced the first declaration of war. Significantly, his second son, the *de facto* Minister of the Marine Grand Duke Constantine, remained at home, checking on the condition of the Baltic fleet and defences.

The immediate problem for Russian diplomacy was that its handling of the Vienna Note had backfired and worsened Russia's position. Curiously, even before the official British reaction to the *Examen* became known, Russian Foreign Ministry officials started to sing a different tune. One subaltern let slip that Nesselrode himself admitted that the imprecise nature of the Vienna Note implied rights for the Emperor regarding the Ottoman Christians that he did not demand. But this rumour was countered by another, namely, that Nicholas was angry with the French and the British for not trusting him, with the Austrians and the Prussians for not fully supporting him, and with his own ambassadors for failing him.[2]

The Tsar still counted on Holy Alliance solidarity and was trying to line up diplomatic support, but he did not even remember what had prompted the *Examen*.[3] Moreover, he and his entourage could not or would not stop thinking in terms of a military showdown with Turkey, even though Russia's back was already against the wall. The Turks could cross the Danube and invade the Principalities, which, after all, were still legally theirs. But if Russia in turn crossed into Bulgaria, the Anglo-French fleets would move to seize control of the Black Sea and might launch an attack in the Baltic as well. The Turks could also attack Russia's positions in Transcaucasia or on the Eastern Black Sea. If Russia, on the other hand, advanced far into Anatolia or threatened Turkey's Black Sea squadron, the British, joined by the French in the second instance, would come to Turkey's aid.[4] The best strategic advice Nicholas could obtain from his confidant Paskevich required luck and Austria's benevolent neutrality to work. Turkish atrocities would produce non-revolutionary Balkan Christian rebels, whom Russia could arm and utilize, presumably, without alienating Austria. The Russians then might invade eastern Bulgaria and move down the coast toward Constantinople and also make a pre-emptive strike at the Turks in Eastern Anatolia even if the Anglo-French fleets took over the Black Sea.[5]

At Olmütz the Tsar saw Franz-Joseph, Buol, the Prussian Heir-Presumptive, Prince William, Westmorland (who had a military background), several British officers, and General Charles-Marie-Augustin de Goyon, Napoleon III's aide-de-camp and personal emissary. Goyon had earlier attended the Prussian manoeuvres and now had come to cement Franco-Austrian relations. The Kaiser and Buol had similar messages for Nicholas and Nesselrode. Vienna wanted nothing more earnestly than good relations with Russia, but not, of course, at the expense of Turkey, and the *Examen* had to be disavowed. Prince William wanted the Tsar to see an analogy between the Principalities and Belgium, which was guaranteed by treaty, and thus evacuate and eliminate the *casus belli*, but the Tsar would hear of nothing but his own bilateral engagements with Turkey. Instead he and Orlov courted the politically naive General Goyon, inviting him and the British officers to Warsaw. The general accepted, and Nicholas even hinted that Napoleon III would be welcome as a 'brother' in St Petersburg.[6]

On the other hand, as was usual in direct dealings with the Russians, the British were more forceful than their French and Austrian counterparts. Westmorland showed Nesselrode Clarendon's crucial dispatches and urged the Russians to accept the modified Note, but the Tsar refused, demanded the original as his reparation and guarantee, and simply promised not to advance against Turkey that year.[7]

Russia's counter-offer was a new variant of the 'Bourqueney expedient'. Nicholas authorized Nesselrode and Buol to draft the four-power declaration that would contain the assurances which many diplomats and statesmen, including Stratford, had earlier thought that the Porte needed in order to accept the Vienna Note. The four powers would vouchsafe that Nicholas claimed no interference in Ottoman affairs and wanted no more rights for the Orthodox Christians than those of 'other Christian communities subject to the Porte'.[8] The Russian *Examen* was thus discounted, and the Turks were supposed to accept what the Russians said under pressure, rather than what they had argued of their own free will three weeks earlier. Typically for a Russian proposal at this time, moreover, its terms were non-negotiable. Hence it was another *de facto* 'Austrian ultimatum', with the Tsar demanding the Porte's unconditional adherence, this time with the four powers guaranteeing that the Russian government had changed its mind and really did not mean what it said earlier.

But if Nicholas really meant what was stated in the Olmütz or 'Buol' project, why not allow the Turkish Modifications and recross the Pruth as soon as possible? Because, at least ostensibly, the Tsar had stated his intentions, demanded to be trusted by those whom he trusted and would not deviate from insisting upon a Turkish affirmation of 'the status quo established by . . . Treaties for the protection of his co-religionaires'.[9] In other words, nothing had really changed since May. Why not accept the Modifications? As angry and impatient parents say to their children: *because*!

If there was any logic to Nicholas's thinking and the conclusions he drew from Brunnow's reports, it was that the Anglo-French decision to send a few war steamers to Constantinople 'to protect the Christians', might be the starting point of five-power coercion of Turkey or a variant of his partition scheme. Considered then by his Saxon colleague Vitzthum von Eckstädt as the most gifted foreign diplomat in London,[10] Brunnow would have been wiser to counsel the Modifications and nothing but the Modifications if he wished to avoid an Anglo–Russian war. Nesselrode was no better. He still thought in terms of refuting and convincing the British ministers, not listening to them, and he lamented their 'bad faith' in taking his expositions seriously, as if he had not done the same with Reshid's circulars.[11] Nevertheless, Nicholas himself must be faulted or credited for gambling with the contradiction between Austria's standing position on evacuation and Buol's formal support of a project that the Turks had already rejected when Stratford suggested it five weeks earlier before the *Examen* was even written.

Buol tried to present this project as a recreation of the beneficient five-power coalition of 1841 and as new concession that he obtained from the Tsar rather than the other way around.[12] Buol of course knew that the Olmütz project had only a miniscule chance of working, since Bourqueney, as well as Westmorland, had already conveyed the word that the Vienna Note was no longer viable. Nesselrode knew this too from his chargé in Vienna, but Nicholas did not care.[13] At any rate, as a result of decisions taken by the Ottoman Grand Council, the Olmütz project was dead before it was ready for transmission to Paris, London and Berlin.

CONSTANTINOPLE: THE TURKS DECLARE

If one could chart war fever for the Turks in 1853, then the period early March to early September would show a crescendo peaking in September and then levelling off into December before declining in the face of several serious military reverses. At the very end of August, three weeks before the anticipated news of Russia's rejection of the Modifications arrived, Clarendon's Turkish political equivalent as the swing man within the Ottoman political high command, the Sheikh–ul–islam (seykülislâm) – the chief religious authority, also declared in favour of war. Anonymous placards urging holy war (*jihad*) against Russia started to appear in the capital, maybe the first poster campaign in Ottoman history. The large body of traditional religious students or *softas*, up to 45,000 by one estimate, became exceedingly restless.[14] Here was an ironic twist of historical logic. The war party within the army and navy, institutions that depended upon Western material and diplomatic support to be effective, allied domestically with traditional Islamic intelligentsia and its youth, who were facing obsolescence.

The Turkish government now balanced domestic fanaticism and Anglo-French counsels. Even before the disturbances, the Porte had refused to countenance la Cour's suggestion that the four powers guarantee the Turkish interpretation of the Vienna Note – an initiative which anticipated French policy at this time and the Olmütz proposals. The Porte also went public again with press articles in Turkish and French. These defended the Modifications as a guarantee of Ottoman sovereignty and attacked the French *Journal de débats* for insisting on the original Vienna Note once the Tsar had accepted it, as if Turkey were 'a fish waiting to be carved up'.[15]

However, neither the military chiefs nor the Sheik-ul-islam wished to be beholden to the Islamic mob, whose unruliness crested around 9–12 September with the support of a minority faction of ulema. So the uneasy Reshid-Mehmed Ali coalition held. Hoping to help tame the crowd and reassure the Porte without giving the Turkish war hawks the full green light that they sought, Stratford got Reshid to agree that the French and British should bring up a token force of two war steamers each to Constantinople. They provided a total of only fifty-seven cannon, but did show support for the Sultan's government and, implicitly, its policy of gradual escalation of measures against Russia. Both la Cour and Stratford agreed that the squadrons themselves should be held back until St Petersburg's response to the modifications arrived.[16]

The Ottoman authorities quickly banished the dissident ulema from Constantinople, started to draft the students into the army, and thus gained control over their militant traditionalists. The Porte, however, was now virtually committed, morally and operationally, to initiate military action sooner rather than later. The motley Ottoman army that was mobilized for the occasion would dissipate its spirits if it sat out the autumn and winter while salary arrears mounted, the diplomats exchanged new, unworkable peace formulas, and the Russian, French and British war machines prepared for serious action. This problem of human organization, not the winds of Besika Bay or any other inclement weather discussed during the summer, mandated the new escalation. Nevertheless, Ottoman preparations for a general offensive, especially in Eastern Anatolia and the eastern edge of the Black Sea, would not be ready until some time in October.[17]

The first reports of the Russian rejection arrived in Constantinople on 18–21 September, but with these came word to la Cour, Bruck and

Wildenbruch that their home governments still wanted the Turks to adhere to the original Vienna Note. Reshid's backing for a peaceful denouement was reduced to the Sultan, the Grand Vizier Mustafa, Rifaat and Stratford. Once more an overwhelming majority in the Grand Council favoured military resistance to Russia and diplomatic stonewalling of the Vienna Conference. No four-power guarantee of an interpretation could justify the indignity of sending such a self-effacing note to the Tsar.[18] If Stratford's Turkish expert Alison is to be believed, the Sultan feared that the ulema would summon the pious to murder him for heeding 'the counsels of the ungodly'. So he symbolically opted for a holy war against Russia by 'girding himself with the sword of the Prophet'.[19]

The diplomats still persevered in their efforts to avoid or delay bloodshed. On 24 September, as soon as the British mission received Clarendon's *No. 184* – his interpretation of the Vienna Note – Stratford joined la Cour in offering a 'hypothetical' guarantee of the Turkish Modifications as the proper reading of the note. Bruck and Wildenbruch lacked the instructions or independence to do this, but they did submit weaker assurances more or less equivalent to the project that Nesselrode and Buol were working out at Olmütz at this time.[20] So the Porte's subsequent moves, made before Clarendon's abandonment of the Vienna Note was known, are a test of the Olmütz project's chances of success.

They were in fact non-existent. On 25 and 26 September, directly after Russia's official reply to the modifications arrived, an expanded Grand Council convened. As many as 172 leading Ottomans, including 'the Pashas out of office' and 'representatives of the Law, the Trades, the Army and the Navy', decided unanimously in favour of war.[21] The reported debates of this quasi-parliament reveal a split between realists, who insisted upon coordination with the maritime powers for their material support, and traditionalist fanatics ready to march into the vast, unknown expanses of the Russian Empire in the name of Allah. The decision was accompanied by the call-up of territorial reserves and a reported 40,000 *softas* and other irregulars.[22]

Stratford meanwhile pursued his own version of London's two-pronged strategy. He prepared the Cabinet for the eventuality of war and the necessity of bringing up the fleet and supplying Turkey with British officers. He also offered two last-minute peace plans, either of which would bring Russia to heel and subordinate the Porte to Britain and Europe. One was a revised and 'truncated' Vienna Note in the spirit of the modifications, with a four-power declaration referring to the 1841 Treaty – a sort of Olmütz Project in reverse. The other proposal was for simple arbitration by the four powers.[23]

Actually at the time of the Ottoman decision to declare war the stock of both the French and British at Constantinople was rather low, due to their failure to convert the nominal Turkish ultimata of late July and late August into real ones. This situation gave the Russians a slight opening. Argyropoulos had been talking with Bruck and Stratford and continuing his shadow negotiations with the Turks, especially Mehmed Ali, who had told the Russian dragoman on 24 September that nothing would be definite for fifteen to twenty days. They projected an exchange of approved letters between Argyropoulos, speaking for Mehmed Ali, and Menshikov, who was then shuttling between Odessa and Sevastopol, to be followed by formal negotiations. The problem here, however, was the same as in every other European capital. Mehmed Ali demanded a substantive modification of the Menshikov Note or the Vienna Note, but Nesselrode and the Tsar, who had a hand in drafting and approving the reply to Argyropoulos, would make no such concession. Argyropoulos also made a bold suggestion, which flew in the face of official Russian policy. If the Turks wished to avoid war, they should send a plenipotentiary to Olmütz to obtain a few small modifications.[24] No one took him up on this, and the Turks did not avoid war. The Tsar, as we already know from Westmorland's *démarche* on the 26th, did not need a Turkish emissary at Olmütz to hear and reject a plea on behalf of the modified Vienna Note.

The Turks, moreover, neither had nor needed the text of the *Examen* to understand Russian thinking. Rather, the Ottoman war manifesto, which was issued on 4 October and published in the *Journal de Constantinople*, attacked the Vienna Note and anticipated correctly the core of Nesselrode's arguments.[25] Clarendon's order to Stratford to summon Dundas's squadron arrived on the same day.[26] On 8 October Omer gave General Gorchakov two weeks to evacuate the Principalities, which was the greatest delay that Stratford claimed he could obtain.[27]

It was precisely during this period when Stratford was trying to postpone the authorization to Omer, that Henry Reeve arrived. He was an eminent English public figure, whom Aberdeen had caused to be sent to check on Her Majesty's Ambassador to the Sublime Porte. Stratford treated Reeve to a pleasant Cook's Tour and sent him packing to Athens. Reeve then wrote to Clarendon that the Turkish army was not very good, that the Turkish hawks were unrealistically optimistic, that Reshid expected the British Cabinet to go along with him, and that Stratford thought that England would have a hand in the upcoming transformation of the Ottoman Empire.[28] All of this was correct.

LONDON: THE CABINET RESOLVES

The British had taken virtual command of Anglo-French policy with the rejection of the Vienna Note on 20 September and the move to promote a new four-power protocol to contain the Russians. Despite the entreaties of Prince Albert, King Leopold, and others, Aberdeen, as well as Clarendon, made it clear that no assurance at Olmütz could revive the original Vienna Note. Russell and Graham now presented the basic British options, given that Russia as well as Turkey appeared to prefer war to the perceived humiliation of diplomatic retreat. Russell, happy that the 'bear had thrown off the mask' and angling to use public opinion as his springboard to displace Aberdeen as Prime Minister, did not let up his pressure for naval support of the Turks. Graham, arrogantly attempting to keep his strategic intentions to himself, was forced to authorize passing the Dardanelles, lest the French with their timetable occupy them alone. He still had hopes for diplomacy, but he started in earnest to plan for a Baltic campaign the next spring. Brunnow, who was becoming almost as irrelevant in London as Argyropoulos was in Constantinople, assayed via yet another wordy memorandum to head off the orders to Stratford to summon the fleet, but to no avail. Rather, the leading British ministers figured that by being vague to Brunnow concerning their intentions, they might frighten the Tsar into meaningful concessions.[29]

When the actual Olmütz project became known, the French hesitated, but waited for England's reaction, where the Tsar's assurances were cancelled out by his continued insistence on the original Vienna Note. Napoleon III, not interested in endangering his *de facto* English alliance or prolonged ambiguities, had already forbidden Goyon to proceed to Warsaw and participate in the Tsar's charades. Nevertheless, Drouyn argued in favour of the Olmütz project as late as 3 October, but was as ready as the British to drop it when the word of the Turks' provisional declaration of war arrived that day.[30]

The news from Constantinople also triggered concrete, cooperative Anglo-French naval planning. Drouyn immediately instructed Walewski to work out a joint plan to protect the approaches to Varna as well as Constantinople. Simultaneously Clarendon and Palmerston told Walewski that the time had come to cease devising notes and to support Turkey with ships and officers. First as usual among the Cabinet members with a set of hypotheses, Russell presented his colleagues with two choices: either act as 'auxiliaries' of the Turks in order to get Nicholas to make a bilateral settlement with them, or, taking off from Stratford's *No. 132* of early July, ally with France militarily and Austria diplomatically, act as 'principles', and impose a European protectorate over the Ottoman Christians. Russell, who had reappointed Stratford back in February, saw the latter option as the only realistic one. So, in fact, did Aberdeen, which is why he reversed track and argued for the Olmütz project.[31]

The key British decisions were taken on 7–8 October at a full Cabinet meeting, minus Graham and the one lone Radical minister, Sir William Molesworth, who for some reason was not informed. Clarendon had already prepared official draft responses to Buol concerning Olmütz and to Drouyn concerning the fleets, as well as corresponding instructions to Stratford. Everybody knew that the real question being debated was that of an Anglo-Russian war over the Eastern Question. No one questioned the Porte's right to declare war and no one argued for Olmütz, which the French had also just definitively rejected, though a few hoped it could be used as a diplomatic opening. Russell and Palmerston played with the line that the British ought to enter the Black Sea as Turkey's 'auxiliaries' and clear it of Russian warships, but here Clarendon had already followed Graham's and Aberdeen's more realistic thinking, which carried the day. The British, once they started fighting Russia, could only be 'principles', and the entry into the Black Sea or the Baltic meant war with Russia. On the other hand, dropping anchor at Buyukdere, north of Constantinople but inside the Bosphorus, would be sufficient to guard the city. The Cabinet thus resolved to allow the squadrons to enter the Black Sea only if the Russians attacked, and this became Anglo-French policy.[32]

Brunnow warned the British not to aid the Turks actively and even credited himself for having prevented the fleets from passing the Bosphorus, but the British similarly warned the Russians against a naval attack on the Turks and urged the Austrians to stop waffling. Nevertheless, frustrated with Turkish intransigence, but hamstrung as well by Russian obstinacy, the Cabinet responded to Stratford's last-ditch peace proposals by authorizing him to pursue them and try to prevent the outbreak of hostilities.[33] British policy in London and Constantinople was now finally coordinated and rested on three options: (1) four-power mediation in favour of the Porte without war; (2) such mediation after the Russo-Turkish war erupted; or (3) Anglo-French participation in that war.

The resolutions of the London Cabinet in early October indicate a determination neither to precipitate hostilities with Russia, nor to lose the diplomatic duel or Western ascendancy in Constantinople. Napoleon III had a powerful lingering urge to impose a concert solution on both the Russians and the Turks and thus avoid war, but was forced to go along with the British or endanger the alliance that secured his domestic power.[34] Buol felt that the only possibility of peace lay in facilitating direct Russo-Turkish negotiations without any coercion. This was also a way of not alienating any of the other powers. Instead, he took the lead in promoting both a financially useful military cutback and sovereign neutrality.[35] These measures basically left the British, French, Turks and Russians free to pursue their own sovereign policies, so long as these did not injure Austria. In the light of respective military capabilities, Turkish offensives did not threaten to harm anyone, but Russian counter-offensives did; so once more the ball was in Russia's court.

THE FIGHTING BEGINS

Once it became clear that the Porte was aiming to declare war and drag the British and French along, the St Petersburg government had four choices consistent with its notion of honour. Russia could (1) remain completely on the defensive; (2) counterattack with great restraint; (3) counterattack with vigour on several fronts, without threatening Austria in the Western Balkans; or (4) attack there as well in concert with insurgent Serbs (as in the next war in 1877). In the event, Nesselrode, the aristocrat–bureaucrat, hinted at the first two safer options, but Nicholas, now acting as a cautious nationalist, selected the third over the fourth.[36]

The Russians had been preparing for Turkish offensives since early September, when the Porte rejected the original Vienna Note. The key Russian strategic move was to contain the summer campaign of the redoubtable insurgent Daghestani Shamyl in the Caucasus and thus free some veterans for action further to the south, and then to reinforce Vorontsov in Transcaucasia by sea with the Thirteenth Division at the end of September. They were still somewhat exposed to the Turks along the frontiers in the Caucasus, Transcaucasia and western Wallachia. The Persian government would have been willing to join a war against Turkey in order to obtain several Ottoman provinces, but Nicholas calculated that such an alliance was not worth the trouble.[37]

The news of Turkey's 4 October declaration and Omer's summons to Gorchakov created some panic within the Russian and foreign mercantile communities, which had to be reassured by the Minister of Finance. It also led to measured Russian diplomatic escalation. Nesselrode immediately asserted that, according to international law, the epoch of notes, declarations and protocols had ended, since wars can only be ended by treaties that supersede earlier treaties. Hoping that Brunnow's suggestion to convert the Vienna Note into a peace treaty might work, Nesselrode unrealistically asked Buol to get the Turks to send a plenipotentiary to Gorchakov's headquarters, as if Russia had just won a major military engagement.[38]

The Tsar as usual approved Nesselrode's dispatches, but he was more interested in the military side of things. Intelligence from Constantinople indicated that the Turks' major offensive would be in Asia. Intelligence from London indicated that the British considered the Black Sea open to the Sultan's allies upon the Porte's declaration of war and that they were ready to cover Turkish ports. An Anglo-French entry into the Black Sea would be the equivalent of a declaration of war, but Nicholas need not provoke London and Paris.[39]

Nicholas's secret orders to Menshikov, however, were very strong and a direct challenge to the Anglo-French: (1) as soon as the Turks initiate action, attack their ships wherever they can be found; (2) sever their communications along the European coast by bombarding Constanza (Kustendji) or Varna; (3) let their entire fleet venture out from the Bosphorus, if they choose, and then sink it; and (4) treat any British or French ships in the Black Sea as enemy vessels.[40] The Tsar thus again rejected Menshikov's cautionary advice, this time to reduce armaments and adopt a purely defensive stance, despite the diplomatic impasse. Meanwhile Russian officials hinted that the Black Sea fleet would stay put for winter, continued to shore up the Baltic defences and tried via back-door channels to ascertain British intentions.[41]

British intentions, of course, were dependent upon what the Russians and Turks would do. In Constantinople, Stratford was doing his utmost to retain the squadrons in order to postpone the outbreak of hostilities, give his peace plans a chance, and at least to maximize his influence over Turkish policy. La Cour, as per instructions, wanted the fleets brought up, but Stratford was able to hold off in principle until 15 October and delay their passing the Dardanelles until the 21st. Receiving Clarendon's wired instructions on the 18th, Stratford summoned the other three ambassadors, obtained their provisional support, elicited an authorized promise from Reshid to order Omer to put off his attack until 1 November and dispatched a draft four-power declaration to the Vienna Conference.[42] Stratford's trump card against the Turks was Clarendon's privately communicated disgust with their attitude that Britain had to support them no matter what.[43]

These machinations hardly constituted a real peace plan, but made sense for Reshid, Stratford and Britain. The delaying order contained an escape clause for the Turks: if hostilities commenced before Omer received it, then it was not valid. On the other hand, the declaration project was precisely that kind of 'Olmütz in reverse' – the modified Vienna Note and guarantees for Turkey – that St Petersburg was resolved to reject, but that the British could use to contain the French and separate the German powers from Russia. The Sultan, by accepting the delaying order, was showing preference for the Reshid–Stratford combination as well as allowing the necessary time for the steamers to tow the sailing vessels up against strong winds and currents. Reshid for his part was hawking a very English line. He called for a naval convention that would combine the British, French and Turkish fleets and take over the Black *and Baltic* Seas in the following year. The result would be the revised 1841 Treaty that would give the Porte the liberty and security to make reforms in the interests of all classes and subjects and to promote the development of commerce and industry – as if containing Russia were the key to saving the Ottoman Empire.[44] No one mentioned that the Turks might get what they wanted and then not reform.

Omer and the Turkish hawks, of course, were determined not to be thwarted. Try as Stratford and Reshid might, the Sultan's order, authorized on 21 October, could not prevent the first Ottoman soldiers from crossing the Danube from Vidin in Western Bulgaria on the 23rd. They skirmished with a few Cossacks and seized the small Wallachian town of Calafat with a view to hampering Russian communications with Serbia.[45]

The Turks at this time had about 90,000 troops in Bulgaria, most of them regulars, and the Russians only about 50,000 in Wallachia, almost all of them, as per Paskevich's thinking, deployed in the eastern part. The Turks also had about 75,000 men in Eastern Anatolia stationed in Erzerum, Kars, Ardahan and Batum; half of them were irregulars, but the total was twice the number of Russian troops deployed in an arc stretching from the border at the coastal fortress of St Nicholas down to Erevan in Armenia. The Batum force attacked St Nicholas on the night of the 27 October and within a few days had taken it and Poti on the Black Sea as well, thereby cutting Russia's sea communications between Sevastopol and Transcaucasia.[46]

Elsewhere the Turks were less successful. In mid-November armies of 18,000 and 36,000 from Ardahan and Kars penetrated Russian territory. General I.M. Andronikov with only 7,000 men immediately counterattacked in two columns from the front and the flank, and dispersed the Ardahan force outside Akhaltsikh, while his superior, V.O. Bebutov, with 10,000 men scared off the troops from Kars by threatening to cut off their retreat. Russian tactical superiority and nerve also prevailed in Central Wallachia. When a Turkish force of about 8,000 took Oltenitsa, right across the Danube, General P.A. Dannenberg with his 6,000 counterattacked on 4 November with heavy losses on both sides. He did not use his reserves, and the battle was registered in the 'sports page' of military commentary as a Russian defeat. Omer, however, feared Russian reinforcements and pulled the remnants of his troops back into Bulgaria. Thus in the first few weeks of warfare the Turks were successful only at Calafat, St Nicholas and Poti, where the Russians were terribly undermanned.[47] This dose of reality dampened Turkish bravado and strengthened the political hand of Reshid and the British and French legations in Constantinople.

Russian policy, however, was not geared to capitalize on the inconclusive military successes that a defensive strategy promised to yield, even though Nesselrode's circular of 31 October and the Tsar's personal letter to Queen Victoria of the next day proclaimed moderation. Rather Nicholas issued a war manifesto of his own on 1 November, with an appeal to Russian religious sentiment and with misinformation regarding the four powers' attitudes towards his dispute with the Porte. This was fully in keeping with the self-righteous, imperious and self-deluding mentality that had informed his diplomacy, but contradicted his military and naval commands that assumed Anglo-French hostility.[48]

Russian society itself was divided over the embroglio with Turkey. On the one hand, educated opinion with access to foreign newspapers, uneasy merchants, and also some of the military élite, doubted the soundness of Russia's policy and feared the upcoming war, but could not influence decision-making. Some mass sentiment, on the other hand, was favourable to the sacred cause and, according to diplomatic reports, was even 'crying havoc and conquest of

St Sophia'. There was a similar gap between Reshid's realism and the mad Turkish dreams of marching into Russia and even toward Moscow.[49]

Overall the Turkish and the Russian shifts over to active hostilities were honest and straightforward moves that had been incubating since 1848 and had gained momentum for almost a year. By late September, the momentum of Ottoman mobilization had itself become a decisive force. Consequently, the Turks had the opportunity to start the shooting, and chose to do so, thus leading the British and the French to the brink of war. The Russians then had the option of remaining on the defensive to facilitate further negotiations or answering in kind. Nicholas chose to answer in kind, and the ninth Russo-Turkish war since 1676 was under way.

NOTES

1. *KfZh* 331–2 (1/13 Sept.–1/13 Oct. 1853); Schiemann IV: 299; Tarlé I: 318); Nes. to Brw., 16/28 Sept. IX 1853 (TsGADA III/115).
2. Du Plat to Cln., 21, 23 Sept. 1853 (PRO FO 65/435).
3. Kis. to Nes., 9/21 Sept. 1853, with Nes. to Nich. I., Nich. I gloss (AVPR K 112)
4. Brw. to Nes., 4/16 Sept. 1853 (AVPR K 75).
5. ZP II.40 (11/23 Sept. 1853).
6. Prince William memo, 26–28, Sept. 1853 (Borries, *Preussen im Krimkrieg*, Stuttgart 1930, pp. 344–6); Brq. to Drn., 28 Sept. 1853 (AMAE CP Autr. 452); cf. Bapst: 447–8, Schroeder *AGBCW*: 77.
7. Cln. to Wst., Wst. to Cln. 20, 26 Sept. 1853 (ClDp. c. 126, 4).
8. Nes. to Brw. 16/28 Sept. (TsGADA III/115); *CORR* III.31.
9. FJ/Nich. I meeting, 27 Sept. 1853 (*CORR* III.23, Incl.).
10. Vitzthum von Eckstaedt, *St Petersburg and London in the Years 1852–1864*, ed. Henry Reeve (2 vols, London 1887), I: 57.
11. Nes. to Brw., 16/28 Sept, 21 Sept./3 Oct. 1853 (TsGADA III/115).
12. Buol to Hüb./Colloredo, 28 Sept. 1853, (*AGK* I.1).
13. Brq. to Drn., Fnt. to Nes. – no gloss, 23 Sept. 1853 (AMAE CP Autr. 451; AVPR K 147, cf. ZP II.111.). Schroeder's explanation that Buol was following Bourqueney's suggestions at Olmütz is thus imprecise: *AGBCW*: 79, note.
14. Saab *OCA*: 81–4.
15. Mollerus to vH., 5, 12 Sept. 1853 (NRA 2.05.01 BZ 2769).
16. Cf. Temperley *ENEC*: 351–2.
17. Str. to Cln., 24 Sept. 1853 (*CORR* III.63).
18. DRA UM Tyrk. Dep. 1853, No. 34 (18 Sept. 1853); Lac. to Drn., 15, 21, 23 (listed 27) Sept. 1853 (AMAE CP Turq. 315); Arg. to Oz., 10/22 Sept. 1853 (AVPR K 20); Mollerus to vH., 21–22 Sept. 1853 (NRA 2.01.05 BZ 2769).

19. To LStr., 28 Sept. 1853, (Lane-Poole II: 301–2); cf. Temperley *ENEC*: 359.
20. Str. to Cln. 24, 26 Sept. 1853 (*CORR* III.63–4).
21. Alison to LStr., 28 Sept. 1853 (Lane-Poole II).
22. DRA UM Tyrk. Dep 1853 (29 Sept. 1853); Saab *OCA*: 88–9.
23. Str. to Cln., 12 Oct. 1853 (*CORR* III.66).
24. Arg. to Oz., Mnsh., Sen., 13/25 Sept–19 Sept./1 Oct. 1853; Draft Arg. to Mnsh., n.d. (AVPR K 20).
25. *CORR* III.80, Incl. 3, trans. Hertslet II.234.
26. Temperley *ENEC*:238 (no source indicated).
27. Str. to Cln. 1, 22 Oct. 1853 (ClDp. c. 10).
28. Str., Reeve to Cln., 4–16 Oct. 1853 (ClDp. c. 10).
29. Cf. Conacher *AC*: 190–5; Schroeder *AGBCW*: 73; Lambert *PRW*: 20–1.
30. Drn. to Wal., 3–5 Oct. 1853 (AMAE CP Angl. 691).
31. Rus. Memo., Ab. to Grm., Cln., 4–6 Oct. 1853 (*AbC* X, ClDp. c. 4).
32. Brw. to Nes., Grm. to Ab., Wal. to Drn., 5–8 Oct. 1853 (AVPR K 75, *AbC* X, AMAE CP Angl. 691).
33. Wal. to Drn., 11, 14 Oct. 1853 (AMAE CP Angl. 691).
34. Cf. Echard: 35–7.
35. Min. Conf. Prot. 9 Oct. 1853; Buol to Crivelli, etc., 18 Oct.–15 Nov. 1853 (*AGK* I.1) cf. Schroeder *AGBCW*: 85–6.
36. Cf. Schiemann IV: 302 (citing Nich. I to Psk.).
37. Baddeley: 449; Tarlé I: 282; Vorontsov to Mnsh. 5/17 Oct. 1853 (ZP II.74); Dolgoruki to Nes. 3/15 Nov. (AVPR K 140).
38. Nes. to Brw. 2/14, 5/17 Oct. (TsGADA III/115), to Buol, 5/17 Oct. 1853 (ZP II.114).
39. Nes. to Nich. I with gloss, 7/19 Oct. 1853 (AVPR K 30).
40. Tarlé I: 282; Nich. I to Mnsh., 9/21 Oct. 1853 (ZP II.48).
41. *DM* 29 Oct./10 Nov. 1853 (TsGAVMF 19/7/32); Pipers to Stierneld, 12 Oct. 1853 (SRA KUB Pet.).
42. *CORR* III.169.
43. Str. to Cln., 22 Oct. 1853 (Lane-Poole II).
44. Rsh. to Lac., 19–21 Oct. (AMAE CP Turq. 316).
45. Beskrovnyi *RVI*: 233; Temperley *ENECL* 364–5.
46. Schefer memo., 13 Oct. 1853 (AMAE CP Turq. 316); Beskrovnyi *RVI*: 221, 235; Allen/Muratoff: 59–61.
47. Allen/Muratoff: 61–3; Tarlé I: 284; Beskrovnyi *RVI*: 233–7.
48. ZP II.24, 78, 96; trans. of Manifesto: Hertslet II.235.
49. Du Plat to Cln., 10, 27 Oct. 1853 (PRO FO 65/435); Pipers to Stierneld, 12 Oct. 1853 (SRA KUB Pet.); Ctb. to Dr., 14 Oct. 1853 (AMAE CP Rus., 210,); also AMAE CCC Pologne 12/52 (from Warsaw, 22 Oct. 1853), and Moscow (5 Nov. 1853); Seym., Reeve to Cln., 12, 16 Nov. 1853 (*CORR* III.307, ClDp. c. 10).

CHAPTER SIXTEEN
Getting Down to Business (October–December 1853)

RUSSIA AND BRITAIN: PLANNING THE INEVITABLE

The October 1853 decisions in London and St Petersburg set Russia and Britain on a virtually unstoppable collision course. London's avowed policy of protecting Turkey from the Russian fleet prompted Nesselrode to put it to Seymour bluntly: 'Are we at peace or at war?'[1] Brunnow warned that Parliament was debating such expansionist options as opening British funds to finance Turkish railroads or even sponsoring Balkan Christian states under British(!) protection. He also confirmed that Stratford had the authority to deploy Dundas's squadron to defend Asian Trebizond as well as European Varna. The Tsar cried 'foul' and himself answered Nesselrode's question: 'C'est la guerre [War]!'[2] This was one day after Nicholas learned that, due to the Anglo-French fleets, Austria could not help Russia at Constantinople any longer and that Buol now favoured a European congress to settle the Eastern Question.[3]

Russia's ambassadors, Buol and Prussia's Manteuffel, were trying to find peace formulas, but Nesselrode saw a resolution only after the Turks had been 'thrashed well'. Thereupon Nicholas would fix the conditions of an honourable settlement, with Russia retaining her 'deserved influence' in Turkey. Russia, after all, had a tradition going back 150 years of ending Turkish wars with bilateral negotiations at Russian headquarters in Ottoman territory,[4] even if no other power considered this a relevant precedent.

The Tsar still planned to wait until the spring to cross the Danube, but wanted immediate counterattacks from Transcaucasia and at sea. While he was willing to allow the British and the French to take command of the Black Sea and expand the war, he was prepared to follow through with his earlier idea of declaring the Principalities, Serbia and Bulgaria independent. All the same, following Nesselrode's warnings, he would only react to native insurgency, not incite it. The Tsar also accepted the intentions of Austria, Prussia, Sweden and Denmark to remain neutral in the upcoming showdown as the best he could obtain from them in the light of the maritime powers' means of inflicting reprisals. Actually he was surprised, angry and even fearful of Turkish boldness, and appealed (unsuccessfully) to the Austrian Emperor to convince the Turks to commence bilateral negotiations, on Russian terms, of course. In short, Nicholas was his usual rigid, but fatalistic, self. His 'hope was in God and His holy will', just as back in April, when it became apparent where British policy was headed.[5] Stratford and Brunnow were thus on the same wave-length, when the one surmised that the Tsar had been 'duping himself', and the other complained that Menshikov really had been working for Napoleon III.[6]

The British leaders, correctly assuming that Nicholas would not retreat, were also headed for war. The question was which operations to emphasize – defensive or offensive – and when to enter the fray. The logic of defensive thinking lay in diplomatic and material realism, as well as lingering fear of Ottoman domestic fragility and of Russian capabilities in the Baltic, in the Black Sea and on land. One military expert wrote back from Constantinople that the Dardanelles were vulnerable to attack by land and had to be secured. Stratford at first envisioned only defending Constantinople with the fleets and not venturing eastward except for reconnaissance. The French were not at all interested in the aggressive schemes in the Black Sea and the Caucasus that had attracted some Englishmen for twenty years, but that were incompatible with diplomatic cooperation with Austria. Vice-Admiral Hamelin (who had replaced la Suisse back in July) was authorized to defend Turkey's Black Sea coast only as far as Varna, if the main Russian fleet ventured out of Sevastopol. Even Rose, who still remained in the shadows as an adviser to Clarendon and was itching to get back to Constantinople, inclined at first to remain on the defensive, but included as 'defensive' such measures as deploying the fleets to deny Russia access to the mouth of the Danube, as well as to Varna and Burgas.[7] In the event, Stratford, Dundas, la Cour and Hamelin met on 1 November and refused the Turkish request to send their squadrons along with the Turkish main fleet toward the Crimea.[8]

The British Admiralty's timetable turned out to be crucial. The battleships needed six months' preparation for war, so the Baltic campaign could not start until spring. Graham exaggerated the Russian threat from that quarter after the hydrographer Captain John Washington had returned from a mission to the Baltic, ostensibly to discuss 'the establishment of an improved form of a lifeboat'. Washington reported a more powerful Russian fleet than Seymour indicated, as well as impregnable walls at Kronstadt. Graham therefore would not send reinforcements to the Mediterranean until late October, when he was certain that the Russians would not venture out from the Baltic. On his own authority he urged Dundas not to budge from the Bosphorus and offend the Tsar. Into early December Graham still leaned toward forcing the Porte to conciliate Russia, especially if the Turks attacked first and were beaten, rather than allow Britain to 'be dragged into hostilities by a barbarian'.[9] Nevertheless, he dispatched the energetic Rear Admiral Edmund Lyons from his diplomatic post in Stockholm to be Dundas's second-in-command.

Graham also had realized since June that Britain lacked the smaller craft necessary for operating in some of the Baltic coastal waters and had been trying to line up experienced Danish and Swedish ship pilots. Clarendon for his part sounded out the Swedes directly for naval aid as early as mid-October. Stockholm and Copenhagen, however, had already decided during the March war jitters to coordinate their neutrality policies. They began their serious deliberations when the Russians occupied the Principalities and by now had decided upon the strictest possible neutrality. But this did not deter Graham from seeking a vulnerable Russian point for a concentrated attack, and he selected Reval (Tallin) in Estonia, where one of Russia's Baltic squadrons normally docked.[10]

Britain's real doves were in a quandary. Queen Victoria, as well as Aberdeen, did not like the Turkish notions of a tripartite military convention and a Baltic campaign, and attributed them to Stratford. Nevertheless, all she could do in response to the Tsar's personal appeal that she trust him was to retort that the common Englishman agreed that no sovereign could assent to what he was asking of the Sultan.[11] Napoleon III and many of the French élite were likewise frustrated by the Tsar's unwillingness to concede diplomatically, which forced them to fall into line with their British ally and honour their commitments to the Porte.[12]

Palmerston, that 'most English' of the Cabinet members, ceded to his worst fears of Russian expansionism. He was relentless in his demands for open military aid to Turkey and in his full support of the Stratford–Reshid plan for a Great Power settlement that would eliminate any of Russia's specific advantages over Turkey.

Once the news of the first shots reached London, he insisted that the admirals have clear instructions to prevent the Russians from attacking the Turks or making landings at any point along the Black Sea coast, lest the Anglo-French appear 'foolish'. Simultaneously Rose allowed his strategic imagination to run wild with news of the first Turkish successes. He called for supporting Omer Pasha from Burgas, blockading Russia's ports, destroying Odessa's naval installations, seizing the huge grain depots, bottling up Sevastopol and the Sea of Azov, then landing in the Crimea, taking Balaklava, besieging Sevastopol and finally trying to link up with insurgent Circassians.[13] This idea intersected with the roll-back schemes of the Polish Emigration, which since 1831 had sought a grand alliance of England, France, Turkey, the small peoples who had been victims of Russian expansion from the Baltic to the Black Sea and anyone else who cared to join. The energetic Polish *emigré* general Adalbert Chrzanowski, who had served the Ottomans in the late 1830s, and who was now in London, may have thrown his daring ideas into the British planning pot.[14] At any rate, diplomacy for peace was giving way to the preliminaries of an Anglo-Russian war.

BRITAIN AND FRANCE: ROPING IN AUSTRIA

The next difficult task for British and French diplomacy was to move Vienna closer to their view of a mediated solution. Buol at first favoured the Russian approach, direct Russo-Turkish negotiations; he would not hear of any of the concrete projects that the British were concocting in Constantinople and London.[15] However, neither the Russians nor the Turks wanted to negotiate until they had won. Russia would not allow either direct Russo-Turkish parleys under the watchful eyes of the four powers or a six-power conference that included Turkey.[16] The British and French, therefore, could only try the standard Stratford–Reshid tactic of routing a project to St Petersburg with the Porte's preliminary adherence. The British Cabinet had adopted such an approach on 20 October instead of Palmerston's more confrontational proposal of summoning Russia to a conference in London. St Petersburg would also reject this mode of action, but at least it could proceed without Russia's participation. The logic of this approach, after the collapse of the Vienna Note, was consistency with (1) Anglo-French naval support of Turkey, (2)

Austria's desire that Russia quit the Principalities and relinquish any notion of a Balkan campaign, and (3) the Berlin Cabinet's backing of these desires in the interest of 'Germany' as well as Prussia. The essence of British diplomacy in October and November was to realise this tactic in some way or other.[17]

Napoleon III's priorities of the English alliance first and cooperation with Vienna and Berlin second, coupled with the force of German and Italian nationalism, rendered Clarendon's task rather easy. There was no change in policy, merely in personnel, as la Cour was replaced at Constantinople by General Baraguay d'Hilliers. This swashbuckling veteran of the Algerian campaigns may have been expected to be independent of Stratford, but could not compete with or displace the Reshid–Stratford duo.[18]

Meanwhile, the Prussian leader Otto Manteuffel played a clever, dissimulating game, promising neutrality to Russia, offering London support in case Vienna were to side with Russia, and manoeuvring both with and against Austria to lead Germany in pursuing a sovereign, self-interested policy in the coming conflict. Simultaneously, Piedmont, which tried to represent 'Italy' at this time and sought a means to expel Austria from Italy, attempted to link up with the incipient Anglo-French–Turkish alliance and even with *emigré* Poles.[19] Prussian and Piedmontese policies thus placed Austria in a precarious position *vis-à-vis* the French and British.

Clarendon, on the other hand, had learned from Palmerston the diplomatic trick of taking outlandishly moral high grounds in order to achieve something more modest, and he regularly accused Vienna (falsely) of being St Petersburg's toady. The French played a similar game. While paying lip-service to Buol's latest peace initiatives, Drouyn and Napoleon threatened not so subtly to 'cooperate with the Revolution' and 'explode Italy' if Austria did not at least join the effort to pressure Russia to evacuate the Principalities and revise the 1841 Treaty in Turkey's interest. Whereas such tactics eventually led Buol to snap back at the French concerning Austria's 'sovereign' policy and seek closer cooperation with the German Confederation, they also did force Austria further into a corner.[20]

Austria's chief concerns were necessarily domestic tranquillity and keeping the Russo-Turkish war away from her borders. As of late November there were no firm commitments from Russia to Vienna's liking concerning the war. So Buol was able to override the Austrian partisans of alliance with Russia. Although he accused the Turks of being more refractory than the Russians, he agreed to Britain's scheme of first asking the Porte to state reasonable peace terms and then pressuring the Russians to accept them.[21]

Both logic and muscle leaned on Vienna. Buol had foresworn a partition deal with Russia months earlier and had already agreed that the original Turkish modifications interpreted the Vienna Note correctly. What grounds, then, could Austria have for not joining to give Turkey diplomatic support in St Petersburg, if the Porte formulated an acceptable settlement on its own? Moreover, if Austria declined, then both Western powers with Prussia might support with arms a combination of Italian, German, Hungarian and Polish nationalism and Ottoman 'independence' against Austria and Russia. Austria's acquiescence was thus a political survival tactic, prompted by the Tsar's armed diplomacy and foreseen by Nesselrode as early as December 1852.[22]

The irony of how this ploy worked out is that Stratford himself, try as he might, had no success in Constantinople in getting the Porte to agree to any specific project that came from London and was conceived in the spirit of the modified Vienna Note. This was because the Turks were rather dizzy with their initial successes on the battlefield, Reshid having become as 'hot upon war' as any other Turk and thus rejecting in November what would have been acceptable in September.[23]

Stratford, though, did obtain one advantage for Britain from Ottoman Cabinet politics. By opting for war, Reshid was able to eclipse Mehmed Ali. Her Majesty's Ambassador could now hope that poor performance on the part of the Ottoman military would render the Porte more amenable to what he suggested as a reasonable solution. The Porte's confidential declaration to Stratford and Baraguay in late November seemed to point in this direction. Turkey would settle for a new arrangement that expanded the 1841 Treaty and disallowed any Russian pretensions to interfere in Ottoman domestic affairs. Clarendon's latest projects, on the other hand, smacked too much of the Vienna Note for Ottoman tastes, but played into Stratford's hands, enabling him to be Britain's 'nice' agent. He simply took control of Buol's initiatives concerning direct Russo-Turkish peace negotiations by preparing Reshid to specify realistic Turkish conditions.[24]

Meanwhile, by 5 December, the reconvened Vienna Conference had produced a Collective Note asking the Porte to state its conditions for a settlement. The accompanying protocol outlined some principles, including the Tsar's Olmütz promises respecting Ottoman sovereignty and the confirmation of existing treaties, as well as strict respect for existing territorial boundaries.[25] This was not as much as Reshid was demanding in late November in the line of treaty revision, but at least the Vienna Conference had finally recognized the legitimacy of Turkish diplomacy.

Meyendorff had hoped that this four-power Vienna initiative would preclude Stratford's personal involvement. The Austrians, and even some French, dreamed of using the protocol to constrain Turkey, but the British, 'in the interest of the European balance', would have none of this. They saw the chief merit of the protocol in its presumed roping in of Austria, not its negligible chances of solving the Russo-Turkish dispute without a wider war.[26]

The beleaguered Buol found himself trying to tie down the sea powers, but was also using their fleets to force the Russians to compromise further, even if he dared not say this outright. The *sine qua non* requirements for his planning to lead to peace were Russian restraint and Turkish military ineptitude, which allowed the French to distance themselves from the British. However, neither the tone of Nicholas I's war manifesto nor his appointment of a governor of the Principalities appeared to be consistent with Russian restraint.[27] The Ottoman armies and navies, moreover, had yet to reveal the fulness of their ineptitude. Thus the four-power initiative, if carried out, was as likely to bind Austria and Prussia to the minimal aims of Anglo-French armed diplomacy as it was to achieve anything else.

RUSSIA AND TURKEY: THE GUNS OF SINOPE

As late as 27 November, Queen Victoria, unaware of the Tsar's standing orders to Menshikov, feared that allowing the Turks to send three steamers toward the Crimea would 'beard the Russian fleet and tempt it to come out of Sevastopol' – as if Stratford controlled the Porte's maritime policy.[28] The Turks in fact longed to force the pace by dispatching their entire navy, except perhaps their two three-deckers. Stratford could only block this by withholding part of the British squadron from Constantinople. The Porte then compromised and also held back its four two-decker battleships from the expedition. But the Turks did send a flotilla of frigates, smaller sail and steamers, manned by 4,000 miserably treated tars. Captain Adolphus Slade, who was still in Ottoman service, commanded one of the steamers.[29]

The queen should also have been worried about the Russians, who remained on the defensive only in the Balkans. General V.I. Bebutov and about 10,000 Russian and native veterans advanced into Eastern Turkey from Aleksandropol. At the so-called Battle of Bashgedikler on 1 December, they smashed a motley Turkish force of 30,000–36,000 by holding the flanks, storming a hill, capturing the main artillery battery, and sending the survivors fleeing back to Kars.[30]

More decisive and fatal was the Russian action at sea. Admiral Nakhimov received orders on 5 November to find the Turkish fleet and destroy it. Capturing a steamer on the 17th, he located the flotilla in Sinope Bay on the 23rd, set a blockade, and sent to Sevastopol for reinforcements. As Sinope lay about 350 miles to the east of Constantinople, but only about 180 miles south of Sevastopol, the Turks were trapped. Within a week Nakhimov had six capital sail and a total of 720 guns, many of them heavy and with explosive shell. The Turks, with no battleships and at most 520 inferior cannon, were little more than target practice and did not even make best use of their reputedly powerful shore batteries.[31]

A valid defensive reason for Nakhimov's attacking was that the flotilla included two transports to ferry men and supplies to the Transcaucasian front. This, any way, was the chief Russian military concern, though the evidence indicates that the real Turkish aim was to acquire prestige or provoke the Russians in order to force the hands of Britain and France. There is no proof at all, however, that Stratford was consciously 'bearding' the Russians by not doing his utmost to disallow a flotilla that was only sailing along the southern coast of the Black Sea. His peace plan presupposed Russian and Turkish restraint. Whatever the case, Nakhimov was skilled and resolute; the Ottoman commander Osman Pasha was neither, but he would not surrender upon demand. Within two hours on the morning of 30 November, the entire flotilla was sunk and at least 2,000 Turks were killed. In this 'legitimate act of war', which the British press would soon call a 'massacre', the Russians lost no ships and very few men.[32]

Only Slade's steamer slipped back to the Bosphorus to tell the tale. The two ambassadors and two admirals quickly met on 3 December, shunned Dundas's urge for revenge in favour of French caution, and agreed to send two steamers apiece to reconnoitre Sinope and Varna, but not provoke battle with a superior Russian unit. Stratford rightly expected this modest show of force in support of his diplomacy would be followed by the entrance of the entire combined fleets to attain uncontested superiority.[33] Turkish 'bearding' had played right into his hands.

STRATFORD VINDICATED: NAPOLEON STRIKES AGAIN

The first word of Sinope reached London and Paris on 10 December. In England this added fuel to a Cabinet crisis, as Russell threatened to resign that day. Palmerston's immediate reaction was that the Russian fleet should be told to remain in port. He submitted his resignation three days later, ostensibly over Russell's proposed Reform Bill to extend the franchise, but in most people's minds over the timidity of British foreign policy.[34] The press in both countries was in an uproar.[35] Brunnow could console himself and Nesselrode with haughty sneers regarding 'the ulema of London . . . (who) greatly resemble their brothers in Constantinople', but Russia's diplomatic position was virtually hopeless, and Brunnow knew it.[36]

After Sinope there was no Anglo-French division. Napoleon and Drouyn agreed with Cowley that the admirals' instructions implicitly would have allowed them to aid the Turks if this had been possible, and that the Russian attack was a moral strike at the British and French and their idle squadrons. Clarendon for his part used the news of Sinope as a splendid device for cutting a Gordian knot even more quickly then he had done with regard to the 'violent interpretation'. He recommended that the squadrons replace the lost Turkish ships in escorting transports and other functions. Walewski assured Thouvenel that any French proposal for action would be approved in London.[37]

Clarendon and Drouyn then worked feverishly to produce similar, strong messages to both Constantinople and St Petersburg, in part to assure that the Tsar knew that Palmerston's resignation was not a signal of British retreat. Drouyn formally adopted Palmerston's line and suggested 'inviting' the Russian fleet to return to Sevastopol as a 'pledge' for the evacuation of the Principalities.[38]

Russell and Napoleon quickly became the most decisive visible actors, and the latter was somewhat embarrassed over word that Hamelin and Baraguay had restrained Stratford from sending ships into the Black Sea before Sinope. Now, despite Cowley's warnings about winter weather, Napoleon authorized orders to enter the Black Sea, and the London Cabinet thereupon instructed Dundas to prevent another Sinope.[39] Drouyn pressed a reluctant Clarendon to agree specifically that war need not be declared on Russia first and that the allies could openly support the Turks because they were in the right. Then on 19 December Napoleon bluffed and called the question again by threatening to double the size of the French squadron and go it alone if the British balked.[40]

There was no such worry. Graham had already accepted the inevitability of war, and Aberdeen had to acquiesce. So did Queen Victoria, who had not really paid attention to the details of Stratford's negotiations and did not understand what he had been doing.[41]

The next day Clarendon, backed by the Cabinet, seconded French policy and responded to Stratford's call by authorizing him to see that the combined fleets obtained 'complete command of the Black Sea' and so inform 'the Russian Admiral'. At the same time Clarendon politely told the Turks to refrain from further independent naval action and cooperate with the protocol process. Walewski and Clarendon parleyed for three hours and agreed that 'complete command of the Black Sea' meant war with Russia.[42]

Aberdeen, at this moment, was no more than a weak chairman of the board, Russell, Graham and Clarendon operating as a big three under him, Cowley being the only ambassador in close contact able to influence policy, and all eyes were on public opinion and future parliamentary debates. Napoleon led again to some extent, but only in the directions that Clarendon's and Russell's initial reactions to Sinope pointed. This was no repeat of late March, when Napoleon answered Rose's invitation to the squadrons only to be scolded by a divided London Cabinet.

What, in fact, might have happened had Nicholas deviated from the course he had set in the summer,[43] ignored the Turkish flotilla and allowed the latest Vienna project to work itself out is an unanswered question. Schroeder thinks that Russian diplomatic rigidity still would have produced Anglo-French war-initiating policies under the pretext that the Tsar was 'the obstacle to peace'.[44] At any rate, Sinope was crucial, and thereby hangs the remainder of our tale. In early December the French were still waiting; *The Times*, at least, had hopes for a peaceful settlement; and Graham had not yet determined that war with Russia was the only solution. Once he had so resolved, he no longer obstructed Clarendon or Stratford, but fixed his sights on the Sevastopol naval base in the Black Sea, naively hoped to destroy it before the Baltic ice melted in early spring, and set in motion the plans for successive maritime campaigns in both seas.[45]

THE TURKS IN TOW AND THE DIE CAST

The Battle of Sinope was, to use a metaphor, the midwife who delivered the Crimea War out of the womb of the Russo-Turkish conflict. Nicholas did not seem to recognize the Pyrrhic nature of his victory, which he celebrated with great fanfare. Rather, he was furious with Vienna over the Collective Note of 5 December and entertained hopes of having Buol replaced. The young Kaiser, however, backed *his* Chancellor with a blunt letter to the Tsar that reiterated Austria's objections to Russian policies. Nicholas and Nesselrode could only retort with the standard arguments, but to no avail. Nicholas, if not Nesselrode, now seemed to have lost hope in a peaceful settlement.[46]

Meanwhile Stratford had already anticipated the 5 December Collective Note in his dealings with Reshid and was ready as usual to orchestrate the four ambassadors' transmission of a Vienna project to the Porte. This time, moreover, he had extra leverage. Having seized the military initiative, the Ottomans were more dependent than ever upon the Anglo-French for naval protection in the Black Sea. Even if the English and French agreed to send in the fleets, it would take time to prepare them, so Turkish aggressiveness was totally stymied.

As soon as the steamers returned from Sinope on 9 December with confirmation of the disaster, Lyons outlined the hazards of the stormy weather and poor visibility in this season. Accordingly, Hamelin proposed that Anglo-French steamers be deployed only to defend the European coast from Varna to the Bosphorus. Dundas agreed. Stratford, however, wished to cover the entire Black Sea, but then compromised by suggesting the establishment of a defensive cordon from Varna to Sinope, which Slade hoped to convert into a naval base as great as Sevastopol.[47]

Stratford used the fleets to press his diplomacy on the Turkish war party. The Collective Note of 5 December, though, was irrelevant, arriving from Vienna only on the 16th, by which time the ambassadors, operating on earlier instructions, had produced a draft much more favourable to the Porte. The clairvoyant Englishman did not even open his dispatch from Westmorland. Rather, as before, Stratford had induced Reshid to play along, then persuaded the French envoy to help draft the text, and finally arranged a meeting or two with Wildenbruch and Bruck and allowed the latter to make a few minor changes before they all agreed that this was the most one could extract from the Turks.[48]

The resulting four-power project of 15 December took the form of identical notes suggesting the bases for a negotiated peace. They represented yet another version of the original *Turkish Ultimatum* of late July or the Modifications cum Reshid's letter of late August, with the two key provisions absent from the Collective Note – preliminary commitment to a speedy evacuation of the Principalities and extension of the 1840–41 treaties relative to Turkish sovereignty.[49]

As Reshid had promised Stratford, a Grand Council met on 17–18 December to consider these proposals. The ulema and Mehmed Ali argued illogically that their military position was too weak to negotiate successfully, so they had to continue the fight – as if that military position could thereby possibly improve without active Anglo-French help. Reshid and his disciple/rivals, Fuad and Aali, did not wish to gamble away Turkey's future in single combat against Russia and won the day by pointing to financial and military realities. Reshid then obtained authorization to accept the four-power initiative, with the identical notes of 15 December serving as the guarantee, and with further domestic reforms an unstated corollary.[50]

Immediately the Muslim war faction, spearheaded by some ulema and *softas* and backed by Mehmed Ali and the Sheik-ul-islam, agitated against Reshid in the mosques and medreshes, creating another threat of anti-Christian pogroms and real panic in the government. One frightened minister even deposited his jewellery at the British mission, while Reshid went into hiding and offered to resign. In response, Stratford, acting as doyen of the diplomatic corps and having nine large war steamers at his disposal, calmed the Sultan and helped the government restore order without bloodshed by forcing Mehmed Ali and the Sheik-ul-islam to act against their own supporters. The ringleaders were exiled to Cyprus; the more turbulent *softas* were given the choice of exile or going to the East Anatolian front; and suspect military units were sent out of the capital. The upshot was a weakening of the militants, with the circumspect Riza replacing the adventurist naval chief, a boon for the Anglo-French fleets, and a moderate brother-in-law of the Sultan entering the Council as a Minister Without Portfolio.[51] The social tensions, the workings of mid-century capitalist imperialism, and the dependency of backward regimes on advanced protectors – all of which accompany Western-supported modernization – could not have been more manifest.

The disturbances delayed the Porte's official response to the four-power initiative, but did not derail it. In fact, Turkey's militants were weakened by the news of the 1 December military disaster at Bashkedikler and the direct threat to Kars, since the Russians retained clear superiority over the Turks on land as well as at sea. In addition, there was the temporarily alarming news that the Persian Shah, presumably at Russian instigation, was planning to mobilize four divisions against different points in Turkish Armenia and Mesopotamia, including Basra near the Persian Gulf. (In fact, facing British pressure and lacking any Russian support, the Persians decided against mobilization.)[52]

Stratford received a welcome Christmas Eve present from Napoleon III, when the new, post-Sinope instructions to Baraguay and Hamelin arrived. Now Baraguay had to agree immediately to the plan to send a superior combined fleet of sail as well as steamers. Decisions followed quickly. On the 26th the Turkish Council took up Reshid's draft response to the identical notes of 15 December. By the 28th Stratford and Baraguay had prepared their instructions to Dundas and Hamelin and their notes informing Menshikov of Anglo-French intent to protect Ottoman territory; however, they concealed the fact that the admirals were also instructed to afford protection to any Turkish vessels that sought it.[53] Stratford envisioned war with Russia now, since he obtained the necessary local plot of land for a British naval cemetery. Bruck and Wildenbruch could only protest in vain that the entry of the fleets was not four-power policy.

While Stratford and Baraguay and the admirals were planning Black Sea operations, the Turks deliberated. A minority of the Grand Council opposed Reshid's approach, so the Sultan was presented with two choices. As expected, he rejected unilateral bellicosity, and he accepted Reshid's reworking of the four-power proposals and a revision of the 1841 Treaty to recognize Turkey as an equal European power to be the desired guarantee against Russia. The Sultan also indicated that further extension of the Tanzimat reforms for the Ottoman Christians would be forthcoming. Finally, in defiance of Russia's rights granted by the 1829 Treaty of Adrianople, which was formally abrogated by the current war, he unilaterally renewed the privileges of Moldavia, Wallachia and Serbia. This quasi-declaration of full Ottoman sovereignty over its autonomous Christian provinces had been in the pipeline for several months. Finally, Reshid wrote to Turkey's ambassadors abroad that this too was another, unalterable ultimatum. He need not have bothered, since Turkey no longer could force the pace of action.[54]

Bruck, who had evaded his instructions in going along with Stratford, viewed this New Year's Eve response as 'satisfactory' and ostensibly saw hope that the fleets somehow would not enter and that Russia would now accede.[55] He was wrong on both counts. The next day the 'weather . . . cleared', and a combined fleet of sixteen battleships, five frigates and twenty-one steamers, five of them Turkish, entered the Black Sea.[56]

Exactly a year, a week and a day earlier Nicholas had ordered the mobilization of the Black Sea fleet and two army corps in response to the Bethlehem decision, the news concerning Montenegro, and the exaggerated appeals from the Russian embassy, which had just lost a round in local patriarchal politics. Half a year later his troops had marched into Moldavia and Wallachia. The results to date were not what he had originally expected, but the most crucial ones followed from his military decisions in November. His intention to wage war across the Danube prompted the Austrians to agree to the Collective Note of 5 December. The order to attack the Ottoman naval squadron and transports close to Turkish shores brought the Anglo-French task-force into the Black Sea with a local ultimatum to the Russian fleet to keep to port. In this sense the Russians lost the Battle of Sinope. British war planning was finally gathering momentum and starting to take on a life of its own. The Tsar now had to accept peace more or less on the basis of the latest Turkish ultimatum or face an expanded war.

NOTES

1. Seym. to Cln., 29 Oct. 1853 (*CORR* III.202).
2. Brw. to Nes., 9/21, 7/29 Oct. 1853, Nich. I gloss. 24 Oct./5 Nov. 1853 (AVPR K 75); cf. Rich: 93, Martens XII: 300–31.
3. Mdf. to Nes., 16/28 Oct. 1853, Nich. I gloss, 23 Oct./4 Nov. 1853 (AVPR K 147).
4. Nes. to Brw., 3l Oct./12 Nov.–4/16 Dec. 1853 (TsGADA III/115).
5. ZP II.67, 66, 139, 140 (Nich. I to Mnsh., Psk., 22 Oct./3 Nov., 7/19 Nov. 1853; memo, by 8/20 Nov. 1853; Nes. memo 8/20 Nov. 1853); cf. Martens XII: 343–5. Monnier mistakenly saw Nesselrode's memo as a response to Pogodin's 7/19 Dec. call for Holy War: 115–16; cf., correctly, Rich: 93–5.
6. Str. to W. Canning, 9 Oct. 1853 (Lane-Poole II); Bunsen to Mnt. 5 Nov. 1853 (*PAP* II).
7. Drn. to Bar., 30 Oct. 1853 (AMAE CP Turq. 316); Str. to Cln., Gen. McIntosh to Col. Aisy, 10–11 Oct. 1853; Rose to Cln., 11 Oct. 1853; Rose memo, surmised between 23 Oct. and 6 Nov. 1853, to Cln., 11 Nov. 1853 (ClDp. c. 10).
8. *CORR* III.293; Lac. to Drn. 4 Nov. 1853 (AMAE CP Turq. 316).
9. Lambert *RCW*: 20–3; Greenhill/Gifford: 56–60; Lane-Poole II: 328–9; Grm. to Ab., 9 Oct. 1853 (*AbC* X); *Herbert* I: 211.
10. Lambert *PRW*: 20–31; Arvel B. Erikson, *The Public career of Sir James Graham* (Oxford 1952, rpt. 1974), p.345; Halicz: 33–6.
11. QV to Ab., Nich. I, 5, 14 Nov. 1853 (*LQV* II).
12. Guizot to (?) Orl., 3 Nov. 1853; Kis. to Nes., 29 Nov./11 Dec. 1853; Seebach to Beust, Nes. 19 Nov., 26 Nov./8 Dec. 1853 (SHSA AM Kanz. Paris Ber., ZP II.81).

13. Plm. to Cln., 25 Sept., 28 Oct., 3, 25 Nov. 1853; Rose to Cln., 11 Nov. 1853, to Ponsonby, 19, 23 Nov. 1853 (ClDp. c. 3, 10).
14. Marcel Handelsmann, *Adam Czartoryski* (4 vols in 3, Warsaw 1948–50), vols II–III; Marian Kukiel, *Czartoryski and European Unity*, pp. 193–281; E. d'Azeglio to Cavour, 12 Nov. 1853 (ASMAE Leg. Londra, Cart. LXXVII, Confid. No. XXIII).
15. Buol to Hüb., Brk., 1, 15 Nov. 1853 (*AGK* I.1).
16. Nes. to Mdf., 14/26 Nov. 1853 (HHSA PA X 38).
17. Cf. Schroeder *AGBCW*: 90–7.
18. Monnier: 112, 120–2; Bapst: 464–5.
19. *Inter alia*, Mnt. to Arnim, 1 Dec. 1853 (PAP II); E. d'Azeglio to Cavour, 26 Sept.–15 Nov. 1853 (ASMAE Leg. Londra, Cart LXXVII, AP and Confid.); Schroeder *AGBCW*: 83–6, 92.
20. Hüb. to Buol. 13 Nov. 1853 (*AGK* I.1); cf. Unckel: 111–12; Schroeder *AGBCW*: 47–51, 101–6.
21. Min. Conf. Prot., 13 Nov. 1853 (*POM* III.175).
22. FJ to Nich. I, 11 Dec. 1853 (*AGK* I.1); cf. ZP I.96–7.
23. Str. to LStr. 19 Nov. 1853 (Lane-Poole II).
24. Cln. Draft Note revised by Str., Lac., 8 Nov. 1853 (AMAE CP Turq. 317); Buol to Brk., 11 Nov. 1853 (*AGK* I.1).
25. *CORR* III.443, Incl. 1–2, 447, Incl. 1–2.
26. Wal. to Thv., Drn., 7, 14 Dec. 1853 (AMAE PA PT 20, CP Angl. 692).
27. Mdf. to Nes., 16/28 Oct., 25 Nov./7 Dec. 29 Nov./11 Dec. 1853 (AVPR K 147); Seym. to Cln., 5 Dec. 1853 (*CORR* III.251).
28. QV to Ab., 27 Nov. 1853 (*AbC* X, *LQV* II).
29. Cf. Saab *OCA*: 112, 116–17.
30. Allen/Muratoff: 63–4; Beskrovnyi *RVI*: 236–7.
31. Kornilov to Mnsh., Nakhimov Orders, 5/17, 17/29 Nov. 1853 (ZP II.52–3); Curtiss *RCW*: 206–7; Beskrovnyi *RVI*: 239–41.
32. Tarlé I: 356–2; Alison to LStr., 25 Dec. 1853 (Lane-Poole II); Saab *OCA*: 112–17; Temperley *SROCW* II: 292; Lambert *CW*: 58; Wailly to Bar., by 9 Dec. 1853 (AMAE CP Turq. 317).
33. Str. to Cln., 4 Dec. (*CORR* II.487); Lambert *PRW*: 24.
34. Schroeder *AGBCW*: 119; Conacher *AC*: 221; Plm. to Cln., 11 Nov. 1853 (ClDp. c. 3); Wal. to Drn., 12 Dec. (AMAE CP Angl. 692).
35. Lynn Case, *French Opinion on War and Diplomacy during the Second Empire* (Philadelphia 1954), pp. 16–18; Marten: 193–7; Conacher *AC*: 234.
36. Brw. to Nes., '13' Dec. 1853 (*NLP* X).
37. Bohl: 196–7; Cln. to Rus., Wal; Wal. to Thv., 13 Dec. 1853 (PRO FO 30/22/11A; AMAE PA PW 14, PT 20).
38. Drn. to Wal., 13 Dec. 1853 (*FR*); Cln. to Cwl., 16 Dec. 1853 (Maxwell II).
39. Drn. to Bar., 13–14 Dec. 1853 (AMAE CP Turq. 317); Cln. to Str., 17 Dec. (*CORR* III.476).
40. Drn. to Wal., 19 Dec. 1853 (AMAE CP Angl. 692).
41. Lambert *PRW*: 25; Conacher *AC*: 236–1; QV to Cln., 17 Dec. 1853 (*LQV* II).
42. Cln. to Str., 20 Dec. 1853 (*CORR* III.492); Wal. to Drn., Cln., 21 Dec. 1853 (AMAE CP Angl. 692).

43. Nich. I to FJ, 8/20 July, 25 July/6 Aug. 1853 (HHSA PA KA GA 8, Russl.).
44. Schroeder *AGBCW*: 126–7.
45. Martin: 193; Conacher *AC*: 221; Lambert *PRW*: 25.
46. FJ to Nich. I, 11 Dec, 1853 (*AGK* I.1); Nes. to Mdf., 12/24 Dec. 1853 (HHSA PA X 38); Rch. to Mnt. 11 Jan. 1854 (*PAP* II).
47. Hamelin to Bar., Slade to Str., 13, 15 Dec. 1853 (AMAE CP Turq. 317).
48. Rsh. to Bar., Brk., Wildenbruch, Str., 12 Dec. (*CORR* III. 609b, cf. Mollerus to vH., 22 Dec. 1853 (NRA 2.05.01 BZ 2773).
49. *CORR* III.566, Incl. 1–2.
50. E. Pisani to Str., 18 Dec. 1853 (*CORR* III.559, Incl.); Bar. to Drn., 24 Dec. 1853 (AMAE CP Turq. 317).
51. Cf. Saab *OCA*: 124–6.
52. L. Tavernier to the French Mission, 30 Nov. 1853 (AMAE CP, Turq. 317); Bar. to Drn., 28 Dec. (AMAE CP Turq. 318B); Dolgoruki to Nes., 3/15 Dec. (AVPR K 140); cf. Garry Alder, 'India and the Crimea War', *Journal of Imperial and Commonwealth History* II.2 (Oct. 1973): 19–25.
53. *CORR* III.615, Incl. 4, 617, Incl. 5.
54. Firman/Hatt-i-sherif to Prince Alexander of Serbia, dated end December; Rsh. to Bar., Bruck, Str., 31 Dec. 1853, to Musurus, 3 Jan. 1854 (AMAE CP Turq. 317; *CORR* III.632, Incl. 1, 667).
55. Brk. to Buol, 1 Jan 1854 (*AGK* I.1); Schroeder, 'Bruck vs. Buol: the Dispute over Austrian Eastern Policy 1853–1855', *JMH* 40 (1968): 201–3.
56. Dundas to Str., 4 Jan. 1854 (*CORR* III.666); Beskrovnyi *RVI*: 248–9.

CHAPTER SEVENTEEN
Calculated Countdown (December 1853–April 1854)

STRATEGIC PLANNING

A point of no return came for the Turks in September, the Russians in November and the British and French in December. Buol still dreamt of bringing the Russians and Turks to the negotiating table, but both camps were planning offensives, and the French and British were contemplating the mechanics of rupture.[1]

Nicholas had expected as early as November that the French would have 15,000 troops in Varna to help guard the coastal route to the Bosphorus and that the Western allies would control the Black Sea. Nevertheless, he determined that he would cross the Danube in early spring 1854, bank on spontaneous local uprisings, and take his chances. He wished to feint a major move across the Lower Danube to open the way for a successful thrust into Western Bulgaria and toward Serbia. Menshikov did not consider using Kornilov and Nakhimov against the tentative Anglo-French in the Black Sea, but thought only in terms of defence.[2]

The same guarded mentalities prevailed regarding the Baltic, when Nicholas directed the Naval Committee to devise a strategy in early December. Kornilov, optimistically reckoning a maximum of twenty-eight Russian and twenty Anglo-French line vessels for the Baltic, recommended a forward policy of confronting and stopping the latter at the Sound and the Belts, but he had no support. This is hardly surprising, for it would have taken a fool or a maritime genius to dare to pit Russia's rickety sailing ships against Britain's new screw-propelled battleships. In fact, Russia was outnumbered in the Baltic as well, twenty-eight (fourteen screw, fourteen sail) to twenty-five (all sail). The two naval chiefs, Menshikov and

Grand Duke Constantine, were more realistic. The Committee reflected their views and resolved to keep the fleet at Kronstadt and Sveaborg, the island-fortress off Helsingfors, not to try to defend Riga or Reval by sea, and not to fortify any further the Åland Islands between Finland and Sweden.[3]

Two sets of aggressive ideas competed in Britain, but only one of them made any sense at all. Palmerston's fanciful concept of a rollback of Russia from the Baltic to the Caucasus was no secret in diplomatic circles, since offensive alliances with Austria, Prussia and Sweden were prerequisites for success. Such notions, however, threatened to involve the Western powers in a long, costly war, which few Englishmen, even fewer Frenchmen desired; only the Polish *emigrés* did, and they counted for very little. Even Palmerston opposed precipitous attacks.[4]

Graham's plans for dramatic naval strikes were more modest and attractive, and he won over the Foreign Office in late December. He had inherited a navy that had been beefed up to knock out Cherbourg in case of a French war. He then hoped to destroy Sevastopol and the Russian Black Sea fleet by the time the Baltic ice melted. In this way an overwhelming Anglo-French armada could launch the northern campaign that would bring Russia to the peace table in one year. Clarendon forgot about Captain Washington's report and even dreamed of dictating peace at Kronstadt. For the present, though, Graham demanded that Gallipoli be garrisoned to protect the squadrons' retreat through the Dardanelles in case of a spectacular Russian advance, and he wanted to be sure that British as well as French troops were there. These defensive plans dovetailed with French desires to send an expeditionary force only to help the Turks defend Constantinople and the Balkan approaches down to Varna.[5]

Graham's long-range schemes required a preponderance of French troops, as well as British ships, so the British had to treat the French as equals. Napoleon refused to risk 20,000–30,000 men in an early strike on Sevastopol. Neither Cowley nor Britain's chief military engineer, Sir John Burgoygne, who stopped off at Paris *en route* to Constantinople, could get Napoleon to commit to an offensive plan, especially as the word was that Sevastopol could not be destroyed so quickly. French terrestrial thinking, as well as public opinion and Napoleon's shaky domestic situation, encouraged a more cautious approach that looked to European alliances and diplomacy to contain Russia. In contrast, English maritime supremacy and public support of vigorous action fostered Graham's forward strategy and London's political leadership in projecting offensives, even if British war plans were still more inchoate than real.[6]

BLUNT MESSAGES

The irony of the entry of combined squadrons into the Black Sea is that they did not thereby attain real control as per instructions. Instead the British and French simply escorted Turkish reinforcements to Batum and then returned to the Bosphorus at the end of January. The only real 'bearding' of the Russians was the delivery of Dundas's and Hamelin's notes to Menshikov, an obvious by-product being some systematic reconnaissance of Sevastopol's defences. As per instructions and Palmerston's reaction to Sinope, these notes requested all Russian warships to return to Sevastopol.[7] This lifted the ambiguities from the ambassadors' original drafts. It was also about as close as one could get to a *de facto* declaration of war – a notification by two Great Powers of intention to enforce a blockade against a third.

The less eager French had pressed for such explicit orders, while Palmerston was waiting on the sideline to return to the government as soon as they were accepted and the Reform Bill tabled. The instructions for Constantinople were also dispatched to St Petersburg to be communicated simultaneously to Nesselrode. As usual, the French courted public opinion and goaded St Petersburg by publishing their dispatch in *Le Moniteur*, while they continued their insurance policy of back-door *plaisanteries* with Russian statesmen and unofficial agents.[8]

Due to heavy snows, the packet from Drouyn to Castelbajac did not arrive until 10 January. Meanwhile the British and French had decided to press Buol to agree to send a collective note to St Petersburg on behalf of the still unknown Turkish reworking of the 5 December Protocol. As soon as the Turkish proposals of 31 December reached London, Russell and Clarendon were ready to treat them as an ultimatum to Russia.[9]

Buol was almost trapped. He disliked Stratford's control of the negotiations in Constantinople, regretted the instructions to the Anglo-French fleets, and rued the Porte's disdain for the latest Vienna project. On the other hand, as Francis Joseph wrote to Nicholas, Vienna was most interested in securing its own neutrality in the upcoming war and a guarantee that Russia would respect the Ottoman ruling dynasty and its territorial integrity.[10] Buol therefore compromised. He allowed the Turkish response of 31 December to the identical notes, all of which Stratford had engineered, to serve as the response to the 5 December Protocol. In return the British and French temporarily dropped the idea of formal, collective pressure on Russia and allowed Buol to transmit the unanimous four-power approval of the Turkish conditions to St Petersburg. This new Protocol of 13 January 1854 carried no sanctions, but did associate the German powers with the Porte's aspirations and hence the minimum goals of the Anglo-French naval intervention, which had just commenced. Buol wrote as if he hoped that Russia would accept this peace initiative, but he knew in fact that the Tsar would not accept it.[11]

Everyone else knew that too. The real question was how Russia would react to the entry of the fleets. Nesselrode, counting on inclement winter weather, tried to temporize. He would be patient if the British and French promised to be neutral and prevent Turkish naval attacks on Russia too. This *was* Anglo-French policy regarding the Turkish fleet on the high seas. However, when Castelbajac and Seymour each saw the ailing Russian Chancellor on 12 January, they informed him that the admirals' instructions were to 'require every Russian ship they meet with to re-enter a Russian port'. Both Seymour and Nesselrode understood that war would soon follow.[12] The Tsar was irate over the French publications in *Le Moniteur* and the blatant English reconnaissance of Sevastopol. Local rumour claimed that only the arguments of Nesselrode, Orlov and the Prussian representative, General Rochow, stopped the enraged Nicholas from expelling Seymour and Castelbajac on the spot.[13]

The diplomacy of rupture then proceeded normally. On 16 January Nesselrode sent instructions to Kiselev and Brunnow to demand explanations from Paris and London. If these proved unsatisfactory, they were to demand their passports. Buol, eager to mediate, had already rejected the ultimatum quality of the Turkish response and now asked the British and French to temper their Black Sea policy if Russia accepted the Porte's conditions for negotiations. He need not have bothered, since Nesselrode had already spurned in principle the Turkish demand for a preliminary commitment to evacuate the Principalities.[14]

The posturing for the moral high ground continued in France and England, where Kiselev and Brunnow communicated Nesselrode's dispatch. On 24 January Brunnow futilely submitted one of his longest, cleverest and most ingratiating of memoranda, in which he smoothed over the aggressiveness of all sides, blamed the events on

Divine Providence, and appealed for further negotiations on the basis of the 5 December Protocol. The English and French, however, were already sketching their military alliance and a four-power convention to bind Austria and Prussia.[15]

The identical replies to the Russian envoys and dispatches to Castelbajac and Seymour, as well as the draft four-power convention, were ready by the end of the month. Clarendon had insisted upon firmness and speed, but the French, having kept up close ties with Vienna, attempted a moderate retreat from what had already been delivered to Sevastopol, Odessa, St Petersburg and the press. They tried to delete the war-inducing 'make the [Russian] vessels return to port' phrase from the dispatch to Castelbajac, but the English caught this 'copyist's error'.[16] The replies, then, were polite affirmations that the combined fleets would restrain the Turks from attacking by sea, while allowing transports to provision Ottoman land forces and forcing the Russian naval vessels to stay put.[17] Brunnow and Kiselev consulted and quickly asked for their passports.

The draft four-power convention envisioned an ultimatum to Russia to make peace on the basis of the 13 January protocol. Prussia had yet to commit, so the British and French could still hope for an expanded war coalition. The minimum to be attained was Austro-Prussian support of Anglo-French war aims. The key clause was an extension of the 1841 Treaty to include Turkey in 'the European equilibrium'.[18] This formulation was sufficiently elastic to allow a modification of the former Russo-Turkish treaties and a territorial rollback of Russia, if circumstances so permitted, or a compromise peace, if this became necessary.

What was now really a headless Clarendon–Russell–Graham–Palmerston team tried to lead the English into war in the face of an angry, pro-Turkish public mood, that had viewed the government as weak and beholden to foreign interests. With the coming rupture, the press campaign against the 'traitor' Prince Albert for his German connections and Austrian orientation died down, and Queen Victoria was able to open Parliament on 31 January without incident.[19] By early February the first diplomatic Blue Books, with over 1,000 documents, were ready, and they served to prove to the public that the Cabinet had been simultaneously conciliatory and vigilant, as well as prudent in its escalations. As the French prepared to publish a few documents of their own in *Le Moniteur*, Walewski urged his superiors to suppress Napoleon's recent threat to double his squadron at the Bosphorus and enter the Black Sea alone. The British, after all, initially concealed the accounts of the potentially compromising

Nicholas–Seymour conversations, though these actually helped the coalition, when the Russians smoked them out in March.[20]

CONTINGENT NEUTRALS

The key decision that brought on the war preceded any secure commitments from the neutral powers. However, Anglo-French maritime and commercial supremacy and the prevailing doctrine that effective wartime blockades were to be respected meant that a *de facto* benevolent neutrality of other maritime states was to be expected. Well aware that they lay in the direct line of fire in any Anglo-Russian war, the Scandinavians took the lead in establishing the principles of non-belligerent maritime rights for the war. The very vulnerable Dutch and Belgians, the smaller German powers, and also three great powers – Prussia, Austria and the United States – followed this lead.[21]

The Swedish–Danish declaration of 20 December, long in the making, was essentially only one of unarmed neutrality, with a total of just five Danish and Swedish–Norwegian harbours closed to the future belligerents. The Danes and Swedes also did their best to avoid giving direct offence to Russia, but stood together on the rights of private citizens to offer services to whomsoever they chose and sheer inability to close all ports to the British and French.[22]

London pushed to convert Scandinavian neutrality into practical logistical support. Until the British were certain that Russia's lighter sailing fleet would not venture out to sea, they wanted Copenhagen and the Sound ports closed too, since the heavier screw-steamers were thought to displace too much water for these harbours. French policy paralleled British. The Russians as well were trying to draw the Scandinavians into alliances and offered twelve to fifteen ships to help them close the Baltic, but the Danish envoy quieted Nesselrode with the spectre of a Baltic 'Sinope'. With English support, the Swedes could also refuse Nesselrode's request that all ports be closed to belligerents. The cost-conscious Graham was not satisfied. He continued to calculate fancifully as if the Swedes would forget their size, their history, their vulnerability and their interests, and sacrifice future tranquillity for the possibility of regaining Finland.[23]

The United States was the potential wild card, but limited its involvement to securing neutral rights. President Pierce had spent 1853 dispatching Admiral Perry to Japan and purchasing 45,000 more square miles of real estate for his land-rich compatriots from the cash-strapped Mexicans. He was ready in December to set in motion a programme for expansion in the Caribbean, Central America, Alaska and Hawaii. The British and French, however, were just as ready, if necessary, to extend their alliance to the New World to stop the Yankees from picking European pockets while the Eastern Question was on fire. Some Russians dreamed of an offensive alliance with America, but this merely helped induce London to compromise with Washington's concept that 'free ships make free goods'. At the same time the British served notice that they would utilize the same criminal definition of privateers and *lettres de marque* that the Americans employed in the Mexican War. All in all, the United States was far more attracted to the inexpensive and profitable policy of selling to both sides and chipping away at Europe's position in the New World than to risking more than 75 per cent of its trade by challenging the new British screw over a mere pittance.[24]

Prussia was the key neutral power in the European north, capable of influencing Swedish and Danish policies. King Frederick William feared the 'Revolution' in general and the French army on the Rhine in particular, and thus had urged the Russians to evacuate the Principalities to end the crisis in late November. Minister President Manteuffel despaired of Russian policy, sought a private arrangement with the London moderates, and was ready in the last resort to join battle against Russia.[25]

Concerned Prussians from various quarters bombarded the king and Manteuffel with unsolicited suggestions. Some ultra-conservatives like Rochow, bought Nesselrode's arguments for Holy Alliance solidarity against the West. Material reality, if not sentiment, neutralized such types, since the Prussian military men did not believe that Russia could supply the needed 200,000 troops Rochow promised against the French. There were only two serious options for Prussia: joining with England, as Berlin's envoy to London, Christian von Bunsen, suggested, or remaining neutral. Several variants of the anti-Russian course circulated, including one that matched the wildest dreams of Palmerston and the Italians. However, in the light of the strength of Prussian conservatism and royalist sentiment, the king would side with England only if Austria were to join Russia, or if England were to guarantee Prussian territory and offer some more. Otherwise the real choice, *faute de mieux*, was between two types of sovereign neutrality: Austro-German and North German.[26]

Otto von Bismarck, who represented Prussia in the Confederation, and the royal heir, Prince William, wished to capitalize on Austria's dilemmas to increase Prussian power in Germany.[27] This was a policy that required patience and nerve, and in the long run worked. In early 1854, however, faction neutralized faction, and Prussian policy wavered, remained guarded, put a brake on both sides, and ensured there would be no land blockade of Russia. Anglo-French pressure curtailed Russia's overland imports from Belgium, whose industrialists sold seven times more *matériel* to France during the war. Berlin and Brussels paid lip-service to the analogy between maritime and terrestrial contraband, but the British themselves did not initially attempt any maritime, commercial blockade. The Russians even found ways to order English products, as well as to float loans in Berlin and Amsterdam.[28]

Austria's problems were more pressing due to Russia's forward policies and Turkey's instability. Standing French and Prussian policies stymied the partisans of Austrian expansion into the Western Balkans. Buol, in fact, was able to convince both the young Kaiser and the Imperial Cabinet on 22–23 January to base policy upon cooperation with the Confederation and with Prussia in order to shield Austria from Anglo-French pressure. Were Russia to cross the Danube, then Austria would establish an observation army and consult with Prussia and the Confederation. If Russia attempted any permanent conquests in the Balkans, then Austria would have to go to war. This was Vienna's version of sovereign, armed neutrality – interposing Austria between Russia and Turkey in the Balkans in the interests of domestic and regional tranquillity.[29]

Vienna's Germany-centred defensive policy required an English loan to finance the observation corps. Still the Austrians were not about to fall for any Anglo-French snares, such as an exchange whereby Piedmont acquired Lombardy and Austria the Principalities, so that London and Paris could obtain a large army to fight Russia at little cost. Rather, Buol wanted Britain and France to restrain the Turks. Yet he also explained to the Russians the limits of Austrian neutrality, appealed to Nicholas to accept the 13 January Protocol, and threatened him with an Anglo-French victory and the opening of the Straits.[30]

The policies of the neutral states established the parameters of the upcoming, expanded war. Russia would be fighting the English, the French and the Turks. The rest of the world was staying out for now. However, Austria, while blocking the ambitions of both sides, was also, in her own interest, crafting a German policy that was more to the advantage of the allies than of Russia, as was the maritime stance of the United States, the Scandinavians and the Dutch.

A TALE OF THREE EMPERORS

The end game of the diplomatic preliminaries of the Crimean War
included a textbook case study in a peculiar kind of futility. Direct
contacts between crowned heads, special missions, and secret feelers
and negotiations cause great stirs and make good copy, but are
no substitute for existing, normal diplomatic channels, when major
state interests are involved. The king of A may sympathize with the
emperor of B but no amount of eloquent French prose can negate
common sense or erase the commitments of the government of A
to C, D and E.

The Tsar, to all intents and purposes, was reduced to desperation
diplomacy by early January. Actually he had been acting somewhat
like a desperado on the international scene since he had mobilized
a fleet and two corps a year earlier and dispatched Menshikov to
Constantinople, but now his blank cheques had been cashed and
he had to pay up. As a result he had been trying his hand at
personal diplomacy, going over the heads or behind the backs of
the regular foreign policy establishments. This too did not work
very well. Queen Victoria and Francis Joseph heeded their foreign
offices in matters of sovereign–sovereign relations; the unstable
Frederick William IV in his heart of hearts wanted a five-power
protectorate over the Ottoman Christians; and the latter's brother
and heir William favoured Britain over Russia.

Nicholas's lone hope of breaking up the British–French–Turkish
coalition lay with his fellow quasi-desperado, Napoleon III. True, the
latter needed his English alliance as a substitute for full legitimacy, but
still was eager to avoid the serious consequences of that alliance, such
as a costly military campaign that France did not need. Moreover, he
sometimes carried on diplomacy independently of Drouyn, or at least
appeared to do so, and his half-brother Morny corresponded with the
unofficial Russian envoy Princesss Lieven and blamed everything on
the British.

The summer had witnessed the commencement of a Franco-Russian
rapprochement gavotte, whereby someone would make a *beau geste* or
utter a *bon mot* on behalf of the other Emperor. It might be the
Emperor himself, or a relative, or a marshal or aide-de-camp, or a
lady with a Paris salon, or a trusted German diplomat. The message
would run somewhat as follows: Nicholas meant nothing personal

when he disputed Napoleon's III, and really desires an *entente* with him and to relate to him as *frère*; Napoleon bears no grudge and longs for peace; 'Albion is perfidious'; France is about to fight England's war; the German powers are puny, while France and Russia are natural allies. Perhaps the most malapropos of these ballroom steps was Castelbajac's congratulating Nicholas for the Christians' victory over the infidel at Sinope – an act which outraged Seymour.[31]

London had no small number of concerns in early 1854 over Napoleon's flirtation with Russia, since the French were lukewarm, indifferent or even hostile towards the British over the impending war. Napoleon, however, was not playing the Russian game, but his own: to find an independent position somewhere between England and Austria. He allowed his Foreign Ministry to help draft a personal letter, which was simultaneously a concession to Buol, an appeal to Nicholas regarding the 13 January Protocol, an offer to him of a future *entente*, and a notice to the French population that its government was doing everything possible to avoid war without shirking its commitments. Clarendon & Co. were upset that the letter offered Anglo-French naval withdrawal all the way to Besika Bay if Nicholas evacuated the Principalities. But Napoleon sent the letter at the end of January, the French government published it and it became the centrepiece of *La France et la Russie*, a little pamphlet and miniature 'blue book' with about fifty diplomatic documents, justifying the approaching war against Russia.[32]

If Nicholas had been willing to compromise he would have separated France and Austria from England, but he had other ideas while Napoleon was composing his celebrated epistle. Soon after Nicholas calmed down from the news of the Anglo-French summons to return to port in the Black Sea, Orlov presented a concrete plan to entice Austria into an active *entente*. Accordingly, Russia would allow Austrian troops to occupy Serbia in case war broke out; Russia and Austria would obtain Prussian support for this scheme; and they could accompany this with declarations based on the 5 December Protocol to cover Austria's obligations to other powers.[33] It is easy to see why Orlov was considered as the 'great cajoler' in England,[34] but it is also obvious what he was doing. While appearing to be offering the Tsar a blueprint for diplomatic victory, which would make the old treaties irrelevant, Orlov was leaving an opening to try to cut his own deal with Berlin and Vienna, and he certainly had the ability. Two years and a million casualties later he would be able to make a few bargains with that other clever fellow, Napoleon III, but not now.

Orlov set off on 20 January with an official proposal for strict, Russian guaranteed, Austro-Prussian neutrality and unofficial Austro-Prussian mediation between Russia and Turkey, so that the Russo-Turkish negotiations would appear to be bilateral. The Turks would explain to Russian satisfaction the meaning of their recent firmans to the Orthodox; and the 1841 Treaty could not be revised. England and France could be disregarded, since they had already violated the 1841 Treaty by entering the Black Sea.[35]

This was another 'mission impossible'. By the time Orlov reached his Vienna on 28 January, Manteuffel had already wired to Vienna that the proposals were inadmissible and offered to resign rather than accept Russian-guaranteed neutrality. In addition, Buol had already consulted Metternich and anticipated Orlov's plan to offer a deal, once his initial proposals failed.[36]

Orlov spent a day with Meyendorff, then saw the Kaiser, who bluntly asked if Nicholas planned to cross the Danube, and finally met with Buol, who demanded in return *'general guarantees'* concerning the Balkan status quo. Nicholas had already expressly forbidden such promises in response to the 13 January Protocol, since the Balkan Christians might be his only allies. On 31 January the Kaiser presided over another extraordinary council, which spurned Orlov's proposals. The military chiefs, Hess and Grünne, wished to occupy Serbia anyway, but Buol and the Finance Minister, Baumgartner, vetoed this as incompatible with cooperation with the Anglo-French and Austria's need for credit. Two days later the Vienna Conference of Buol, Bourquenay, Westmorland and the Prussian Arnim also disallowed Orlov's proposals as incompatible with the earlier Protocol.[37]

Then the real bargaining began. Napoleon III's letter and Buol's convincing the English and French to defer the four-power convention enabled Orlov to send back to St Petersburg a plan for Austria to try to broker a Russo-Turkish peace on the basis of the 13 January Protocol.[38] In this way at least a conservative Central European monarchy could be the handmaiden of Russia's retreat from her pretensions and the Principalities. Simultaneously, Seebach, the Saxon envoy to Paris, was urging his father-in-law Nesselrode to accept Napoleon's offer. Brunnow, meanwhile, had been trying to get Nicholas to see that the main thing to negotiate in the Eastern Question was not the extortion of a Turkish diplomatic note, but the withdrawal of the Anglo-French squadron back to the Mediterranean.[39]

The Tsar, however, refused to allow the Austrians and the French to save Russia from the more ambitious British and Turks. He rejected

Napoleon's offer as beneath Russia's honour and merely promised no more offensives if France restrained the Turks – as if the occupation of the Principalities were not *the* main issue. Nesselrode had already stated that Orlov's official instructions represented Russia's final offer to Turkey, and criticized him for not doing the impossible – extracting some promissory note of neutrality from Berlin and Vienna. By the time that Orlov returned in mid-February, Nicholas had confirmed that the Russian troops would cross the Danube. He vowed again that he would make no conquests, but would not promise to respect Ottoman territorial integrity.[40] The two other emperors, Napoleon and Francis Joseph, thus had no grounds to change course.

FROM RUPTURE TO SUMMONS

The diplomacy of rupture and the preparations for war proceeded as if there were no epistolary exchanges under way among the emperors and other crowned heads and no extraordinary missions. While Napoleon's letter was *en route* to St Petersburg and Orlov was still in Vienna, Brunnow and Kiselev suspended Russia's relations with England and France, leaving London and Paris on 6 February. Thereupon Clarendon and Drouyn instructed Seymour and Castelbajac to return home. Nicholas showed his greater displeasure at England by expelling Seymour, albeit courteously, while bestowing the prestigious Order of St Andrew on Castelbajac. These gestures, were however, mere formalities.[41]

Both sides were acting as if war had just been declared. The British preparations for the Baltic expedition had begun quietly, but by early February were obvious. The Anglo-French had hoped that Turkish troops with European officers and aided by the squadrons could take Sevastopol, but the Turks, with only 10,000–15,000 soldiers to spare, demanded French and British troops too. The original Anglo-French minimum was set at 30,000, two-thirds of them French – chiefly veterans from Algeria. Realists saw that many more would be needed.[42]

In mid-February the British started to parade units, which were destined for Constantinople via Malta. The British and French missions abroad were notified to protect each other's subjects. The Baltic expeditionary squadron set sail in early March, with Clarendon pressing the French to contribute at least one screw battleship.[43]

An infectious war fever swept Britain, but not France, where only the military professionals were roused. Queen Victoria and Graham were stricken by the mood of the country. Unrealistic dreams of a massive reduction of Russian power and a hypocritical reading of the perniciousness of Russian intent prevailed. There was anger at Austria, Prussia and the Scandinavians for not participating. After all, it is easier to mobilize troops in a free country for lofty goals, than for what even Palmerston recognized had to be the realistic ones, namely, the revision of the Russo-Turkish treaties and a measured reduction of Russia's local preponderance. Palmerston's *beau idéal*, though, remained that of Rose, the Polish Emigration, and now Seymour: a grand alliance and general rolling back of Russian territory, with a large, Polish–Lithuanian barrier to Russian expansion.[44]

Nicholas knew what was afoot in the West, but made little effort to cut his losses. He too was also angry with the neutral powers. His chief strategic move in response to Austria's new stance was to redirect his offensive plans toward south-eastern Bulgaria, as if this could assuage Vienna. He focused on the Turkish strongholds there at Silistria and Ruschuk, with the aim of blocking the Anglo-French troops who would be in Varna and eventually effecting a junction with Serbian insurgents. On 21 February the Tsar issued his third manifesto, this time announcing rupture and imminent war 'for the Orthodox faith' against Britain and France, who are 'on the side of the enemies of Christianity'. However, even Russians in some of the core provinces, not to say borderland peoples, were uneasy or indifferent. Paskevich, now named Commander-in-Chief, wished to await further information concerning Austrian intentions before committing himself to cross the Danube, but the Tsar proceeded to elaborate his plans. Paskevich then tried to sandbag them by using extreme caution in preparing supplies; nevertheless he was ordered to cross.[45]

Britain and France continued to treat the 13 January Protocol as an ultimatum which Russia had rejected. However, while the English were still trying to organize a war coalition with expanded aims, the French remained closer to Austria and her limited goals. Recognizing that a *guerre à outrance* would be needed to force major territorial revisions, the French confidentially proposed lesser aims on 25 February. These became the celebrated Four Points, worked out by the Austrians with the French and British in the summer as the basic peace aims. Russia would have to relinquish only the vague religious protectorate; the specific territorial protectorates over

Moldavia, Wallachia and Serbia; control over the Sulina Channel at the mouth of the Danube; and the preponderance in the Black Sea that resulted from Straits closure and the possession of Sevastopol. London, meanwhile, did not take up Stratford's suggestion to include an indemnity and Russian withdrawal from the western Caucasus as initial war aims.[46]

The French and the Austrians at the same time issued a proposal for four-power mediation on the basis of the revision of the 1841 Treaty 'so as to bind the existence of the Ottoman Empire to the general equilibrium of Europe'. Buol tried to mask the fact that this represented a significant escalation in Turkey's favour.[47]

Nothing could now stop the Anglo-French war clock from ticking away. London and Paris issued their summons to evacuate the Principalities on 27 February. The key ingredient was a six-day expiration period for the reply, after which a state of war was automatically in existence. Since Russia's rejection was a foregone conclusion, the date of evacuation was immaterial, and Walewski and Cowley allowed the French summons to read 15 April and the English the 30th. Napoleon brought the pre-declaration Anglo-French preliminaries to a climax by disclaiming annexationist aims at a personal appearance in the Legislative Corps, which responded by authorizing a war loan of 250 million French francs (£10 million – more than the normal annual army and navy allocations.[48]

ENABLING ALLIANCES

The ultimata only reached St Petersburg in mid-March, since the British hoped to elicit full Austrian and Prussian support, and the couriers passed through Vienna and Berlin *en route*. The Austrians, however, stuck to their German orientation and tried to get the Prussians to support the convention and a limited war, if necessary, to expel Russia from the Principalities. Buol also pressed the French to leave Italy alone.[49]

St Petersburg's diplomacy towards the neighbouring neutrals was now reduced to asking them not to take up arms against Russia, and this ploy worked. Prussia would not touch the draft convention, which thus hung in abeyance. Meanwhile the ultimata crisscrossed Nesselrode's official response of 26 February to Buol's latest proposal, stemming from Orlov's mission. Given Bruck's pro-Russian views, the Turks were nervous about an Austrian reversal, and even Drouyn would have considered Nesselrode's offer, had the Russians been willing to evacuate the Principalities and thus stop the war before it started. They were not, and he did not.[50]

The later claims of Sydney Herbert, then British Minister at War, clouded our historiography by claiming that these Russian proposals were a serious peace effort that the English and French refused to consider. A simple examination of the texts, however, shows that Nesselrode only proposed a modification of what he had sent to Orlov in Vienna in late January as a response to the 13 January protocol. The new Russian project even fudged concerning the old 'subjects of the Porte' problem and demanded that the Anglo-French squadrons return to Malta and Toulon at the same time the last Russian troops left the Principalities. This might have worked in August or even November 1853, but not in March 1854, when the Western powers planned to redress the 'European equilibrium' and had no intention of allowing Russia to return to a modified status quo *ante* mobilization.[51]

If anything, both sides were hardening. There was no question of a retreat to the Mediterranean in return for an evacuation that left the Sevastopol installations and Kornilov's fleet alive and well in the Black Sea. Consequently, the King of Prussia got nowhere with his plan for five-power recognition of the Sultan's sovereign emancipation of the Ottoman Christians, since the Tsar insisted upon mutual withdrawal as well.[52]

Queen Victoria lamented to Frederick William on 17 March that Nesselrode's latest proposals were basically incompatible with Anglo-French intent – not that she really understood the Russian game either. At any rate, the first French troops were on their way to Gallipoli, the British armada almost inside the Baltic, and the ultimata about to expire in two days. On the 27th and 28th Queen Victoria and Napoleon issued their formal declarations of war to Parliament and the Legislative Corps. Clarendon lied through his teeth with his altruistic 'We want nothing for our trade, and we fear nothing for our Indian possessions', and the British voted their first extraordinary war credits.[53] In addition, with the Russians poised to strike across the Danube, Reshid had initialled Stratford's draft of an Anglo-French–Turkish alliance treaty, while Baraguay, lacking instructions, looked on. It contained the usual disavowals of separate peace negotiations and specific Anglo-French promises to respect local customs and to evacuate Ottoman territory at the end of the war.[54]

Stratford, it should be noted, was no longer central to the diplomacy in Europe, but by early April had helped Reshid eliminate Rifaat and Mehmed Ali from the Turkish Cabinet and replace the current Sheik-ul-islam. England's ascendancy over the Ottoman political and military high command was as great as possible for a foreign government. Stratford shared both Palmerston's maximum war goals and his realism regarding the need to accommodate Austria, and the Porte was unlikely henceforth to lead allied war policy or hinder peace efforts. The Anglo-French loan to Turkey, moreover, had still not been consummated, so the Porte's hands were virtually tied. The French and Austrians could only compete with British influence at Constantinople by doing more to drive the Russians from the Principalities and the Crimea.[55]

What forced Austria's hand was not the expiration of the Anglo-French ultimata to Russia on 19 March or the declarations of war, but Russian troops crossing the Danube on the 22nd. The day before Buol had outlined a plan of allying first with Prussia to protect Austrian and German interests and then with the English and French to join the war against Russia. Ministerial conferences on 22 and 25 March, however, heeded the more cautious Hess, who wanted an agreement with Berlin to guarantee Habsburg possessions and force the Russians to quit the Principalities without a war. The Prussian leaders debated the nuances of such an alliance and hoped it might restrain Buol, but needed it as the surest guarantee of their own neutrality.[56]

The Austro-Prussian *entente* freed both to pursue their local and Balkan interests without further compulsion on the part of the French and British. On 9 April the four powers reaffirmed the earlier Vienna protocols, but only in support of getting Russia out of the Principalities. The next day Clarendon and Walewski concluded the Anglo-French offensive–defensive alliance, which would last for the duration of the Russian war and be open to other countries to join. On the 20th, despite intense Russian entreaties, Hess and Manteuffel signed their own offensive–defensive alliance open to all-German participation, with a secret article authorizing Austria to summon Russia to evacuate Wallachia and Moldavia and use force if necessary.[57]

The Franco-Austrian cooperation thus led to Anglo-French and Austro-Prussian alliances that complemented each other against Russian intransigence. On 22 April a combined squadron of six English and six French war steamers and smaller craft armed with rockets attacked the Russian naval installations at Odessa. Both sides claimed success. Now the *Crimean* War was under way.[58]

NOTES

1. Wal. to Drn., 6 Jan. 1854 (AMAE CP Angl. 693).
2. Nich. I glosses and memo, ca. 21 Nov./3 Dec. 1853 (ZP II.64, 129–30, 140); Beskrovnyi *RVI*: 248–50.
3. Beskrovnyi *RVI*: 228–30; cf. Greenhill/Giffard: 52–5.
4. Balan Diary, 26 Nov., 27 Dec. 1853 (*AGK* II.1); Plm. to Cln., 16 Jan. 1854 (ClDp. c. 15); Lambert *PRW*: 31–3.
5. Wal. to Drn., 13 Jan. 1853 (AMAE CP Angl. 693); Lambert: *PRW*: 23–9; Greenhill/Giffard: 57–61.
6. Cf. Lambert *PRW*: 28, *CW*: 55–6, 84; Gooch *NBG*: 58–9, 66–8.
7. Dundas and Hamelin to Mnsh., ca. 9 Jan. 1854 (*CORR* IVa. 45); English Description of Sevastopol, by 25 Jan. 1854 (AMAE CP Turq. 318B); Plessen to Bluhme, 18 Jan. 1854 (DRA UM Russl. Dep.).
8. Drn. to Ctb., 26 Dec. 1853 (*FR* 33); Cln. to Seym., Cwl. to Cln., 27, 30 Dec. 1853 (*CORR* III.507, 545).
9. Str. to Cln., 31 Dec. 1853 (*CORR* III.613); Wal. to Drn., 13.I 1854 (AMAE CP Angl. 693).
10. Buol to Brk., FJ to Nich. I, 2, 7 Jan. 1854 (*AGK* I.1).
11. Buol to Lbz., Brk., 13, 16 Jan. 1854 (*AGK* I.1).
12. Seym. to Cln., 13 Jan. 1854 (*CORR* III.659).
13. Ctb. to Drn., 13, 16 Jan. 1854 (AMAE CP Russ. 211); Nes. to Rch., 4/16 Jan. 1854 (*PAP* II); Bray-Steinberg to Pfordten, 17.Jan. 1854 (BHSA OA II).
14. Nes. to Brw., Kis., 16 Jan. 1854 (ZP II.102–03); Buol to Hüb., etc., 17, 24 Jan. 1854; Lbz. to Buol, 23 Jan. 1854 (*AGK* I.1).
15. Brw. to Cln., 24 Jan. 1854 (*CORR* IVa.2, Incl. 3); Wal. to Thv., 12, 20, 27 Jan. 1854 (AMAE PA PT 20).
16. Wal.–Drn. correspondence, 27 Jan.–3 Feb. 1853 (AMAE CP Angl. 693).
17. Drn. to Kis., Ctb.; Cln. to Brw., Seym., 1 Feb. 1854 (*CORR* IVa.83–6).
18. Cln. to Wst., 1 Feb. 1854 (*CORR* IVa.90).
19. Greville VII: 127–36; Martin: 203–14; Conacher *AC*: 270–3.
20. Wal. to Drn., 9–10 Feb., 13 March 1854 (AMAE CP Angl. 693); Greville VII: 127–37; Conacher *AC*: 273–4; Plessen to Bluhme, 31 March 1854 (DRA UM Russl. Dep.); Nolan I: 111–14.
21. Halicz: 36–8, 43–4, 187–8; Prussian reports, 2 Dec. 1853–13 Jan. 1854 (*AGK* II.1.86, 91, 112, 120); for texts, ASMAE, Busta 3/115, Documenti varii, 1815–61 (Danish, Swedish Declarations, 20 Dec. 1853, and the adherence of other neutrals).
22. Plessen–Bluhme correspondence, 3 Jan.–22 Feb. 1854 (DRA UM Russl.).
23. Moltke-Hvitfeldt, Plessen to Bluhme, 5 Dec. 1853, 3 Jan. 1854 (DRA UM Frankr., Russl. Dep.); Drn. to Wal., 4 Jan. 1854; Wal. to Drn., 6, 27 Feb. 1854 (AMAE CP Angl. 693–4); Münster to Gerlach, 16 Feb. 1854 (*AGK*.II.1); Halicz: 46–7; Walker: 259; Lambert *PRW*: 30–4.
24. Alan Dowty, *The Limits of American Isolation: the United States and the Crimean War* (New York 1971), pp. 41–63; Tarlé I: 423–4;Wal. to Drn., 16 Feb., 2 March 1854 (AMAE CP Angl. 694); Conacher *AC*: 254–5.

25. FW IV, Mnt. to Rch., 29 Nov., 2 Dec. 1853; Balan Diary, 12 Dec. 1853 (*AGK* II.1); Mnt. to Arnim, 1 Dec. 1853 (*PAP* II: 188–98); FW IV to Nich. I, 8 Dec. 1853 (Schiemann VI: 423–5).

26. Cf. Rch., Münster, Bunsen, Pourtalès, Bonin, Usedom, and FW IV, 19 Dec. 1853–29 Jan. 1854 (*AGK* II.1.98, 102–3, 108, 110, 116, 123–4, 131, 136, 148; *PAP* II: 268–70, 307–8).

27. *AGK* II.1.154, 178 (15 Feb., 12 March 1854).

28. *AGK* II.1.221, 313 and notes; Thomas: 131, Olive Anderson, 'Economic Warfare in the Crimean War', *Economic History Review* XIV (1961): 34–7.

29. Buol to FJ, Min. Conf. Prot., 16, 23 Jan. 1854 (*AGK* I.1).

30. Buol to Colloredo/Hüb., Esterházy, 24 Jan. 1854 9*AGK* I.1).

31. *Inter alia*, Seebach to Beust, 6, 19 July, 25 Nov. 1853 (SHSA AM Kanz. Paris Ber.); Nap. III to Ctb., Nes. to Seebach, 28 Dec. 1853, 4 Jan. 1854; (ZP II.82, 87); Seebach to Nes., Poggenpol to Dir. of Chancery, 7 Feb., 20 March 1854 (*NLP* XI); Bapst: 433–4, 448, 450; Tarlé I: 332–3; Geneviève Dille, 'Au temps de la guerre de Crimée: correspondance inédite du Comte de Morny et de la Princesse de Lieven', *Revue des deux mondes* (1966): 328–45. Cf. Curtiss.

32. Plm. to Cln., 19, 25, 29 Jan. 1854 (ClDp.c. 15); Nap. III to Nich. I, 29 Jan. 1853 (ZP II.89); Wal. to Thv., 30 Jan. 1854 (AMAE PA PT 20); Case, *French Opinion*, p. 18; Bohl: 242–9.

33. Orl. memo, 7/19 Jan. 1854 (ZP II.119).

34. Wal. to Thv., 27 Jan. 1854 (AMAE PA PT 20); Greville VII: 132–5.

35. Nes. to Orl. 8/20 Jan. 1854 (TsGADA XV/324).

36. Mnt. to Arnim, FW IV, 25, 28 Jan. 1853 (*AGK* I.1); Buol–Metternich exchange, 27 Jan. 1854 (*AGK* I.1).

37. Orl. to Nich. I, 22 Jan./3 Feb. 1854 (ZP II.123–4); Min. Conf. Prot., 31 Jan. 1854 (*AGK* I.1); Wst. to Cln., 2 Feb. 1854 (*CORR* IVa. 97).

38. Orl. to Nes., 26 Jan./7 Feb. 1854 (AVPR K 160).

39. Brw., 'Aperçu', 1/13 Jan. 1854 (ZP II.101); Wst. to Cln., 1 Feb. 1854 (*CORR* IVa.96); Seebach to Nes., 7 Feb. 1854 (*NLP* XI).

40. Esterházy to Buol. 5, 12 Feb. 1854 (*AGK* I.1); Nich. I to Nap. III, 28 Jan./9 Feb. 1853 (ZP II.89).

41. Seym. to Cln., 14 Feb. 1853 (*CORR* IVa.271–2); Bapst: 484–5.

42. Greville VII: 136–7; Thv. to Bar., 19 Jan. 1854, Bar. to Drn., 2, 24 Feb. 1854 (AMAE CP Turq. 318B); Gooch *NBG*: 68–72.

43. Cln. circ., 23 Feb. 1853 (*CORR* IVa.273); Wal. to Drn., 16 Feb., 2, 8, 13 March 1854 (AMAE CP Angl. 694).

44. QV to Leopold I, 18 Feb., 14 March 1854 (*LQV* III); Gooch *NBG*: 68; Greville VII: 145–7; Conacher *AC*: 257; Palmer *BB*: 41–7; Erikson, *The Public Career of Sir James Graham*, pp. 345–7; Plm. to Cln., 17 Feb., 4, 20 March 1854 (ClDp. c. 15).

45. Nich. I to Gorchakov and memo, 1/13 Feb. 1854; Manifesto, 11/23 Feb. 1854; Psk. to Gorchakov, 8/20 March 1854 (ZP II.94, 136–8); Third Section Reports, 22 Feb./6 March–6/16 March 1854 (TsGAOR 3/1/109/399–2).

46. Drn. to Wal., etc., 25 Feb. 1854 (AMAE CP Angl. 694); Str. to Cln. and memo, 3 Feb. 1854 (*CORR* IVa.258 and Incl.).

47. Draft Convention, Buol to Thun, 25 Feb. 1854 (*AGK* I.1).

48. Drn., Cln. to Nes., 27 Feb. 1853 (ZP II.93, 104); L'a Gorce *HSE* I: 216.

49. Buol–Hüb., Thun exchange, 5–7 March 1854 (*AGK* I.1).
50. Nes. to Mdf., 13/25 Feb. 1854 (*NLP* XI); Bar. to Drn., 27 Feb., 7, 11 March 1854 (AMAE CP Turq., 318B); Mnt. to Arnim, 5 March 1854 (*AGK* II.1); Drn. to Wal., 5 March 1854 (*AMAE CP* Angl. 694).
51. *Herbert*: 189–2; Russian Draft Preliminaries, late Feb. 1854 (*CORR* IVa.386); cf. Rich: 103–4.
52. Gröben, Münster, to FW IV, 11, 24 March 1854 (*AGK* II.1); Rch., Bunsen, to Mnt., 15 March, 7 April 1854; FW IV to Nich. I, 16 March 1854 (*PAP* II).
53. QV to FW IV, 17 March (*LQV* III); Greenhill/Giffard: 133–34; *London Gazette*, 28 March 1854, Suppl.; La Gorce *HSE* I: 218; Nolan I: 101; Seton-Watson *BE*: 323; Hertslet II: 238–40.
54. Draft Conv., 12 March 1854 (*CORR* IVa.453); Hertslet II.237.
55. Bar. to Drn., 25 March 1854 (AMAE CP Turq. 318B); Str. to LStr., 15 April 1854 (Lane-Poole II).
56. Buol, Hess to FJ; Min. Conf. Prots.; Buol to Hess, 21–25 March 1854; E. Manteuffel to FW IV; Balan, Gerlach, memos, 27 March–3 April 1854 (*AGK* I.1, II.1); cf. Schroeder, 'A Turning Point in Austrian Policy in the Crimean War: the Conferences of March 1854' *AHY* 4/5 (1968/69): 161–4.
57. ZP II.106, 146–8; Hertslet II: 241–2, 244.
58. Nolan I: 167–8; Beskrovnyi *RVI*: 250.

PART SIX
Conclusions and Consequences

CHAPTER EIGHTEEN

The Origins of the Crimean War

PERSONAL RESPONSIBILITIES: I – THE EMPERORS

The Crimean War, as a 'modern' war, was not an isolated event, but one waiting to be fought in some fashion in the light of the 1848–49 crises, the Bonapartist challenge to the 1815 settlement, the Anglo-Russian 'great game', and the legacy of Russo-Turkish hostilities. Nevertheless, the outbreak of this war was especially the result of the power, policies and personality of an autocrat, who exhibited plenty of 'ill will' as well as pride and poor judgement, and who, like his Western counterparts, understood the implications of his armed diplomacy:[1] Nicholas I is thus in the company of three other nineteenth-century strong men without whom certain European wars would have been inconceivable: Napoleon I, Napoleon III and Bismarck.

A review of the role of several other key figures only points to the central role of Nicholas I. Twice when La Valette threatened to use warships in the Holy Places dispute, Louis Napoleon followed British counsels of moderation. When Fuad, Mehmed Ali and Omer Pasha provoked Austria and Russia by attempting to extend Ottoman power into Montenegro, all the Great Powers restrained the Turks. When Rose, Napoleon, Palmerston and Russell first wanted to send the fleets to Turkish waters, Aberdeen, Graham, Clarendon and Stratford, supported by a wide body of influential Englishmen and other Europeans, held back. Stratford and the diplomatic community at Constantinople reined in the Turkish war party for five months after the Menshikov Mission flopped.

Nicholas, on the other hand, served notice that he would defeat the Turks by diplomacy or arms and gave the other powers the choice of joining him or stopping him. His repudiation of Menshikov's earlier advice to seize an Asian province or port, rather than the Principalities, or Orlov's compromise project shows that even the top Russian nationalists could not alter the course. Moreover, the Tsar knew what British and French policy was concerning naval action in the Black Sea when he gave the orders that led to Sinope.

Explanations of the other powers' support of Turkey and of their willingness to use confrontational diplomacy against Russia unfailingly leads us to the same spot: Nicholas's refusal to evacuate the Principalities except on his own terms. Reshid's proposals in themselves always appeared perfectly acceptable to most Western and Central Europeans who wished to preserve the Ottoman Empire and were only set aside as impractical in the light of the peace process or Nicholas's prestige needs.

What of that other emperor, Napoleon III? Did he 'probably desire war', as the even-handed Bernadotte Schmitt concluded?[2] The role of the new Napoleon is peculiarly problematic because he is often seen as having initiated the quarrel in a manner calculated to enhance his power in France and Europe, while the escalated Anglo-French goals were essentially British ones. In fact, the two emperors, except for their pride of office, could not have been more different in 1852–53. Napoleon inherited and intensified France's forward policy concerning the Holy Places and tolerated la Valette's hyperbole, but would compromise and not let his legation in Constantinople determine his policy. Nicholas's response to alleged Turkish chicanery was to allow the French gains in a few shrines in order to justify his own enhanced demands for the protectorate. Neither wished to be defrauded, but Nicholas would not listen to the combined voices of Europe. Napoleon did not pick the fight over his own imperial title or the number III. Nicholas did. Napoleon, was careful not to run the risk of another humiliation for France in an Eastern crisis as in 1840–41. Nicholas set the stage for a greater humiliation than in the 1849 refugee crisis.

Each wished to rule the pre-eminent power on the continent, but the insecure Napoleon sought the appearance of prudence in foreign policy and sound relations with England – the only state that could hurt him. Nicholas felt somewhat insecure as of 1848, due to domestic events outside Russia, but was trigger-happy with his diplomatic offers and designs. Napoleon's 'ideas' for a Europe of nations were an inherent threat to Russia's Western provinces, but his normal probing tactic was to jab, feint or insinuate, as with Belgium, but then pull back or make a bargain. His reaction to the coincidence of the culmination of the disputes over the Holy Places and his imperial title in late 1852 was to capitalize on British and Austrian wariness of Nicholas's agenda for the Ottoman Christians. Nicholas's reaction was to push his potential allies against French aggression into the Franco-Turkish camp. When the chips were down in 1853–54, Napoleon preferred the security of *entente* with Austria and *détente* with Prussia to his 'ideas', whereas Nicholas opted for his illusions about the Ottoman Christians and the 'Holy Alliance' over his real community of interests with Austria.[3]

Napoleon had a peculiar penchant in 1852–53 for making a point with battleships in the Mediterranean, but to single out the *Charlemagne* and Tripoli incidents for escalating the Holy Places dispute, as does Temperley, without noting Russia's standing threat to use the army, is one-sided.[4] Moreover, Napoleon's decisive naval decisions in March and December 1853 were measured reactions to Russian escalations, whereby France honoured commitments to Turkey and hoped first to obtain and then to reinforce the English alliance. The British did not need to send any ships in March, because Stratford with a squadron at Malta was still worth more than la Cour with one at Salamis. On the other hand, to have withheld the combined squadrons after the engagement at Sinope would have compelled the Sultan to make peace on Russian terms. Napoleon certainly did not shrink from international violence, but he was readier than most British to seek an accommodation with the Russians from September 1853 until the Crimean War ended.

Nicholas did not need a foreign alliance to consolidate domestic power and thus did not have to listen to anybody. His initial mobilization was connected with aggressive designs on Turkey, including the seizure of the Principalities and Dobrudja if he did not get his way, and should not be discounted by a misreading of Nicholas's crucial memorandum.[5]

The most dovish, realistic judgement on Nicholas I is that he planned a war with Turkey to expel her from Europe and/or partition her with the other Great Powers, but that he would have settled for a diplomatic victory and an expended protectorate over the Ottoman Christians. The fact that in 1853 Nicholas considered this to be the minimum due to him as 'reparation' for putative Turkish bad faith and preferred war with England and France to retreat is a sign that he had 'lost it'. The most hawkish, solid judgement on Napoleon in this crisis is that he planned for diplomatic success to elevate French prestige in Europe at the expense of Russia's and that he was prepared to use armed diplomacy and fight with British support or cooperation on Turkey's side. Had Prussia or Austria joined with Russia, he also would have been ready, with England as an ally, to march into the Rhineland or Italy and reacquire territory lost by France in 1814. However, his diplomacy in 1853 reveals an urge to ally with the German powers in order to defeat Russian diplomatically without war, while his fleet would be at the Bosphorus as a sign that France had saved Turkey. Brunnow's and Nesselrode's hypotheses that Napoleon was planning a coalition war with England in the Black Sea in defence of Turkey against Russia were really veiled warnings to Nicholas. They do not constitute the missing Bonapartist smoking gun that no one has found to date.[6] Napoleon eventually 'lost it' too, but not in 1853–54.

PERSONAL RESPONSIBILITIES:
II – THE ENGLISHMEN

English and French propaganda would have had everyone believing that those countries were forced by Russian policies to go to war. Surely, however, even after Sinope and with the combined squadrons in the Black Sea, the English and French had the option of following Austrian counsels, as Paul Schroeder laments.[7] They could have continued measured, gradual escalation and attempted without an immediate Baltic campaign or landing in the Crimea to compel or induce Russia to accept a peace on the basis of one of the Vienna protocols or Constantinople notes.

Such a policy, however, ran the risk of a very protracted crisis, Ottoman domestic troubles, a shift in public opinion, and maybe even Austrian defection from the anti-Russian camp to stricter neutrality, as well as the overthrow of the London Cabinet. It was simpler and safer for the British and their French allies to choose the method of offensives with the enhanced if modest war aims of reducing Russia's strategic assets in the Black and Baltic Seas. The French and the English, especially the latter, were thus reactively aggressive in establishing their minimal goals, not to mention the fanciful schemes mounting a super-coalition war against Russia.

Accordingly, two English statesmen are often given peculiar blame for having brought on the war: Palmerston and Stratford. Palmerston is much more problematic to evaluate than Napoleon, because of a surfeit of smoking guns. Like some Americans of the Cold War era he combined an essentially aggressive combination of contempt for

Russia as a 'humbug' and fear of her expansionist potential.[8] He had risked war with the Russians and 'bearded' them twice in the Black Sea and the Dardanelles by 1850 and sent the Malta squadron to Besika Bay on two other occasions. In 1853–54 he among British politicians was the most consistent in imagining an expanded war to remake the map of Europe. In 1856 he did not want to cease hostilities, even though most of his Cabinet were in favour of doing so. But this does not mean that he had long sought war with Russia, as Monnier claimed.[9]

Nesselrode fretted that Palmerston 'came into this world to create misery', and Nicholas suspected 'that Palmerston was really sick in the head'.[10] He was, in fact, the quintessence of a politician who rides the crests of popular nationalism while despising the masses and allowing others to take the lead in devising democratizing reforms. His established role was that of England's imperial champion, his attitude toward most foreign obstacles or prospective prey being pugilistic. Making liberal use of gunboat diplomacy and initiating two wars with hapless China over commercial policy, he did not fear maritime rivals and risked war with France over the Levant and with the United States over Central America. All the same, up to 1853 he asserted British interests while avoiding war with any major power.

The major question, then, is whether this 'most English Minister' actively sought war in 1853 before the Russians occupied the Principalities and refused to leave. It seems not. His initial security task as Home Secretary was to form a special committee to recommend measures to strengthen home island defences at a time when the main threat seemed to come from France, not Russia. Until the autumn his policies were reactive, his basic principle being that words should be met with words and facts with facts. When official word arrived in London, in late May, of Menshikov's real demands, Palmerston correctly assumed from experience with Nicholas I that these represented St Petersburg's instructions and wanted England and France to commit themselves to protect Turkey by arms if necessary.[11]

Palmerston's role in shaping public opinion is controversial. As soon as he was certain that the Russians meant to push for the protectorate, he was unwilling to cede to them the moral high ground and encouraged strong responses to their manifestos and circulars.[12] He was also a central figure in England's alarmist press campaign, but the British press was much more than his mouthpiece, *The Morning Post*, and revived its russophobia in response to Russia's mobilization and Menshikov's mission. Everyone who counted had the means to air his views in the London papers. *The Morning Post* was willing to exit the crisis with the Vienna Note until Nesselrode's *Examen* surfaced. It was other papers, such as *The Morning Advertiser*, that printed David Urquhart's extremist position and showed themselves quite 'Turkish' by denouncing the Vienna Note, after Nicholas accepted it, for omitting a provision for evacuation of the Principalities. To single out Palmerston's influence over the popular mind as a major factor in the origin of the Crimean War may be an over-simplification of the diversity of press and society in mid-nineteenth-century England.[13]

On the other hand, Paul Schroeder is certainly correct that Palmerston and his protégé Clarendon in no way considered Austria's role as one of mediating.[14] But Schroeder, in my opinion, misses the most important point for the people involved in 1853: *there was nothing to mediate*. Turkey was right, Russia was wrong, and that was that, though diplomats hoped to avoid smearing mud in the Tsar's face by putting it this way. Palmerston was ahead of everyone else in London and Paris in calling for a four-power interpretation of the Vienna Note, were it to be of any use, and viewing the Turkish Modifications as coming from an endangered ally. Likewise, and here is the rub, he was ahead of everyone else in conceiving a coalition war in the Black Sea, with the illusion that the Anglo-French squadrons and Turkish troops officered by Europeans would be sufficient.[15]

Palmerston was thus the most confident and blatantly partisan strong man within the Anglo-French war factions, since Russell and Napoleon despised the Turks, and the latter really wanted some kind of *entente* with Russia too. However, Palmerston could not make his entire policy England's policy and was ready to settle at first for more modest war aims, await developments and see how the campaigns went. He was as much to blame as anyone else for Britain's maximal goals for the war, but not for the war's breaking out in the first place.

Stratford is even more problematic than Palmerston for several reasons. The 'Great Ambassador' seemingly dominated and orchestrated Reshid's actions from May 1853 onward; he pre-empted, anticipated or thwarted opponents in Constantinople, London and everywhere else; and he got first London and then the Vienna Conference to adopt his own policies. He certainly was not seeking a war out of personal animosity toward Nicholas – a common myth then and later. Stratford claimed he was too little a personage to wage such a vendetta, but actually he was too big to waste his time on what he saw as such a secondary issue. He was after the largest of prizes:

the settling of the Eastern Question in Britain's favour.[16] This meant opening Turkey up to Western commercial, industrial and financial penetration, and forcing a domestic reform, which many observers, including Turks, saw as hastening the collapse of the Ottoman Empire – the death of a barbarian from civilization.

Such *was*, more or less, British policy towards the backward world. Other countries were expected to play by English rules, but Nicholas chose to break rules accepted by all the other European powers in his attempt to increase Russian influence in Turkey. Stratford thereby had a golden opportunity to further British interests, and his unique achievement was to direct Turkish bellicosity, diplomacy, domestic policy and public relations in such a way as to prevent self-defeating initiatives and allow for coalition support.

The real questions concerning Stratford are these. What did he mean with his appeal in early July to stop at no sacrifice to solve 'the great Eastern Question'? Was he saying that once Russian troops had crossed the Pruth, England should not let Nicholas off the hook without a major strategic setback that could only result from a costly war? And, worse still, was Stratford such a clairvoyant, determined and successful anti-Russian conspirator that he 'lured' Menshikov,[17] advised him to be brusque[18] and orchestrated his last seven weeks on the Bosphorus to produce the Russian occupation and/or engineer the Ottoman responses so that the Tsar, to quote Russell, 'having announced a play . . . must go on with the performance'?[19]

Certainly Stratford did not cause the Menshikov Mission to fail: the latter's instructions and standing Anglo-French policy did. Then, starting in May, Stratford helped the Turks prepare clever two-pronged diplomatic weapons to ready the ground for either a diplomatic victory or a coalition war. His attempts to prevent the Turks from starting hostilities in October were connected with his sense of proper timing and his desire to control the Turkish military. He was not responsible for the Russian gamble at Sinope, which paved the way for full Anglo-French involvement in the war. However, he had been ready since July to promote a costly coalition conflict to eliminate Russian power from the Black Sea and most of its shores. J.L. Herkless's recent defence of Stratford falters precisely because it neglects his memoranda which aimed to influence the British Cabinet and public opinion.[20]

The basic case against Stratford, one that has been made since the eve of Menshikov's departure from Constantinople to the present time, boils down to this: without such an ambassador in Constantinople, the Meyendorffs, the Buols, the Bourqueneys and their backers might have had a free hand with their projects and expedients; the Turks might have accepted a humiliating denouement and gone on trying to cheat everyone; and then Nicholas might have evacuated the Principalities, dredged the Sulina Channel, and thereby accommodated European and Ottoman sensibilities. In other words, Stratford's ultimate offence was his ability to outwit Europe's diplomatic establishments and not allow Europe to exit this embroglio via the Vienna Note.

There are two things wrong with this supposition. The first is the erroneous assumption that the wording of the Vienna Note, or even the Menshikov Note, did not matter or was no threat to Turkey. Thus have argued Vinogradov, Schroeder, Curtiss, Rich and others – as if the Turks had no experience with the Russian legation, no memory, no judgement, and no free will. The second problem is that the real alternative to Stratford in Constaninople after Nicholas mobilized in early 1853 was a genuine Palmerstonian, such as Rose. International European court politics had lost out. Fair or foul, British opinion in 1853 would not have tolerated a wishy-washy, pro-Austrian 'bug' like Aberdeen in Stratford's place.[21] La Cour, Bruck and Baraguay were instructed to represent an independent policy, but Stratford was able to string them along precisely because they dared not abandon their home country's commitments to the Turks. He knew that supporting Ottoman mobilization and armaments from late May onward would lead ineluctably to backing the Turks militarily at some point. However, if the Porte could or would not help defend itself, then the Ottoman Empire had no *raison d'être* and only deserved to be carved up – something that only Nicholas and one faction of Russians really desired.

In sum, Stratford agreed with the moderate Turks that the Menshikov and Nesselrode ultimata and the invasion of the Princi-palities were ideal grounds for getting rid of Kuchuk-Kainarji, but would settle for limiting its meaning, as with the Turkish Modifications. Stratford was also ready to escalate Anglo-French diplomacy and armaments, as Turkey geared up for war, and ready to turn any war into a strategic one; nevertheless, he would settle for the diplomatic victory inherent in any of his or Reshid's proposals. Like Palmerston, Stratford personally is partly responsible for the enhanced war aims and expanded war, but not for its genesis.

None of the other major figures is worth discussing as a key instigator of the Crimean War. Nesselrode and Russia's ambassadors could have been blunter, but they gave Nicholas the necessary information to make the rational judgements he refused to make.

Their choices all along were to resign or be his accomplices. In fact, most of the ambassadors attempted on their own, within the boundaries of their instructions, to initiate policies to avoid war or to limit it. One might just as easily blame a Castelbajac or a Rochow for coddling Nicholas, or a Buol or a Francis Joseph for fence-straddling, or a Westmorland, who could not forcefully represent British policy in Vienna, or his superiors, who left him at his post and wished to pretend that they were 'drifting toward war', when they were really engaging in measured escalation.[22]

LESS PERSONAL FORCES

If English policy is at all to blame for the Crimean War, then the culprits are two-fold, neither one strictly personal. First of all, British imperialism and expansionism, like those of other Great Powers, courted war with more backward rivals or potential victims. But in this case the primary clash was between Russian and Turkish ambitions within the Ottoman Empire, while the French, British and Austrians were able to capitalize on Turkish goals. Secondly, the peculiar constellation of domestic British politics resulted in a shaky coalition of dovish Peelites, such as Graham and Gladstone, more hawkish Whigs, such as Russell and Clarendon, and two characteristic and opposing relics, who had held various offices on and off since the first Napoleonic era: Aberdeen and Palmerston. Those waiting in the wings were not the critics of Stratford, but Tories like Clanricarde, Malmesbury and Disraeli – ready to pounce upon the coalition for being soft on Russia. The Aberdeen coalition at least gave Nicholas a chance to prove that his mobilization was for show, but he failed to do this and left Brunnow with egg on his face. Aberdeen may have been an ineffectual constable, but he was not, in this case, the armed extortionist who brought on the war over a contrived issue that was produced by his own subalterns.

The developing press in the initial age of the telegraph and steamship played an ancillary role. The press enabled the informed public of Austria, Russia and Turkey, as well as England and France, to learn of the comings and goings of open diplomacy and the views of a variety of statesmen. The press forced all states, including Russia and Turkey, to justify their actions in the eyes of their people. The press, with its reports coming in from all over the world, also ensured that the views of the important European commercial colonies on the Bosphorus were aired in the home countries. The press was a vital element in the Porte's keeping the British and French to their commitments. It thereby helped prevent one of those imaginatively concocted solutions that some diplomats and historians love, in this case one allowing Russia to withdraw from the crisis with some gain at the expense of a very unwilling Turkey – the basis of every compromise proposal.

Commerce and economic imperialism were only indirect determinants of the Crimean War. Economics underlay Britain's position in the 'Great Game', but the cost-conscious London government was not about to start a Great Power war to accelerate the economic penetration of the Ottoman Empire or to force free trade policies upon Russia. Gladstone, who ran the exchequer in 1854, would not even grant the Turks a loan until the French forced his hand. On the Russian side, moreover, the negotiating strategy of Menshikov's mission was to accommodate England's economic interests and only press for political goals.

In one place only did economic interests figure directly. Austria, Britain, Turkey and the Romanians opposed the obstruction of the Sulina Channel – a policy of malign neglect, which favoured Russian grain exports from Odessa. Freeing the mouth of the Danube would eventually have become a serious issue, but in the event merely became the specific, limited, Austrian aim in supporting the Anglo-French war effort in 1854.

The Great Power arms races also played a tangential, if interesting, role in the genesis of the Crimean War. Since the mid-1840s, war steamers had put teeth into the standing Russian threat to launch an attack on Varna, Sizopol or the Bosphorus from Sevastopol and Odessa in case of a crisis. On the other hand, Russian expertise had called for more such vessels before a surprise attack might be launched. Nicholas initiated armed diplomacy in 1853 before his forces were ready to do their assigned job, which is one reason why his plans failed.

War steamers and screw battleships also gave the French in the early 1850s a certain daring in the Mediterranean that had been lacking since 1841. When the chips were down, however, the French admirals were loath to test their mettle in combat against the Russians in the Black Sea. Napoleon's usually cautious diplomacy reflected this maritime insecurity.

England's new complement of fifteen big screw battleships turned the French threat temporarily into a sorry joke, but made a Baltic expedition much more promising than in the 1830s or 1849, when Palmerston only operated in Besika Bay. Russell's comment in March

1853 that if the Tsar proved a cheat, he would face action in the Baltic as well as the Black Sea was no empty threat. But this fleet had been built up to fight France or America at virtually any place on the globe, not Russia in the Baltic, where Nicholas was satisfied with Russian control over Finland and the Åland Islands, and enjoyed good relations with the conservative courts of Stockholm and Copenhagen. Had the British, nonetheless, sought a war to test the new warships, they would have at least encouraged the French in the Holy Places dispute. In the event, even Rose tried to temper both sides, and the London statesmen, as well as Stratford, tilted toward Russia. When the occupation of the Principalities made war likely, then the new battle fleet propelled Graham and the Admiralty to centre stage and provided a strategy for the Baltic, but the fleet was no more the cause of the war than a gun is the cause of a hold-up. If anything, the time necessary for a full naval mobilization after September meant that the diplomats had ample further opportunity to talk.

IDEAS

Ideas had but a secondary role in causing the war and can hardly be separated from the social movements or competitive imperialism that underlay the mid-century domestic and international crises. British and European russophobia were merely one set of political notions related to the international competition of the day. This russophobia rose and fell in direct proportion to the growth of Russian external influence and naval power in the 1830s, was dormant in the 1840s, and revived as a result of the interventions of 1848–49. It then died down once more, only to be rekindled by Russia's mobilization, Menshikov's mission and military moves in 1853. To credit russophobia for the outbreak of the Crimean War is to neglect the real course of politics and diplomacy in 1852–1853. If anything, Nicholas's misplaced on-and-off gallophobia, which he projected onto other powers, contributed more to the origin of the war than did British and European russophobia.

The most powerful of the disruptive ideologies of the time was nationalism in its various forms, which promoted the forward policies of England, France and Russia. Nationalism also threatened the very existence of the Austrian and Ottoman Empires and Russian control over her border provinces. On the other hand, the clash between demands for democracy and domestic reform and existing establishments meant that exporting tensions to the international arena was an attractive policy option for ruling cliques. But this observation says very little, since the external projection of domestic tensions has been a standing option for most great powers in modern times and has underlain every modern European war.

Actually the greatest of the unfulfilled nationalisms in 1853, that of the Germans, had created a community of British–French–Russian interest that operated in the 1848–52 Danish crises. Only with this question shelved could the British, French and Russians afford to allow the Eastern Question to get out of hand. Even in 1853–54, the greater German Question kept the lesser Eastern Question within certain bounds. Since the seventeenth century all major wars in Europe have been at least partially German wars. The Crimean War was not a 'great' war because the Germans themselves did not wish it to be one.

As it turned out, nationalism, a growing force in Europe at this time, played a paradoxical role in the genesis of the Crimean War. Nicholas's domestic and foreign policies during 1848–53 were those of counter-revolutionary containment of nationalism. Nevertheless, the specific policies he pursued to block the Ottoman counter-revolutionary resurgence in the Balkans threatened Austria's counter-revolutionary revival, which he had aided with arms, blood and treasure. As the Austrians were the first to note, Nicholas started to ally *de facto* with the Balkan nationalism that he was trying to control. France and England were also prepared to ally themselves either with third-party nationalism or with the European counter-revolution, as their geopolitical interests might demand. In short, both nationalism and the counter-revolution were pervasive forces during 1848–53, but they did not have to result in a Russo-Turkish or Crimean war.

Perhaps the most important of the ideologies that helped bring on the war were the peculiar concepts of the semi-modernizing empire represented by Official Nationality in Russia and the Tanzimat in Turkey. Guided by the principles of 'autocracy, Orthodoxy and nationality', His Imperial Majesty in St Petersburg sought to extend the benefits of his enlightened rule to his Orthodox co-religionists in Turkey. On the other hand, since 1839 His Highness the Sultan had theoretically considered all of his subjects, regardless of religion, equal citizens before the law: 'Muslims in the mosque, Christians in the church, Jews in the synagogue, but there is no difference among them in any other way.'[23] Official Nationality, however, kept religion as a special category and foregrounded Kuchuk-Kainarji.

Without an intellectual package like Official Nationality, the Russian government could not have combined the outlook of a nineteenth-century conservative European Great Power with the obsessive illusions concerning the Ottoman Orthodox. Without Tanzimat ideals and fictions, there was no justification for Ottoman sovereignty over Christians in the mid-nineteenth century, and the Ottoman resurgence in the Balkans would have obtained less support from Europe.

It should not be forgotten, however, that Official Nationality and the Tanzimat had clashed from 1839 to 1847 without any war crisis, and the problems after 1848 were prompted by revolutionary upheaval in south-eastern Europe. The 1849 Convention of Balta Liman and the resolution of the refugee crisis were Russo-Turkish compromises, with the British and French supporting the Turks and the Austrians more or less supporting the Russians. Leiningen's mission in February 1853 produced a parallel Austro-Turkish compromise, with the British and French again backing the Turks and the Russians backing the Austrians. Menshikov's mission got rid of a liberal ministry in Serbia and prepared the way for a Russian–Ottoman–French compromise over the Holy Places. All of this shows that, even under the impact of revolutionary movements and counter-revolutionary paranoia, the pretensions of Official Nationality and the Tanzimat – that is, Russian and Russian-backed Austrian imperialism and the confluence of British, French and Ottoman imperialism – could and did compromise over concrete issues.

ATAVISM AND MEDIEVALISM

The Roses, la Valettes, Slades, Balabins and other strident and bellicose agents of imperialism played a part in exacerbating the situation that brought on the war. So did the Ozerovs, Bottas and Valergas, those generals and colonels of the cold war over the Holy Places and their bigoted minions and lobbyists who had a crusading mentality towards rival Christians. However, it was the Ottomans who initially were the most eager of all to give battle, even though most Turks who understood weaponry recognized their own weakness and Russia's qualitative and quantitative superiority.

The Turkish urge to fight, represented by Omer Pasha and Mehmed Ali, was as atavistic as rational. In so far as it was calculating, in the hands of Fuad or Reshid, its calculus was political and diplomatic, not military. The actual drive towards war represented an explosion of frustrations against all Europeans, which was cleverly directed toward the traditional and visible Russian enemy. The British and French, whose influence bore away from within at traditional Ottoman society, institutions and thought, were more or less spared. The superficial Westernization and modernization of some of the Ottoman élite and parts of the army and navy fed illusions that somehow Turkey could pacify the Balkan peoples and even regain control of the Black Sea. Western military aid was thus a contributing factor to the Ottoman resurgence in the Balkans and Turkish confidence in adopting a French orientation in late 1852.

Tsar Nicholas's reaction to this Turkish 'insolence' was also atavistic, connected with both counter-revolutionary paranoia and the frustrated megalomania of a middle-aged autocrat who imagined himself the senior monarch of Europe and Western Asia. Not surprisingly, the twin symbolic cores of the medieval value structure, religion and honour, figured heavily in both Russian and Turkish bellicosity. But the sense of injured national honour was also not absent from the Anglo-French speeches or public diplomacy. After Sinope, civilian crowds in England clamoured for their soldiers to be shipped off to die on distant battlefields for the sake of the nation's dignity as well as Turkey's and India's security. Supporters of the British Empire had thus made Turkey's battle their battle. Napoleon III was always looking over his shoulder at the fate of Louis-Philippe, whom the British had humiliated over the Eastern Question, even when compromising with him. To deny these irrational psycho-political elements, which constitute effective 'ill will', in the origin of the Crimean War is to ignore human realities and probably miss part of the essence of the story. But since these realities are also constants, we must redirect our focus to concrete human actions. And when we do this, we find that Nicholas I, by violating Ottoman territorial sovereignty after his initial armed diplomacy had achieved modest results, and by refusing to retreat diplomatically or withdraw from Ottoman territory, is more responsible than any other person for the Crimean War.

NOTES

1. Cf. Anderson, *The Eastern Question*, pp. 125, 131–2: 'None of them had the slightest desire for war, but all were now using their armies and navies for essentially diplomatic purposes without any real understanding of the dangers this involved. . . . The Crimean War was thus the

outcome of a series of misjudgements, misunderstandings, and blunders, of stupidity, pride, and obstinacy, rather than ill will.' Hardly. In contrast, the contemporary liberal historian, T.N. Granovsky, 'Zapiska o Vostochnom voprose', 20 Nov./2 Dec. 1856 (GPB, 869/16/3).

2. Schmitt: 46.
3. Cf. A.J.P. Taylor, *The Struggle for Mastery in Europe*, pp. 59–62, for commentary more than facts.
4. Temperley *ENEC*: 508, 511; Michael Florinsky, whose fine general history of Russia relied heavily on Temperley, was more balanced: *Russia. A History and Interpretation* (2 vols, New York 1947), II: 858–69.
5. Nich. I, Notes, n.d., but ca. 1 Jan. 1853 (ZP I.98), where it is clear that he envisioned the fall of the Ottoman Empire resulting from Turkish opposition to his demands; cf. Rich: 22. Schroeder, rather, characterizes the Tsar's initial moves as 'criminally rash': *AGBCW*: 29.
6. Cf. above, ch. 6.
7. Schroeder *AGBCW*: 115–36.
8. Henry Lytton Bulwer (Lord Dalling), *The Life of Henry John Temple, Viscount Palmerston* (3 vols – vol. III, ed. Evelyn Ashley, London 1870–74) III: 5 (Plm. to William Temple, 21 April 1835).
9. Monnier: 19.
10. Nes. to Brw., 8/20 Oct. 1849 (TsGADA III/115); Nes. memo, Nich I. gloss, 2/14 Nov. 1851 (AVPR K 39).
11. Plm. to Cln., Rus., 22 May, 7 July 1853 (Ashley II); Lambert *PRW*: 17.
12. Wal. to Drn., 19, 23, 26 May, 13 July 1853 (AMAE CP Angl. 689–90).
13. Cf. Rich: 8; Seton-Watson *BE*: 6, note 19; Henderson, 'The Seymour Conversations', *History* XVIII.71 (1933): 339, 343; Martin: 85–102, 117–33, 143–54; Palmer *BB*: 13, 20–1.
14. Schroeder *AGBCW*: 136–7.
15. Plm. memos, 20 June, 12 July 1853; to Cln., 27–28 July, 26 Aug. 1853 (PRO 30/22/11A, *AbC* X, ClDp. c.3); Wal. to Drn., 24 June 1853 (AMAE CP Angl. 690).
16. Str. to Cln., 4 July 1853 (*CORR* II.107), to LStr., 4 July 1853 (Lane-Poole II), et al; Gooch's indictment of Stratford missed this key point: *CHOCW*: 232–41; Marriott's did not: 231.
17. Marriott: 231–2 – sans source: but seemingly from Lane-Poole's hero-worship and ignorance of Menshikov's instructions: II: 255: 'He [Stratford] conducted himself as a debonair diplomatist, and with gentle tact drew the Prince on to his fate.'
18. Bourgeois, *Manuel* II: 36 – sans source: certainly not in La Cour's reports.
19. Rus. to Ab., 10 July 1853 (*AbC* X).
20. J.L. Herkless, 'Stratford, the Cabinet, and the Outbreak of the Crimean War', *HJ* XVIII (Sept. 1975): 497–523.
21. Martin: 232: 'Bad luck they say all night and day/To the Cobugs and the humbugs/To the Witermbugs and the Scarembugs/And all the German horserugs/And the old bug of Aberdeen/The Peterbugs and Prussians/May Providence protect the Turks/and massacre the Russians.'
22. Ab. to Cln., 7 June 1853 (Maxwell II).
23. Riasanovsky, *Nicholas I*, pp. 235–65; Davison *ROE*: 31.

CHAPTER NINETEEN
The Strange Sequel

THE ILLUSIONS OF WAR

Nicholas sent his troops across the Danube into Eastern Bulgaria on 23 March 1854 and immediately besieged Silistria, which was only seventy miles north of Varna. He hoped that some quick victories would stir up the natives, demoralize the Turks, disabuse the British and French of any thoughts of an easy success, and create the conditions for a negotiated settlement. However, the Prussian-backed Austrian threat to attack Russian positions and the counsels of Paskevich and Nesselrode convinced the Tsar to retreat. He called off the promising siege in mid-June and then withdrew his two well-supplied but disease-ridden corps from the Principalities in August. Henceforth Russian troops were on the defensive, 600,000, among them some of the best being deployed from Finland to Bessarabia to guard against Swedish, Prussian and Austrian eventualities.[1] Only in the Caucasus and Transcaucasia did the Russians mount counterattacks, invariably with outnumbered forces, initially to protect Georgia and Armenia and then to advance into eastern Anatolia. Russian armies temporarily held Bayazid, which traversed an important caravan route, and prepared to invest Kars, the key regional stronghold.[2]

The British and French did not have an easy time. The Baltic expeditionary squadron under the timid, superannuated Charles Napier with his ten screw battleships and 3,500 guns, accomplished little in the first year, save for reconnoitring Kronstadt and destroying the new Russian fortifications at Bomarsund on the Åland Islands.[3] Down in the Black Sea theatre, the bombardment of Odessa was more noise than damage. Then 85,000 Allied troops went to Varna, where over 7,000 died from cholera after the Russians had retired from Silistria. A Franco-Turkish foray eastward into disease-infested Dobrudja was also a wasteful operation.[4]

An Anglo-French war council on 17 July then decided to invade the Crimea and invest Sevastopol even though they lacked any good maps or estimations of Russian forces. In early September 62,000 unopposed British and French with 130 artillery pieces disembarked at Evpatoria, about forty miles north of Sevastopol by land. Menshikov had 55,000–60,000 men at Sevastopol and about 4,000 guns, three-quarters of them naval and very few of them facing the land approaches. He also had six months' supply of food for the garrison, but lacked staff, maps, construction tools, sufficient powder and the means of keeping his fleet functional. The French were reasonably well provisioned, but the English did not have transportation and siege equipment. All sides suffered from inadequate medical facilities.

Menshikov deployed 35,000 of his troops along the Alma River, half way between Evpatoria and Sevastopol. His columns were savaged by French artillery and British line tactics, but the Allies also paid for a spirited drive against the Russian artillery batteries. Following the retreat from the Alma, the Russians concentrated on shoring up Sevastopol, sinking their heavy ships in the harbour, converting the sailors into soldiers, and constructing a set of earthworks with heavy guns on the northern side under the direction of engineer Adjutant E.I. Totleben. Menshikov himself departed from the stronghold and turned the command over to Admiral Kornilov.[5]

On 17 October the Allies, who had redeployed to Balaklava about twelve miles southwest of Sevastopol, started to bombard the fortress. Russian direct hits on the French artillery demoralized them and prevented any assault. Kornilov was killed on one of the key outer defences, the Malakhov Kurgan, and the supreme command passed to Admiral Nakhimov.

Eight days later the celebrated Battle of Balaklava took place, in which a 16,000-man Russian force tried and failed to drive off the British and Turks with a surprise attack. The suicidal British 'Charge of the Light Brigade' through cross-fire had in fact a 'reason why' – to attempt to recapture several artillery pieces. The Russians 'won' Balaklava in terms of casualities, but the overall result was to strengthen the British position, since they reinforced and were now on the lookout.

Following Balaklava, the Allies advanced towards Sevastopol from the south and dug in near the Inkerman ruins, about ten miles from the stronghold. Two Russian units totalling 35,000 men, one a field army under Menshikov, the other a troop from Sevastopol, made uncoordinated, inconclusive, and costly bayonet attacks uphill against two lines of 23,000 British backed by an equal number of French reserves. The Allies were stunned, the under-supplied British now quite demoralized. But the Russians were in a far worse position to resupply *on their own turf* than the Allies, whose ships ferried between Marseilles and Balaklava.

The Allies proceeded to build trenches, tunnels and mines opposite the Sevastopol towers. Despite an especially rough winter for the poorly clad British, the Allies did find reinforcements. Piedmont, under pressure not to cause any problems for Austria, but still eager to raise the Italian Question again, joined the war alliance and sent 15,000 troops. The Allies were also able to bring in a Turkish corps, while Paskevich's fear of Austria stopped him from reinforcing the Crimea in time.

Nicholas's last move was to order the Crimean field army to take Evpatoria in February to prevent a full Turkish corps from landing there. However, in view of poor reconnaissance and the twin problems caused to any advance by a water-filled ditch and strong Franco-Turkish artillery, the Russian commander, K.A. Khrulev, called off the siege. It is said that this failure pushed Nicholas over the brink from his normal melancholy to a depression that sapped his strength, after he caught a bad cold. He died on 18 February/2 March 1855.[6]

Investing Sevastopol was a tedious and difficult process, since it was never totally cut off from provisions and thousands of reinforcements. Ingenious French attempts in February and March to outflank the Russian redoubts and earthworks were met with successful countermeasures. Allied bombardments in March failed to breach the main walls. Ten days of fierce Allied bombardments in April did not break resistance. On the other hand, Admiral Lyons, who was in charge of the British Black Sea squadron, succeeded in a daring campaign in May along the Straits of Kerch and into the Sea of Azov in weakening Russian supply lines. This enabled the new French Commander-in-Chief, A.J.J. Pélissier, to wear down Sevastopol in stages.

On 15 August, as ordered by Nicholas's son Alexander II, the Sevastopol forces tried a final, hopeless counterattack with 60,000 troops near the River Chernaia. There was only a faint possibility of the Russians holding any heights they might have taken from the well-entrenched Allies. They did succeed momentarily against the Piedmontese, but misinterpreted a set of orders and sent infantry straight uphill into French artillery, before the defeatist General Gorchakov called off another one-sided battle.

Now nothing could prevent the fall of Sevastopol, but the Russians did have the foresight to bring in timbers and construct a bridge across the bay for the retreat. As the Allies resumed their bombardment on 18 August, the Russian shell supply was fast dwindling, and the garrison was losing, 1,000–2,500 men per day. Then, on 8 September, the French finally captured the key Malakhov Kurgan. Thereupon Gorchakov, now Russia's supreme commander, resolved to abandon the city, sink the remainder of the fleet, lay sea mines and take up new positions further to the north in the Crimea. Both sides continued to skirmish in the Crimea, but avoided pitched battles. The total casualties for a year's fighting at Sevastopol were 102,000 Russians and 71,000 Allies, making it one of the bloodiest scenes of battle ever until the First World War. The British waged some maritime operations against other Russian Black Sea strongholds and were successful against Kinburn and Ochakov at the mouth of the Dnieper estuary, but did not attack Odessa again, partially because Napoleon vetoed the idea.[7]

Outside the northern Black Sea theatre, the British probed Kronstadt and Russia's innovative sea mines once more in June 1855, but feared the Paixhans guns there and bombarded Sveaborg off Helsingfors instead. Modest attempts to land in Finland were easily beaten off, and the chief English gain remained the destruction of Russian commercial shipping. Meanwhile the Russians had held their positions in the western Caucasus and Transcaucasia, and began a lackadaisical siege of Kars. With the fall of Sevastopol, Omer Pasha's 40,000-man army was free to leave the Crimea, and time was critical. The new local Commander-in-Chief, N.N. Muraviev, tried an immediate, costly assault and then laid a regular siege that led, at the end of December, both to capitulation and to the end of the Turkish Anatolian Army as an effective force. For Russia Kars was both a point of honour and a bargaining chip at the peace table. Meanwhile Omer Pasha's army landed at Sukhumi in September, preparatory to campaigns into the heart of Georgia that the British hardliners favoured, but the Turks were unable to execute.

All fighting ended in early 1856. The grim reaper had collected about 450,000 Russian subjects, 80,000–95,000 French, 20,000–25,000 British, 2,000 Italians, and an unknown number of Ottomans (200,000–400,000), most of all of these unfortunates from disease.[8] Excluding the Tai-Ping Rebellion in China, but including the American Civil War and the Franco-Prussian and Russo-Japanese clashes, the Crimean War was the costliest conflict in human terms between 1815 and 1914.

THE LOGIC OF PEACE . . . OR . . . ANOTHER WAR AVERTED

The Crimean War was a classic case of diplomacy interrupted by warfare. The Vienna Conference operated on and off throughout, and Russian diplomats talked with the British and French in many capitals. An almost constant chain reaction was in effect – Russia restraining Prussia, restraining Austria, restraining France, restraining Britain, restraining Turkey. After Austria threatened to join the war to force Russia from the Principalities, Nicholas replaced Meyendorff in Vienna with Alexander Gorchakov, a partisan of *entente* with France. Buol, however, was able to gain Turkish and Anglo-French concurrence to an Austrian wartime occupation of the Principalities. This move made Vienna an equal protector of Turkey with London and Paris. Meanwhile Prussia and the German Confederation saw to it that Buol did not lead Austria into full participation in the war on the Allied side.[9]

The Russians had been ready as early as March to drop exclusive protectorates and accept the Prussian plan for five-power supervision of the Ottoman Christians in return for mutual withdrawal. The British, French and Austrians, however, had already added the freeing of the Sulina Channel and some reduction of Russia's regional preponderance, as well as a firm guarantee for Turkey to their list of peace terms. On 8 August 1854, before the landings in the Crimea, these demands were formalized into Four Points. By 29 November, after the Russian reverses at Bomarsund, Alma and Inkerman, St Petersburg was willing in principle to accept these terms too, but not unconditionally, since Point Three regarding the balance of power in the Black Sea was dangerously elastic. Here is where Sevastopol became crucial. So long as it held, Russia refused anything but a restricted interpretation of this condition.

Austria's joining the Anglo-French alliance in early December 1854 and Nicholas's death in January 1855 had no immediate effect, while Palmerston's replacing Aberdeen then was merely symptomatic of a British public annoyed that Russia was not crying 'uncle'. The British in fact had to pressure Napoleon not to accept Austria's loose interpretation of Point Three, leading to Drouyn's resignation and replacement by Walewski. The French, however, would still promise no more than to press the siege of Sevastopol to a successful conclusion.

Once Sevastopol fell, Russian political disarray and inertia prevented any immediate concessions, while Palmerston's Cabinet wished to continue the war until Russia was driven from the Black and Baltic Seas. Napoleon now was ready to back the English, if the Russians would not agree to Allied terms. Austria, Prussia and (to a lesser extent) Sweden, however, remained crucial partners for any widened war, but they all held back. Then in November 1855, Napoleon, bolstered by a new type of steamship, whose big guns might offset Russian shore batteries, seduced King Oscar I of Sweden into a defensive alliance.[10] However, other Frenchmen, backed by financial circles, made simultaneous overtures to Gorchakov. The French generals, moreover, who commanded the largest Allied land forces, doubted that the Allies could do much more on land – let alone take the entire Crimea. Then Buol and Morny finally reconciled divergent Austrian and French war aims, agreeing upon a 'weak' interpretation of Point Three, whereby Turkey and Russia would be equal powers in a 'neutralized' Black Sea, Russia also relinquishing control over the mouth of the Danube. The additional British 'Point Five' or 'particular conditions' was thus effectively diluted.

Armed with the agreement with the French and a very reluctant British compromise and facing the financial strains of continuous mobilization, Buol sent Russia another ultimatum in December. Fearing a possible Franco-Russian deal at his expense or the domestic fallout from a general war, the King of Prussia vehemently urged the Russians to concede. Some Russian statesmen took this as a threat and thus favoured guarded acceptance at an extraordinary council in late December. The Austrians, however, insisted upon absolute compliance, while Nesselrode demolished the argument that Russia could delay and bargain separately with the French, who now were asking the least from Russia.[11] The Russians had almost two million men mobilized, but were in no position to fight a war of attrition against a coalition with twice their population and more than three times their national income. A second special council, comprising Russia's civil and military élite, provisionally accepted Austria's terms to avoid the potential loss of Finnish, Baltic and Polish provinces.

The incipient Franco-Russian *entente* led to the official peace conference meeting at Paris, where many of the key actors from before the war represented their countries: Clarendon and Cowley,

Walewski and Bourgueney, Buol and Hübner, Orlov and Brunnow, Fuad, Camillo Cavour from Piedmont and, eventually, Manteuffel. Napoleon also loomed in the background.[12]

The victorious coalition obtained the abolition of the bilateral Russo-Turkish treaties: Kuchuk-Kainarji, Adrianople and the 1849 Convention of Balta Liman. The autonomy of Moldavia, Wallachia and Serbia, as well as general rights of Ottoman Christians were placed under the protection of the five Great Powers and also Piedmont. Turkey, having ceded at last to Stratford's pressures and granted civil equality to all subjects, was now a recognized European power, with an unworkable six-power limitation on the Sultan's sovereignty over his Christians.

Austria's and Turkey's specific pay-off was that the Sulina Channel and the southern chunk of Bessarabia, Russia's sole territorial loss, was returned to (Ottoman) Moldavia and Russia ceased to be a Danubian power. A Commission of riparian powers only, dominated by Austria, was established to oversee the Danube and its traffic. Russia evacuated Eastern Anatolia and Kars, and the Allies left the Crimea and Sevastopol.

The revision of the 1841 Treaty in the interest of the 'European equilibrium' and the 'neutralization' of the Black Sea were tricky, the choices being to open the Straits to all fleets or eliminate local Russian sea power. The Russians and Turks on their own agreed to demilitarize the Black Sea and continue Straits closure in peace time. These 'Black Sea Clauses' were thus a partial concession to Russia, as well as a humiliation. Open Straits would have been chiefly to Britain's advantage.

England's 'particular conditions' proved less tractable. The fruit of two seasons of Baltic campaigns was demilitarization of the Åland Islands. The British fleet also remained in the Black Sea into 1857, in the hope of weakening the Russians in Transcaucasia and thereby supposedly increasing the security of India. The only result of this action was that Russia ceded a few fine points concerning what constituted Southern Bessarabia.[13]

Turkey, saddled with wartime debt, was an anomaly. Reshid had resigned during the war over Mehmed Ali's rehabilitation, Fuad and Aali were back in power, and the Porte was pursuing its own interests, while the French finally dispatched to Constantinople an ambassador – Thouvenel – who proved to be a match for Stratford. The irony of Stratford's diplomacy was the Porte's clear disdain for his imperiousness, request for his recall and blockage of any effective Great Power protectorate over the subject Christians. In this regard,

Stratford did not consider his career to have been a success,[14] for his 'pig' had bolted and slipped away.

The French, whose demands regarding the Holy Places ignited the pre-war crisis, demanded little in particular, and even kept a leash on their aggressive clerics in the Levant. Napoleon's real victory was restoring Paris to the central place of European politics on the Continent. He was more interested in courting the Russians on the side than in following the details of the negotiations. The Holy Places settlement, which the Turks desired and Stratford had brokered in 1853, held – and more or less still does in the Church of the Holy Sepulchre, where the Greeks, Latins and Armenians are together overseeing the present redecoration of the inside of the dome. The Russians were able to construct their church and hospice under the protection of their local consul. Twelve years later Napoleon III and Alexander II presided over the restoration of the cupola. As a fitting tribute to the power of industry, which had enabled the Catholics to recover some lost ground in Jerusalem, the basic reconstruction material was steel.

NATIONALISM AND IMPERIALISM TRIUMPHANT

The real victor of the Crimean War in Europe, as many people recognized, was Germany. Prussia and the Confederation had facilitated Austria's successful diplomacy by standing up to France, England and Russia. The Italians gained too from Piedmont's participation and seat at the peace Congress. Balkan nationalism as a whole profited from Great Power protection of the Serbian and Romanian states. Moreover, both Russia and Austria emerged from the war financially strapped and soon had to initiate reforms which benefited most East and East Central European national movements and also touched off another rebellion in Tsarist Poland. Ironically, it was the Crimean War, rather than the Revolutions of 1848–49, that created the real 'springtime of nations' and also hastened the abolition of serfdom in Russia, Russian Poland and the Principalities.

Imperialism as a whole was the big winner outside of Europe and North America. The British and French succeeded via their loans to the Turks to bind them more securely to Europe and promote policies that opened their empire further to economic and cultural penetration. The British and French also increased their influence within Egypt and other Ottoman provinces.[15]

A fact which is often neglected in analyses of the Crimean War is that Russia may have lost in the Baltic and the Black Sea, but really won in Asia. The last great Daghestani and Circassian offensives failed before the war erupted. Anglo-Turkish attempts to support the Shamyl and some of the Caucasus peoples against Russia flopped. Once the war was over the Russians had a surplus of trained veterans who were to finish the subjugation of the Caucasus in 1864. This freed some of the troops there to move across the Caspian Sea, where the Russian conquest of Central Asia south of the Kazakh Steppe began the next year. The British Imperial and Indian lobbies objected, but the English as a whole had lost their taste for Russian wars.[16]

The Caucasus and Central Asia are only part of this story. Immediately after the Crimean War the Russians supported another Persian march on Afghanistan. The Britain army's loss of prestige during the war and the mobilization of the Anglo-Indians to counter the Persians helped touch off the Great Mutiny or Sepoy Rebellion. This uprising may have led eventually to a more effective English raj in India, but it also immediately drew British attention away from the Black Sea and limited Russia's losses there. Palmerston's *beau idéal* of a major rollback of Russia thus petered out completely as a result of a sepoy jacquerie. This was another one of those explosions resulting from the clash of Western values, military modernization and native traditions, including in this case some very elemental taboos.[17]

The imperialist repercussions of the Crimean War stretched to East Asia as well. After Commodore Matthew C. Perry with only three steamers, four sail, 2,000 men and 144 solid guns, 'opened' Japan for the United States in late 1853, small British, French and Russian squadrons nearby were able to acquire similar rights.[18] Meanwhile 300 Russians beat off an Anglo-French landing on Kamchatka in northeastern Siberia with 900 men, and Admiral Putiatin activated a flotilla along the River Amur, well to the south of the Russian–Manchurian boundary that had been stable since 1689. When the war ended in 1856 the British and the French moved to extort more treaty ports from the Chinese, leading to the second 'Opium War'. The Manchu–Chinese regime at this time was coping with the extensive Tai-Ping Rebellion, which had started in 1850 in the south, partially under the impact of Western ideas. Russian diplomacy in turn activated a protection racket under Putiatin and Nicholas Ignatiev, a young officer, who after the Crimean War had been posted in London to study the methods of British imperialism in Asia. The overall results were the following: fifteen Chinese 'treaty ports' were opened to the maritime nations with extraterritoriality; a special tariff administration was established under an Englishman to finance China's war indemnity; the British then helped the Chinese to suppress the rebellion; and the Russians annexed the Amur-Ussuri region (comprising as much territory as Italy and France put together), including the future Vladivostok, with its potential as a naval base.[19]

An offshoot of the Russian consolidation and expansion of holdings in north-east Asia was the decision to sell Alaska to the United States. California had been supplying Russian America since the 1840s. In order to accommodate the interests of the United States, the British had agreed in 1854 to a wartime truce between the Russian–American and Hudson Bay Companies, whose respective domains met in northwestern Canada. The Anglo-French alliance prevented the Americans from moving into Cuba or Hawaii during the war, but America's version of sovereign neutrality ensured that Alaska would not fall into British hands.[20]

A generally neglected transoceanic linkage concerns the revolutionary effects of the Crimean War in North America, where the wartime export and shipping boom in the United States North was followed by the return of Russian grain to European markets, a post-war British credit squeeze on railroad expansion, and the Panic of 1857. The subsequent depression destroyed not only the growing national trade union movement, but also the Democratic Party's old alliance of Northern workers and Southern planters, and with it the political Compromise of 1850 over the expansion of slavery. The less severely affected South gained in the confidence that it no longer needed the Union. Just as important, the Northern workers allied politically for the first time with the Free Soil farmers of the Midwest, capturing for the Republicans first many seats in Congress in 1858 and then the White House in 1860. The result of this temporary worker–peasant alliance was the central event in American history and a new stimulus for industrial development and territorial expansion. Whether the secession of the South was inevitable before or after the 1857 Panic will be debated by historians for many years to come.[21] At any rate, before the dust had settled in 1867, a bloody Civil War had been fought, slavery abolished, Alaska transferred by Russia to the United States for $7,200,000 earmarked for railroad construction and the core of Canada had achieved Dominion status with meaningful autonomy for French-speaking Quebec.

In sum, all the Great Powers (including British India) benefited from the Crimean War and its aftermath – if of course one discounts the human cost from the casualties. The real losers were the Ottoman Empire, the native Indian states, China, Persia and the American South. Austria won too, though she was unable to compete with Prussia in Germany. Early industrial imperialism was alive and well, Russia was rejuvenating, and the so-called New Imperialism that would subjugate most of Asia, the Middle East, Africa and the Pacific islands to Europe, the United States and Japan, was soon to take off.

REPERCUSSIONS AND LEGACIES

One of the most sarcastic of diplomatic historians has quipped: 'Men always learn from their mistakes how to make new ones.'[22] And so it was, but only in part, after the Crimean War. The Russians learned the real costs of comparative backwardness for the first time since Peter the Great and tried to do something about it by instituting a gamut of reforms, including military ones. The English learned how ramshackle their army was in comparison to the French and had started to accelerate reform during the war. Anybody who so desired could learn the utility of railroads, telegraphs, steamships, rifles, citizen armies, reserve systems and more professionalized medical services in warfare. The English and the Russians also basically learned to be more careful with each other in their 'Great Game'.

Napoleon III concluded that he learned that he could get away with adventurism and playing with combinations that supported and opposed the same power simultaneously. This worked more or less through 1862, as long as he had his English alliance. By 1867 his ploys with Italy, Austria, Russian Poland, Mexico and Germany had succeeded in angering and alienating all the other Great Powers. When cornered by Bismarck in 1870 and pressed by outraged, ill-informed and hypocritical nationalist opinion at home, Napoleon III gambled on single combat with a militarily more prepared opponent, and lost badly.[23]

Buol thought (or hoped) that the Crimean War showed that Austria was an essential element of England's containment of Russia and that Prussia and the Confederation would back a Vienna that mobilized or fought for 'German' interests. In fact, however, Austria had been in a position to protect German interests in 1854 only because Nicholas I had helped put down the Hungarians in 1849–50. Many English still sympathized with the Italians, while Prussians cared for Prussia or Germany, and few people cared for Austria except as a factor in the balance of power. Nevertheless, Buol allowed Cavour and Napoleon III to manoeuvre Austria into the same position with respect to Piedmont in 1859 as Russia had been *vis-à-vis* Turkey in 1853. A resentful Russia refused to support Austria. By the end of 1860 the French and English had aided the unification of most of Italy under Piedmont, Germany and Prussia, allowing Austria to retain just Venetia. Six years later Bismarck used Venetia as bait to obtain Italian aid in expelling Austria from North Germany. Austria had to find her 'compensation' in the Balkans, something she had rejected when offered as an enticement by both the Russians and the Anglo–French in 1853.

The Russians had already learned in 1849 that the Straits Convention of 1841 would not prevent the Turks from inviting in a friendly squadron if they felt menaced. Now, without a Black Sea fleet or fortifications, the Russians were even more threatened, and so could not give up the idea that only their own control of the Straits could secure their Black Sea commerce and coasts. The Russians also discovered from this crisis that their communities of interest lay more with Prussia, France, Piedmont/Italy or the United States than with Austria or England. The Russians additionally found that they could live without the legal fictions of Kuchuk-Kainarji and compete as another Great Power in the Balkans by utilizing real assets and common interests with either the native Christians or the Ottoman Empire.[24] The Russians even learned from Jomini's confidential Foreign Ministry history that Nicholas I had made some mistakes in not taking other powers' views seriously in 1853 and that his ambassadors had been less than forthright with him concerning the pitfalls of his policies.

Most importantly, the Russians learned that the 'Crimean Coalition' of France, Britain and Austria was highly unlikely (if able at all) to mobilize the necessary resources to threaten the Russian heartland. When Russia's Poles revolted again in 1863, the British and French wanted to support them and attempted to activate Austria to force Russia to restore 'Poland' as a separate state on the basis of the 1815 Treaty. Austria, possessing her own Poles, only supported Polish rights in principle; Prussia, also having Polish provinces, leaned toward Russia; Nesselrode's successor Alexander Gorchakov threatened the British and French with a new edition of 1812; and the plan for coalition intervention collapsed.[25]

The Turkish hold over the Balkans was quite shaky after the Crimean War, as European pressure to execute the essentially paper reforms only increased domestic unrest. The French shepherded a unification of the two Romanian Principalities in 1859, which were able to install their own Hohenzollern prince in 1866. The Serbian principality almost engineered rebellion by a Balkan League in 1868. Native revolts continually threatened to erupt and during a Bosnian uprising in 1860 Gorchakov proclaimed: 'the eleventh hour of the Ottoman Empire' was at hand. In 1868 he tried to revive the Convention of München grätz and initiate talks about spheres of influence with Austria.[26]

One of the ironies of post-Crimean War Turkey is that Ignatiev, as Russia's ambassador in Constantinople (1864–77), was sometimes the dominant foreign envoy there. This is because without the Kuchuk-Kainarji nonsense, the Russian argument that Western reform advice was worse than the opium the British forced upon the Chinese made good sense to many Turks. During his period of ascendancy Ignatiev was able to effect far more in peacetime for subject Orthodox Slavs than any of his predecessors had done. His crowning achievement was aiding the establishment of an ecclesiastical Exarchate of Bulgaria in 1870, freeing these Slavs from the Greek patriarchal administration and creating an incipient Bulgarian principality under Russian protection.[27]

Russian policy, though, was conditioned by two overriding strategic goals, which were also points of honour: Southern Bessarabia and the 'Black Sea Clauses'. Hoping to obtain support against the chief obstacles to treaty revision, Austria and Britain, the Russians backed France, Italy, Prussia and the United States in a variety of ways. The first real pay-off came during the Franco-Prussian War of 1870–71, when Gorchakov, backed by Bismarck, threatened unilaterally to abrogate the Clauses, but agreed to a new London conference to authorize remilitarization with continued Straits closure in peacetime.[28]

Russia's next pay-off came when Bismarck, with his new German Empire, presided over a reconciliation of Austria and Russia, creating a loose *Dreikaiserbund* ('Three Emperors' League') in 1873. This 'Neo-Holy alliance' fulfilled one of Nicholas I's dreams by activating the secret clause of the Convention of München grätz, whereby Russia and Austria would consult if the Ottoman Empire started to collapse in the Balkans.[29] The upshot of this arrangement was initial Austro-Russian cooperation, when native revolts against Turkey erupted first in Herzegovina and Bosnia in 1875 and then in Bulgaria in 1876. The Austrians had a hand in inciting the first, and the Russians in setting off the second. When the Serbians declared war in 1875 in support of the Bosnians, 2,000 Russian volunteers went to Serbia under General

Mikhail Cherniaev, one of Russia's conquistadors in Central Asia. Neither Serb nor Russian fought very effectively against the Ottoman regulars, but the Austrian and Russian governments finally started discussing spheres of influence in the Western Balkans, spearheading a Great Power move to prevent the Turks from exploiting their military defeat of the Serbs.[30]

Tsar Alexander II (1855–81) now faced tremendous pressure from Russia's nationalists and the military to go to war against Turkey, especially after the Bulgarian rebellion erupted. Due to one-sided press reports of 'Bulgarian Horrors' inflicted by the Turks, English opinion also swung in favour of the rebels. This gave Russia a situation similar to the one of 1826–28, when the well-publicized Greek rebellion preceded an Eastern crisis and a Russo-Turkish war, rather than that of 1853, when the recent Bosnian disturbances had not created any international stir. Russian policy in turn was reminiscent of 1826–28. Russia cooperated with other Great Powers to suggest new autonomy schemes, but prepared for war and made special engagements concerning the peace terms. Gorchakov assured the Austrian (now Austro-Hungarian) Foreign Minister, Count Andrassy, that Vienna could dominate Bosnia–Herzegovina and that Russia would not create a 'big Slavic or other state'. On this basis, Austria agreed to facilitate Russia's crossing the Danube – a reversal of the policy of 1853–54. Meanwhile, Brunnow's successor in London, Count Peter Shuvalov, told the British that Russia would not threaten the Straits. The Russians also promised Romania full independence and pretended that they would not reannex Southern Bessarabia.[31]

The Turks, like good reactionaries, having neither learned nor forgotten anything, did what had worked in 1853 but failed in 1826–28. They rejected Great Power projects in the name of sovereignty, decreed more reforms, prepared to fight and gambled on the 'conditional neutrality' of England – a source of mixed messages – to save them from Russia.[32] This tactic would have been problematic, had the Liberals under Gladstone (a disciple of Peel and Aberdeen) been in power in London. The Conservative Disraeli, however, was more in the tradition of George Canning and Palmerston in outlook and very much wanted to preserve Turkey and dominate Egypt for the sake of India, if nothing else. Stratford de Redcliffe, now ninety years old and apparently still lucid, fearful of Russian power and bitter over Ottoman failure to reform, recommended his original policy of early 1853: trust Russian assurances, but 'observe their movement with vigilance and prepare to counter any failure in the promises'.[33]

Twenty-three years after Paskevich called off the siege of Silistria,

Nicholas I's great plan was put into effect. In April 1877 Russian troops crossed the Danube again in several places, aiming to take the Turkish fortresses in Eastern Bulgaria, proceed past Varna along the coast, and also to march directly south over the central Balkans towards the Bosphorus. Eastern Bulgaria held, but the southward campaign worked. Although the Russians were temporarily held up by a new Turkish stronghold at Plevna in central Bulgaria, they were joined by Romanian troops, some Bulgarian volunteers and eventually Serbs and Montenegrins. By January the advance guard had taken Adrianople.[34]

At this point, as in 1853, the Russians forgot the experience of 1829. Under pressure from élite and popular nationalist and Panslavic opinion, the Russian government had started in the summer to expand war aims regarding Serbian and Montenegrin territorial expansion and the extent of Bulgarian and Bosnian–Herzegovinian autonomy, and also talked of a temporary occupation of Constantinople. In December the Tsar authorized his generals and Ignatiev to forward peace preliminaries on the basis of these goals, contradicting some of the earlier commitments to London and Vienna. The autonomous Bulgaria envisioned, based on the Exarchate, was a 'big Slavic state', bordering on the Black Sea and the Aegean Sea, only a hundred miles from the Bosphorus.[35]

As the Russian troops approached the Straits, Disraeli sent the Malta squadron to Besika Bay. The new British ambassador there, Assyriologist Austin Henry Layard, who had been more hawkish than Stratford in 1853, brought the warships almost up to Constantinople. The Russians then advanced almost to the suburbs. In order to get them to pull back, the Porte signed the Treaty of San Stefano in March 1878 on Russian terms, which also included full Serbian, Montenegrin and Romanian independence, expanded reforms for Bosnia–Herzegovina, the retrocession of Southern Bessarabia and the cession of Batum, Ardahan, Kars and Bayazid to Russia, but nothing for Austria. When these conditions became known, the British threatened to go to war. The Austrians straddled the fence and tempered the British hawks, but eventually agreed to work with London. As in 1853, British public opinion was split, but the moderate newspapers like *The Times* reacted less to the flow of Russian military moves and diplomacy.

Russian was now in an analogous position to the second half of 1853, San Stefano representing precisely the same kind of unacceptable interpretation of Russia's earlier commitments that the Menshikov Note and Nesselrode's *Examen* had done. Certain factors, however, were now different for Russia. The press was much freer and divided over continuing the war. More importantly, the Ministers of War and Finance told the Tsar that Russia was in no position to fight further and this neutralized the pressure of bellicose nationalists, who were ready to challenge Britain. Facing domestic discontent from social radicals as well, the Tsar accepted Bismarck's offer to host a congress in Berlin, where Russia could retreat more or less back to her original promises. Alexander II was not Nicholas I, and Russia was no longer the same kind of autocracy. Bismarck thus succeeded where Buol had failed: preventing the expansion of a Russo–Turkish war into a coalition war against Russia.[36]

The fate of the Balkan and Ottoman Christians, as well as vulnerability at the Straits, subsequently bedevilled Russian foreign policy until the fall of the Russian Empire in 1917. The British wanted the Turks to open the Straits during the 1884–85 Afghan crisis, after the Russians occupied Merv in eastern Turkmenistan, but Bismarck's diplomatic pressure would not allow it. Ignatiev's successor at Constantinople in the 1880s and 1890s, Alexander Nelidov, who had formulated Russia's demands at San Stefano, tried no less than four times to induce his more cautious superiors in St Petersburg to attempt a *coup de main* at the Bosphorus.[37] The Balkan crises of 1908–14 that preceded the First World War were due in part to Russia's trying first to acquire greater power over the Straits in 1908–09 and, this failing, to renege on a secret promise made to Austria in 1881 regarding the latter's eventual annexation of Bosnia–Herzegovina.[38] A Russian government, however, never initiated hostilities over the Balkans or the Straits after 1877. In the light of the growth of German and then American power in Europe, starting a war over the Eastern Question became for Russia a luxury of a bygone age.

THE IRONY OF 'SICKNESS'

Curiously, after the First World War, with both Russia and Turkey defeated and facing revolution and civil war, the victorious British attempted again to become a Black Sea power and patronize independent states in the Caucasus. This British game was doomed, however, when the Bolsheviks, with tremendous losses, drove the main remaining force of Russia's White Army from the Crimea in 1920. In 1942 the Germans occupied the Crimea by land and took Sevastopol after another long and costly siege, but were forced to evacuate two years later. Then in 1945 Stalin's Foreign Minister, Viacheslav Molotov, invoked the Russo-Turkish Treaties of 1805 and 1833 in a bid for a base at the Straits, only to find in Winston Churchill an able successor to Castlereagh, Palmerston and Disraeli.[39]

By late 1991 the Soviet Union had rather unexpectedly become a very sick man and disintegrated into national states. Russia remains very large and still contains many restless minority Muslims, including Daghestanis and Chechens, whose ancestors had supported Shamyl against Nicholas I. Semi-capitalist, national Turkey, on the other hand, has only one real minority left – the Muslim Kurds, some of whom have been in rebellion for decades. Turkey also still controls the Straits and is toying with the idea of becoming a regional economic power in the Black Sea region, where every other state is committed to institute a market economy. Behind Turkey stand the fully capitalist countries of Europe, together with America and some oil-rich Arab states. Meanwhile, at the time of writing (autumn 1992), Russia has been squabbling on and off with Ukraine over respective shares of the former Soviet Black Sea fleet, which neither can afford, the fate of Sevastopol, which neither really needs for deterrence in the nuclear age, and the Crimea itself, whose minority Tatars desire sovereignty. It would be another great act of folly if the Black Sea states failed to cooperate and compromise, and this book had to be renamed: 'The Origin of the First Crimean War'.

NOTES

1. For the military side of the war from the Russian standpoint, see Curtiss, *The Russian Army under Nicholas I*, pp. 315–56, and *RCW*: 299–341, 408–71; Beskrovnyi *RVI*: 224–89, almost entirely from Russian archival sources; from the standpoints of all three major powers, Palmer *BB*: 80–308.
2. For the Transcaucasia front, also Allen/Muratoff: 68–102.
3. Greenville/Giffard: 109–337; Lambert *CW*: 158–93.
4. For a set of French viewpoints, Gooch *NBG*: 81–251.
5. For the defence of Sevastopol, Eduard Totleben, *Opsanie oborony goroda Sevastopola* (2 vols in 3, St Petersburg 1863).
6. Lincoln, *Nicholas I*, pp. 348–50.
7. For the Black Sea operations, Lambert *CW*: 223–34, 251–63.
8. Palmer *BB*: 242–3.
9. The wartime diplomacy is covered brilliantly by Schroeder *AGBCW*: 169–346; also Curtiss *RCW*: 238–96, 342–407, 472–501; more irreverently, Wetzel: 99–181, and more succinctly and very clearly, Rich: 107–23, 140–81.

10. Paul Knaplund, 'Finnmark in British Diplomacy', pp. 493–502.

11. Cf. Curtiss *RCW*: 498–9.

12. Winfried Baumgart, *The Peace of Paris, 1856, Studies in War, Diplomacy, and Peacemaking* (Santa Barbara 1981), pp. 101–77; also Curtiss *RCW*: 502–29; Wetzel: 183–200; Rich: 182–97; for the 30 March 1856 Treaty and Russo-Turkish Conventions, *CTS* CXIV: 101–35, trans., Hertslet II.264–7, *MENA* I.105.

13. Werner E. Mosse, 'Britain, Russia, and the Questions of Serpents Island and Bolgrad', *SEER* XXX (Dec. 1950): 89–98.

14. Temperley, 'The Last Phase of Stratford de Redcliffe, 1853–1858', *EHR* 47 (1932): 216–33, 257; Lynn Case, 'The Duel of Giants in old Stambul: Stratford Versus Thouvenel', *JMH* XXXV (1953): 262–73.

15. Donald C. Blaisdell, *European Financial Control in the Ottoman Empire: a Study of the Establishment, Activities, and Significance of the Ottoman Public Debt* (New York 1929).

16. Baddeley: 458–72; Allen/Muratoff: 105–6; N.S. Kiniapina, M.M. Bliev and V.V. Degoev, *Kavkaz i Sredniaia Aziia vo vneshnoi politike Rossii. Vtoraia polovina XVIII-80-e gody XIX v.* (Moscow 1982), pp. 189–98, 252–315.

17. Christopher Hibbet, *The Great Mutiny. India 1857* (Middlesex UK/New York 1978/80), and many other works.

18. Arthur Walworth, *Black Ships of Japan* (New York 1946), p. 239.

19. R.K.I. Quested, *The Expansion of Russia in East Asia, 1857–1860*, pp. 64–174.

20. Dowty, *The Limits of Isolation*, pp. 81–3; Bolkhovitinov: 91–103.

21. Kenneth M. Stampp, *America in 1857. A Nation on the Brink* (Oxford 1990), pp. 231–331.

22. Taylor, *Struggle for Mastery*, p. 111.

23. Carr, *Wars of German Unification*, pp. 151–203.

24. I.V. Koz'menko, 'Rossiiskaia diplomatiia v oborone', *Mezhdunarodnye otnosheniia na Balkanakh, 1856–78 gg.* (ed. V.N. Vinogradov, Moscow 1986), pp. 52–73.

25. R.F. Leslie, *Reform and Insurrection in Poland 1856–1865* (London 1963), pp. 170–202.

26. Kathryn Schach, *Russian Foreign Policy under Prince Alexander M. Gorchakov. The Diplomatic Game Plan vs. Austria* (Dissertation, Univ. of Nebraska 1973), pp. 191, 364–466.

27. Jelavich, *Russia's Balkan Entanglements*, pp. 147–66; Thomas A. Meininger, *Ignatiev and the Establishment of the Bulgarian Exarchate, 1864–1872: a Study in Personal Diplomacy* (Madison WI 1970).

28. Barbara Jelavich, *The Ottoman Empire, the Great Powers, and the Straits Question* (Bloomington 1973), pp. 25–84.

29. William Langer, *European Alliances and Alignments, 1871–1890* (2nd edn, New York 1956), pp. 19–26, 59–72.

30. David MacKenzie, *The Serbs and Russian Pan-Slavism* (Ithaca NY 1967), pp. 61–193; B.H. Sumner, *Russia and the Balkans, 1870–80* (Oxford 1937), pp. 99, 137–45.

31. Sumner, *Russia and the Balkans*, pp. 196–308; cf. AVPR Sek. Arkh. 20, 22, for the Russian commitments to Austria in 1876–77.

32. For the Ottoman side of developments, Davison *ROE*: 270–408; on

Britain during this war, Richard Millman, *Britain and the Eastern Question, 1875–1878* (Oxford 1979); also R.W. Seton-Watson, *Disraeli, Gladstone, and the Eastern Question* (London 1935).

33. Stratford de Redcliffe, *The Eastern Question* (London 1878), p. 133.

34. For military side of the war, Beskrovnyi *RVI*: 309–54, supplemented by Allen/Muratoff: 105–217; for a new assessment, Fuller: 317–27.

35. For a Russian view of these diplomatic manoeuvres, S.L. Chernov, *Rossiia na zavershaiushchem etape Vostochnogo krizisa, 1875–1878 gg.* (Moscow 1984), pp. 25–55; also Barbara Jelavich, 'Negotiating the Treaty of San Stefano', *Southeastern Europe* VI.2 (1979): 171–93.

36. W.N. Medlicott, *The Congress of Berlin and After. A Diplomatic History of the Near Eastern Settlement, 1878–1880* (2nd edn, London 1963).

37. Barbara Jelavich, *The Ottoman Empire, the Great Powers and the Straits Question, 1870–1887* (Bloomington 1973), pp. 35–45, and *Russia's Balkan Entanglements*, pp. 173, 205.

38. Alfred F. Pribam, *The Secret Treaties of Austria-Hungary, 1879–1914* (Cambridge MA 1920), p. 43 (Secret Convention of Berlin, 18 June 1881, Separate Protocol, art. 1); Robert E. Langer, *The Diplomacy of Imperialism* (2 vols, New York 1935): I: 373–5; Andrew Rossos, *Russia and the Balkans: Inter-Russian Rivalries and Russian Foreign Policy, 1908–1914* (Toronto 1981).

39. On Anglo-French intervention in the Black Sea and the Crimea after the First World War, see Richard Henry Ullman, *Anglo-Soviet Relations, 1917–1921* (3 vols, Princeton NJ 1961–73), for 1945, Hurewitz, 'Russia and the Turkish Straits', pp. 605–6.

Bibliography*

(1) MANUSCRIPT COLLECTIONS AND ABBREVIATIONS†

AAT: Archives de l'Armée de terre, Paris.

AdMss: British Library, London, Manuscript Division (for the Aberdeen Papers).

AMAE: Archive du Ministère des affaires étrangères, Paris.

AMAE Blg.: Archive du Ministère des affaires étrangères, Brussels, Correspondance politique.

AMAE CC: AMAE. Correspondance consulaire.

AMAE CP: AMAE. Correspondance politique.

AMAE PA PC, PT, PW: AMAE. Papiers d'agents. Papiers Castelbajac, Thouvenel, Walewski.

ASMAE: Archivio Storico del Ministerio degli Affari Esteri, Rome.

ARB: Archives royales belges, Brussels.

AVPR: Arkhiv vneshnei politiki Rossii, Moscow.

AVPR K: AVPR, fond Kantseliariia.

AVPR GA-V2; AVPR, fond Glavnyi arkhiv-V2.

AVPR Pos. Konst. AVPR, fond Posol'stvo v Konstantinopole.

BHSA OA: Bayerisches Hauptstaatsarchiv, Munich . . . Orientalische Angelegenheiten.

---

*Not all of the works cited in the footnotes are listed here.
†Some of the Russian archives have recently undergone or are in the process of undergoing insignificant name changes, which will not negate the utility of the standard acronyms used here; for example, AVPR to AVPRI (Arkhiv vneshnei politiki Rossiiskoi imperii), and TsGAVMF to RGAVMF (Russkii gosudarstvennyi arckhiv Voenno-morskogo flota).

305

ClDp: Bodleian Library, Oxford, Clarendon Papers.

DRA UM: Rigsarchivet, Copenhagen, Udenrigsministeriet.

GPB: Gosudarstvennaia publichnaia biblioteka, St Petersburg. Rukopisnyi otdel.

HHSA PA: Haus- Hof- und Staatsarchiv, Vienna. Politische Abteilung.

HHSA PA KA GA: HHSA PA, Kabinettsarchiv, Geheimakten.

NRA . . . BZ: Nederland Algemeen Rijksarchief . . . Buitenlandse Zaken.

PRO: Public Record Office, London.

PRO FO: PRO, Foreign Office.

SHSA AM Kanz.: Sächsisches Hauptstaatsarchiv, Dresden, Aussenministerium, Kanzlei.

SRA KUB: Riksarchivet, Stockholm, Kabinett för utrikes Brevvätslikngebn.

TsGADA: Tsentral'yi gosudarstvennyi arkhiv drevnykh aktov, Moscow.

TsGAOR: Tsentral'yi gosudarstvennyi arkhiv Okt'iabrskoi revoliutsii, Moscow.

TsGAVMF: Tsentral'yi gosudarstvennyi voenno-morskoi arkhiv, St Petersburg.

TsGIA: Tsentral'yi gosudarstvennyi istoricheskii arkhiv, St Petersburg.

TsGVIA: Tsentral'yi gosudarstvennyi voenno-istoricheskii arkhiv, Moscow.

ZSAM HA: Zentrales Staatsarchiv, Merseburg, Historische Abteilung.

(2) COLLECTIONS OF PUBLISHED OFFICIAL SOURCES

AGK: Winfried Baumgart, Anna Maria Schop Soler, et al. (eds), *Akten zur Geschichte des Krimkriegs*. Munich/Vienna 1980. This series covers/will cover Austria (in 3 vols, 1980), Prussia (2 vols, 1990), Britain (4 vols: vol. 3, 1988), and France (3 vols), while the editors hope that *VPR* can provide companion volumes for Russian sources; has created new standards for Crimean War publication and annotation of documents: necessarily selective; includes official and unofficial material; begins at the end of 1852 and early 1853 for Austria and Prussia, but will go back to the development of the Holy Places dispute for Britain and France.

CORR: Great Britain, Foreign Office, *Correspondence Respecting the*

Rights and Privileges of the Latin and Greek Churches in Turkey, 1853–1856. 8 vols. Surprisingly rich for a contemporary, official publication and still an indispensable collection – especially for the Holy Places dispute, Anglo-Russian and Anglo-Turkish relations, and the various compromise proposals of 1853–54.

CTS: Clive Perry (ed.), *The Consolidated Treaty Series*. 231 vols, Dobbs Ferry NY 1969–81. Reprinted from other collections; for this period misses only the 1851 Austro–Prussian Treaty.

EP: Great Britain, House of Commons, *Eastern Papers (Parliamentary Papers: Accounts and Papers, 1854* LXXI–LXXII). Almost the same set of documents as in *CORR*.

FR: France, Ministry of Foreign Affaires, *La France et la Russie*. Paris 1854. Scanty but vital collection of the chief pieces of French public diplomacy, 1853–Feb. 1854.

Hertslet: Edward Hertslet (ed.), *Map of Europe by Treaty*. 4 vols, London 1875–91. English translations of major treaties and memoranda, starting 1814; with detailed maps.

Julius von Jasmond, *Aktenstücke zur orientalischen Frage*. 3 vols, Berlin 1855–59. Mostly in German translation, now supplanted.

Martens: F.F. Martens, *Recueil des traités conclus par la Russie avec les puissances étrangères*. 15 vols, St Petersburg 1874–1906. All kinds of extracts from diplomatic correspondence, as well as many treaties; not always reliable commentary: in both French and Russian.

MENA: Jacob C. Hurwitz, *The Middle East and North Africa in World Politics. A Documentary Record*. 2nd edn, 3 vols, New Haven/London 1975–. English translation of key documents, starting with 1535.

Nouradounghian: Gabriel Effendi Nouradounghian, *Recueil d'actes internationaux de l'Empire Ottoman*. 4 vols, Paris 1897–1903. Supplements Testa.

POM: Friedrich Engel-Janosi (ed.), *Die Protokolle des österreichischen Ministerrates, 1848–1867*. Vienna 1970–.

Testa: Baron I. Testa, *Recueil des traités de la Porte Ottomane avec les puissances étrangères*. 11 vols, Paris 1864–1911. Fills important gaps.

VPR: USSR/Russia, Ministry of Foreign Affairs, *Vneshniaia politika Rossii XIX i nachale XX veka. Dokumenty ministerstva inostrannykh del*. Moscow 1960–. Comprehensive, well annotated, indexed and cross-referenced, but unlikely to reach the 1850s until some time in the twenty-first century.

ZP: A.M. Zaionchkovskii, *Vostochnaia voina 1853–1856 gg. Prilozheniia*. 2 vols, 3 suppl., St Petersburg 1908–13. The supplementary volumes are poorly organized, but very rich for military as well as diplomatic developments; the two narrative volumes are also useful, with some interesting photographs.

(3) ORIGINAL SOURCES CITED IN ABBREVIATION

DM: TsGAVMF 19/7/135, *Dnevnik Menshikova* (Menshikov's Diary).
KfZh: TsGIA 516//1/120/2322//306–340 *Kamerfur'erskie zhurnaly* (Journals of the Court Chamberlain), 1/13 Aug 1851–Jan. 1854.
MQLS: 'Mémoire sur la question des lieux saints', attributed to Fuad Pasha (Aug. 1853/Zilcadé 1269), Testa III: 294–312.
PHQSL: 'Précis historique de la question des Saints-Lieux' (Jan. 1853), ZP I.83.

(4) ABBREVIATIONS OF NAMES IN NOTES

Ab.	Aberdeen (British Prime Minister)
Arg.	Argyropoulos (Russian First Dragoman, Constantinople)
Bar.	Baraguay d'Hilliers (French Ambassador, Constantinople)
Bkr.	Brouckère (Belgian Prime/Foreign Minister)
BlC.	Blondeel van Cuelebroeck (Belgian Minister, Constantinople)
Brk.	Bruck (Austrian Internuncio, Constantinople)
Brq.	Bourqueney (French Minister, Vienna)
Brw.	Brunnow (Russian Minister, London)
Cln.	Clarendon (British Foreign Secretary)
Const.	Grand Duke Constantine (Acting Russian Minister of the Marine)
Ctb.	Castelbajac (French Minister, St Petersburg)
Cwl.	Cowley (British Ambassador, Paris)
Drn.	Drouyn de Lhuys (French Foreign Minister)
FJ	Francis Joseph I (Emperor of Austria)
Fnt.	Fonton (Russian First Secretary/Chargé, Vienna)
FW IV	Frederick William IV (King of Prussia)
Grm.	Graham (British First Lord of the Admiralty)
Hüb.	Hübner (Austrian Minister, Paris)
Kis.	Kiselev (Russian Minister, Paris)
Lac.	La [de la] Cour (French Ambassador, Constantinople)

Lav.   La [de la] Valette (French Ambassador, Constantinople)
Lbz.   Lebzeltern (Austrian Chargé, St Petersburg)
LStr.   Lady Stratford (Wife of Stratford de Redcliffe)
Mdf.   Meyendorff (Russian Minister, Vienna)
Mlm.   Malmesbury (British Foreign Secretary)
Mnsh.   Menshikov (Russian Minister of the Marine, Extraordinary
         Ambassador, Constantinople)
Mnt.   Manteuffel (Prussian Minister President)
Nap. III Napoleon III (Emperor of France)
Nes.   Nesselrode (Russian Chancellor)
Nich. I. Nicholas I (Emperor of Russia)
Orl.   Orlov (Russian Director, Third Section; Extraordinary
         Ambassador, Vienna).
Oz.   Ozerov (Russian Chargé/First Secretary, Constantinople)
Plm.   Palmerston (British Foreign Secretary; Home Secretary)
Psk.   Paskevich (Russian Viceroy, Warsaw; Commander-in/
         Chief)
QV   Victoria (British Queen)
Rch.   Rochow (Prussian Minister, St Petersburg)
Rsh.   Reshid Pasha (Turkish Foreign Minister)
Rus.   Russell (British Foreign Secretary; Commons Leader)
Sen.   Seniavin (Russian Deputy Foreign Minister/Chief of Asiatic
         Department)
Seym.   Seymour (British Minister, St Petersburg)
Str.   Stratford de Redcliffe (British Ambassador, Constan-
         tinople)
Thv.   Thouvenel (French Political Director, Foreign Ministry)
Tit.   Titov (Russian Minister, Constantinople)
vH.   van Hall (Dutch Foreign Minister)
Wal.   Walewski (French Ambassador, Constantinople)
Wst.   Westmorland (British Minister, Vienna)

(5) REFERENCE WORKS CITED IN ABBREVIATION

EB: *Encyclopaedia Britannica* (London, etc. 1911 and 1947
         edns).
ES: *Entsiklopedicheskii slovar'* (St Petersburg 1890–1914).
GJ: *Gothaisches genealisches Taschenbuch nebst diplomatisch-statis-
         tischem Jahrbuch.* Not the best statistics, but very informa-
         tive for comparisons.

(6) PUBLISHED COLLECTIONS OF PRIVATE CORRESPONDENCE, MEMOIRS AND BIOGRAPHIES WITH SOURCES

AbC: Lord Stanmore, *Selections from the Correspondence of the Earl of Aberdeen*. 13 vols, London, n.d. and 1885.

Albert, Prince Consort of Victoria, *Letters of the Prince Consort*. ed. Kurt von Jagow, trans. E.T.S. Dugdale. 2 vols, London 1906.

Ashley: Evelyn Ashley, *The Life of Henry John Temple, Viscount Palmerston: 1846–1865*. 2 vols, London 1876.

Herbert, C.F. Bell, *Lord Palmerston*. 2 vols, London 1888, repr. 1936, 1966. Judicious review of his foreign policy during 1853–54.

Christian Carl Josias Freiherr von Bunsen. Aus seinen Briefen und nach eigener Erinnerungen geschildert von seiner Witwe. ed. Freidrich Nippod. 3 vols, Leipzig 1868–71.

Greville: Charles C.F. Greville, *The Greville Memoirs*. ed. Henry Reeve. 8 vols, London 1888. Critical of Stratford and of British war hysteria.

Herbert: Lord Stanmore, Arthur Hamilton Gordon, *Sydney Herbert. Lord Herbert of Lea. A Memoir*. 2 vols, London 1906. Critical of the policy he helped to implement.

Graf Joseph Alexander von Hübner, *Neuf ans de souvenirs d'un ambassadeur d'Autriche à Paris sous le Second Empire, 1851–1859*. 2 vols, Paris 1904. Widely utilized, slightly distrusted.

Alexander Jomini, *Diplomatic Study in the Crimean War*. 2 vols, London 1882, originally Russian, 1863. Represents a Russian Foreign Ministry memoir, without footnotes: as Lane-Poole wrote, 'as a happy mixture of candour and misrecital of facts . . . perhaps unequalled'; has been trusted too much.

Lane-Poole: Stanley Lane-Poole, *The Life of the Right Honourable Stratford Canning, Viscount Stratford de Recliffe. From his Memoirs and Private Papers*. 2 vols. London 1888. Court history, indispensable for the extracts of correspondence later lost; hero-worshipping editor.

LQV: Arthur C. Benson and Viscount Esher (eds), *The Letters of Queen Victoria*. 3 vols, New York 1907.

NLP: Comte Anatole de Nesselrode (ed.), *Lettres et papiers du chancelier Comte de Nesselrode, 1760–1856*, 11 vols, Paris 1904–12. Chiefly his private (really semi-official) correspondence with Meyendorff for the period under consideration.

PAP: Heinrich Ritter von Poschinger (ed.), *Preussens auswärtige Politik, 1850–1858. Unveröffentliche Dokumente aus dem Nachlasse Manteuffels*.

2 vols, Berlin 1902. Private correspondence, mainly diplomatic, now supplements *AGK* II.1–2.

Charles Stuart Parker, *Life and Letters of Sir James Graham, Second Baronet of Netherby, P.C., G.C.B., 1792–1861.* 2 vols, London 1907.

PASK: A.P. Shcherbatov, *General-fel'dmarshal Kniaz' Paskevich i ego zhizn' i diatel'nost': po neizdannym istochnikam.* 7 vols. St Petersburg 1888–1904. With much of the Nicholas I–Paskevich correspondence.

Jean Gilbert Victor Fialin, Duc de Persigny, *Mémoires du Duc de Persigny publiés avec des documents inédits.* Paris 1896. More important for contemporary attitudes than for the key moves by Napoleon.

PM: *Peter von Meyendorff: Ein russischer Diplomat an den Höfen von Berlin und Wien. Politischer und Privater Briefwechsel, 1826–1863.* ed. Otto Hoetzsch. 3 vols, Berlin 1923. For this period, many private letters to Nesselrode; companion to NLP; reveals the contradictions of a loyal court diplomat.

Graf Anton Franz von Prokesch-Osten, *Aus den Breifen des Grafen Prokesch von Osten, k.u.k. österr. Botschafter und Feldzeugmeister (1849–1855).* Vienna 1896.

Captain Adolphus Slade, *Turkey and the Crimean War.* London 1867. Employed by the Turks, but collaborated with Rose and Stratford in 1853 and then with the British commanders during the war.

Thouvenel: Louis Thouvenel, *Nicolas I et Napoléon III: les préliminaires de la Guerre de Crimée.* Paris 1891. Contains extracts from Edouard Thouvenel's private correspondence with the envoys to St Petersburg and Constantinople.

Carl Friedrich Vitzthum von Eckstaedt, *St Petersburg and London in the Years 1852–1864.* Originally in German (1886); ed. Henry Reeve. 2 vols, London 1887. Fascinating, questionably reliable.

Walpole: Spencer Walpole, *The Life of Lord John Russell.* 2 vols, London 1889.

Wellesley, D.A. (ed.), *The Paris Embassy under the Second Empire.* London 1928. Cowley deserves to have more of his private papers printed than are found here.

(7) JOURNALS FREQUENTLY CITED

AHR: American Historical Review
AHY: Austria History Yearbook

CHJ: Cambridge Historical Journal
EHR: English Historical Review
HJ: Historical Journal
JGO: Jahrbücher für Geschichte Osteuropas
JMH: Journal of Modern History
SEER/SR: Slavonic and East European Review (formerly Slavonic Review)

(8) MONOGRAPHS AND GENERAL STUDIES

Allen/Muratoff: W.E.D. Allen and Paul Muratoff, *Caucasian Battlefields. A History of the Wars on the Turco-Caucasian Border, 1828–1921*. Cambridge UK 1953. Details, maps, no citations, just a critical bibliography.

M.S. Anderson, *The Eastern Question, 1774–1923*. New York 1966. Corrects Marriott with an Ottoman perspective; derivative for the origin of the war.

Baddeley: John F. Baddeley, *The Russian Conquest of the Caucasus*. London 1908. Shamyl and the Circassians from the Russian viewpoint; no citations.

Frank Edgar Bailey, *British Policy and the Turkish Reform Movement. A Study in Anglo-Turkish Relations*. Cambridge MA 1942. Useful, but anglo-centric.

Bapst: Edmond Bapst, *Les origines de la guerre de Crimée: La France et la Russie de 1848 à 1854*. Paris 1912. Overplays the Nicholas I–Napoleon III relationship; mixed source base, including French archives; no use of ZP I.

C.J. Bartlett, *Great Britain and Sea Power, 1815–1853*. Oxford 1963. Perfect companion volume for the approach in this book.

Winfried Baumgart, *The Peace of Paris, 1856. Studies in War, Diplomacy, and Peacemaking*. Trans. A.P. Saab, Santa Barbara 1981. German original, 1972. Topical and analytical presentation of the Crimean War problem by the editor-in-chief of *AGK*.

Yehoshua Ben-Arieh, *Jerusalem in the 19th Century*, 2 vols, Jerusalem/New York 1984–86. Encyclopedic, derivative.

A.L. Beskrovnyi, *Russkaia armiia i flot v XIX veke*. Moscow 1973. Archive based, lots of statistics.

Beskrovnyi *RVI*: A.L. Beskrovnyi, *Russkoe voennoe iskusstvo XIX v*. Moscow 1974. Analytical account of Russia's nineteenth-century wars based entirely on Russian archives.

M.I. Bogdanovich, *Vostochnaia voina 1853–1856 gg.* 4 vols in 2, St Petersburg 1876. Brief on origins, but useful citations; now superseded.

Bohl: Robert Bohl, *Anglo-French Relations and the Crimean War Alliance.* Dissertation, Univ. of Pennsylvania 1974. Many citations from the Cowley–Clarendon and Walewski–Drouyn correspondence.

Bolkhovitinov: Nikolai N. Bolkhovitinov, *Russko-amerikanskie otnosheniia i prodazha Aliaski, 1834–1867.* Moscow 1990. Interesting focus on the North Pacific and the Alaska–Hudson Bay Company problem.

Kurt Borries, *Preussen im Krimkrieg.* Stuttgart 1930. A few key documents.

Emile Bourgeois, *Manuel historique de politique étrangère.* 3 vols, Paris 1892–1905. Needs to be superseded by a more reliable documented, detailed, general diplomatic history.

Kenneth Bourne, *Britain and the Balance of Power in North America, 1815–1908.* Berkeley/Los Angeles 1967. Illustrates Britain's dilemmas and advantages when competing with Russia and the United States simultaneously.

Philip Marshall Brown, *Foreigners in Turkey, Their Juridical Status.* Princeton/London 1914.

Lynn M. Case, *Edouard Thouvenel et la diplomatie du Second Empire.* Paris 1976. Background to a key French figure.

_____, *French Opinion on War and Diplomacy during the Second Empire.* Philadelphia 1954. Complements Kingsley Martin.

Richard Charmatz, *Minister Freiherr von Bruck: Der Vorkämpfer Mitteleuropas.* Leipzig 1916.

James B. Conacher, *The Aberdeen Coalition. A Study in Mid-Nineteenth-Century Party Politics.* Cambridge UK 1968. Masterful monograph, essential for following British decision-making; interesting evaluation of Stratford; elucidates the effect of Cabinet divisions.

John Shelton Curtiss, *The Russian Army under Nicholas I, 1825–1855.* Durham 1965. Based on published sources, concludes with the Crimean War.

Curtiss *RCW*: John Shelton Curtiss, *Russia's Crimean War.* Durham 1979. Some interesting use of AVPR, HHSA and AMAE; for Russian documents otherwise one-sidedly relies on Jomini, Martens, and ZP at the expense of even published French, English, and Turkish sources for the origins of the war, Vienna Note, etc.

Davison *ROE*: Roderic H. Davison, *Reform in the Ottoman Empire, 1856–1876.* Princeton 1963. Fine pre-1856 background too.

Alan Dowty, *The Limits of American Isolation: the United States and the Crimean War*. New York 1971. Could be more detailed.

Echard: William E. Echard, *Napoleon III and the Concert of Europe*; Baton Rouge and London 1983. Foregrounds Napoleon's attempt to square the circle by recrafting the European 'concert' to meet the post-1848 realities.

Arvil B. Erikson, *The Public Career of Sir James Graham*. Oxford/Cleveland 1952. Too brief on 1853–54.

Franz Eckhart, *Die Deutsche Frage und der Krimkrieg*. Berlin/Königsberg 1931.

Radu Florescu, *The Struggle against Russia in the Roumanian Principalities, 1821–1854*. Munich 1962. Slanted title, useful background.

Fuller: William C. Fuller, Jr, *Strategy and Power in Russia, 1600–1914*. New York 1992. Serious re-evaluation, based on an understanding of Russia's weaknesses; used archival sources for the army which this author did not see.

B.A. Georgiev, N.S. Kiniapina, M.T. Panchencko, and V.I. Sheremet, *Vostochnyi vopros vo vneshnei politike Rossii konets XVIII–nachalo XX v.* Moscow 1978. The Eastern Question from a Russian perspective; fresh research in AVPR.

David Gillard, *The Struggle for Asia, 1828–1914*. London 1977/80. Comprehensive overview of the 'Great Game'.

John H. Gleason, *The Genesis of Russophobia in Great Britain*. Cambridge MA 1950. Chiefly the 1830s; chronicles the rise *and* decline before 1848.

Gooch *NBG*: Brison D. Gooch, *The New Bonapartist Generals in the Crimean War. Distrust and Decision-Making in the Anglo-French Alliance*. The Hague 1959. The French perspective – a good antidote to the standard anglo-centric works; based on memoirs and secondary sources, not AAT research.

———, *The Origins of the Crimean War*. Lexington MA 1969. Heath and Company 'Problems in European Civilization' volume of selections from historians, nothing later than 1956, mostly syntheses, without citations, even when they are found in the original works; no indication of factual mistakes, so how can the reader make valid judgements?

La Gorce *HSE*: Pierre de la Gorce, *Histoire du Second Empire*. 6 vols, mixed edn, Paris 1901–03. Rich for domestic history, but dated.

M.S. Gorianov, *Le Bosphore et les Dardanelles*. Paris 1910. Often cited, but says nothing important about 1848–54.

Basil Greenhill and Ann Giffard, *The British Assault on Finland*,

1854–1855. London 1988. A fresh, archive-based detailed examination and presentation of the Baltic campaign.

Emmanuel Halicz, *Danish Neutrality During the Crimean War (1853–1856). Denmark Between the Hammer and the Anvil*. Janet Cave, trans. Odense DK 1977. Archive based, informative; useful bibliography for Sweden as well as Denmark.

Heindl: Waltraud Heindl, *Graf Buol-Schauenstein in St Petersburg und London 1848–1852*. Vienna/Cologne/Graz 1970. Essential background for a critical player in 1853–54; well documented from HHSA by one of the editors of *POM*.

HM: Österreichische Akademie der Wissenschaften, *Die Habsburgermonarchie 1848–1918*. Vienna 1973—. Very informative, collective, multi-volume history; topically organized.

Derek Hopwood, *The Russian Presence in Syria and Palestine, 1843–1914: Church and Politics in the Near East*. Oxford 1969. Reliable, based on published Russian and Arabic sources, but no use of the Russian Holy Synod collection in TsGIA.

Harold Ingle, *Nesselrode and the Russian Rapproachment with Britain, 1836–1844*. Berkeley 1978. Based on published Russian sources, but comprehensive and judicious.

Barbara Jelavich, *Russian's Balkan Entanglements, 1806–1914*. Cambridge UK 1991. Thoughtful synthesis; original research is from the Balkan side; views Nicholas from the standpoint of 'defence of the status quo'.

Charles and Barbara Jelavich, *The Establishment of Balkan National States*. Seattle 1977. More a textbook, but also a companion to B. Jelavich, *Balkan Entanglements*.

Kinglake, *Invasion of the Crimea*: Arthur W. Kinglake, *The Invasion of the Crimea: Its Origin and Account of its Progress down to the death of Lord Raglan*. 14 vols, Leipzig 1863–69. Detailed, based on British sources, with many extracts from documents, not kind to Napoleon III.

N.S. Kiniapina, M.M. Bliev and V.V. Degoev, *Kavkaz i Sredniaia Aziia vo vneshnoi politike Rossii. Vtoraia polovina XVIII-80-e gody XIX v*. Moscow 1982. Archive-based for Central Asia.

Marian Kukiel, *Czartoryski and European Unity*. Princeton 1955. Slightly overrates the impact of the energetic and active anti-tsarism of the Polish Emigration.

Lambert *CW*: Andrew Lambert, *The Crimean War, British Grand Strategy, 1853–1856*. Manchester UK/New York 1990. Fresh analysis, based chiefly on British naval and other archives; military imperatives inform outlook on origins; companion French and Russian volumes would be most useful.

W. Bruce Lincoln, *Nicholas I: Emperor and Autocrat of all the Russias*. Bloomington 1978. Scholarly, sympathetic; brief and derivative for foreign policy.

David MacKenzie, *Ilija Garašanin: Balkan Bismarck*. New York/Boulder 1985. The subject is important for his opposition to Russian interference in Ottoman Serbia in the 1840s–50s; archive-based.

Alyce E. Mange, *The Near Eastern Policy of Napoleon III* (Urbana 1940) – straightforward overview; better for the Holy Places dispute than for the origins of the war.

Marriott: J.A.R. Marriott, *The Eastern Question. A Historical Study of European Diplomacy*. Oxford 1917. The view from Europe; poorly documented for origins of this war.

Martin: B. Kingsley Martin, *The Triumph of Lord Palmerston. A Study of Public Opinion in England before the Crimean War*. New York 1924. Rich in data on the English press.

Monnier: Luc Monnier, *Etude sur les origines de la guerre de Crimée*. Geneva 1977. Uses AMAE and some rare sources, as well as insight; not always accurate; Napoleon's family archive yielded a few gems.

Nolan: E.H. Nolan, *Illustrated History of the War Against Russia*. 2 vols, London 1857. Detailed dated chronicle, with many documents.

Palmer *BB*: Alan Palmer, *The Banner of Battle. The Story of the Crimean War*. London 1987. Broadly researched and readable, by a prolific and erudite historian who has found new sources, such as the diaries of Seymour and Rose; fair concerning the chief actors; passes over the sticky problems regarding the origins rather quickly.

G. Pélisse du Rausas, *Le régime des capitulations dans l'Empire Ottoman*. Paris 1902. Essential background.

Puryear *ERSQ*: Vernon Puryear, *England, Russia, and the Straits Question, 1844–1856*. Berkeley 1931. The seminal scholarly indictment of British policy; gives Russian interpretations of treaty rights and informal agreements more than the benefit of doubt.

———, *France and the Levant, 1820–1845*. Berkeley 1941.

———, *International Economics and Diplomacy in the Near East: A Study of British Commercial Policy in the Levant, 1834–1853*. Stanford 1935. Supplements his *ERSQ*.

Nicholas Riasanovsky, *Nicholas I and Official Nationality in Russia, 1825–1855*. Berkeley 1959. Penetrating study of Nicholas I's ideological world, including the ideas behind his foreign policy.

Rich: Norman Rich, *Why the Crimean War? A Cautionary Tale*. Hanover/London 1985. About as good as possible for a short study based completely on published documents in English, French, and German and on secondary sources; maybe skirts too quickly over the May–September 1853 compromise proposals; excellent treatment of the war itself and the peace process; fine annotated bibliography.

Gunther Rothenberg, *The Army of Francis Joseph*. West Lafayette 1976. Excellent historian, not very detailed work.

Saab *OCA*: Ann Pottinger Saab, *The Origins of the Crimean – Alliance*. Charlottesville 1977. Essential turco-centric monograph, using AMAE, HHSA, and Ottoman sources; emphasizes Turkish freedom of action; well documented; bibliography includes Turkish works, council protocols, references to diplomatic correspondence that very few people have used.

Schroeder *AGBCW*: Paul W. Schroeder, *Austria, Great Britain and the Crimean War. The Destruction of the Concert of Europe*. Ithaca 1972. Brilliant, thorough diplomatic history based on HHSA, AMAE, PRO, ClDp, *inter alia*. Exposes the cynicism and consistent inconsistencies of British policies and thinking, as well as Austria's dilemmas.

Schiemann: Theodor Schiemann, *Geschichte Russlands unter Kaiser Nikolaus I*. 4 vols, Berlin, Leipzig 1904–19. Still a standard work.

Albert Seaton, *The Crimean War. A Russian Chronicle*. London 1977. Good, brief military history from the Russian side, derivative for origins.

Seton-Watson *BE*: R.W. Seton-Watson, *Britain in Europe, 1789–1914*. Cambridge UK 1937. Attempts to be both balanced and critical of British statesmen and journalists.

Sheremet: V.I. Sheremet, *Osmanskaia imperiia i zapadnaia Evropa, vtoraia tret' XIX veka*. Moscow 1986. Uses Russian mission reports; analyses the interplay of treaty rights, economic interests, and international relations.

F.A. Simpson, *Louis Napoleon and the Recovery of France, 1848–1856*. New York 1923. Based on evidence, not prejudice, concerning his subject; less reliable on the origins of the war.

Hew Strachan, *Wellington's Legacy: The Reform of the British Army, 1830–1854*. Manchester UK 1984. Useful companion to Bartlett.

Tarlé: Evgenii Tarlé, *Krymskaia voina*. 2 vols, Moscow 1941–44; repr. as *Sochineniia*, vols 8–9, 1959. Brilliant; wide use of Russian primary sources; marred by conspiracy thinking.

A.J.P. Taylor, *The Struggle for Mastery in Europe*. Oxford 1954. Witty, sarcastic, judgemental, uneven; real value is in foregrounding the German Question.

Temperley *ENEC*: Harold Temperley, *England and the Near East: the Crimea*. London 1936, repr. 1964. Classic based chiefly on British sources, with pioneering manuscript work on British motivation; too credulous regarding diplomatic rumours and too free in assigning motives, almost as if one were creating *belles-lettres*.

Thomas: Daniel H. Thomas, *The Guarantee of Belgian Independence and Neutrality in European Diplomacy, 1830s–1930s*. Kingston RI 1983. Useful data.

Unckel: Bernhard Unckel, *Österreich und der Krimkrieg. Studien zur Politik der Donaumonarchie in den Jahren 1852–1856*. Lübeck/Hamburg 1969. Solid monograph using HHSA, with a footnote for every fact; most helpful.

V.N. Vinogradov, *Velikobritaniia i Balkany ot Venskogo kongresa do Krymskoi voiny*. Moscow 1985. Re-examination of Anglo-Russian rivalry in the Balkans; uses AVPR and published sources; emphasizes British expansionism.

———, et al. (eds), *Mezhdunarodnye otnosheniia na Balkanakh, 1830–1856 gg*. AVPR as the basic great power source; sympathetic to Balkan aspirations; nothing new on origins of the war.

Philip Warner, *The Crimean War. A Reappraisal*. New York 1972. Derivative for origins; good military history.

Walker: Charles Emerson Walker, *The Role of Karl Nesselrode in the Formulation and Implementation of Russian Foreign Policy, 1850–1856*. Dissertation, Univ of West Virginia 1973. Used PRO and AMAE for the origins period; some good citations.

Webster, *Palmerston*: Charles Webster, *The Foreign Policy of Palmerston, 1830–1841*. 2 vols, London 1951. Detailed view from PRO FO sources; similarly detailed volumes on Palmerston, 1846–1851, Clarendon, 1853–1856, and French foreign policy, 1848–1856, would be most useful.

Hermann Wentkler, *Vom Wiener Kongress zur Pariser Konferenz. England, die deutsche Frage und das Mächtesystem, 1815–1856*. Göttingen/Zürich 1991. Has a section on war aims formulation, 1853–54, not seen by this author.

Wetzel: David Wetzel, *The Crimean War: A Diplomatic History*. Boulder/New York 1985; writes bitingly and judgementally as if he were A.J.P. Taylor's *alter ego*; no use of the available *AGK* I.1–3; many, many inaccuracies; should have cited more sources in order to be trustworthy history.

Zaionchkovskii *VV*: See above, (2), under ZP: the narrative volumes.

Sergei Zhigarev, *Russkaia politika v Vostochnom voprose*. 2 vols, Moscow 1896. The best of the Imperial Russian treatments of the Eastern Question.

(9) ARTICLES

Garry J. Alder, 'India and the Crimean War', *Journal of Imperial and Commonwealth History* II.2 (Oct. 1973): 15–37. Indicates Calcutta's relative calm in 1853.

Olive Anderson, 'Great Britain and the Beginning of the Ottoman Public Debt, 1854–1855', *HJ* VII.1 (1964): 42–64. Supplements Rodkey.

Winfried Baumgart, 'Probleme der Krimkriegsforschung. Eine Studie über die Literatur des letzen Jahrzehnts (1961–1970)', *JGO* XIX (1971): 49–109, 243–64, 371–400. Rich sequel to Hösch's article by the general editor of *AGK*.

G.H. Bolsover, 'Nicholas I and the Partition of Turkey', *SR/SEER* XXVIII (1948): 115–45. Covers 1833, 1843–44, 1853.

Radu Florescu, 'The Rumanian Principalities and the Origin of the Crimean War', *SEER/SR* XLIII (1964): 46–67. Correct about the centrality of the Principalities, but no proof that Stratford's frustrations from 1848–49 were decisive in 1853.

Gooch *CHOCW*: Brison D. Gooch, 'A Century of Historiography on the Origins of the Crimean War', *AHR* LX.3 (Oct. 1956): 33–58. Judicious on the French side; neglects Tarlé, insufficiently critical.

_____, 'An 1853 Formula for Ottoman Victory', *AHY* XIV (1978): 79–88. A glimpse at the Hungarian emigration at work.

C.I. Hamilton, 'The Royal Navy, *La Royale*, and the Militarization of Naval Warfare, 1840–1870', *Journal of Strategic Studies* VI (1983): 183–94. Supplements Bartlett.

Henderson: Gavin B. Henderson, 'The Seymour Conversations', *History* XVIII.71 (1933): 241–7; rev. and repr in *Crimean War Diplomacy and Other Historical Essays*, Glasgow 1947. Only English sources; Nicholas as 'blunderer' not 'plotter' thesis – perhaps a false dichotomy; some imprecise dates.

J.L. Herkless, 'Stratford, the Cabinet and the Outbreak of the Crimean War', *HJ* XVIII (1975): 497–523. On the apologetic side.

Edgar Hösch, 'Neuere Literatur (1940–1960) über den Krimkrieg', *JGO* IX (1969): 399–434. Comprehensive, judicious.

H.E. Howard, 'Brunnow's Reports on Aberdeen, 1853', *CHJ* IV (1932–34): 312–21. The extracts of documents, copied with permission from anti-Bolsheviks in the Russian mission in London soon after the November 1917 coup, are somewhat slanted; the thesis that the origin of the war lies in Brunnow's reports is not substantiated.

Jacob C. Hurewitz, 'Ottoman Diplomacy and the European State System', *Middle East Journal* XV (1961): 141–52. Good summary.

_____, 'Russia and the Turkish Straits: A Reevaluation of the Origin of the Problem', *World Politics* XIV (1961–62): 605–33. Serious focus on the 1798/99 and 1805 treaties by the editor of *MENA*; makes use of Turkish archives.

Paul Knaplund, 'Finnmark in British Diplomacy, 1832–1855', *AHR* XXX (1925): 478–502. The northwesternmost point in the 'Great Game'.

Lambert *PRW*: Andrew Lambert, 'Preparing for the Russian War. British Strategic Planning, March 1853–March 1854', *War and Society* VII.2 (Sept. 1989): 15–39. Supplements his *Crimean War*.

Vernon Puryear, 'New Light on the Origins of the Crimean War', *JMH* III.2 (June 1931): 219–34: Precursor to *ERSQ* thesis about a genuine Anglo-Russian understanding as of 1844; forced.

Rodkey: Frederick Stanley, 'Ottoman Concern about Western Economic Penetration in the Levant, 1849–1856', *JMH* XXX.4 (1958): 348–53. Shows the problems on both the Anglo-French and Turkish sides in initiating Ottoman state borrowing.

Ann Pottinger Saab, John M. Knapp and Françoise de Bourqueney Knapp, 'A Reassessment of French Foreign Policy During the Crimean War Based on the Papers of Adolphe de Bourqueney', *French Historical Studies* XIV.4 (Fall 1986): 468–96. Useful information and extracts from documents, not just from Bourqueney.

_____, 'Review of Winfried Baumgart, *Der Fried von Paris, 1856;* Paul W. Schroeder, *Austria, Great Britain, and the Crimean War,*' *Central European History* 8 (1975): 51–68. Notes differences over the analytical utility of the 'Concert of Europe'.

Richard Salomon, 'Die Anerkennung Napoleons III: ein Beitrag zur Geschichte der Politik Nikolaus I, *Zeitschrift für osteuropäische Geschichte* II (1912): 312–66. Utilized ZP I fruitfully.

Schmitt: Bernard Schmitt, 'Diplomatic Preliminaries of the Crimean War', *AHR* XXV.1 (Oct. 1919): 33–67. Neglected to use ZP I–II or to discern source bases, but even-handed.

Paul W. Schroeder, 'Austria and the Danubian Principalities, 1853–1856', *Central European History* 2 (1969): 216–36.

_____, 'Bruck vs. Buol: the Dispute over Austrian Eastern Policy 1853–1855', *JMH* 40 (1968): 193–217.

_____, 'A Turning Point in Austrian Eastern Policy in the Crimean War. The Conferences of March, 1854', *AHY* 4–5 (1968–69): 159–202. All three articles have a certain mark of scholarly distinction.

John J. Stephan, 'The Crimean War in the Far East', *Modern Asian Studies* III.3 (July 1969): 257–77. Elucidates the Amur connection.

Harold Temperley, 'The Alleged Violations of the Straits Convention by Stratford de Redcliffe between June and September, 1853', *EHR* 49 (1934): 637–42. Challenges Puryear over interpretation; elucidates maritime communication problems.

_____, 'The Last Phase of Stratford de Redcliffe, 1853–1858', *EHR* 47 (1932): 216–59. Almost ironical outcome.

Temperley *SROCW*: —, 'Stratford de Redcliffe and the Origins of the Crimean War', *EHR* 48 (1933): 601–21, 49 (1934): 265–98. Pro-Stratford; too little attention to his ideas; dramatic; not superseded to date concerning this diplomat, but flippant about Menshikov, Rifaat, Argyropoulos and others.

Hermann Wentkler, 'Russland vor dem Krimkrieg: Die russische Aussenpolitik 1853/54 im Urteil des britischen Gesandten George Hamilton Seymour', *JGO* 40.3 (1992): 366–80. Fresh material from Seymour's private correspondence; reveals his mounting, albeit well-concealed, aggressive russophobia in 1853, as well as his perplexity over Nicholas I and disgust with Russia's autocracy.

Maps

Map 1 Europe 1848–1855

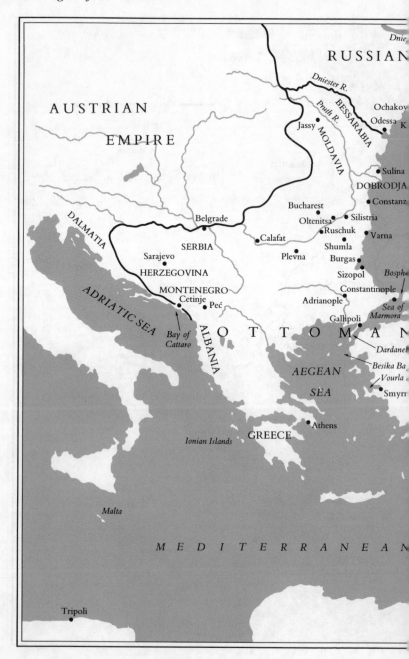

Map 2 The Eastern Question and the Crimean War

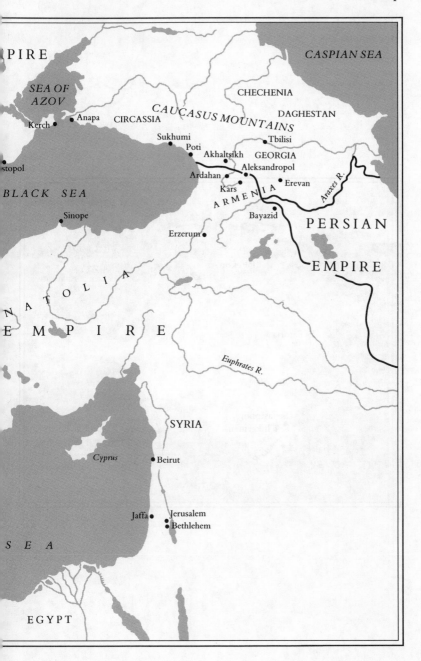

EMPIRE

SEA OF
AZOV

CASPIAN SEA

Kerch •   • Anapa   CIRCASSIA

CHECHENIA

DAGHESTAN

CAUCASUS MOUNTAINS

stopol

Sukhumi
Poti •
        Akhaltsikh
    Ardahan •
           Kars •
      ARMENIA
            • Bayazid
• Tbilisi

GEORGIA
Aleksandropol
          • Erevan

Araxes R.

PERSIAN

EMPIRE

BLACK   SEA

• Sinope

Erzerum •

NATOLIA

EMPIRE

Euphrates R.

SYRIA

Cyprus   • Beirut

Jaffa • • Jerusalem
        • Bethlehem

SEA

EGYPT

327

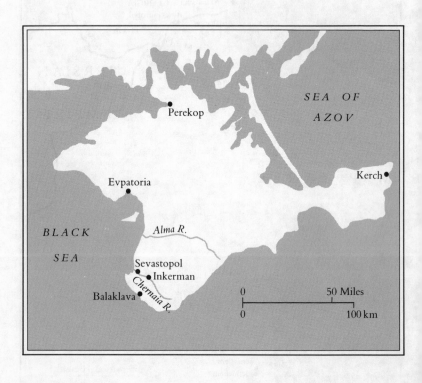

Map 3 The Crimean Peninsula

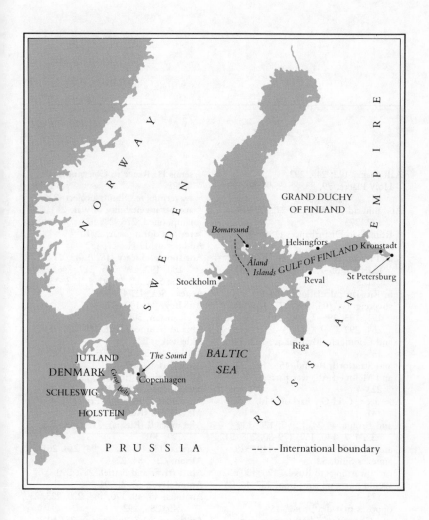

Map 4 The Baltic and the Crimean War

Index

Index

Index

Index